The Lorette Wilmot Library
Nazareth College of Rochester

VALUES
in
SELECTED
CHILDREN'S BOOKS
of
FICTION *and* FANTASY

VALUES
in
SELECTED
CHILDREN'S BOOKS
of
FICTION *and* FANTASY

CAROLYN W. FIELD
JAQUELINE SHACHTER WEISS

LIBRARY
PROFESSIONAL
PUBLICATIONS
1987

First published 1987 as a Library Professional Publication,
an imprint of The Shoe String Press, Inc.
Hamden, Connecticut 06514

Printed in the United States of America

Library of Congress Cataloging-in-Publication Data

Field, Carolyn W., 1916–
Values in selected children's books of
fiction and fantasy.
Includes bibliographies and index.
1. Children's stories—History and criticism.
2. Values in literature. I. Weiss, Jaqueline Shachter.
II. Title.
PN3347.F54   1987   809.3'9353   87-3874
ISBN 0-208-02100-0
ISBN 0-208-02101-9 (pbk.)

To the thousands of librarians who dedicate their lives to introduce children
and adults to the joys and values of quality children's books

C. W. F.

To my devoted husband, George, our children, Sherry,
Stuart, Ross, Ruth, Scott, and Steven, and our future grandchildren,
a lineage of readers, with love

J. S. W.

Contents

Acknowledgments

Without the cooperation of The Free Library of Philadelphia, this book would not have been possible. Special thanks go to Barbara Maxwell and her staff of the Northwest Regional Library, Ellen Whitney and Dianejude McDowell and their staff of the Central Children's Department, and Kit Breckenridge and Adrienne Jenness in the Office of Work with Children.

Gratitude is also warmly expressed to Marian Peck and her staff at the Montgomery County–Norristown Public Library.

Introduction

This is a practical guide to children's books used in preschool through middle grades. Its purpose is to make users aware of readable books, including little-known ones, that highlight positive values and to help young people develop their own standards. The book can serve as a bibliotherapeutic aid, introducing titles that assist children in coping with stress and problems in today's complex world. It can also be a springboard for discussion between children and adults.

In the book we discuss 713 titles of children's fiction and fantasy. That total is divided among three categories: 142 books for early years (preschool through second grade), 213 books for middle years (grades 3–4), and 358 books for later years (grades 5–8). There is a progressive increase in the number of books from early to later years since older children and adolescents are more experienced, better readers, more mature in their thinking than young children, and more challenging books with more complex values are available for them. Out-of-print books are included if they are appropriate to the examined value since most are on the shelves of established libraries.

This book appears to be the only known published study that deals solely with values in children's books. Values, interpreted as ethical ideals that motivate personal effectiveness or social commitment, are considered to be the "glue" of civilization. *The American College Dictionary* defines values as "the things of social life (ideals . . .) toward which the people of the group have an effective regard." Individuals do not learn values only intellectually but internalize them into unconscious and subconscious behavior. Basically this complicated identification process stems from the home, the school, and the community. Young, impressionable minds may also develop a value system through the medium of trade books. People determine what is good or right according to their own personal values.

Each chapter in this book focuses on one of the following defined values, listed here along with the number of books discussed on that topic:

1. cooperation (working together or sharing), sixty-two books
2. courage (surviving or showing tenacity and spirit), ninety-six books
3. friendship and love of animals (caring about mammals, birds, reptiles, etc.), fifty-one books
4. friendship and love of people (caring about human beings), ninety-three books
5. humaneness (opposing prejudice, being fair or showing kindness, and interpersonal and intercultural understanding), fifty-seven books
6. ingenuity (being resourceful in solving problems), eighty-nine books
7. loyalty (being faithful to individuals, country, or ideals), twenty-five books
8. maturing (growing physically and mentally), one hundred books
9. responsibility (being reliable or self-reliant), sixty-nine books
10. self-respect (acquiring a good self-image and self-esteem), seventy-one books

It is encouraging to note that the most popular values in the selected children's books appear to be courage, friendship, love of people, humaneness, ingenuity, and maturing. Perhaps maturing is the most all-encompassing value. Honesty is not generally found as a stressed value that can serve as the subject of a chapter but is often associated with other values. All of the listed values are positive ones which are respected by followers of various life styles in our society. Impressionable young people who read about others with ideals may be more willing to accept these ideals in their own lives.

We have discussed in this book values in selected literature for children published or distributed in the United States from 1930 through 1984 with emphasis on fairly recent titles. Modern classics may be included. Among books considered were those originally published in other countries and republished in the United States. The authors made these selections after extensive reading and years of working with children and adolescents, and after referring to the following respected sources:

The Bookfinder: A Guide to Children's Literature About the Needs and Problems of Youth Aged 2–15, Vol. I (books through 1974) and Vol. II (books through 1978)

Bulletin of the Center for Children's Books, 1979–1984 editions

The Free Library of Philadelphia master file in the Office of Work with Children, 1980–1984

More Notes from a Different Drummer: A Guide to Juvenile Fiction Portraying the Disabled, 1984

Notes from a Different Drummer: A Guide to Juvenile Fiction Portraying the Handicapped, 1977

Prizewinning Books for Children: Themes and Stereotypes in U.S. Prize-winning Prose Fiction for Children, 1983

Reading Ladders for Human Relations, various editions, 1947–1981

In choosing a book for a chapter, the authors considered whether or not it appeals to intended readers or is popular with them. The project does not include early classics, short stories, drama, poetry, nonfiction, wordless books, or almost-wordless books. Focus is on the text of realistic fiction and fantasy, not the illustrations.

Illustrators are cited in the text only for the early years because of their key role in picture storybooks. Books that stress a selected value are grouped in each chapter according to intended readers' age levels. Quotations are reproduced verbatim from the books themselves. Where it is important, selected sequels are identified, even if the sequel's stressed value is in the category of another chapter. Cross references are not made for series books.

In the text, there is frequent use of quotations to support the emphasized value with an author's own words. Quotations are used also to introduce an author's writing style. The page number is in parentheses after each quotation, but for brevity's sake, the word "page" is omitted. If a quotation is from an unpaged picture storybook, "unp" appears in parentheses.

References at the end of each chapter are for hardcover editions unless otherwise indicated. The name of an author, book title, illustrator, and/or translator in the reference is identical with wording on the book's title page. The publisher's name in a reference also comes directly from the book's title page or the citation in *Cumulative Book*

Index. (Often the publisher cites the company's name in a variety of ways unrelated to a merger.) Due to mergers and conglomerates among publishers, addresses are not given but are available in the current *Books in Print* or *Literary Market Place*.

Part of the reference is an abbreviation indicating if the intended readers are in their early (E), middle (M), or later (L) years. The number of pages (abbreviated as "p.") for each reference is based on text and illustrations essential to the text. References acknowledge all illustrators. If the author is also the illustrator, the citation merely states that the book is "Illustrated."

Where it is appropriate, the reference lists values for each book other than the one discussed in that particular chapter. The authors have made the decision as to major or minor values. Unless otherwise indicated, the value *friendship* refers to friendship with and love of people. *Animal friendship*, of course, is our concise way of stating friendship with and love of animals.

Unlike a collection of annotations used for reference only, this book invites cover-to-cover reading. Cited selections show a variety of experiences and may be recommended with assurance by those who are too busy to read for themselves the broad base from which they are culled.

References

Barnhart, C. L., ed. *The American College Dictionary*. Random House, 1963.

Baskin, Barbara H., and Karen H. Harris, eds. *More Notes from a Different Drummer: A Guide to Juvenile Fiction Portraying the Disabled*. Bowker, 1984.

———. *Notes from a Different Drummer: A Guide to Juvenile Fiction Portraying the Handicapped*. Bowker, 1977.

Dreyer, Sharon Spredemann, ed. *The Bookfinder: A Guide to Children's Literature About the Needs and Problems of Youth Aged 2–15*. American Guidance Service, Vol. I. 1977, Vol. II, 1981.

Reading Ladders for Human Relations. American Council on Education, 1947–1981.

Sutherland, Zena, ed. *Bulletin of the Center for Children's Books*. University of Chicago Graduate Library School, 1979–1984.

Weiss, Jaqueline Shachter. *Prizewinning Books for Children: Themes and Stereotypes in U.S. Prizewinning Prose Fiction for Children*. Lexington Books, 1983.

I

Cooperation

Cooperation takes different forms. Books for early, middle, and later years emphasize the positive value of cooperation or working together with unity. Many tales deal with working harmoniously for survival or in the performance of tasks, and others with the sharing of items. Some focus on combining efforts in sports or an exchange of services as well as cooperation in the interest of fairness, family tranquility, support of the needy, or another common goal. Finally, there are stories that stress sublimation of individual to collective needs.

BOOKS FOR EARLY YEARS

In *Swimmy*, by author-illustrator Leo Lionni, a lonely little fish, Swimmy, is the only black fish to survive when a large tuna eats his friends. After Swimmy meets fearful small red fish hiding from predators, he teaches them to cooperate. He says, "We are going to swim all together like the biggest fish in the sea" (22). The black fish becomes the eye of the group that succeeds in chasing away big fish.

Emphasizing the same value in a second book, *Tico and the Golden Wings*, author-illustrator Leo Lionni tells about a bird, Tico, who is born without wings, and who receives golden wings from a wishingbird. When Tico contributes a single golden feather to a needy person, a black feather grows in its place, until he looks like other birds. Tico concludes, "Now my wings are black, and yet I am not like my friends. We are *all* different. Each for his own memories and his own invisible golden dreams" (unp).

It is with contributions from the costumes of his friends that poor Harlequin makes his patchwork suit in Remy Charlip's and Burton

Supree's *Harlequin and the Gift of Many Colors*, illustrated by Charlip. In Italy, during the holiday of Carnival, the widow's son wears his costume made of shared, bright scraps of material. "And Harlequin was the happiest of them all [revelers] on this happy night, for he was clothed in the love of his friends" (36).

Pelle gets cloth for an outfit in a different way in *Pelle's New Suit* by author-illustrator Elsa Beskow. After the Swedish boy, Pelle, shears his lamb, he does chores in exchange for getting one grandmother to card wool, another grandmother to spin wool into yarn, his mother to weave yarn into cloth, and the tailor to sew a suit. When Pelle wears his new clothes on Sunday, he tells the lamb, "Thank you very much for my new suit, little lamb" (unp).

The setting shifts to Mexico for Clyde Robert Bulla's *The Poppy Seeds*, illustrated by Jean Charlot. After young Pablo receives poppy seeds, he plants them in his neighbors' yards and beside the spring belonging to selfish, aged Antonio who accuses him of stealing water. When poppies bloom in his yard, Antonio delivers some to sick Pablo. The boy recovers, rejoicing when Antonio, now generous, says of his spring water, "There *is* enough for all" (unp).

In *King Wacky*, a fantasy by author-illustrator Dick Gackenbach, residents of Woosey cooperate with their beloved king whose head is on backwards and who has a backward way of walking, talking, and behaving. His subjects grow rich as he declares, "From now on, the king will pay taxes to the people" (unp). If the king says, "Good," he means, "Bad," but his prospective bride, Princess Honey from Bumble, does not understand. He insults her as he praises, "Honey, you are the ugliest thing I've ever seen!" (unp). After her father declares war, King Wacky tells his people, "I HAVE GOOD NEWS. WE ARE AT PEACE!" (unp). Forgetting he speaks in opposite terms, his subjects kiss enemy soldiers, ending the war. They remember to reverse words, however, after he weds Honey, for they pin on the back of the honeymooners' carriage, "Married Just" (unp).

Animals do favors for each other in Judy Delton's *Two Good Friends*, illustrated by Guilo Maestro. Duck, a spotless housekeeper, visits Bear, a fine cook, whose floor is sticky with honey. The next day, Bear calls on Duck with raspberry muffins but finds no one home since Duck is cleaning Bear's house as a surprise. In the end, Bear tells Duck, "Let's celebrate! Come in and have some cookies. But first, . . . wipe your feet on the mat" (31–32).

Two personified dogs are in *Ton and Pon: Two Good Friends* by author-illustrator Kazuo Iwamura. Their mothers ask big Ton and little Pon to carry a heavy basket of apples to a friend, Mickie, for her birthday. Ton suggests putting a pole under the basket's handle so each dog can support an end of the pole. Pon asks, "Working together is easier, isn't it, Ton?" (unp). The dogs eat the apples, deliver wild flowers instead, and return home with apples from Mickie's mother.

A giraffe is Mr. Tall and a mouse, Mr. Small, in Barbara Brenner's *Mr. Tall and Mr. Small*, illustrated by Tomi Ungerer. They cooperate to escape a forest fire since Mr. Small puts his ear to the ground and says, "Yes, I hear them. . . . The animals are running west" (unp). Mr. Tall looks over burning trees before declaring, "There is a lake on the western side. That's the way we can escape" (unp). They survive by running west together.

The Church Mice Adrift, part of a series by author-illustrator Graham Oakley, tells about mice who lose their home to rats and win it back with unusual help from Sampson, a cat. After rats displace the mice in the Wortlethorpe Church, Sampson marches into a trap, an open plastic bag held by the rats, who then dump the cat outside. Sampson finds shelter for the mice in the playroom of a vacant house. Two mice, Humphrey and Arthur, are unsuccessful when they try to get the other mice to fight the rats, but Sampson offers a more exciting plan that wins support. The mice wheel the playroom dollhouse to the riverbank, attach a sign, "Riverside Restaurant," and advertise, "Free grub for all rats!" (unp). Sampson leads scavenger mice who get food from trash cans, Arthur leads construction workers, and Humphrey, restaurant decorators. When the rats come to eat in the restaurant, the mice set the restaurant adrift. Sampson rescues two mice waiters still aboard, Arthur and Humphrey. The group returns to the vestry, working four days to clean the rats' mess.

The six Fieldmouse children are in Franz Brandenberg's *Nice New Neighbors*, illustrated by Aliki. The children win a place in their new neighborhood by assigning parts in their "Three Blind Mice" play fairly to next-door peers. When they run out of parts, they conclude, "We could always make one up" (33). After the performance, "The Fieldmouse children played with the Frog child, the Lizard children, the Grasshopper children, and the Snail children" (50).

Two five-year-old girls, Sara and Ann, learn to share in Betty Miles's *Having a Friend*, illustrated by Erik Blegvad. At first, the girls play separately. But then "Sara and Ann made a pie together. . . . They gave each other drinks at the fountain. . . . They made each other valentines. . . . They dressed almost alike" (unp).

Emily McCully's illustrations show how a boy and girl learn to be a team in *That's Mine!* by Elizabeth Winthrop. As the two build separate towers, both reach for the last block and angrily destroy each other's work. Then they discover the joy of cooperating when they construct a huge castle together.

Siblings learn to relate in *Jungle Day; or How I Learned to Love My Nosey Little Brother* by author-illustrator Barbara Bottner. When young Jackie has to bring a cutout jungle animal to Miss Naomi's class, she asks her little brother, Wayne, to leave her alone. He suggests:

> If I were you, I would cut up all the animals [she previously drew] that don't look like what they're supposed to look like, paste the best parts together, and make something nobody's ever seen before. (unp)

Jackie accepts Wayne's idea, calling him back to help, and says of her results, "There's never been anything like it before in the whole entire world!" (unp).

June Jordan's *New Life: New Room*, illustrated by Ray Cruz, tells how a family cooperates to accommodate a new baby. When the Robinsons can't get a three-bedroom project apartment, they rearrange their two bedrooms. There is a crib in the parents' bedroom for the new baby girl. Three other children, ten-year-old Rudy, nine-year-old Tyrone, and six-year-old Linda, learn to share what used to be the boys' room. After Daddy buys Linda a cot, he gets poster paint that the three children use on their windows and toy box. As Daddy serves refreshments, Linda exclaims, "It was like a party. A pajama party with ice cream and soda and Daddy . . . and a brand-new room that would look like a rainbow in the morning" (46).

Author-illustrator Charles E. Martin, in *Summer Business*, focuses on a group of children who pool their earnings. Young Sam tells his friends, "My father says everyone ought to learn how to work" (unp). There are no summer jobs left, so the group follows the librarian's suggestion to sell things.

> They finally decided that Lulu and Hamilton would sell painted rocks and shells. Jonathan, May, and Sam would run

a flea market. Kate and Heather would sell lemonade and cookies. Rita would dogsit, pick up mail, and fill in wherever she was needed. She would also be treasurer. They decided they would save their earnings till the end of summer. (unp)

The children spend their combined savings at the Harvest Fair. With leftover money, they buy ice cream for all, including the librarian.

BOOKS FOR MIDDLE YEARS

In Roger W. Drury's *The Champion of Merrimack County*, at least seven people help a champion mouse, O'Crispin, who ruins Mr. Berryfield's bathtub after using it as a bicycle racetrack. Dr. Norton, a dentist, repairs the damaged tub enamel. Mrs. Berryfield and her daughter, Janet, get the hospital to bandage O'Crispin's tail, which he dislocates when he slips on soap. Three craftsmen and the dentist repair the wrecked bicycle. Even Mr. Berryfield, who has a mouse-trapping reputation, helps O'Crispin retain his title as Champion of Merrimack County. Mr. Berryfield says, "This is a champion, that's what! Why didn't anybody tell me? What luck for us that he came to live in our house!" (196)

Cooperation extends from fantasy to realistic fiction in Peggy Mann's two books set in Manhattan, *The Street of the Flower Boxes* and *When Carlos Closed the Street*. In the first, nine-year-old Carlos Gomez and his five-year-old brother, Luis, uproot flowers belonging to new neighbors, the Mitchells. After Carlos's grandmother forces him to apologize, the Mitchells hire Carlos to replant flowers. The Mitchells give Carlos extra flowers and planters, which he sells to neighbors. He finds he has not charged enough for expenses, so he raises the balance with a street carnival. Neighbors make punch, bake cookies, donate prizes, plan games, and clean up afterwards. The *Times* cites: "As a result, fourteen more city blocks had now been brightened by window boxes of their own" (72).

Mann's sequel, *When Carlos Closed the Street*, shows Carlos a year later. East of a fire hydrant on his block live black youths in the Young Kings's gang and west, Puerto Ricans in the Spanish Angels. When Carlos's ball rolls on the Kings's turf, Carlos gets it and agrees to a stickball championship game between the two gangs. The police help by closing the street that day, and crowds come in Sunday-best clothes. "Looking around him, Carlos realized that he hardly cared who won this Big Game. What was important was that it was really happening" (70).

Nine-year-old Renfroe learns to share in Robert Burch's *Renfroe's Christmas*. In the beginning, he says he would rather receive gifts than give them. Renfroe gets three for Christmas but does not donate to the poor. Nathan, a classmate's retarded fifteen-year-old brother, wants Renfroe's new Mickey Mouse watch, and Renfroe lets him take it, knowing the boy is leaving for a training institute. After Renfroe returns home, he believes he sees an old Christmas angel on a woodshed door waving at him.

Louise A. Stinetorf's *A Charm for Paco's Mother* is about a boy, Paco, who helps his blind mother sell cacti to tourists in Oaxaca, Mexico. When a tourist tells Paco about an operation to restore Mother's sight, Paco thinks the operation is like a charm for which he must pray on Christmas Eve; thus he travels to pray at a distant cross. As he begins his walk, he stops to free a goat caught in a rabbit trap and sits with the goat until a shepherd comes. Next, he waits with little Malinchina while her father repairs a wagon wheel. Later, he gives his *serape* to a needy boy and helps him deliver coal. Then Paco realizes Christmas Eve is over. He returns home to see that the tourist, a doctor, has completed Mother's operation. Mother tells him there is no better charm than his kind deeds.

There are four nine-year-old boys—black, white, and Hispanic—in Osmond Molarsky's *Where the Good Luck Was*. They clean Mr. Pendleton's attic to buy aluminum crutches for a friend, Arnold McWilliams, who has a broken ankle and is using a hospital's wooden crutches. When they find old silverware in a box and give it to Mr. Pendleton, he buys aluminum crutches as a reward. Arnold prefers the wooden ones, so they donate the new ones to the hospital.

Eddie Wilson calls his items "valuable property," but his family calls them "junk" in Carolyn Haywood's *Eddie and His Big Deals*, one of thirteen books in her series about Eddie. Eddie learns to cooperate with a friend, Anna Patricia Wallace, who acquires a free printing press but is willing to trade it for a fine doll. She offers to help Eddie publish a paper, and he agrees, saying, "But you'll have to work. You'll have to go around and get all the news of this street, and it has to be good. I'm going to call this newspaper *Hot News.* . . . And you have to go out and sell it" (86). Anna Patricia trades the press for a doll that Eddie finds.

Unusual teacher-pupil cooperation is the essence of Susan

Shreve's *The Flunking of Joshua T. Bates*. Before school starts, Joshua T. Bates learns that he must repeat third grade, and his new teacher, Mrs. Goodwin, arranges to tutor him every afternoon. (She is depressed because Mr. Goodwin is leaving her.) Joshua improves so much that, after Thanksgiving, he advances to fourth grade. Joshua continues tutoring, telling Mrs. Goodwin, "I want you to make me as smart as anyone in the fourth grade" (40). As they work together, Joshua understands some of her problems and tells her that at least she will not flunk. She replies, "That's not necessarily true. There're all kinds of flunking" (63).

Red-headed ten-year-old Larry Pryor from Hazleton, Connecticut, featured in Betty Miles's *The Secret Life of the Underwear Champ*, is visiting New York City when the Zigmund Model Agency invites him to do a commercial for ChampWin Knitting Mills with a red-headed television "family." When he learns that he is to advertise underwear, he worries about peer reaction. The television cast is helpful, including young Suzanne Ridley, who asks, "Did you ever see 'Oliver!' . . . It's a neat show. If you wanted, I could probably get you a ticket, so you could come to it" (77). He reciprocates by inviting her to a ball game, and when she attends, the first-base player lets Larry assume first base, so she does not see him in his usual substitute's bench-warming role. When Larry bats in place of another teammate and scores a home run, fellow players no longer call him "underwear champ," just "Champ."

C. S. Adler tells about siblings and friends who learn to work together in *Get Lost, Little Brother*. Eighth-grade twins, Leon and Michael Lewis, dominate their brother, Todd, who is two years younger. When they lock Todd in the bathroom for the day so he cannot give a school report, he sees from a window a small river island behind his home which he wants to claim. A tax assessor issues him a title to the 33' × 12' shoe-shaped sandbar. His eleven-year-old friend, Louanne ("Louie") LaVoy, attracts a reporter to an island-naming event. Todd tells the reporter:

> I couldn't have built the place up by myself, and—it's more fun doing it together. . . . You see, Leon figured out how to shore up the end when the river started eating it. And then Leon showed us how to build the shack. . . . I claim this island . . . in the name of our club. . . . And I name it, uh, Shoe Island (144–146).

When Leon invites him, "How about going tonight? You and me and Michael could camp out together" (152), Todd is too happy to sleep. "In his whole life he [Todd] couldn't remember a night as wonderful as this one had been. Somehow he had gained a treasure even better than an island of his own" (154).

Ten-year-old Brooklynite Tybee Trimble learns to cooperate with her parents in Lila Perl's *Tybee Trimble's Hard Times*. Tybee, whose name means dove, is disappointed that her family cannot afford circus tickets while Father is on leave of absence to study for bar exams. Planning a school essay on circus elephants, she secretly tries to get circus money by washing cars and delivering groceries. There is more insecurity when Mother quits her library job to work as a house painter, falls off a ladder, and goes to a hospital, though not in serious condition. Finally ready to attend the circus, Tybee learns that Mother had been pregnant and lost her baby in the fall. Shocked, Tybee decides on her family as her essay topic, writing how ". . . everybody ought to try to pull together" (141). She decides to "buy something pretty and cheerful for her mother with part of her circus money" (142).

Children often work together for fair play. In Aidan Chambers's *The Present Takers*, a group exposes a bully, Melanie Prosser, and her cohorts, who demand presents when eleven-year-old Lucy Hall celebrates her birthday. Melanie even shoplifts a cassette at Woolworth's, hiding it on Lucy's person. Clare Tonks, who has also been bullied by the girls, Angus Burns, and Lucy expose Melanie in the class newspaper in a feature article, "Bullies," and a poem. Melanie goes beserk arguing that "things put in writing for everybody to see were different from things that were only said" (138). Melanie enrolls in another school amid rumors that she moved into a foster home due to friction with her father.

On a more positive note is Eleanor Clymer's *The Horse in the Attic*. When the Keatings move from New York City to an old Bridgeton home, every family member goes to work. Mother sells plants in a shop, sixteen-year-old Tom does carpentry and house painting, twelve-year-old Caroline gets a stable job, and Father at first commutes to and from a New York City job. But when Caroline finds in their stable attic a horse and jockey painting done around 1894, Father restores the painting, sells it for a good price, and plans an artistic career.

Another book by Eleanor Clymer, *The Get-away Car*, shows how

Susan Crouse Miklusky, twelve-year-old Maggie Fisher's grandmother, helps solve others' problems and her own. For seven years after her parents' separation, Maggie has chosen to live with Grandmother rather than with stern Aunt Ruby ("Rhubarb") Fisher. Maggie refuses to go to California with her aunt. To avoid her, Maggie and Grandmother leave New York City by renting a "get-away" car. Their trip ends in Mountainside, New York at the decrepit home of Cousin Bertha, who faces dispossession for tax delinquency. Grandmother finds jewels from a robbery in the car and realizes the reward will pay Bertha's taxes. Staying with Bertha, Maggie does the housework and Grandmother gets a job, feeling as she always has, "It's lucky I have you, Maggie. . . . I need somebody to keep me in order" (5).

A second book about a grandmother's and granddaughter's cooperation is Elizabeth Winthrop's *Belinda's Hurricane*. Belinda, who is spending August with Granny May on Fox Island, goes to a gift shop to buy Granny a birthday seashell necklace. She finds none left and no one will identify a local man who makes such jewelry. After a hurricane strikes, Granny May shelters a reclusive neighbor, Mr. Fletcher, and his dog, Fishface. During the storm, Belinda tries to make a shell necklace and Mr. Fletcher helps. She, in turn, rescues Fishface from hurricane waters. Mr. Fletcher rewards her by finishing the necklace, admitting he is the gift shop jeweler and offering, "Maybe next year, we could go into business together. I'm getting too old to tramp around the island looking for shells" (50).

An African author, Moses L. Howard, depicts cooperation between a grandmother, Gaushe, and her granddaughter, Khuana, in *The Ostrich Chase*. Khuana, one of the Bushmen of Africa's Kalahari Desert, dreams of helping on an ostrich hunt. Gaushe becomes gravely ill while fixing poisonous arrowheads. The Bushmen abandon Gaushe when they travel to find water, so Khuana secretly returns and leads her by a short, dangerous route. When they come to a water hole, Khuana kills an ostrich. The two live on dried ostrich meat and water carried in ostrich eggshells, rejoining Bushmen with enough meat for a feast.

The scene shifts to the French Alps for Claire Huchet Bishop's *All Alone*. Ten-year-old Marcel Mabout tends three heifers on Little Giant while his friend, Pierre Pascal, herds his three on Big Giant. Because their fathers revere independence, the boys feel guilty when they weather a storm together on Big Giant. Their fathers rescue them, telling them that the storm destroyed Little Giant and that Marcel was wise to join Pierre. Their two families, inspired by Marcel and Pierre, now share baby-sitting, herding, and crops. The mayor, who gives the boys a tractor honoring their cooperative spirit, declares:

> We, the people of Monestier, have decided to tear down the age-old fences and hedges which enclose and separate our fields, and to work the whole land of the valley together—one common field under the sun. (88)

Meindert DeJong's *The Wheel on the School* shows a similar spirit in the Netherlands. During the first quarter of this century, a teacher inspires six pupils to cooperate in order to attract storks back to their village, Shora. The odds are against them because Shora's storms are severe and house roofs slant. Determined, the children place a wheel on their school roof as a nesting place and watch two storks arrive. "And the long dream—storks on every roof in Shora—begins to come true" (298).

In another book, *The House of Sixty Fathers*, Meindert DeJong tells of a Chinese lad, Tien Pao, who is separated from his family during World War II. While his parents work at an airfield near Hengyang, Tien Pao and his pet pig stay on the family sampan which drifts into Japanese territory. Abandoning the boat, he wanders on land, bringing water to a wounded American airman, Lieutenant Hamsun. Chinese guerillas take Tien Pao to Hengyang, where he and his pig stay in a barracks with sixty American soldiers. An interpreter says, "The men of the Sixteenth Bombardment Squadron—that is what your sixty fathers are called—last night adopted you" (146). The soldiers give him food, medicine, a miniature uniform, and money. Lieutenant Hamsun, now recovered, helps him find his parents. Since Hamsun does not speak Chinese, he imagines the parents' gratitude, for "the heart understands without words" (189).

It is a time change from World War II to World War I, the period of Eleanor Estes's Moffat family. The first of four books in her episodic series set in Cranbury, Connecticut, *The Moffats* introduces four siblings: Sylvie, aged fifteen; Joey, twelve; Jane, ten; and five-and-a-half-year-old Rufus. They cooperate with their widowed mother, a seamstress, whom they admire, even for the way she peels apples. Financial plight pulls the family together, for when Mama thinks Joey lost the coal money, she does not scold. She says, "Well, if it's gone, it's gone. We'll manage somehow. If I work late tonight, I might finish some of the suits by tomorrow" (205). After Joey finds the money, he and Jane go into the cold night to bring coal home, and Mama rewards them with steaming pancakes.

Jane, continuing their story in *The Middle Moffat*, is anxious to see the town's oldest inhabitant, Hannibal Buckley, through to his hundredth birthday. She and he cooperate in a game, always saying, "Sh-sh!" as a greeting since she introduces herself to him as "the mysterious middle Moffat" (16). When Jane, who can play only the national anthem, posts a sign inviting neighbors to an organ recital, Mr. Buckley and the Browning Society ladies attend, but the organ's pedal breaks and a horde of moths fly from the instrument. Mama serves refreshments, and guests laugh as they leave. After Mr. Buckley's centennial birthday celebration, the Moffats ride in his automobile—a new experience for Rufus.

Rufus M. is the third book in the Moffat series. The title reflects the fact that Rufus can write only the initial of his last name when he applies for a library card. In his World War I victory garden, Rufus, now seven years old, grows Rufus beans, a hardy vegetable that thrives despite his interference. With a dollar Rufus finds in the ice, Mama pays the plumber to repair their frozen pipes, and he buys kindling, hard coal, apples, oranges, eggs, and potatoes, returning home "feeling like Santa Claus" (180).

In the last Moffat book, *The Moffat Museum*, Rufus and Joey cooperate with Jane by converting the family's barn into the town's only museum. The day the museum opens, June 14, 1919, Mr. Eugene Pennypepper, superintendent of schools, leads children there as part of his annual tour of important places. The highlight is Rufus as the waxworks boy. Later, every Moffat participates in Sylvie's wedding to Reverend Ray Abbot. Mama makes the wedding dress, Joey gives away the bride, Jane is flower girl, and Rufus throws rose pedals from the church balcony. The book ends as the boys help Mama financially. Joey, now sixteen, gets his working papers, takes a messenger's job, and studies draftsmanship by correspondence. Rufus delivers the *Saturday Evening Post* and gets paid for singing in a choir.

The pioneering days of 1873 are those that Laura Ingalls Wilder describes in *Little House in the Big Woods*. Laura is six years old and living with her sisters, Mary and Carrie, in Wisconsin in the first of nine books about American pioneer cooperation for survival. Pa hunts, traps, and farms while Ma makes her own cheese, sugar, and aromatic bread. The author evokes the harmony in the snug log cabin Pa built: "But Laura lay awake . . . listening to Pa's fiddle softly playing and to the lonely sound of the wind in the Big Woods. . . . She looked at Ma, gently rocking and knitting" (238).

In the second Wilder book, *Little House on the Prairie*, Pa wants to go West where it is not crowded and where there are plenty of animals. So the Ingalls family travels by covered wagon to a spot near the Verdigris River in Kansas where Pa builds a house with glass windows. "Every day Pa went hunting and trapping. In the cozy, firelit house Mary and Laura helped Ma with the work. Then they sewed quiltpatches" (253). When they hear the government is sending soldiers to get settlers out of Indian territory, the family heads north.

Laura Ingalls Wilder interrupts her own story to describe the childhood of her future husband, Almanzo Wilder, in *Farmer Boy*. She focuses on northern New York State where Almanzo, who is about nine years old, lives on a farm with his brother, Royal, and two sisters, Eliza Jane and Alice. The Wilder children go to school when their parents can spare them from spring plowing and sowing, summer sheep shearing, fall harvesting, and winter threshing. While Royal becomes a storekeeper, Almanzo wants to be a farmer, like his father.

About ten years later, Almanzo meets Laura Ingalls, whose next book about her own family is *On the Banks of Plum Creek*. After her folks leave Kansas, they go to Minnesota, and Laura picks plums near Plum Creek. When an ox strays on the roof of their underground home, "Pa had to stay at home to build a new roof. Laura helped him carry fresh willow boughs and she handed them to him while he wedged them into place" (51). Expecting a good wheat harvest, Pa goes into debt to build a house with store-bought lumber, but grasshoppers ruin his crop. He has to walk several hundred miles east and harvest others' crops to pay what he owes.

Wilder's *By the Shores of Silver Lake* announces a new baby, Grace Ingalls, born in Minnesota. Mary becomes blind when scarlet fever strikes. Pa's sister, Docia, visits, and he returns with her to Dakota territory to work for the railroad. When Mary is stronger, Ma and the four girls take their first train ride so they can join Pa. He files for a homestead and erects part of a house. Thirteen-year-old Laura never forgets, "Pa had said that she must be eyes for Mary" (2).

In *The Long Winter*, Laura's family survives the 1880–81 blizzards in the Dakota territory town where Royal Wilder has a feed store and his brother, Almanzo, spends the winter. (Almanzo has applied for his own homestead.) When there is a desperate need for food, Almanzo Wilder and Cap Garland make the dangerous trip across a frozen prairie to secure wheat. It is not until May that the train gets through with supplies, and Pa tells Ma, "You not only make the wheat come out even with the very last meal before the train comes, but you make the biscuits in sizes to fit the six of us" (319). The train brings the Ingalls family a Christmas barrel with a frozen turkey and gifts, so they celebrate Christmas in May.

In *Little Town on the Prairie*, fifteen-year-old Laura contributes earnings from sewing and teaching to a family fund for Mary to have a seven-year college and manual training course for the blind. Mary leaves for Vinton, Iowa. When Laura gets her teaching certificate and a job, she thinks, "Now Mary can have everything she needs, and she can come home this next summer" (307). Laura exchanges name cards with Almanzo who tells her his name's origin. During the Crusades, an Arab, El Manzoor, saved a Wilder and ever since, the Wilder family preserves the Anglicized version of his name. It is Almanzo who regularly walks Laura home from church.

BOOKS FOR LATER YEARS

The content of Laura Ingalls Wilder's last two books in her series suits mature readers. *These Happy Golden Years* tells how Laura, as she teaches school for three terms, always wants her salary to benefit Mary. Laura agrees with Pa who says, "We should have an organ when Mary comes home, so she can keep up the music she's learning in college. . . . If you will pay your school money for it, I can make up the other twenty-five dollars" (154). Before Laura leaves home at the age of eighteen to marry Almanzo Wilder, Pa assures her his homestead will belong to him next year, "So you need never worry about helping any more, Half-Pint. You have done your share and then some" (245).

Wilder's *The First Four Years*, published posthumously, discusses her early years of marriage. Laura does not want the harsh farm life, so Manly (her name for Almanzo) promises to evaluate their finances with her at the end of three years, but they continue farming because of debts and lack of a suitable alternative. She is nineteen and Manly, twenty-nine, when their first child, Rose, is born. Their second child dies when he is three weeks old. Laura describes how she assists Manly while he has post-diphtheria temporary limb paralysis: "It was a busy summer for Laura, what with the housework, caring for Rose, and helping Manly whenever he needed her" (91). The years, 1885 to 1889, end with Manly regaining his health.

Athena V. Lord's story, *A Spirit to Ride the Whirlwind*, takes place in 1836 in Lowell, Massachusetts. Lowell is a textile town where young women come to earn mill workers' wages while living in company boarding houses, like the one run by the mother of young Arabinia ("Binnie") Howe. After her twelfth birthday, Binnie becomes a doffer, bringing empty bobbins to spinners and removing full ones. A cut in wages and an increase in daily boarding rates force workers to talk about cooperating in a union. If Binnie joins, mill owners may blacklist her and force her family from their home. Since Mother encourages self-decision, Binnie "turns-out" or strikes with 2,000 employees, responding to the call, "Sisters, . . . in Union there is power . . ." (175). She becomes a messenger, collecting dues for a Factory Girls' Association. During a month-long strike, many strikers leave, but Mrs. Howe does not replace such boarders with strike breakers. Finally, the corporations rescind higher daily boarding rates, and employees who are not union leaders go back to work. Binnie returns for a time, planning to continue her formal education.

The setting shifts to northern Canada for Farley Mowat's *Lost in the Barrens*, an adventurous tale of cooperation between three lads who are Cree, Caucasian, and Eskimo. When his uncle goes fur trading, sixteen-year-old Jamie Macnair, recently arrived in the subarctic forests from Toronto, lives with the English-speaking Cree chief's son, Awasin. After the Crees give food to starving Deer Eaters, they send Awasin and Jamie by canoe to the Deer Eaters' camp. Starting home, the lads get lost in the Barrens and their canoe smashes in the rapids. It is bleeding Awasin who saves unconscious Jamie. Jamie asks Awasin to abandon him, but the chief's son replies, "You must be crazy!" (62). The two kill deer, travel by sled, develop snow blindness, and find shelter in an Eskimo igloo. Peetyuk, the igloo's owner, leads them home. Awasin, taught to fear Eskimos, is surprised at such cooperation. After telling his father, "It was Peetyuk and the Kazon Eskimos who saved our lives, and now he has come south to live" (242), the chief welcomes Peetyuk as another son.

The locale changes to a small Australian lumbering village for Ivan Southall's *Hills End*, a story of cooperation among seven children, aged nine to thirteen. When other villagers picnic, the seven and their teacher, Miss Goodwin, remain to look for aboriginal pictures in local caves. After a cyclone strikes, the seven return to the ruined village with their teacher, who has collapsed. One of the students, Adrian Fiddler, admits that he lied about having seen cave drawings, devises a survival plan, and the young people execute it. Adults, returning despite a washed-out bridge and raging river, find the children rebuilding amid devastation. Adrian's father refers to the "death of a town," but the boy says, "It's not dead, Dad. We're rebuilding already. We've started!" (171)

Janet McNeill's *Goodbye, Dove Square* portrays characters in an English urban-renewal program helping their former Dove Square neighbors. Sixteen-year-old Matt, Madge, and their friends cooperate to care for the Flint children. Mr. Flint is in the hospital and Mrs. Flint has deserted her family. Matt and his chums help the Flint children avoid foster homes by getting a responsible adult, Miss Harrison, to be with them. Matt buys the youngsters groceries and Madge buys them Christmas presents.

K. M. Peyton's *'Who, Sir? Me, Sir?'* is another tale set in England. Sam Sylvester, a form master at Hawkwood Comprehensive, a school for poor children, bets Master Plumpton of Grey Coats, a school for rich students, that [Sam] can randomly pick four Hawkwood pupils and train them in a year to beat Grey Coats's tetrathlon competitors in running, swimming, shooting, and riding cross-country. A girl, Nutty McTavish, becomes captain of the team of thirteen-year-old Hawkwood boys. Nutty works to get the team needed sports teachers, like police who instruct in shooting. Team members learn to ride on four horses which are due to be slaughtered. Nutty's sister, Gloria, spies for her, questions opponents she is dating, and reports to Nutty. Teammates genuinely cooperate, refusing to allow "Sam's amazing brainchild [the bet] . . . to be flushed down the pan . . ." (79).

An English mother, Sarah Lattimer, and an American father, Robert Graham, marry, and their children from previous marriages learn to cooperate in Barbara Willard's *Storm from the West*. Sixteen-year-old Nicholas and fourteen-year-old Charlotte have doubts when they learn their widowed mother is marrying a widower with four children. His children—Nan, aged sixteen, Alan and Roderick, aged twelve and eleven, and Lucy, aged ten—have the same fears, which seem justified when the two groups meet at the Lattimer cottage in

Kilmorah, Scotland. Leaving their tense offspring behind to resolve differences without adults, the parents tour Scotland alone. When the youngest of the six children, Lucy gets caught in a storm, the other children want to send their parents a message signed "The Clan," but telegraph lines are down and their folks are en route home. Charlotte endorses "The Clan" signature explaining, "A clan was made up of families and sometimes the families squabbled—but it was still the clan and the laird was head" (188).

In *Hang on, Harvey!* by Nancy J. Hopper, Harvey Smucker, a flutist in eighth grade, learns to cooperate in his J. F. Kennedy Middle School orchestra. Harvey is disappointed when a retired teacher, Eileen Hamilton, becomes the orchestra's conductor and lets Tina be first flutist. To get even, he plans with two orchestra members, Denny May and Fats Scarlotti, to ruin a dress rehearsal for the December concert. When Denny fires the starter pistol at the beginning of the "1812 Overture," he aims the gun at Fats, a drummer, who pretends to collapse. Unperturbed, Miss Hamilton tells Harvey privately:

> All you need is to learn to consider the performance of the orchestra as a whole as well as your own private achievement. . . . You have the ability. You can learn cooperation. That is one of the purposes of a middle-school orchestra. That is one of the reasons I am letting you stay. . . . Hang on, Harvey. (77–78)

Reflecting on these words, Harvey thinks, "She [Tina] was always cooperative, . . . I was afraid Tina could play the flute better than I did" (78). Harvey and the other musicians perform well in the concert, replaying "Jesu Joy of Man's Desiring" as an encore.

Two school sports stories are by R. R. Knudson: *Zanbanger* and *Zanboomer*. At high school, Suzanne ("Zan") Hagen's private student coach is Arthur Rinehart. In *Zanbanger*, Arthur wins a judge's support when he pleads in court for Zan's right to play with the Generals, formerly an all-male basketball team. Zan joins the team and by season's end two male holdouts cooperate so that the Generals become league champions. After winning the tournament, Zan says, "We had won. . . . We had won each other" (162).

In the sequel, Knudson's *Zanboomer*, Zan is shortstop and a power hitter on the high school baseball team throughout the exhibition season. In the first conference game, she dislocates her shoulder while sliding into first base and can no longer play for the year. Arthur trains her for cross-country running and through effort, she wins a trophy in her first race.

Two adolescent boys, Clay and Paul, learn to work together in *Sail, Calypso!* by Adrienne Jones. Clay is walking on the beach when he finds an abandoned sailboat he decides to repair. Before he begins Paul claims the boat, so they restore it together as the *Calypso*, laboring at Bert Showell's boatyard in exchange for materials. At summer's end, before the boys go their separate ways, Clay and Paul sail their restored boat to an island. On their return journey, there is a storm in which Paul falls overboard and Clay saves him. Then both swim ashore while the *Calypso* drifts out to sea.

Another boat enthusiast is twelve-year-old Tim, the brother of sixteen-year-old Vinny Waters, in Bianca Bradbury's "*I'm Vinny, I'm Me.*" The two live in a northeastern resort town where their deceased father grew up and their mother, who is now dead, bought an old motel. The orphans run the motel with Judge Tyson Haskell as their guardian, but the state welfare department considers placing them in a foster home. Despite the department's objection, Tim begins to work full-time on a boat, quitting his job when the department withdraws from the orphans' case. After pledging to help with the motel, Tim demonstrates affection to Vinny:

> He came to her. Usually he would rather be shot than show affection to his sister, but he came at her from behind and put his arms around her. She turned to face him and clutched him tight. . . . He was a tough kid, one a girl could lean on. What more could anyone want than to be loved tenderly by another human being? (199)

Anne Alexander shows other struggling children who unite in *Trouble on Treat Street*, which is set in San Francisco. The book features two elementary school boys who receive gang threats: a short, slight Chicano lad, Manolo Gomez, and his new black neighbor, tall, thin Clemuel ("Clem") Jackson. Clem is forlorn since his parents were killed in an automobile accident and he has to live with a grandmother he scarcely knows. At school, gang members threaten Clem, demanding a daily payoff, but he has no money or job. When the gang tries to start a fight between Manolo and Clem, passing police prevent it. Later, the boys team up, fearing the gang, and feeling safer with each other. The hovering gang abducts the two, makes them ride in a stolen car, forces Clem to strip, throws his clothes out of a moving vehicle, and dumps the schoolmates miles from home. After Manolo recovers as many of Clem's clothes as he can, the boys walk home, fearful of gang retaliation if they discuss the incident. It is not until Granny Jackson helps Manolo's baby brother, Pedro, recover from a seizure that the families become as cooperative as Manolo and Clem.

A tragedy, Gail Graham's *Cross-fire: A Vietnam Novel*, shows unusual American-Vietnamese cooperation. The story takes place during the Vietnam War. A young American soldier, Harry, is looking for his outfit in the jungle when he comes upon Vietnamese siblings led by thirteen-year-old Mi. She is holding a baby and accompanies her nine-year-old brother, Ton, and her three-year-old sister, Bong. American bombers have destroyed their village. Although they do not speak each other's language, Mi and Harry learn to communicate while walking toward civilization. After the baby dies, Harry tries to save Ton. When American planes strafe Harry, he dies, despite Mi's efforts to help him. Later, American soldiers shoot the children, thinking they are Viet Cong.

The tone is not tragic in Robert C. O'Brien's *Mrs. Frisby and the Rats of NIMH*, a fantasy about super-intelligent rats who cooperate to create a self-sufficient community. Widowed Mrs. Frisby learns that her deceased husband was one of the rats led by Nicodemus who got injections to increase their intelligence at the National Institute of Mental Health (NIMH). These special reading rats help Mrs. Frisby relocate her home and children where it is safe from the plow, and she reciprocates by supplying overheard information so that the rats can escape to Thorn Valley. There the independent rats develop their own civilization without using human resources, ". . . without stealing, of course. That's the whole idea. That's the Plan" (157).

SUMMARY

Among the sixty-two books discussed that concern cooperation as a value, sixteen are appropriate for early years, thirty are for middle years, and sixteen are for later years. Books that show animal cooperation are the only fantasies among the selections.

References

Adler, C. S. *Get Lost, Little Brother.* Clarion Books, 1983. 144 p. (M) (Maturing)

Alexander, Anne. *Trouble on Treat Street.* Atheneum Publishers, 1974. 116 p. (L) (Friendship, Humaneness)

Beskow, Elsa. *Pelle's New Suit.* Illustrated. Translated from Swedish by Marion Letcher Woodburn. Harper & Row, Publishers, 1929. 15 p. (E)

Bishop, Claire Huchet. *All Alone.* Illustrated by Feodor Rojankovsky. The Viking Press, 1953. 95 p. (M) (Responsibility)

Bottner, Barbara. *Jungle Day; or How I Learned to Love My Nosey Little Brother.* Illustrated. Delacorte Press, 1978. Unpaged. (E) (Friendship)

Bradbury, Bianca. *"I'm Vinny, I'm Me."* Illustrated by Richard Cuffari, Houghton Mifflin Company, 1977. 200 p. (L) (Ingenuity, Responsibility)

Brandenberg, Franz. *Nice New Neighbors.* Illustrated by Aliki. Greenwillow Books, 1977. 56 p. (E) (Animal Friendship)

Brenner, Barbara. *Mr. Tall and Mr. Small.* Illustrated by Tomi Ungerer. Young Scott Books, 1966. Unpaged. (E)

Bulla, Clyde Robert. *The Poppy Seeds.* Illustrated by Jean Charlot. The Thomas Y. Crowell Co., 1955. Unpaged. (E)

Burch, Robert. *Renfroe's Christmas.* Illustrated by Rocco Negri. The Viking Press, 1968. 59 p. (M)

Chambers, Aidan. *The Present Takers.* Harper & Row, Publishers, 1983. 156 p. (M) (Courage)

Charlip, Remy, and Burton Supree. *Harlequin and the Gift of Many Colors.* Illustrated by Remy Charlip. Parents Magazine Press, 1973. Unpaged. (E) (Friendship, Ingenuity)

Clymer, Eleanor. *The Get-away Car.* E. P. Dutton, 1978. 149 p. (M) (Friendship, Ingenuity)

————. *The Horse in the Attic.* Illustrated by Ted Lewin. Bradbury Press, 1983. 87 p. (M) (Ingenuity)

DeJong, Meindert. *The House of Sixty Fathers.* Illustrated by Maurice Sendak. Harper & Row, Publishers, 1956. 189 p. (M)

————. *The Wheel on the School.* Illustrated by Maurice Sendak. Harper & Row, Publishers, 1954. 298 p. (M)

Delton, Judy. *Two Good Friends*. Illustrated by Guilo Maestro. Crown
Publishers, 1974. 32 p. (E) (Animal Friendship)

Drury, Roger W. *The Champion of Merrimack County*. Illustrated by
Fritz Wegner. Little, Brown & Company, 1976. 199 p. (M)

Estes, Eleanor. *The Middle Moffat*. Illustrated by Louis Slobodkin.
Harcourt, Brace & Company, 1942. 317 p. (M) (Friendship)

————. *The Moffat Museum*. Illustrated. Harcourt Brace Jovanovich,
1983. 262 p. (M) (Ingenuity)

————. *The Moffats*. Illustrated by Louis Slobodkin. Harcourt, Brace
& World, 1941. 290 p. (M) (Friendship)

————. *Rufus M.* Illustrated by Louis Slobodkin. Harcourt, Brace &
World, 1943. 320 p. (M) (Friendship)

Gackenbach, Dick. *King Wacky*. Illustrated. Crown Publishers, 1984.
32 p. (E)

Graham, Gail. *Cross-fire: A Vietnam Novel*. Illustrated by David
Martin Stone. Pantheon, 1972. 135 p. (L) (Courage, Humaneness, Responsibility)

Haywood, Carolyn. *Eddie and His Big Deals*. Illustrated. William
Morrow & Company, 1955. 190 p. (M) (Ingenuity)

Hopper, Nancy J. *Hang on, Harvey!* E. P. Dutton, 1983. 86 p. (L)

Howard, Moses L. *The Ostrich Chase*. Illustrated by Barbara Seuling.
Holt, Rinehart & Winston, 1974. 118 p. (M) (Courage, Ingenuity,
Loyalty, Responsibility)

Iwamura, Kazuo. *Ton and Pon: Two Good Friends*. Illustrated. Bradbury Press, 1984. 52 p. (E) (Animal Friendship)

Jones, Adrienne. *Sail, Calypso!* Illustrated by Adolph LeMoult. Little,
Brown & Company, 1968. 210 p. (L) (Friendship)

Jordan, June. *New Life: New Room*. Illustrated by Ray Cruz. Thomas
Y. Crowell, 1975. 52 p. (E) (Friendship)

Knudson, R. R. *Zanbanger*. Harper & Row, Publishers, 1977. 162 p.
(L) (Humaneness)

————. *Zanboomer*. Harper & Row, Publishers, 1978. 183 p. (L)
(Friendship)

Lionni, Leo. *Swimmy*. Illustrated. Pantheon, 1963. Unpaged. (E)

————. *Tico and the Golden Wings*. Illustrated. Pantheon, 1964.
Unpaged. (E) (Animal Friendship)

Lord, Athena V. *A Spirit to Ride the Whirlwind*. Macmillan Publishing
Company, 1981. 205 p. (L) (Friendship)

McNeill, Janet. *Goodbye, Dove Square*. Illustrated by Mary Russon. Little, Brown & Company, 1969. 196 p. (L) (Responsibility)

Mann, Peggy. *The Street of the Flower Boxes*. Illustrated by Peter Burchard. Coward-McCann, 1966. 71 p. (M) (Ingenuity)

———. *When Carlos Closed the Street*. Illustrated by Peter Burchard. Coward-McCann, 1969. 71 p. (M) (Ingenuity)

Martin, Charles E. *Summer Business*. Illustrated. Greenwillow Books, 1984. Unpaged. (E) (Ingenuity)

Miles, Betty. *Having a Friend*. Illustrated by Erik Blegvad. Alfred A. Knopf, 1959. Unpaged. (E) (Friendship)

———. *The Secret Life of the Underwear Champ*. Illustrated by Dan Jones. Alfred A. Knopf, 1981. 117 p. (M) (Friendship)

Molarsky, Osmond. *Where the Good Luck Was*. Illustrated by Ingrid Fetz. Henry Z. Walck, 1970. 63 p. (M) (Friendship)

Mowat, Farley. *Lost in the Barrens*. Little, Brown & Company, 1956. 244 p. (L) (Courage, Humaneness, Maturing)

Oakley, Graham. *The Church Mice Adrift*. Illustrated. Atheneum, 1977. Unpaged. (E) (Ingenuity)

O'Brien, Robert C. *Mrs. Frisby and the Rats of NIMH*. Illustrated by Zena Bernstein. Atheneum, 1971. 233 p. (L)

Perl, Lila. *Tybee Trimble's Hard Times*. Houghton Mifflin Company, 1984. 143 p. (M) (Friendship)

Peyton, K. M. *'Who, Sir? Me, Sir?'* Oxford Univ. Press, 1983. 171 p. (L)

Shreve, Susan. *The Flunking of Joshua T. Bates*. Illustrated by Diane de Groat. Alfred A. Knopf, 1984. 82 p. (M) (Friendship)

Southall, Ivan. *Hills End*. St. Martin's Press, 1963. 174 p. (L) (Courage, Ingenuity, Maturing, Responsibility)

Stinetorf, Louise A. *A Charm for Paco's Mother*. Illustrated by Joseph Escourido. The John Day Company, 1965. 127 p. (M) (Responsibility)

Wilder, Laura Ingalls. *By the Shores of Silver Lake*. Rev. ed. Illustrated by Garth Williams. Harper & Row, Publishers, 1953 (Text 1939). 291 p. (M) (Friendship)

———. *Farmer Boy*. Rev. ed. Illustrated by Garth Williams. Harper & Row, Publishers, 1953 (Text 1933). 372 p. (M) (Friendship)

———. *The First Four Years*. Harper & Row, Publishers, 1971. 134 p. (L) (Friendship)

————. *Little House in the Big Woods*. Rev. ed. Illustrated by Garth Williams. Harper & Row, Publishers, 1953 (Text 1932). 238 p. (M) (Friendship)

————. *Little House on the Prairie*. Rev. ed. Illustrated by Garth Williams. Harper & Row, Publishers, 1953 (Text 1935). 335 p. (M) (Friendship)

————. *Little Town on the Prairie*. Rev. ed. Illustrated by Garth Williams. Harper & Row, Publishers, 1953 (Text 1941). 307 p. (M) (Friendship)

————. *The Long Winter*. Rev. ed. Illustrated by Garth Williams. Harper & Row, Publishers, 1953 (Text 1940). 335 p. (M) (Friendship, Ingenuity)

————. *On the Banks of Plum Creek*. Rev. ed. Illustrated by Garth Williams. Harper & Row, Publishers, 1953 (Text 1937). 339 p. (M) (Friendship)

————. *These Happy Golden Years*. Rev. ed. Illustrated by Garth Williams. Harper & Row, Publishers, 1953 (Text 1943). 289 p. (L) (Friendship)

Willard, Barbara. *Storm from the West*. Illustrated by Douglas Hall. Harcourt, Brace & World, 1963. 189 p. (L) (Ingenuity)

Winthrop, Elizabeth. *Belinda's Hurricane*. Illustrated by Wendy Watson. E. P. Dutton, 1984. 54 p. (M) (Friendship)

————. *That's Mine!* Illustrated by Emily McCully. Holiday House, 1977. Unpaged. (E)

II

Courage

The *American College Dictionary* defines courage as "the quality of mind that enables one to encounter difficulties and danger with firmness or without fear." In the majority of children's books with courage as a central theme, the protagonist may be afraid but despite this, faces dangers. Often remaining silent or still in a particular situation requires greater courage than showing bravado.

BOOKS FOR EARLY YEARS

A popular preschool book is *The Little Engine that Could* by Watty Piper, with illustrations by George and Doris Hauman. When an engine, taking toys and food to tots on the other side of the mountain, cannot make it to the top, no train will help until the little blue engine appears. Children enjoy chanting as it chugs up the mountain, "I think I can. I think I can. I think I can" (unp). Then they proudly echo as it descends, "I thought I could. I thought I could. I thought I could" (unp).

Marjorie Flack's pictures of vivid Easter eggs mesh with DuBose Heyward's words in telling a story of *The Country Bunny and the Little Gold Shoes*. Every year, when Grandfather Bunny chooses the five kindest, swiftest, and wisest bunnies to deliver Easter eggs, a country girl bunny with brown skin and white tail wants to be named. Instead, she becomes a married Lady Cottontail with twenty-one babies whom she teaches to do housework. When it is time to replace a retiring Easter Bunny, Grandfather chooses Cottontail because she proves she has trained her children to work happily together. Cottontail's work seems complete on Easter Eve, but Grandfather asks her to deliver a beautiful egg to a sick boy who lives atop a mountain. While ascending the icy mountain, Cottontail slips, injuring a leg. As she struggles up, Grandfather appears and says, "You are not only wise, and kind, and swift, but you are also the bravest of all the bunnies. And I shall make you my very own Gold Shoe Easter Bunny" (unp). Wearing gold shoes, Cottontail flies up the mountain to put an egg in the sleeping boy's hands.

Author-illustrator Bill Peet has a horse as his hero in *Cowardly Clyde*. Clyde is an aloof horse as he prances, hoping to keep his cowardice a secret. Wearing armor, Sir Galavant rides Clyde, looking for a monster to conquer. He finds a monster that chases him in the woods. When Clyde realizes Sir Galavant has been knocked from his back by a branch, the horse returns for his master. After the monster chases Clyde into a sunny meadow and vanishes in "KER-PUFFLE," Clyde feels brave.

Little Owl, an American Indian boy in upstate New York, and White One, his horse, are heroes in *Little Owl Indian* by author-illustrator Hetty Burlingame Beatty. When they are riding in the forest one day, Little Owl discovers a forest fire. He warns people of his village and his animal friends, leading them across a river to safety. Big Chief Great Eagle thanks the rider and his horse "for their courage and skill in finding the fire and riding to warn all the animals and all the Indians and leading them to safety" (31).

Fear of heights prevents Michael from climbing atop a slide or bars in *Michael Is Brave* by Helen E. Buckley, illustrated by Emily McCully. When a small girl climbs atop a slide and is afraid to come down, the teacher asks Michael to climb and stand behind her. Slowly he climbs. After the girl sees him behind, she smiles and slides down to her teacher. As Michael stands at the top, the girl ascends again. Michael says to no one in particular, "I was afraid, too" (unp). Before he thinks about it, down the slide he goes.

Brendan is another boy afraid of heights in Carol Carrick's *The Climb*, a book with soft illustrations by Donald Carrick. Four years younger than his cousin Nora, Brendan fearfully climbs a mountain while she says, "Don't look down, Brendan. Look at me" (unp). As she descends, Nora tries to hide, is stuck in a cave entrance, and gets out with Brendan's help.

In *Harry and the Terrible Whatzit*, author-illustrator Dick Gackenbach shows little Harry warning his mother about something frightening in the cellar, but she still goes down to get pickles. When Harry follows her with a broom, he finds her gone, but there is a double-headed, three-clawed, six-toed, long-horned Whatzit. As Harry attacks with his broom, the Whatzit diminishes because Harry is no longer afraid. The boy discovers Mother in the garden and she says, "I will never worry about a Whatzit as long as you are around" (unp).

Taro Yashima's *Crow Boy*, with the author's illustrations of rural Japan, describes a shy boy's courage. Chibi is in the sixth grade before a kind teacher, Mr. Isobe, notices that he can imitate crows. Though the friendless, poor boy lives far from school, he attends every day—rain or shine—for six years. With Mr. Isobe's encouragement, shy Chibi imitates crow sounds in a talent show. Thereafter, townspeople call him Crow Boy, and he always remembers his day of glory after he leaves school to work in the fields.

BOOKS FOR MIDDLE YEARS

In text and through illustrations, William Pène du Bois tells a story of bravery in *The Forbidden Forest*. An enterprising man, Spider Max, takes his kangaroo, Lady Adelaide, to Europe where she becomes a lightweight boxing champion. After they save a bulldog, Buckingham, from a cruel owner, the three prevent the Great War. In the Forbidden Forest, Lady Adelaide hits a German officer in the eye with a grape from a slingshot, making him give an arm signal prematurely which, in turn, causes a cannon to misfire and destroy ammunition intended to shell Paris. Captured, Lady Adelaide faces a firing squad. At the right moment, Spider Max calls, "Mouse, Lady Adelaide" (49). She leaps over the wall and "the Stoppers of the Great War" return to Australia in triumph.

Bernard, Mouse Prisoner's Aid Society secretary, narrowly escapes death in Margery Sharp's *Bernard the Brave: A Miss Bianca Story*. Another mouse, old Nicodemus, gets Bernard to rescue a friend, Miss Tomasina, from bandits. Bernard and a teddy bear, Algernon, go to the bandits' Wolf Range hideout. "It needed some courage and resolution on both of their parts to leave the railway station—their last link with civilization!—and begin the long slog in search of the bandits' lair" (55). In spite of their capture by wolves and other misadventures, Bernard and Algernon rescue Miss Tomasina.

Mary Stolz has created four books about two timid mice, Asa and Rambo; a cat, Siri; and a Chihuahua pup, Maximilian. In *Belling the Tiger*, other mice order Asa and Rambo, lowly cellar dwellers, to "bell" Siri. With the collar and bell they got at a hardware store, Asa and Rambo run from a street cat to a ship. They sail to a foreign land where they make friends with a large cat, Tiger. He lets them bell his tail and explains an elephant's fear of mice. "He's simply terrified of mice. But a brave fellow for all that. It's nothing to be ashamed of . . . a fear or two. Most of us have them" (52).

When Asa and Rambo return home, they feel important enough to move to the pantry. In Stolz's *The Great Rebellion*, the two leave the dictatorship of Portman, head mouse at home, and become field mice. After encountering a fox, an owl, and a raccoon, Asa and Rambo decide they are really house mice and take refuge in Benn's delicatessen—where Siri lives. They feel safe from him as long as he talks because, as Rambo says, "He's a talker first and a cat second" (15). In the end, the mice and cat live together. In the third book, they actually are friends.

Before Siri and the mice can relax, Benn's delicatessen gets a pup, Maximilian. In Mary Stolz's *Siri, the Conquistador*, the three friends face the dog. Siri commands, "First I'll terrify him and then we'll coexist" (39). Siri later adds, "I am certainly glad that we decided to coexist before we saw Maximilian, that is Maxie. Now we need never doubt our courage again" (48).

In Stolz's *Maximilian's World*, the pup and Asa explore the outdoors despite Siri's and Rambo's objections. When no harm comes to them, Siri and Rambo apologize.

Eight-year-old Sarah Noble is the heroine in Alice Dalgliesh's *The Courage of Sarah Noble*. In 1707, before Sarah goes with her father, who is building a new wilderness home in Connecticut, her mother wraps a cloak about her and says, "Keep up your courage, Sarah Noble" (2). When Sarah is afraid, she wears the red cloak and repeats Mother's words. Her father prepares to return for the rest of his family, leaving Sarah with the Indians, but she complains, "Stay here. Alone? I am afraid. I have lost my courage" (36). Father replies, "To be afraid and to be brave is the best courage of all" (36). After her family returns, Sarah looks at the cloak and realizes that "she had kept up her courage and it was something that would always be with her. Always—even when the cloak was all worn out" (54).

In Avi's *Night Journeys*, a Quaker justice of the peace, Everett Shinn, offers a home to orphaned, twelve-year-old Peter York and his horse, Jumper. In 1768, Peter joins a search party for two escaped New Jersey bondsmen, discovering eleven-year-old Elizabeth Mawes and ten-year-old Robert Linnly. Peter gives them his horse, helping them escape to Easton, Pennsylvania where they will be free. Returning to Shinn to take his punishment, Peter learns that Shinn is aware of his acts and could have stopped him. He understands Shinn's words, "It is not for me to say this law, that law. I'm required to uphold all laws" (100).

Avi's sequel, *Encounter at Easton*, depicts Robert and Elizabeth going toward Easton when frightened Jumper, their horse, runs away. Elizabeth, ill from a gunshot wound, takes refuge with a woman, Mad Moll, who lives in a cave. Robert gets a job working for Nathaniel Hill, who is in Easton to capture the children for their master, Mr. Tolliver. Despite Robert's precautions, Mr. Hill finds the cave, shoots Mad Moll, and learns that Elizabeth is dead. Mr. Grey, the inn's tapman, befriends Robert, helps him bury Elizabeth and Moll, and buys Robert's contract from Mr. Tolliver.

In Kathryn Lasky's *The Night Journey*, thirteen-year-old Rachel Lewis encourages her great-grandmother, Nana Sachie, to relate her escape from Russia when Nana was nine years old. Nana proposed that her family dress for the Purim holiday to cross the border on the fourteenth day of the Hebrew month, Adar, when Purim occurs. Nana suggested putting gold pieces in cookies to pay border guards, and Nana accidentally mixed the cookies so that the family escaped with the gold. This is a story about the courage and ingenuity needed to seek freedom.

In a blizzard on March 11, 1888, Katie waits for her father so that she can redeem her mother's brooch at a pawn shop. "Dependable Kate," as her mother calls her, is caring for her sick mother and five-year-old brother in *Day of the Blizzard* by Marietta D. Moskin. Since her father does not return, Katie starts out in the storm. The storm nearly defeats her, but Katie says, "I can't give up . . . not after coming this far" (45). After nearly freezing to death and being helped by others, she reaches the shop where she redeems her mother's brooch.

In Marilyn Sachs's *Call Me Ruth*, eight-year-old Rifka admires her mother, Faigel, in 1908 as she leads passengers in Yiddish songs on a boat bringing them to America. After her father dies, Rifka's mother becomes an exploited garment worker who joins a 1909 Shirtwaist

Makers Union strike. Rifka, now called Ruth, is ashamed of her
mother's broken English and union activity. She secretly gives a napkin
her mother embroidered to her teacher, Miss Baxter, as a Christmas
present. But when the strike is successful and Mother may serve as a
union organizer, Ruth asks her teacher to return the napkin, saying,
"My mother made the napkin for my trousseau. There was a tablecloth
and five other napkins too, but somebody stole it on the boat. She cried
for days. I think she would die if she knew I gave it away" (128). Miss
Baxter, while condemning the strike, admires Ruth's courage and
returns the napkin.

Priscilla Homola's *The Willow Whistle*, set in South Dakota about
1900 tells about eleven-year-old Annie and her strict father. Her father
refuses to let her go to a church social because he hears she has a
thirteen-year-old boyfriend, Conrad. After she insists upon going, Papa
whips her until she says, "I'm—not going" (57). Papa changes his mind
about Conrad when the boy and Annie ride her horse in a raging
blizzard to get Papa. Then Papa and Conrad go on the boy's sleigh to
save children at school who are caught in the storm. As they force their
way through drifts, Conrad tells Papa about a willow whistle he made
for Annie. Later, Papa praises Conrad, "Annie's fond of you. I can see
why now" (107).

A poignant story of courage during World War II is Arnold A.
Griese's *The Wind Is Not a River*. Thirteen-year-old Sasan and her ten-
year-old brother, Sidak, live with their grandmother on the island of
Attu. After Grandmother dies, Sasan takes her brother to their summer
camp on the other side of the island. When the Japanese control the
island, the children find an unconscious Japanese soldier. The two
delay their own departure to hide the soldier and help him recover.
Then, as the children paddle toward the U.S. naval base on Kiska
Island, a U.S. submarine rescues them. Sasan tells her brother,
"Troubles are like the wind, they do not go on forever. And so we must
always remember what Grandmother told us: the wind is not a river"
(108).

In another World War II story, *Twenty and Ten* by Claire Huchet
Bishop, twenty French children who have been evacuated to the
mountains with a nun, Sister Gabriel, hide ten Jewish children sought
by the Nazis. After the French pupils agree to hide the others, Sister
Gabriel says:

I did not expect less from you boys and girls. But you must
understand what this means. The Nazis are looking for those
children. If we take them, we must never let on that they are
here. Never. Even if we are questioned, we can never betray
them, no matter what the Nazis do to us. (21)

The French children play a favorite game, Flight into Egypt, and the
Nazis never suspect Jewish children are hiding in a cave.

Benjamin ("Mouse") Fawley and his friend, Ezzie, have thought
of seventeen ways to handle emergencies, such as swim fast if attacked
by a killer shark. In *The 18th Emergency* by Betsy Byars, Mouse cannot
cope with a class bully, Marvin Hammerman. Mouse, who decorates
walls with smart remarks, puts Marvin's name on a chart outside the
history room, drawing an arrow to a Neanderthal man. When he sees
Marvin behind him, he runs. He explains to Ezzie, "My problem is
that I have a *thing* about being hit . . . I just hate to be hurt" (80–81).
For a time he avoids Marvin but knows he cannot indefinitely. After he
hunts for Marvin to take a beating, he decides to stop writing captions.
He begins to understand that Marvin must feel as he did when first
called Mouse.

Young Barney Windsor, the new boy in town, faces a bully, Lenny
Coots, in *What a Wimp!* by Carol Carrick. Tired of being scorned,
Barney turns to Lenny, saying, "I'm not running. . . . I don't care
anymore what you do. . . . I'm not going to run. You'll have to kill me
first, 'cause I'm not going to run away" (87–88). Lenny is so surprised,
he hastily exits.

Twelve-year-old Paul Mather tells his story to a tape recorder as he
lies in a hospital dying of leukemia in *Hang Tough, Paul Mather* by
Alfred Slote. The Mathers move to Michigan to be near Dr. Kinsella, a
leukemia specialist. Paul, an excellent baseball player, loves the game.
Because he does not believe his father will sign an entry form for him to
join a local team, he forges Mr. Mather's signature and plays in a game.
He gets involved when he sees three boys in baseball uniforms talking to
his brother, Larry. He says, "I knew it would be a mistake to go over
there. I'd been sent to get Larry, not to meet a bunch of baseball
players. If I hadn't gone, it might have made all the difference in the
world, though Dr. Kinsella keeps telling me no" (210–211). Luckily,
Mr. Mather is at the game in which Paul plays, sees him collide with

the first baseman, and rushes his son to the hospital. Dr. Kinsella helps Paul face his impending death with courage and dignity.

A happy story about a disabled child is *Windows for Rosemary* by Marguerite Vance. Nine-year-old Rosemary has been blind since birth. Her parents and younger brother, Billy, have given her a sense of security, independence, and courage. For her birthday, Rosemary hopes for a Braille typewriter, and she is not disappointed.

Shy and lonely, twelve-year-old Alison lives with her mother in a council flat, or apartment, in England. She is fascinated by a German shepherd that stares from a third-story window as she goes to school. In *The Dog at the Window* by Helen Griffiths, Alison finally gathers courage to go to the flat of a stranger, Mrs. Bailey. The dog, Wolf, belongs to Mrs. Bailey's grandson, Bobby, who is in an institution for the mentally retarded. When she convinces Mrs. Bailey to let her walk Wolf daily, Alison changes for she feels, "She'd take on the whole world to save Wolf if she had to" (46). Mrs. Bailey, beaten down by life, commits suicide, and the S.P.C.A. claims Wolf. Uncle Reg, the boyfriend of Alison's mother, understands Alison's need for Wolf and tells her after Wolf gets a new master, "Love is knowing when to give up, as well as when to hold on" (116). In the end, Uncle Reg not only becomes her stepfather but obtains Wolf for her.

In *Courage, Dana* by Susan Beth Pfeffer, twelve-year-old Dana Parker becomes an instant heroine when she saves a little boy from being killed by a car. Tired of her being a celebrity, her best friend, Sharon, says, "We all know you're just a little coward who did one brave thing once and will never do another brave thing again" (58). To prove she is not cowardly, Dana stays in a graveyard after dark and stands up to a bully, Charlie, who has been teasing a classmate, Brian. She sees Brian writing on the school wall, signing Charlie's initials. She is torn between revealing Brian as the culprit or letting Charlie be unfairly punished. She discovers that being brave can involve choosing between right and wrong as well as being physically brave. When Dana confronts Charlie, Sharon declares, "That's real bravery. I'll never call you a coward again" (132).

Her New York City grandmother treats twelve-year-old Gertie Warshefsky like a servant in Barbara Cohen's *Queen for a Day*. Her mother is in an asylum and her father is seeking his fortune in the West. Her two mean aunts are only a few years older than she is. When Aunt Lilly is to be Queen Esther in a Purim holiday celebration, Gertie helps so much with her lines that she memorizes the part. Lilly gets stage fright and Gertie assumes the role. Unhappy because she is still treated like a servant, she feels better when Mr. Neufeld, a boarder, tells her, "You're a brave girl, Gertie, and you're a smart one. Your chance to show everyone that you're really a Queen will come again, and when it does, you'll have two eyes to see it and the nerve to take it" (121). After Mr. Neufeld moves to Chicago, he sends money so Gertie can stay in school.

Nine-year-old Jeffrey Post runs away to an island's closed amusement park in Eth Clifford's *Just Tell Me When We're Dead*. Jeff, who lives with his grandmother, is afraid she will not return from the hospital, so he will be abandoned again. His Uncle Harry Onetree comes with his daughters, seven-year-old Jo-Beth and ten-year-old Mary Rose, to take him to their home for the present. When the girls discover his rowboat is gone, they suspect he is on the island and they go after him. Two bank robbers come to the island to get their loot, discover Jeff, and tie him up in the amusement park's control room. As the girls sit in the Tunnel-of-Terror train wondering where to look for him, Jeff moves switches to turn on music and start the train. Frightened, Jo-Beth wants her sister to "Just tell me when we're dead" (61). Alerted by the music, the island's caretaker comes, rescues Jeff, and gets the sheriff to capture the robbers. Back on the mainland, Jeff learns his grandmother is recovering, so he is willing to visit his uncle.

In *The Middle Sister* by Miriam E. Mason, a little girl discovers that caring can lead to bravery. Eight-year-old Sarah Samantha is fearful. Her Uncle Romeo, who travels with a circus, promises a lion's tooth to make her brave if she bakes an apple dumpling from the fruit of an apple tree he gave her. When the family moves to Minnesota, each member chooses one thing to take, and Sarah Samantha chooses her apple tree. In her new home, she cares for her tree and one night, chases a pig that is trying to eat her tree's apples. That night, she discovers an Indian boy crying under a bush and brings him home, though her father returns the child to his people. In the fall, she bakes an apple dumpling, discovering she is no longer afraid. While Big Buffalo visits her house, he says, "You are a brave girl. Your name is Buffalo Woman" (154).

Just as children in America have fears, so do those in other lands. In Marietta Moskin's *Toto*, seven-year-old Suku will not help herd the tribe's cattle because he is afraid of lions. One day, he finds a baby lion,

Toto, caught in a poacher's trap. He frees it and leads it back to the game preserve. He sees a lion that runs away when an elephant herd appears. After his father and a game warden arrive in a Landrover, the game warden tells Suku, "You did right, Suku. I get so angry too when I catch these poachers. You would make a good game warden some day, Suku. You love animals and you are brave" (unp). Suku overcomes his fear by placing an animal's safety above his own.

In Armstrong Sperry's classic, *Call It Courage*, fifteen-year-old Mafatu, a South Sea Islander, proves his courage. Ever since his mother drowned when he was three years old, he has been afraid of the sea. He hears a friend, Kana, say, "I have tried to be friendly with him. But he is good only for making spears. Mafatu is a coward" (11). Stealing a boat, Mafatu leaves with his mongrel dog and an albatross, only to be shipwrecked in a storm, landing on Forbidden Island. He survives, makes a canoe, and returns home to hear his father proclaim, "Here is my son come home from the sea, Mafatu, Stout Heart. A brave name for a brave boy" (94).

Fear of the sea is also Li Lun's problem in Carolyn Treffinger's *Li Lun, Lad of Courage*. He refuses to join the "man-making" fishing trip expected of ten-year-old boys. His angry father punishes him by having him plant seven grains of rice atop Lao Shan or Sorrow Mountain and not return until he has seven times as many grains. Following the advice of wise old Sun Ling, he climbs the mountain, plants his grains, and guards the young shoots for three and a half months. Gulls and rats destroy six, but the seventh bears ninety-nine grains. When he returns, the Keeper of the Temple arranges a ceremony at which he tells the community, "We are fisher folk. We have brought our rice across the sea over rough and teacherous waters. But now I shall ask Li Lun to teach other boys how to grow rice. Not on Lao Shan, but right here on our Temple grounds" (93).

BOOKS FOR LATER YEARS

A fantasy often portrays moral values clearer than a realistic story, as exemplified in Lloyd Alexander's trilogy about Theo, a printer's apprentice, and Mickle, heir apparent to Westmark's throne. In *Westmark*, the king becomes ill when his evil chief minister, Cabbarus, secretly kidnaps the princess, Augusta. Meanwhile, a former apprentice, Theo, saves the life of a waif, Mickle, and presents her as a ventriloquist to two quack medicine vendors, Count Las Bombas and his dwarf, Musket. Fearful of becoming as much a rogue as his male companions, Theo leaves to follow a rebel leader, Florian. When Mickle, Las Bombas, and Musket are imprisoned, Florian and his men rescue them. Theo, brave without killing soldiers, tells Florian, "Killing is wrong. I believe that. I still do but now I wonder. Do I believe it because I want to be a decent man? Or because I am a coward?" (136). To encourage the king's abdication, cruel Cabbarus brings Mickle to court to pretend she is the spirit of the princess, but she confesses she *is* the princess. Theo asks the king to banish, not kill, Cabbarus. Theo says, "I want no one's death on my conscience, not even his" (176). The king banishes Cabbarus and lets Theo tour the kingdom "to find out what the people want and what's to be done about it" (183).

In *The Kestrel,* the second book in Alexander's trilogy, Theo is touring the country when he learns that General Erzcour is planning a coup with the military and aristocracy. After the king's death, Theo starts for the capitol, but a Cabbarus spy, Skeit, shoots him en route. Theo's rescuer, Florian, explains:

> I want our freedom spelled out in laws. I want the equality for every man and woman in Westmark. I want your word, that come what may, you'll support our cause. Against the aristocracy. Against the monarchy. Against the queen herself. Do I have your promise? (44)

Theo promises. Then Mickle, worried about Theo, puts on urchin's clothes and joins Las Bombas and Musket to search for him. Cabbarus escapes to Regia where he directs an invasion. Theo, called the Kestrel, Florian, and Justin lead rebels against Regians. Mickle commands her country's troops, not realizing this "Colonel Kestrel . . . a real madman, a bloodthirsty fellow" (156), is Theo. Mickle, now Queen Augusta, meets with sixteen-year-old Constantine, the Regian king, and ends the war. Theo and Mickle decide to marry. She will retain the monarchy with three consuls: Florian, Justin, and Theo. "But I'm not a statesman," says Theo. And Mickle replies, "I know, that's one of your better qualities" (244)

The Beggar Queen concludes the Alexander trilogy. The war is over, but Regia's Duke Conrad, King Constantine's uncle, plots with Cabbarus to overthrow the queen and her consuls. When Cabbarus rules from the palace, Queen Augusta uses a pawnshop as headquarters for her government in exile, enlisting support from street fiddlers, beggars, washerwomen, and match girls. Once again, Theo assumes Colonel Kestrel's qualities to save Westmark and kill Cabbarus. Theo realizes that

> he could not leave it to chance or accident. He could not
> tolerate the idea that the man might escape. It was Theo's last
> obligation, he hoped he would not be cheated out of it. If it
> cost his own life, that, too, was as it should be. (140)

After the people rise up and win the battle, Mickle abdicates to let them decide what to do with their country. Mickle and Theo leave with Count Las Bombas and Musket to see the world.

In a timeless fantasy, Natalie Babbitt's *Tuck Everlasting*, the main character is ten-year-old Winnie Foster. She must choose between drinking water from a spring, Tregap, which offers immortality, and living a normal life ending in death. After Winnie meets the Tuck family at the spring, Mr. Tuck stresses the importance of the life cycle and the burden of immortality, saying, "You can't have living without dying. Can you imagine? All the little ones little forever, all the old ones old forever" (64). Mrs. Tuck accidentally kills a stranger who discovers the secret of the spring and wants the water for an evil purpose. Sentenced to die, immortal Mrs. Tuck rejoices when Winnie takes her place to allow the family to escape and the spring to remain a secret. Authorities grant Winnie her freedom, and she dies as an old woman.

Two realistic books with supernatural qualities are Anne Knowles's *The Halcyon Island* and Margaret Mahy's *The Changeover: A Supernatural Romance*. In the Knowles book, twelve-year-old Ken stays with the housekeeper at a vacation cottage near a river while his parents are away. Since he almost drowned when he was three years old, Ken wants to conquer his fear of water. He tries river boating but loses his paddles. "It seemed he was fated to drown, and now he'd drift downstream and go over the weir and that would be that" (38). But another boy, Giles, rescues the paddles, teaching Ken to swim and handle boats. They spend wonderful days on the river and watch kingfishers on Halcyon Island where Giles lives. After Ken's parents return, Giles disappears and Ken wonders whether Giles had been real after all.

Fourteen-year-old Laura Chant, who has had several premonitions come true, knows that she has psychic powers. In Mahy's *The Changeover: A Supernatural Romance*, Laura is sure that the new boy, sixteen-year-old Sorry Carlisle, is a witch. When an antique dealer, Carmody, puts his mark on her three-year-old brother, Jacko, and he becomes ill, Laura asks for Sorry's help. The doctors cannot find what is wrong though they smell peppermint near him, the same odor that pervades Carmody's shop. After Laura goes to the Carlisle home and sees locked gates, she says the house's name, Juana Caeli, "like a magic spell" (57), only to find the bolt releases. Laura asks old Mrs. Carlisle and her daughter to break the spell. Mrs. Carlisle replies, "We are not without our powers, you know. . . . We are the daughters of the moon. But we'll talk it over later on" (88). Sorry predicts Laura's success, "because you'll make it come right, won't you? Your brother will catch survival from you. You know what you are, Chant, you're a born survivor" (17). Laura puts her mark on Carmody and saves her brother.

Elizabeth George Speare shows religious persecution and fear based on superstition in *The Witch of Blackbird Pond*. In 1687, sixteen-year-old Kit Tyler leaves her home in Barbados when her grandfather dies and moves to Wethersfield, Connecticut, a Puritan town, to live with her aunt. While still en route, she dives from the ship to rescue Prudence Cruff's doll which had been thrown overboard. The little girl's mother, Goodwife Cruff, is horrified. Nat Eaton, the captain's son, who dives into the water to save Kit, tells her later that Goodwife Cruff has been accusing her of being a witch. "She says no respectable woman can keep afloat in the water like that" (13). Kit, who has difficulty adjusting to Puritan life, befriends Hannah Tupper, an isolated Quaker widow. Feeling sorry for little Prudence Cruff, Kit secretly introduces her to Hannah and teaches her to read. When King James plans to withdraw the town charter, Nat explains to Kit why people are upset:

> If the King respects our rights and keeps his word to us, then he will retain our loyalty. But if he revokes the laws he has made and tacks and comes about till the ship is on the beam ends, then finally we will be forced to cut the hawser. (121)

After a few sudden deaths in Wethersfield, people accuse Hannah and Kit of being witches. Kit and Nat help Hannah escape, but authorities arrest Kit and hold her for an inquiry on witchcraft. Though she refuses to implicate Prudence in her relationship with Hannah, Nat brings Prudence to testify that Kit has taught her to read and write, and the case is dismissed.

War fosters courage in soldiers and in their families at home. Fourteen-year-old Rebecca Ransome is a fine girls' role model in *Rebecca's War* by Ann Finlayson. Father and Will are privateering, Tom is a rebel, Mother is dead, and Rebecca is at home in Philadelphia with Ursula Keim, a bound girl, to care for four-year-old Peter along with eight-year-old Amelia, her siblings. Rebecca hides a fortune in lead-covered gold ingots for the rebels. British officers control the house, but with ingenuity, Rebecca finds food for family members and prisoners. She is cheerful with the British, particularly with a severely wounded captain, the Honourable Frederick Augustus Towne. When the British finally leave, Rebecca reflects:

> It had been a hard eight and a half months, but Rebecca had come through. She had done everything they had asked of her, held the family together, protected the secret of the gold. Every time, they'd call for one more little effort, she'd carried it through somehow. She'd even saved some of the Honourable Frederick's esteem. (278)

Like many families during the American Revolution, the Bishops are divided in loyalties. In Scott O'Dell's *Sarah Bishop*, Sarah's father is a Tory and a Long Island farmer. Her younger brother, Chad, runs away to join the rebels. Feelings run high in town. One night, Colonel Ben Birdsall and a cutthroat gang come to the farm, reminding the father that he had destroyed Thomas Paine's pamphlet, *Common Sense*, and has the king's picture over his bed. They set fire to the house, tie Sarah to a tree, and tar and feather her father, who dies. Sarah searches for her brother in New York City and finds that he has died on a prison ship. Falsely accused of setting fire to a rooming house, she runs away, earns money in a tavern, and goes to the wilderness of the mainland, armed with a musket and supplies. She lives alone all winter, rescuing a trapper caught in his own trap. She confesses to a young Quaker friend that people make her afraid, so he replies, "Fear is something that encourages people to harm thee. Fear causes hatred" (139). After promising to attend some Quaker meetings, Sarah returns to her cave. She starts to shoot a copperhead but "putting the musket under [her] arm, [she] made a wide circle around the pool and went on" (184).

In *Johnny Tremain*, Esther Forbes pictures Boston in 1773 when orphaned, fourteen-year-old Johnny Tremain apprentices to a silver-smith, Mr. Lapham. Arrogant at first, Johnny injures his right hand while pouring molten silver and becomes depressed. He seeks help from a rich relative who accuses him of stealing a silver cup, one actually given to Johnny by his mother. Josiah Quincy defends Johnny in court and wins the case. After Johnny becomes a friend of Rob, a young printer for the rebel *Observer* newspaper, he joins in the Boston Tea Party. When he sees his British soldier friend, Pumpkin, shot as a deserter, he confesses:

> That night for one horrible moment he was glad his hand was crippled. He would never have to face the round eye of death at the end of a musket. For days he felt his own inadequacy. Was the bold Johnny Tremain a coward at heart? (201)

Johnny brings a gun to Rob, who was wounded in the Battle of Lexington, and meets Dr. Warren, Rob's physician. Dr. Warren gives Johnny hope that his crippled hand can be restored.

Another powerful Revolutionary War story is *War Comes to Willy Freeman* by James L. Collier and Christopher Collier. When Willy's father enlists in the American militia in 1780, his owner frees him, his wife, and their thirteen-year-old daughter, Willy. She sees the British shoot her father at Groton and returns home to New London, Connecticut only to discover her mother is a prisoner in New York City. Disguised as a boy, Willy goes to New York City where she learns she must be courageous to be black, free, and a woman. She thinks, "When you was a woman you was half a slave, anyway" (63).

Russia in the 1920s during the Bolshevik Revolution is the setting for Felice Holman's *The Wild Children*. Twelve-year-old Alex descends from a hidden storage room, which is his bedroom, to find his mother, father, sister, and grandmother taken away. "He often wondered how life could be so perilous for the people, even though his father had told him that the new government was a 'people's government' " (3). His teacher hides him and sends him to his uncle in Moscow, giving him the name of her St. Petersburg brother, who can arrange his escape from Russia. When Alex gets to Moscow, his uncle is gone, so he joins a band of homeless, desperate, criminal children, living in filthy cellars and caves, a group led by Peter. After Alex recovers from illness, he goes south with Peter's group and then on to St. Petersburg. When his teacher's brother arranges for Alex to cross to Finland without making provisions for the other children, Alex says, "But I can't leave them. It was my idea to come here. I can't leave them now, they are my friends, and yes, my family" (130). Then all go to Finland.

Jaap ter Haar's *Boris* takes place in 1942 as the Germans besiege Leningrad (formerly St. Petersburg). Twelve-year-old Boris Makarenko cares for his sick mother and spends most of the day standing in food lines. Nadia, his friend, knows where there are potatoes in a suburban field. Fearful Boris remembers his father's words, "The courage that we show will give courage to other people" (19). He accompanies Nadia, and when she collapses in the field, three German soldiers kindly carry her to the Russian line. Russians break through German lines, saving Boris. As he sees German prisoners herded through streets, he remembers the helpful German soldiers and gives chocolate to a German. He ignores nasty remarks from others, and draws comfort from an old woman's remark, "What use is our freedom to us if we still live in hate?" (149).

Fourteen-year-old Erik Hansen is on a school trip from Denmark to Germany in 1937 when he becomes involved in the anti-Nazi underground in *Chase Me, Catch Nobody!* by Erik Christian Haugaard. Shy, quiet Erik constantly prays, "Oh God, make me invisible until the bell rings and the lesson is over" (5). Erik makes friends with a boy from another school, Nicolai Linde. A man in a shabby gray raincoat gives Erik a package to hold until they disembark from the ferry. When they land, two members of the S.S. take the man away. Erik knows that he must deliver the package (Danish passports) to the Hamburg address the man had whispered to him. After delivering the passports, Erik discovers that the S.S. wants him. He runs away with the help of a barmaid who asks him to help her thirteen-year-old niece escape to Denmark. The niece, calling herself Nobody, is wanted by the S.S. because she is part Jewish. With Nikolai's assistance, Erik and Nobody, dressed as German youths, reach Kiel, find a boat, and cross to Denmark. Since the boat starts to sink near the shore, Erik swims and discovers the water is just waist deep.

During the Nazi occupation of a small Dutch town, fourteen-year-old Arnold Westervoort is torn between his father's support of Germany and the hostility of his classmates and neighbors. In *War Without Friends* by Evert Hartman, Arnold begins to believe in the Resistance and in an underground newspaper's stories of German concentration camp atrocities. His father defends wartime lack of normal justice, saying, "Anyone who thinks differently is wrong and a danger to society.

. . . We must have authority and leadership. A nation without a leader is a house of cards and collapses in the first puff of wind" (148). Arnold, beaten when he discovers a houseboat of stolen goods, befriends an injured Resistance fighter in the hospital. Arnold sneaks him a gun so that he can escape. When Arnold's parents leave by train with other departing Germans, Arnold hides until they are gone.

The title of Margaret Balderson's *When the Jays Fly to Bárbmo* derives from a Lapp saying which means that people will return to their birthplace. The title is appropriate because fourteen-year-old Ingeborg Mygaard tries to learn about the mysterious background of her dead mother, a Laplander despised by Norwegians. Her father strikes her when she wears a Lapland costume which she finds in a storage shed. Ingeborg is so angry that she refuses to say goodbye to him as he leaves on a fishing trip. She thinks, "I had come to a point in my life when I felt it was my right to know the truth about certain things. If I didn't make a stand now, perhaps I never would" (66). Nazis invade Norway and her father dies while helping people flee the country. Ingeborg cries when she reads in her father's last letter, "Too much time is wasted over futile quarrels—too much of our energies consumed by bitter regrets, . . . [that] will destroy the roots you have put down in your childhood" (93). The Nazis come for the Nygaard's Jewish handy man, burning the barn and slaughtering cattle. Aunt Anne-Sigri dies and Ingeborg is alone in a vacuum of nothingness. "But the will to survive cannot be denied. It is strongest in creatures that are young" (168). The girl decides to go to her mother's Lapland family, burning her farm to prevent Nazi acquisition. She leaves on skiis, nearly dying in a blizzard, and reflects, "The only conscious thought in my mind was to keep going" (200). Although her mother's family welcomes her, the image of the burned farm stays with her, so she plans to return.

A family's wartime survival is the theme of Christine Nöstlinger's *Fly Away Home*, set in Vienna in 1945. Following Russian rule, a German family, the Goths, move to a suburban villa while eight-year-old Christel remains in Vienna. Since Russian officers stay in the villa, Christel becomes fond of Cohen, their pleasant cook, once a Leningrad tailor. This is a story of daily courage during occupation.

A poignant tale of wartime children, based on accounts from over 400 youths, is *Max's Gang* by Frank Baer. Between April and October 1945, five children return home to Berlin from a Czech Children's Evacuation Camp, leaving by train with all their belongings. After an airplane strafes the train, they have to walk. They get a few rides but most of the time they walk. Max loses

> a pair of shoes, brown half-boots made of sturdy skiver leather. They were double-stitched, laced with leather thong overhooks, and had strong soles with metal at front and back.
> . . . His father had made them for his qualifying exam for journeyman cobbler. (103)

A farmer imprisons the children. They escape, rescue an ill woman, and get involved with the black market. When Max finally reaches Berlin and walks home, his family is eating dinner. His father slaps him for losing the boots, so Max gets his knapsack and leaves.

It takes great courage to suffer discrimination without retaliating, as eleven-year-old Rinko Tsujimura discovers in Yoshiko Uchida's *A Jar of Dreams* and *The Best Bad Thing*, stories set in California in 1935. Rinko's father, a barber, is five months behind in paying rent. Her mother starts a hand laundry and her father opens a repair shop in his garage. The family perseveres when faced with vandalism and signs saying, "GET OUT OF OUR TERRITORY JAP LAUNDRY OR YOU'LL BE SORRY," engineered by a local laundry competitor, Wilbur Starr. Cal, Rinko's older brother, wants to quit college, but Father says, "You know, in spite of everything, we never gave up. The more we were despised, the harder we worked. We always had hopes that some day things would be better. If not for us, then for our children" (82). Visiting from Japan, Aunt Waka helps Rinko understand why her parents take chances or risk losing their dreams forever. She tells Rinko, "They are strong. They endured because they have patience and courage. And they have managed to hold on to their Japanese selves" (107).

In Uchida's sequel, *The Best Bad Thing*, Rinko helps a widow, Mrs. Hata, and her two sons who raise cucumbers. An old man, living secretly in Mrs. Hata's barn, rescues the children when a stranger attacks them as they gather railroad ties. While befriending the old man, Rinko learns about herself. She thinks:

> Actually I guess I am about five different people depending on who I'm with. With Joji I can be mean and bossy. With Mama and Papa I can be stubborn and ornery. With Mrs. Sugar I can be cheerful and sweet, and with a big bully, I

really tried to be strong and brave the way Aunt Waka told me
to be. (52)

In the end, Papa gets Mrs. Hata a job in the church dormitory so that
she does not have to go on welfare.

Discrimination based on color is difficult to combat. In *Sounder*,
William H. Armstrong, the author, repeats an old story told to him in
which a black family and their dog are courageous. After the sheriff
arrests the boy's father because he stole a ham for his hungry family,
Sounder, a Georgia redbone hound and bulldog, chases the sheriff's
wagon, only to be shot. Two months later, the mutilated dog comes
home. It is six years before the return of the black sharecropper, also
mutilated. The boy, his mother, and three younger siblings survive
while the sharecropper is in a chain gang. The mother often hums:

> You've gotta walk that lonesome valley,
> You've gotta walk it by yourself,
> Ain't nobody else gonna walk it for you. (69)

During the long trips the boy makes to try to find where his father is
imprisoned, he becomes determined to learn to read and discovers:

> His journeys in search of his father accomplished one won-
> derful thing. In the towns he found that people threw newspa-
> pers and magazines into trashbarrels, so he could always find
> something with which to practice his reading. (80)

When the boy returns after each trip, the crippled coon hound greets
him. Eventually, a school teacher lets the boy live with him, educates
him, and gives him hope for the future.

In Armstrong's sequel, *Sour Land*, the former boy, now Moses
Waters in his sixties, comes to town to teach in a black school. Anson
Stone, a white man, widowed with three children, hires Moses to help
him. Moses teaches the Stone children to love books and develop
intellectual curiosity. When some poor whites harass Moses, the white
owner of a general store, Enoch Morris, befriends the teacher. Anson
says of Enoch, "When something gets too heavy for ordinary men to
carry, Enoch steps in and carries the extra weight. And I don't mean
sacks of potatoes and grain, though he does that too, I mean troubles"
(27). Quiet young David Stone lets a squirrel bite him to prove he is
unafraid and comments:

Moses put turpentine on it. I didn't tell him why I did it. Just
that I did it to show that I had courage. He said he didn't think
it was as much courage as foolish. Then I asked him what
courage was and he said it was different things. (73)

It is 1933 in Mississippi and a black family, the Logans, own a 400-
acre cotton farm, formerly belonging to a white man, Harlan Granger.
In *Roll of Thunder, Hear My Cry* by Mildred D. Taylor, eight-year-old
Cassie Logan learns why her father, David Logan, works on the railroad
to earn money to keep his land. He tells her:

Look out there, Cassie girl. All that belongs to you. You ain't
never had to live on nobody's place but your own and long as
I live and the family survives, you'll never have to. That's
important. You may not understand that now, but one day
you will. Then you'll see. (7)

David Logan tries to help sharecroppers do cooperative buying in
Vicksburg. When T. J. Avery, a friend of Cassie's brother, and two
white boys rob a store, killing the owner, a witness recognizes only the
black thief. To prevent a lynch mob from storming T. J.'s home, David
Logan sets part of his cotton fields afire. Cassie says, "I cried for T. J.
For T. J. and the land" (276).

In Ouida Sebestyen's story of the early 1900s, *Words by Heart*, Ben
Sills moves his family from an all-black southern community to an all-
white western one. With faith in God, he encourages his daughter,
Lena, to enter a Biblical verse competition. Lena wins, only to find the
prize is a bow tie. Afterwards, someone poisons the Sills's dog and
breaks into their house, putting a knife in a cake. Ben Sills explains to
Lena why he left discrimination in the South and came West:

It was easier there, but I wasn't proud of myself. . . . The
promised land where people would see us, not our color. Last
night you stood up there, the equal of any person in the
world, because you were good at something, you had worked
at till you excelled. That was a proud moment. (30–31)

When Lena's father does not return from repairing fences, she looks for
him, finds him shot, and discovers the boy who did it to him. It is Tater
Haney, a poor white lad, who lies on the field injured by his own horse.
It requires courage for Lena to obey her father and take Tater in the
same wagon with Ben Sills.

Ten-year-old Janey Larkin, in *Blue Willow* by Doris Gates, learns about the discrimination toward migrant workers. When she moves with her stepmother and Dad in a one-room shack near the cotton fields where Dad works, Janey hopes she can go to school. A blue willow-patterned plate, her mother's family heirloom for generations, is her only possession from former days when Dad had his own ranch. She displays the plate only when they stay at a decent place, and she is hopeful when they move into a shack on a ranch that hires Dad. Bounce, the ranch foreman, demands shack rent. Mrs. Larkin becomes ill so there is no rent money, and Janey gives Bounce the blue willow plate instead. When Dad says they must move after the harvest, Janey visits Mr. Anderson, the ranch owner, to say goodbye to her plate. Mr. Anderson learns about Bounce's actions, fires him, and hires Mr. Larkin as foreman instead.

In *Tiger Eyes: A Novel* by Judy Blume, characters seek courage to face sudden death and death after a long-term illness. Fifteen-year-old Davy Wexler is devastated when her father dies from a robber's bullet in his 7-Eleven store in Atlantic City. Her mother takes Davy and her seven-year-old brother, Jason, to Los Alamos, New Mexico to visit Aunt Bitsy and Uncle Walter. The relatives welcome them but smother Davy with overpossessiveness and rigid rules. While serving as a hospital candy striper, Davy meets Mr. Ortiz, who is dying of terminal cancer, and his son, Martin. After the father dies, she writes these words to Martin:

> Here is something I found in a magazine: Each of us must confront our own fears, we must come face to face with them. How we handle our fears will determine where we go with the rest of our lives. To experience adventure or to be limited by the fear of it. (64)

Determined to remember the good times with her father, Davy is ready to return to Atlantic City with her mother and Jason.

Another juvenile who deals with a parent's death is eleven-year-old Grace O'Malley in *The Gift of the Pirate Queen* by Patricia Reilly Giff. After her mother's death, Grace tends the house and her younger, diabetic sister, Amy. While alone in her schoolroom, Grace accidentally drops and breaks a glass bell from the desk of her teacher, Mrs. Raphael, and plans to buy her a new one for Christmas. Grace dislikes her father's cousin from Ireland, Fiona, until Fiona tells the story of an ancestor, Grace O'Malley, a pirate queen. Meanwhile, Lisa, a poor, unloved child in her class, helps Grace after Amy goes into insulin shock, so Grace's doubtful reward is to put Lisa's name on the Christmas bell. The teacher thinks Lisa broke the original bell. Grace remembers Fiona's words: "You're like the other Grace O'Malley. . . . She was a fierce one all right. She was brave and bold" (55). After Grace confesses with difficulty that she broke the bell, the teacher replies, "Sometimes we have to do hard things in life" (52).

May I Cross Your Golden River? by Paige Dixon is a story of eighteen-year-old Jordan Phillips, a victim of incurable, fatal Lou Gehrig's disease, amyotrophic lateral sclerosis. His family helps without pitying him. After considering suicide, Jordon decides to "spend all his time and energy learning and experiencing all he could while he still had a chance" (88). Knowing he causes others pain, he draws comfort from comments by his brother, Tony, "When people love other people, they're bound to get hurt" (104). Tony quotes from Byron, "He did the best he could, with things not very subject to control" (104). Jordan's three goals are to serve as best man at the wedding of his brother, Alex; to be godfather for the child of his sister, Terry; and to die with dignity in his own home. He accomplishes all three.

Between remission periods, sixteen-year-old Mike Rankin suffers an agony of treatments for leukemia. In *Hunter in the Dark* by Monica Hughes, Mike resents his parents' failure to disclose the nature of his disease to him. Finally, armed with information from a library book, he forces his doctor to tell him the truth. Helped by his buddy, Doug O'Reilly, he secretly plans a trip to the Swan Hills in Alberta, Canada to shoot a deer of trophy size before he dies. At his campfire the first night, he looks skyward and thinks, "God, how empty space was, on and on forever. Was eternity going to be like that? Was that what was waiting for him out there?" (48). Caught in a snowstorm, stalking deer, he takes refuge among tree roots, screaming to himself, "I don't want to die. He hurled a silent shout up into the uncaring sky. He knew it was uncaring, that no one was listening, because he had been screaming the same silent phrase and it hadn't helped" (68). On his last day in the woods with a buck centered on his scope, he disengages the bolt head. "There was a loud click. It seemed to Mike that the click echoed round the world, that the whole universe had waited for his decision" (129)

In *Winning* by Robin F. Brancato, Gary H. Madden, paralyzed by a football accident, struggles to accept the reality of his condition. His mother is overprotective, but friends and his recently widowed English teacher, Ann Treer, try to give him courage. Ann teaches him a word game, anagrams with people's names, in which he transposes his name as Damm Raggedy. At Phillip's Institute of Rehabilitation, he suffers when one of his three roommates commits suicide and another's wife leaves him. Gary, who wants to commit suicide himself, tells Ann:

> I'm beat. Some want to lose, remember? You said it once: I'm beat. No endurance. Wish I had it in like your metaphor— Swimming grace and ease and all that. What's mine? What's my metaphor, Mrs. Treer? I never found one. (207)

Ann talks him out of suicide and adds:

> Speaking of anagrams, ever since you came up with Damm Raggedy I've been trying for one that suits you better, but I don't think I can get one out of those letters. I guess it's impossible. We'll live with Damm Raggedy and play a different game. (209)

Fly, Wheels, Fly! by Harriet May Savitz offers hope to all in wheelchairs. Fourteen-year-old Jeff Cobb, paralyzed since birth and a Hollie House resident since he was three, sees no future for himself. To curb his anger, nurses give him a single room which he likes "because dignity was the one thing he found in that room alone and he guarded it jealously" (5). Meanwhile, Chuck Robbins, a college-bound high school senior, is paralyzed when the second-floor railing at his girl friend's apartment gives way and he falls two flights. A doctor suggests to Coach Joe Johnson that Chuck and Jeff become Paraolympics basketball players for The Rollers. In spite of their attitudes, Joe takes them to a practice session, and they get involved in National Olympics training. Jeff tells himself, "Don't let him get to you. Joe was temporary—he mustn't forget it—and someday, without warning, he could leave just as he had come" (46). In a game, Chuck falls. Jeff helps him back into his chair and whispers, "Fly, wheels, fly!" (53). Chuck and Jeff visit stores to raise money for the Nationals, which they attend. Chuck wins second place in javelin throwing and Jeff, first in the sixty-yard dash.

Four misfits become friends and help one another in *The Alfred Summer* by Jan Slepian. Fourteen-year-old Lester has cerebral palsy. Fat, clumsy thirteen-year-old Myron is smothered by his mother. Eleven-year-old Alfred, who has a crippled hand, is mentally slow.

Boyish thirteen-year-old Claire feels out of place with female classmates. Lester and Alfred become friends after Lester's father rescues
Alfred at the beach. As Myron builds a boat in his basement, he gets the
other three to join him. Myron takes the finished boat to the beach
where it sinks, and though nonplussed by the others' laughter, he
changes ridicule into success in the following way:

> He stood there at the water's edge dripping wet. . . . Then,
> incredibly, he smiled at his audience and raised his arms. He
> clasped his hands in a victory salute. Then he bowed as if
> acknowledging applause and again lifted his arms. But now
> the laughter was completely for him instead of at him. (119)

A different kind of story involving an accident is Joan Lowery
Nixon's *The Ghosts of Now*. After the Duprees move to a small Texas
town where Mr. Dupree works for an oil company, they find antagonism between local people and company employees. Sixteen-year-old
Angie discovers that her brother, Jeremy, is in a gang. When he is a hit-
and-run accident victim and left in a coma, Angie determines to find
out who is to blame. Helped by a friend, Del Scully, she learns that
stolen items from robberies by Jeremy and his gang are hidden in an
abandoned house. In Jeremy's room she discovers a stolen watch, but
also some poems he wrote which show how much he has been affected
by the family's constant moving. One poem says:

> The house is haunted by the Ghosts of Now
> Whose shadows no one wants to see,
> Whose screams no one wants to hear,
> Until tomorrow. (79)

Angie learns who hit her brother and prods her parents to change,
warning, "We're not a family. We're four people living in the same
house. We're the ghosts of now" (178).
    Two powerful survival stories are *Scrub Fire* by Ann DeRoo, set in
the New Zealand wilds, and *Climb a Lonely Hill* by Lilith Norman,
laid in the Australian outback. In *Scrub Fire*, fourteen-year-old Michelle Seton and her two brothers, twelve-year-old Andrew and nine-
year-old Jason, go camping in the bush with Aunt Celia and Uncle
Don. After a campfire, Jason, who is asked to bring a can of water to
extinguish the fire, accidentally brings petrol. When a bush fire results,
all flee in different directions. Eventually, the children find each other.

Andrew has camping experience, but when Jason becomes ill, it is Michelle who drags Andrew from a gorge, entertains Jason with make believe, and pushes Andrew to the limit. Before their rescue, Andrew feels hopeless. "Michelle's mind worked slowly but with a clarity that surprised her. . . . She had to ask the impossible of Andrew and give him the strength to do it" (97). After twelve days, the youngsters are united with their parents and their aunt and uncle.

In *Climb a Lonely Hill*, fourteen-year-old Jack Clarke and his twelve-year-old sister Sue go gold prospecting in the outback with their uncle. In their truck's freak accident, Uncle Bert dies and Sue injures a foot. Jack has never before had such a challenge, having often played the fool to hide shame which he feels about his father's drunkenness. When he acknowledges his uncle's death, he unpacks provisions, trying to decide what to carry, and makes Sue crude crutches. They head for distant hills to get off the blazing plain and to find water. After three agonizing days, they reach a cave and water. At times, Jack looks at Sue with hatred and realizes that "behind the hatred lay fear. Fear of not knowing what to do" (53). For eleven days they live in the cave, keep a fire burning, and eat lizards to save canned food. "It was only anger and frustration that prevented [Jack] from giving into the icy hopelessness of his and Sue's insane journey" (84). One day, they hear a plane, throw leaves on the fire, and know rescue is at hand.

A scrawny, fifteen-year-old boy, whose real name the author never discloses, lives with his father on a 2100-square-mile Arizona ranch in *Whichaway* by Glendon and Kathryn Swarthout. During the summer, the boy's father makes him bunk with the men and work on the ranch. Beans, the cook, asks him "whichaway" he is going each day, so that becomes his nickname. His job is to inspect and grease the thirty-one windmills. Beans repeats:

> A windmill's like a man. It don't matter how hard the wind blows or whichaway, that mill's got to go on turnin'. The cattle depends on it. An' a man's got t'go on doing his job, too. No matter what. Folks depend on him. (13)

One day, Whichaway starts for Crittenden's on his horse, Dub, but changes his mind and heads in the opposite direction for Crazy Horse Mesa. While he is atop a windmill on a platform, a dust devil storm throws him around and breaks both his legs. Cattle rustlers appear and leave him to die. An old prospector shoots at him. For two days and two nights, he lies on the platform. He tears his clothes into strips to make a rope which he fortifies with string from the bird's nest he finds under the platform and the wire frames of his glasses. With the rope, he lowers himself to Dub's back. Just then his father and the men appear. Though his father makes him ride, Whichaway thinks, "He might not make the fifteen miles to the ranch, but even if he fell off he wouldn't holler. Not even for his father. Ever again. He was man enough now to cut his own mustard" (101)

James Houston writes and illustrates stories about Eskimo courage and survival tactics. In *Akavak: An Eskimo Journey*, thirteen-year-old Akavak goes with Grandfather to visit Grandfather's brother. Before Akavak leaves, his father tells him to "avoid the high mountains that stretch inland" (10). Noting that Grandfather is old, the boy's father warns, "If he does not seem to hear you, and his spirit appears to leave him, you must then be careful and decide everything for him" (12). He adds, "Remain on the sea ice and follow the coast. That way you should not get lost" (16). The trip begins, but they find a food cache has been destroyed. Grandfather says they must cross the mountain or they will die of starvation along the coast. "What could Akavak say to such a wise and powerful man, the one who had taught his father. He could say no more. He could only help him to reach the far camp of his brother, or he would surely seem to be a coward" (30). In a mountain crevasse, they save only one dog, Kojo, and a sled. Akavak harnesses himself with Kojo to pull the sled bearing Grandfather. Akavak "thought at times he could walk no more. But in his mind he kept thinking, 'We are closer now, this journey nears its end' " (69). When they arrive at camp, Grandfather dies.

In another book, *Frozen Fire: A Tale of Courage*, James Houston tells about thirteen-year-old Matt Morgan who flies with his father, a geologist, to Frobisher Bay seeking a copper vein. Matt makes friends with Kayak, an Eskimo boy. Father and Charlie, a helicopter pilot, give a false flight plan as they leave the village; only Matt knows the actual plan. When Father does not return, the Air Force's rescue planes look in the wrong direction until Matt tells the truth. He and Kayak borrow a snowmobile to look for Father. After they hit a blizzard and exhaust their gas supply, they start walking home. Kayak uses survival techniques learned from his grandfather. Discouraged, Matt thinks, "They had come looking for his father, and now they, themselves faced death" (100). Caught on an ice floe floating to sea, they are lucky when a helicopter pilot sees Matt's signal with a mirror and Kayak's circle with seal blood on the ice. After the rescue of Father and his pilot, Father decides to stay to teach in the local school.

Knowing that surviving is a way of life in Scandanavia, Leif Hamre writes stories of the courage of survivors facing death in the North. In *Leap into Danger*, Lieutenant Geir Grand and Flight Sergeant Peter Hovden begin a routine ambulance rescue mission in northern Norway. After the plane's engine fails, they have to bail out. Peter breaks a leg, but Geir finds him, builds a hut, and tries to trap ptarmigan and fish. As Geir searches in the plane for items he needs, such as an ax and torch, he gets caught in a blizzard and starts back to Peter. He thinks, "The temptation to lie down in the snow was overpowering. . . . He *must* hold out" (79). Lost in the storm, he hears Peter whistle to guide him. The weather clears before the Air Rescue Service saves them. Before leaving, Geir destroys his snares and fish traps, saying, "Now, we'll be leaving the animals in peace, in gratitude to them for giving us what we needed while we were here" (151).

In *Operation Arctic*, Leif Hamre portrays children surviving alone in the wilds. Fourteen-year-old Torgeir Solheim and his eight-year-old twin siblings, Terji and Lisa, think they are stowing away on a Norwegian Air Force plane to visit Father in Sola. They board a plane to Half Moon Island off the Icelandic coast to rescue a sick trapper. After they debark and see the plane ascend without them, they take refuge in the trapper's cabin. Torgeir, who knows they are not at Sola, worries about limited food. In fighting a bear with a ski, he discovers an underground food cache. One day, a flight sergeant remembers that he talked to the children the day they disappeared and that he exchanged his plane to Half Moon Island for the one to Sola. When the children hear a plane, they ignite a kerosene drum in a bonfire. The pilot sees the explosion and rescues them.

In the 1940s, sixth graders, Ted Stavros and Joe Sokol, shine shoes to earn money for L. L. Bean camping equipment in David Kherdian's *It Started with Old Man Bean*. Ted says, "In a way, old Joe and I don't have a lot in common. . . . We do have something in common—besides liking to go to the movies and that's exploring" (29). Ted reads in a library about camping and the outdoors. The boys plan to go to Snake River but tell their parents they are going only to McCable River. When a storm engulfs them, Joe breaks his elbow and wrist. Ted tries to take them downstream on a log but steps in a snag. The log floats only with

Joe who is saved. After Ted heads for the highway and hails rescuers, he wonders, "how much I've changed and if I'm going to keep on changing right up until the time I'm an adult. Do adults change once they get to be adults?" (217).

Surviving alone is a challenge for sixteen-year-old Peter Torin in J. Allan Bosworth's *All the Dark Places*. When Peter decides to explore the Appalachian cave, Preacher's End, he is angry because his brother, Jack, and friends fail to join him. He has been in the cave with Jack, but it fascinates him because of its large size. He describes his problems after damaging his carbide lamp and flashlight, "Groping and feeling the walls, he almost came to panic again. But he fought it off. And, on that thin edge of control he remembered the matches" (90). In total darkness, except for eighteen matches, he moves cautiously, fighting cold, hunger, and exhaustion. He must "strike a match, commit to memory shapes and directions and crawl" (100). "Once he hears voices only to discover the voices were nothing more than the sound of falling water" (124). Jack and friends arrive as Peter collapses near the cave entrance.

In *The Island Keeper* by Harry Mazer, sixteen-year-old Cleo Murphy survives for months on a Canadian island. Rich, fat Cleo, unhappy since her younger sister's death in a boat accident, hides on an island her father owns in a lake. She cancels her camp reservation by pretending to be her grandmother, buys camp equipment and food, steals a canoe, and reaches the island. She housekeeps in a cave, hiding when a caretaker looks for her. After a raccoon steals most of her food, she fishes and eats wild greens until a violent storm erupts. She finds that "The island which had been so green and lush, full of birds and insects, activity and sound, was like an empty house whose tenants had fled. Now it *was* time to leave" (103). However, the storm destroys her canoe and she has to return to the island because she cannot complete a swim of five miles to the mainland. Even the raft she makes falls apart. Realizing she has to stay until the lake freezes, she kills animals to survive. After seven months, she trudges across the frozen lake and, still unable to communicate well with Father and Grandmother, returns to boarding school, thinking "There was a progression to things. She'd learned it on the island. One step, and then the next, and then the one after that. . . . School was a part of the progression for her" (163).

In another book by Harry Mazer, *Snow Bound*, fifteen-year-old Tony Laporte, angry because his parents will not let him keep a dog that follows him home, steals his mother's car and heads for the Canadian border to visit an uncle. In a snowstorm, he picks up a hitchhiker, Cindy Reichert. When a blizzard begins, Tony takes a shortcut, drives into a field, and smashes into a rock. Peeved, Cindy starts walking but returns with frostbitten feet. She says to Tony, "We have to cooperate. . . . We got into this mess and there's no use blaming anyone" (61). Tony leaves Cindy in the car for several days until he finds a hunter's hut. After he returns for her, he uses the car hood as a sled, falls into a ravine with the sled, and hurts his ankle. They fight wild dogs and eleven days later, reach a house near a state park. They separate, but Cindy writes Tony:

> We nearly died, Tony. . . . We did a lot of dumb things, and a lot of good smart things. . . . Here's the thing, Tony, we were born once to our mothers, as everyone is. But this time we gave birth to ourselves. (145)

Life is grim in *Cold Hazard* by Richard Armstrong when a tramp steamer, *Drumlogan*, hits an iceberg and all escape in a lifeboat except for five crew members. The third mate, seventeen-year-old Jim Naylor, is charged with making decisions and takes the five in a jolly boat toward the mainland. Jim feels

> not exactly fear, though there was an element of that in it. It was awe for the immensity of the sea; it was an awareness of the littleness of man and his temerity in confronting it. This and underneath it all, the queer warming feeling of pride that he was of the breed that dared to challenge these forces. (40)

After six days, the five crew members land on an island, uninhabited except for goats. They carry the jolly boat to the island's other side. Then they start to row toward the mainland. A coastguard cutter finds them, but they are determined to finish rowing. "And finish it they did with the cutter steaming rings round them all the way while her skipper alternately cursed their obstinacy and applauded their guts and seamanship" (180). It is exactly five weeks, three days, and thirteen and a half hours since the *Drumlogan*'s accident.

In *Mayday! Mayday!* by Hilary Milton, two children are the only ones able to travel when the small plane in which they are passengers from New Orleans to Birmingham crashes on a wooded mountainside. Although Mark has a broken arm and bruised Alison later sprains her ankle, the two descend the mountain followed by wild dogs. After losing their way in a mine tunnel, they exit, cross a river, and leave the dogs on the other side. Mark does not want to abandon Alison who cannot walk, but she says, "It's right, you don't have a choice. Take it. Find somebody, please. And hurry—I'm freezing cold" (115). Mark "stood there for a moment, looking down at her trying to make himself accept the truth of what she said" (115). Finally, he gets the help she needs.

Eleven-year-old David seldom sees his father, a great sportsman, and is afraid of him in *The Grizzly* by Annabel and Edgar Johnson. While having nightmares about his father, David thinks about the fact that "he only knew he dreaded the time when the nightmare man would come back and he would have to meet him face to face" (4). As his father comes to take him fishing in the Montana Mountains, his mother warns, "You mustn't be afraid of him. He's so strong himself that he never has understood any sort of weakness" (13). At the fishing spot, a bear ruins their food and a mother grizzly chases David up a tree, clawing his father's leg and damaging their truck. After his Father faints from pain, David dresses the man's wound. Together they repair the truck, and the father appreciates his son's efforts, though unsuccessful, to land a big trout. On the way home, when David's father calls his mother, he says, "Well we did run into some trouble, but you've got a boy who can take it" (160).

Among her books on nature or human and animal survival is Jean Craighead George's *Julie of the Wolves*, a tale of an Eskimo girl enduring the Arctic wilds, fed and protected by wolves. Julie is thirteen years old when she complies with an arranged marriage to a retarded boy. To escape him, she plans a trip across the tundra from Barrow to Point Hope where she can get a ship to San Francisco to visit Amy, her pen pal. Julie's mother is dead and her father, a great hunter, left to hunt seals and never returned. He "had taught her that fear can so cripple a person that he cannot think or act. . . . Change your ways when fear seizes you for it usually means you are doing something wrong" (51–52). He said, "Wolves are brotherly. They love each other and if you learn to speak to them, they will love you too" (97). By following wolves and watching bird flight directions, Julie finds civilization and her father. At first, feeling he has betrayed his Eskimo heritage by marrying a white woman, Julie heads for the tundra but returns to him when she realizes she cannot survive alone.

Another book by Jean Craighead George, *The Talking Earth*,

focuses on Billie Wind, a Seminole in Florida. She disavows ancestral legends after attending school at the Kennedy Space Center where her father works and where she learns about the earth's pollution. Charlie Wind, a medicine man, sends her to the Everglades in a dugout for one night and two days to hear animals talk, see a serpent, and meet little people living underground. She lands on an island where she finds a cave with antiquities, but after a fire destroys her dugout, she builds a canoe and leaves with a pet otter, Petang. She lives on the water for twenty weeks while birds and animals tell her what is happening. Adding another pet, a turtle named Burden, she says as she nears a highway, "I don't want to be found now. I've gone too far and am too close to the answer I seek. The animals talk that I do know" (112). After she meets Oats Tiger on his name-seeking quest, they ride out a hurricane. Heading home, she knows that "the earth will not blow up and die" (151).

In *Tundra* by William F. Hallstead, a story of a courageous animal's survival, Jamie Harwood's Tundra is a Siberian husky. During a storm, the dog escapes from a fenced area. A car hits him, a farmer shoots at him, a dogcatcher gets him, and two men steal him to use in a pit where dogs fight until death. Jamie, who never stops hoping for Tundra's return, advertises for the dog. His mother says, "Promise me that in the back of your mind, you'll realize that he may not come back no matter how strongly you believe he will" (62). After Tundra escapes from the pit, a man hunting raccoons catches him and takes him to an animal shelter. A young employee buys Tundra on the day he would be put to sleep. The young employee, however, cannot keep a dog in his apartment, so he takes Tundra to a dog show, hoping to find an owner. Since Jamie and his mother are there, Tundra recognizes them, and he and Jamie joyously reunite.

When Danny gives police his name after fighting an old lady's attacker, he does not know the attacker's brother is in his high school's toughest gang, the Outlaws. In Eve Bunting's *Someone Is Hiding on Alcatraz Island*, the gang overtakes Danny at Fisherman's Wharf and chases him to Alcatraz Island. Staying on the island after the last boat leaves, Danny discovers the Outlaws are there too. Hiding in the morgue, he "shivered and tried not to bawl. No kidding. [He] was so scared and lonely. [He] felt about six years old" (48). The Outlaws capture Danny and Biddy, a Park Ranger, locking them both in cells. Digging through a rotting back wall, Danny escapes, locks up the

Outlaw leader, Cowboy, and is on his way to free Biddy. When Cowboy taunts his captor, Danny replies, "Liking to hurt and scare doesn't make you a hero, Cowboy" (135). Asked what it takes to be a hero, Danny answers, "I don't know. Maybe being afraid, and doing what you have to do anyway" (135).

In *Winter of the Owl* by June Andrea Hanson, Janey wants to train a colt she names Fire Dancer. Her father, a depot agent, tells her grandfather to sell all horses not needed to run the Montana ranch. Janey gets the hired man's son, John Yellowfeather, to help train the colt. After John shows her a great horned owl on the ranch, her Uncle Ed tries to shoot the owl, but Janey deflects his aim. The owl seems to symbolize saving animals, like the colt. Finally, her father lets Janey keep Fire Dancer, declaring, "I'm proud of you, Janey. . . . I'm proud of the courage and intelligence you are showing" (111).

Cross-country Runner by Leon McClinton features Vern Mansfield, a star football player, who relinquishes the game for cross-country running and endures animosity from the football team, his classmates, his girl friend, his father, and even track team members. When asked why he is giving up football, Vern says, "All I know is I don't get the satisfaction out of playing football that the other guys get. . . . After practice or a game, I don't even feel good about it" (16). Despite attacks by the Speaker boys, who resent him on the track team, Vern perseveres to become a top runner. At one point, when ready to concede in a race, Vern changes his mind. "Taking a shuddering breath, Vern began to sprint. Miraculously, his legs responded. He called on a strength of reserve he didn't know he had" (131–132).

A story of friendship between two seventeen-year-old boys with different interests is Joan Phipson's *Fly Free*, set in Australia. Wilfred Manning, a headmaster's son, is quick, witty, and scholarly. Johnny Johnson, a farmer's boy, is slow, cheerful, and active, enjoying trapping rabbits and foxes. Johnny gets Wilfred to join him in trapping rabbits so that both can earn money for a school trip. Wilfred has a horror of enclosed places and hates to kill animals, but "Johnny said the rabbits had to be killed. It was his own weakness that always put him in the place of the trapped animal" (55). Beyond rabbits, the boys agree to sell birds they catch to two crooks, Gus and Tal, for sale overseas although Wilfred feels it is illegal and refuses to check bird traps. After the boys fight, Wilfred accidentally gets locked in a tool shed. Johnny gets caught in a trap himself, lying there from Friday until Sunday, thinking, "It was the birth of the courage that was to grow in him and that would in the end carry him through the night. And the one comfort he had as the darkness crept into the clearing was that he was not alone" (105). A rabbit and a trapped parrot are there too. When his father finally finds Johnny, Gus and Tal arrive in a van full of captive birds. Mr. Johnson insists on freeing the birds. "As they lifted Johnny out, there was a whirr of wings about their heads and the air was full of rainbow colours" (131).

Rosemary Sutcliff's *The Witch's Brat* describes the England of 1066, as eleven-year-old crippled Lovel has to leave his village upon his grandmother's death. Grandmother, called a witch because of her healing ability, taught Lovel many skills. She confided to him, "Not even I can mend a broken butterfly. But one day you will mend other things. You will be one of the menders of the world; not the makers, nor yet the breakers, first one of the menders" (6). A swineherd rescues ill, hungry Lovel, taking him to the Abbey for the Holy Fathers where he learns to read and write. Eventually, he leaves for Smithfield, outside London's walls, to help Rahere, former jongleur or minstrel to King Henry I, to build a hospital and priory where Lovel mends bodies.

India is the setting for Aimée Sommerfelt's story of Lalu's courage in *The Road to Agra* and *The White Bungalow*. After seven-year-old Maya begins to lose her vision, in *The Road to Agra*, her thirteen-year-old brother, Lalu, worries that she will become a blind beggar. He wants her to continue in school because she teaches him. Grandmother encourages their trip to doctors in Agra, saying, "He who has patience may easily lose it on a long journey. But he who has none, like Lalu, can perhaps acquire it. A journey such as this may make a man of Lalu" (26). With their dog, Kanga, the children travel the long road to Agra, only to be rejected by the hospital. On the way home, they stop for milk at a United Nations World Health Organization clinic, where Dr. Prasad, a female physician, takes an interest in Maya, returns her to the hospital, and helps restore her sight. Lalu works for Dr. Prasad to earn money for the return trip.

In Sommerfelt's *The White Bungalow*, Lalu wants to become a doctor. His best friend, Ram, daily sits outside the school, too poor to enroll. Dr. Prasad says there will soon be room for Lalu in boarding school but not for Ram. When Lalu's father, a farmer, hurts his back, Lalu must help at home and asks if Ram can take his place. Lalu writes Dr. Prasad, "I must stay in Katura. I must plow and harrow. . . . Could

Ram have it? He has no one to care for him and he has a good brain"
(114).

Manolo Olivar's father, Spain's greatest bullfighter, was killed in a
bullring at age twenty-two. In *Shadow of a Bull* by Maia Wojciechowska, townspeople expect Manolo to follow in his father's footsteps,
killing his first bull on his twelfth birthday. When that day comes,
Manolo faces a bull and conquers his fear. Then he realizes he does not
want to be a bullfighter but a doctor, a healer. He thinks, "His father's
life, bullfighting, would stay a part of him, as it always had been, but in
a different way than anyone had planned" (155).

Mountain climbing is a Swiss way of life, and in James Ramsey
Ullman's *Banner in the Sky*, sixteen-year-old Rudi wants to reach the
Citadel's peak where his father died. After he raises Captain Winter
from a deep crevasse, Rudi secretly joins Winter and a guide when they
climb the Citadel. His Uncle Franz and several guides try to bring the
group back before Franz decides to join them. On the ascent, Rudi stays
with an injured climber while the others go to the top.

In Phyllis Reynolds Naylor's *Night Cry*, which is set in Mississippi,
thirteen-year-old Ellen Stump discovers the kidnapping of Jason Cory,
son of the town's most famous personage. Ellen is often alone on a five-
acre farm because her father is a traveling salesman and her mother is
dead. Her brother died after falling from his horse, Sleet, who was
spooked in a storm. A recently hired man who helps Ellen on the farm
is squatting at the nearby empty Brody place. One night, Ellen hears
crying from there, suspects Jason is captive, and sees the hired man
packing his car as if to leave. She rescues Jason, and rides on Sleet with
the child to town. Afterwards, Maureen Sinclair, interviewing Ellen on
television, says, "I hope, if I'm ever called on to be courageous, that I'll
carry it off as well as you did, Ellen" (149). When Ellen gets an award,
she tells her father, "It's embarrassing is what it is. Wasn't one ounce of
courage in me, Dad. I was scared as a polecat up a tree over a river"
(151). Dad replies, "That's what I mean. You were scared half out of
your mind, but you went and did it anyways" (151).

In Susan Lowry Rardin's *Captives in a Foreign Land*, an Arab
terrorist group in Rome captures six sightseeing American children
whose parents are attending an international symposium on nuclear
arms control. The terrorists, opposed to the arms race, take the children
to a Middle East hideaway. One of them says of the Americans, "So,
you don't want more weapons because it uses up your money. . . . Not

because those weapons threaten millions of people who aren't even your enemies" (40). Assad explains that some Arab groups "unite to preserve the world which Allah created so that there will be human voices left to praise him" (42). For two months, the children live in a hut, help build a dam, and devise ways to disclose their location. For Tawbah, the terrorist group, they write a statement to be sent to the United States which begins:

> This statement will talk about fear, and what it can make people do. It is because fear itself has become so dangerous, that we now support immediate unilateral U.S. disarmament of nuclear weapons. (186)

Rescue occurs after Martha, one of the captive children becomes seriously ill and the Arab terrorists take her to a hospital.

SUMMARY

Of the ninety-six books presented in this chapter, eight are for readers in their early years, twenty-seven are for those in their middle years, and sixty-one are for older boys and girls. Characters show great courage in these stories that are set in various countries and in historical periods ranging from the eleventh century to the present.

References

Alexander, Lloyd. *The Beggar Queen*. E. P. Dutton, 1984. 237 p. (L) (Maturing, Responsibility)

———. *The Kestrel*. E. P. Dutton, 1982. 244 p. (L)

———. *Westmark*. E. P. Dutton, 1981. 184 p. (L)

Armstrong, Richard. *Cold Hazard*. Illustrated by C. Walter Hodges. Houghton Mifflin Company, 1956. 180 p. (L) (Responsibility)

Armstrong, William H. *Sounder*. Illustrated by James Barkley. Harper & Row, Publishers, 1969. 116 p. (L)

———. *Sour Land*. Harper & Row, Publishers, 1971. 116 p. (L)

Avi. *Encounter at Easton*. Pantheon Books, 1980. 138 p. (M)

———. *Night Journeys*. Pantheon Books, 1979. 143 p. (M) (Ingenuity, Loyalty)

Babbitt, Natalie. *Tuck Everlasting*. Farrar, Straus, Giroux, 1975. 139 p. (L) (Maturing)

Baer, Frank. *Max's Gang*. Translated from German by Ivanka Roberts. Little, Brown & Company, 1983. 298 p. (L) (Friendship)

Balderson, Margaret. *When Jays Fly to Bárbmo*. Illustrated by Victor G.

Ambrus. The World Publishing Company, 1968. 238 p. (L)
(Maturing, Responsibility)

Beatty, Hetty Burlingame. *Little Owl Indian*. Illustrated. Houghton
Mifflin Company, 1951. 32 p. (E)

Bishop, Claire Huchet. *Twenty and Ten*. Illustrated by William Pene
duBois. The Viking Press, 1952. 76 p. (M)

Blume, Judy. *Tiger Eyes: A Novel*. Bradbury Press, 1981. 206 p. (L)

Bosworth, J. Allan. *All the Dark Places*. Doubleday, 1963. 166 p. (L)
(Ingenuity)

Brancato, Robin F. *Winning*. Alfred A. Knopf, 1977. 211 p. (L) (Self-
respect)

Buckley, Helen E. *Michael Is Brave*. Illustrated by Emily McCully.
Lothrop, Lee & Shepard Company, 1971. Unpaged. (E)

Bunting, Eve. *Someone Is Hiding on Alcatraz Island*. Clarion Books,
1984. 136 p. (L)

Byars, Betsy. *The 18th Emergency*. Illustrated by Robert Grossman. The
Viking Press, 1973. 126 p. (M)

Carrick, Carol. *The Climb*. Illustrated by Donald Carrick. Houghton
Mifflin/Clarion Books, 1980. Unpaged. (E)

————. *What a Wimp!* Illustrated by Donald Carrick. Clarion Books,
1983. 89 p. (M)

Clifford, Eth. *Just Tell Me When We're Dead*. Illustrated by George
Hughes. Houghton Mifflin Company, 1983. 130 p. (M)

Cohen, Barbara. *Queen for a Day*. Lothrop, Lee & Shepard Books,
1981. 158 p. (M)

Collier, James L. and Christopher Collier. *War Comes to Willy Freeman*. Delacorte Press, 1983. 178 p. (L)

Dalgliesh, Alice. *The Courage of Sarah Noble*. Illustrated by Leonard
Weisgard. Charles Scribner's Sons, 1954. 54 p. (M) (Friendship,
Humaneness)

DeRoo, Ann. *Scrub Fire*. Atheneum, 1977. 106 p. (L) (Responsibility)

Dixon, Paige. *May I Cross Your Golden River?* Atheneum, 1975. 262
p. (L)

du Bois, William Pène. *The Forbidden Forest*. Illustrated. Harper &
Row, Publishers, 1978. 56 p. (M)

Finlayson, Ann. *Rebecca's War*. Illustrated by Sherry Streeter. Frederick Warne & Company, 1972. 280 p. (L) (Ingenuity, Responsibility)

Forbes, Esther. *Johnny Tremain*. Illustrated by Lynd Ward. Houghton Mifflin Company, 1943. 256 p. (L) (Maturing, Responsibility)

Gackenbach, Dick. *Harry and the Terrible Whatzit*. Illustrated. The Seabury Press, 1977. 32 p. (E)

Gates, Doris. *Blue Willow*. Illustrated by Paul Lantz. The Viking Press, 1940. 172 p. (L)

George, Jean Craighead. *Julie of the Wolves*. Illustrated by John Schoenherr. Harper & Row, Publishers, 1972. 170 p. (L) (Ingenuity, Maturing)

————. *The Talking Earth*. Harper & Row, Publishers, 1983. 151 p. (L) (Ingenuity)

Giff, Patricia Reilly. *The Gift of the Pirate Queen*. Illustrated by Jenny Rutherford. Delacorte Press, 1982. 164 p. (L)

Griese, Arnold A. *The Wind Is Not a River*. Illustrated by Glo Coalson. Thomas Y. Crowell, 1978. 108 p. (M) (Ingenuity, Responsibility)

Griffiths, Helen. *The Dog at the Window*. Holiday House, 1984. 123 p. (M)

Hallstead, William F. *Tundra*. Crown Publishers, 1984. 121 p. (L)

Hamre, Leif. *Leap into Danger*. Translated from Norwegian by Evelyn Ramsden. Harcourt, Brace & Company, 1959. 156 p. (L) (Ingenuity)

————. *Operation Arctic*. Translated from Norwegian by Dag Ryen. Atheneum, 1973. 154 p. (L) (Ingenuity, Responsibility)

Hanson, June Andrea. *Winter of the Owl*. Macmillan Publishing Company, 1980. 126 p. (L) (Ingenuity)

Hartman, Evert. *War Without Friends*. Translated from Dutch by Patricia Crampton. Crown Publishers, 1982. 218 p. (L)

Haugaard, Erik Christian. *Chase Me, Catch Nobody!* Houghton Mifflin Company, 1980. 209 p. (L) (Loyalty, Maturing)

Heyward, DuBose. *The Country Bunny and the Little Gold Shoes*. Illustrated by Marjorie Flack. Houghton Mifflin Company, 1939. Unpaged. (E)

Holman, Felice. *The Wild Children*. Charles Scribner's Sons, 1983. 149 p. (L) (Ingenuity, Responsibility)

Homola, Priscilla. *The Willow Whistle*. Illustrated by Ted Lewin. Dodd, Mead & Company, 1983. 109 p. (M) (Friendship)

Houston, James. *Akavak: An Eskimo Journey*. Illustrated. Harcourt, Brace & World, 1968. 79 p. (L) (Responsibility)

———. *Frozen Fire: A Tale of Courage*. Illustrated. Atheneum, 1977. 149 p. (L) (Ingenuity, Friendship)

Hughes, Monica. *Hunter in the Dark*. Atheneum, 1982. 131 p. (L)

Johnson, Annabel and Edgar. *The Grizzly*. Illustrated by Gilbert Riswold. Harper & Row, Publishers, 1964. 160 p. (L)

Kherdian, David. *It Started with Old Man Bean*. Greenwillow Books, 1980. 217 p. (L) (Friendship, Ingenuity)

Knowles, Anne. *The Halcyon Island*. Harper & Row, 1980. 120 p. (L)

Lasky, Kathryn. *The Night Journey*. Illustrated by Trina Schart Hyman. Frederick Warne, 1981. 150 p. (M) (Ingenuity)

McClinton, Leon. *Cross-country Runner*. E. P. Dutton & Co., 1974. 217 p. (L)

Mahy, Margaret. *The Changeover: A Supernatural Romance*. Atheneum, 1984. 214 p. (L)

Mason, Miriam E. *The Middle Sister*. Illustrated by Grace Paull. The Macmillan Company, 1947. 160 p. (M)

Mazer, Harry. *The Island Keeper*. Delacorte Press, 1981. 165 p. (L)

———. *Snow Bound*. Delacorte Press, 1973. 146 p. (L) (Maturing)

Milton, Hilary. *Mayday! Mayday!* Franklin Watts, 1979. 152 p. (L)

Moskin, Marietta D. *Day of the Blizzard*. Illustrated by Stephen Gammell. Coward, McCann & Geoghegan, 1978. 79 p. (M) (Responsibility)

———. *Toto*. Illustrated by Rocco Negri. Coward, McCann & Geogehegan, 1971. Unpaged. (M)

Naylor, Phyllis Reynolds. *Night Cry*. Atheneum, 1984. 154 p. (L) (Loyalty)

Nixon, Joan Lowery. *The Ghosts of Now*. Delacorte Press, 1984. 179 p. (L)

Norman, Lilith. *Climb a Lonely Hill*. Henry Z. Walck, 1970. 159 p. (L) (Ingenuity, Responsibility)

Nöstlinger, Christine, *Fly Away Home*. Translated from German by Anthea Bell. Franklin Watts, 1975. 134 p. (L)

O'Dell, Scott. *Sarah Bishop*. Houghton Mifflin Company, 1980. 184 p. (L)

Peet, Bill. *Cowardly Clyde*. Illustrated. Houghton Mifflin Company, 1979. 38 p. (E)

Pfeffer, Susan Beth. *Courage, Dana*. Illustrated by Jenny Rutherford. Delacorte Press, 1983. 160 p. (M)

Phipson, Joan. *Fly Free*. Atheneum, 1979. 134 p. (L) (Friendship, Maturing)

Piper, Watty. *The Little Engine That Could*. Illustrated by George & Doris Hauman. Platt & Munk, 1961. Unpaged. (E) (Cooperation)

Rardin, Susan Lowry. *Captives in a Foreign Land*. Houghton Mifflin Company, 1984. 218 p. (L) (Cooperation, Ingenuity)

Sachs, Marilyn. *Call Me Ruth*. Doubleday & Company, 1982. 134 p. (M)

Savitz, Harriet May. *Fly, Wheels, Fly!* The John Day Company, 1970. 90 p. (L)

Sebestyen, Ouida. *Words by Heart*. Little, Brown & Company, 1979. 162 p. (L) (Humaneness, Maturing)

Sharp, Margery. *Bernard the Brave: A Miss Bianca Story*. Illustrated by Leslie Morrill. Little, Brown & Company, 1977. 128 p. (M)

Slepian, Jan. *The Alfred Summer*. Macmillan Publishing Company, 1980. 119 p. (L) (Friendship)

Slote, Alfred. *Hang Tough, Paul Mather*. J. B. Lippincott Company, 1973. 156 p. (M)

Sommerfelt, Aimée. *The Road to Agra*. Translated from Norwegian. Illustrated by Ulf Aas. Criterion Books, 1961. 191 p. (L) (Responsibility)

———. *The White Bungalow*. Translated from Norwegian by Evelyn Ramsden. Illustrated by Ulf Aas. Criterion Books, 1964. 126 p. (L) (Maturing, Responsibility)

Speare, Elizabeth George. *The Witch of Blackbird Pond*. Houghton Mifflin Company, 1958. 250 p. (L) (Humaneness)

Sperry, Armstrong. *Call It Courage*. Illustrated. The Macmillan Company, 1940. 95 p. (M) (Ingenuity, Self-respect)

Stolz, Mary. *Belling the Tiger*. Illustrated by Beni Montresor. Harper & Row, Publishers, 1961. 64 p. (M)

———. *The Great Rebellion*. Illustrated by Beni Montresor. Harper & Row, Publishers, 1961. 63 p. (M)

———. *Maximilian's World*. Illustrated by Uri Shulevitz. Harper & Row, Publishers, 1966. 60 p. (M) (Friendship)

———. *Siri, the Conquistador*. Illustrated by Beni Montresor. Harper & Row, Publishers, 1978. 51 p. (M) (Friendship)

Sutcliff, Rosemary. *The Witch's Brat*. Illustrated by Richard Lebenson. Henry Z. Walck, Publisher, 1970. 143 p. (L)

Swarthout, Glendon and Kathryn. *Whichaway*. Illustrated by Richard
    M. Powers. Random House, 1966. 101 p. (L) (Ingenuity, Self-
    respect)

Taylor, Mildred D. *Roll of Thunder, Hear My Cry*. The Dial Press,
    1976. 276 p. (L) (Humaneness, Self-respect)

ter Haar, Jaap. *Boris*. Translated by Martha Mearns. Illustrated by Rien
    Poortvliet. Delacorte Press, 1966. 152 p. (L)

Treffinger, Carolyn. *Li Lun, Lad of Courage*. Illustrated by Kurt Wiese.
    Abingdon-Cokesbury Press, 1947. 96 p. (M) (Ingenuity, Self-
    respect)

Uchida, Yoshiko. *The Best Bad Thing*. Atheneum, 1983. 120 p. (L)
    (Cooperation, Maturing).

————. *A Jar of Dreams*. Atheneum, 1981. 131 p. (L) (Humaneness)

Ullman, James Ramsey. *Banner in the Sky*. J. B. Lippincott Company,
    1954. 252 p. (L) (Maturing)

Vance, Marguerite. *Windows for Rosemary*. Illustrated by Robert
    Doares. E. P. Dutton & Company, 1956. 60 p. (M)

Wojciechowska, Maia. *Shadow of a Bull*. Illustrated by Alvin Smith.
    Atheneum, 1964. 165 p. (L) (Self-respect)

Yashima, Taro. *Crow Boy*. Illustrated. The Viking Press, 1955. 37 p.
    (E)

III

Friendship and Love of Animals

This chapter encompasses books about the value of friendship and love among animals themselves and between animals and people. Most of the animal characters are personified.

BOOKS FOR EARLY YEARS

Arnold Lobel is author-illustrator of a series of three "I Can Read" episodic picture storybooks: *Frog and Toad Are Friends, Frog and Toad Together,* and *Frog and Toad All Year.* In the first book, when Toad complains about not getting mail, Frog writes this letter which a snail delivers four days later: "Dear Toad, I am glad that you are my best friend. Your best friend, Frog" (62). In the second book, Frog and Toad try to prove their bravery by climbing a mountain, but frightened by snakes, hawks, and a rock avalanche, they run to Toad's house. "They stayed there for a long time, just feeling brave together" (51). The third book traces friendship in various seasons. After Frog arrives late with a clock as a Christmas gift for Toad, the book concludes, "The two friends sat by the fire. The hands of the clock moved to show the hours of a merry Christmas Eve" (64).

Friendship develops among other woodland creatures (possibly two raccoons) in *Benjamin and Tulip* by author-illustrator Rosemary Wells. Benjamin's aunt refers to "sweet little Tulip," unaware that Tulip fights Benjamin whenever she can. After Benjamin resists Tulip, he enjoys equality and shares his watermelon with her.

Russell Hoban makes a commentary on the arbitrary use of gender roles in *Best Friends for Frances,* illustrated by Lillian Hoban, a story of some young badgers. After being snubbed twice by Albert, who refuses to play baseball with her because she is a girl, Frances becomes friends with her younger sister, Gloria, and the two picnic with a sign, "BEST FRIENDS OUTING. NO BOYS" (16). Later, they let Albert join them.

Again Russell Hoban writes and Lillian Hoban illustrates a picture storybook, *Emmet Otter's Jug-band Christmas*. A poor otter mother and her son both secretly enter a talent show hoping to use prize money for each other's Christmas gifts. When both lose, each appreciates the other's motive. Ma says, "I guess I ought to feel pretty bad, but the funny thing is that I don't" (32). When they sing together on the way home, Doc Bullfrog hears them and hires both to perform at Riverside Rest.

From the woodlands come two possums depicted humorously in Barbara Cooney's illustrations for Marjorie Weinman Sharmat's *Burton and Dudley*. It is Dudley who persuades armchair-prone Burton to join him on a walk. They enjoy nature and each other, reversing roles when Dudley tires and Burton announces, "I want to see the whole world. . . . I don't want to see the whole world without you" (unp).

Another Marjorie Weinman Sharmat book, *Bartholomew, the Bossy*, illustrated by Normand Chartier, portrays other personified animals. Friends, "too numerous to count" (3), elect Bartholomew Skunk to be the Block Club's president. However, Bartholomew becomes so bossy that no one attends his second meeting. After he consults Fabian Owl, he reforms and again is popular.

In Rebecca Caudill's *A Pocketful of Cricket*, illustrated by Evaline Ness, six-year-old Jay begins first grade with a cricket in his pocket. After the cricket chirps, the kind teacher asks, "Is this cricket your friend?" (unp). He nods his head and displays his cricket at show-and-tell.

An adult who respects animals is Mr. Bobbin in *The Happy Hunter* by author-illustrator Roger Duvoisin. Mr. Bobbin, who lives by himself in the woods, buys a hunting outfit and gun, but he never pulls the trigger. After "hunting" his animal friends, he says, "Well, that was another beautiful hunting day. I had a lovely walk through the forest" (23). When he becomes too old to hunt, he sits on his porch and animals visit him. "So the years were still full of happy days for Mr. Bobbin" (29).

A preschool girl wants to play with a grasshopper, frog, turtle, chipmunk, blue jay, rabbit, and snake in *Play with Me* by author-illustrator Marie Hall Ets. The animals lose their fear and sit beside her, joined by a fawn who licks her cheek. The girl exclaims, "Oh, now I was happy—as happy could be! For all of them—ALL OF THEM— were playing with me" (30–31).

Another book by Ets with her fine lithographs is *Mr. T. W. Anthony Woo*. As Michael, a cobbler, works at his bench, Rodrigo, a dog, and Meola, a cat, sit nearby. Mr. T. W. Anthony Woo, a mouse, sits on Michael's shoulder. Miss Dora, who moves in with them, favors only her parrot, Pollyandrew. It is Mr. T. W. who scares Miss Dora away, earning Rodrigo's and Meola's gratitude, for now, "They all lived together in peace" (54).

Alexander stays alone in a mouse hole in *Alexander and the Wind-up Mouse* by author-illustrator Leo Lionni. Alexander's first request to a magic lizard is to be changed into a wind-up mouse like Willie, but when he hears about plans to discard Willie (who is broken), he asks that Willie become a fellow live mouse. After Alexander gets his wish, "he hugged Willie and . . . they danced until dawn" (unp).

Friends of a different size appear in *Amos & Boris* by author-illustrator William Steig. Amos is a mouse who falls overboard from his ship, *The Rodent*, and gets rescued by Boris, a whale. Later, when hurricane Yetta beaches Boris on Amos's shore, the mouse gets help to save Boris. Before departing, Boris tells Amos, "We *will* be friends forever, but we can't be together. . . . I'll never forget you, though" (unp).

Another rodent craves companions in *Wilfred the Rat* by author-illustrator James Stevenson. During a winter stop at an amusement park, Wilfred meets Dwayne, a squirrel, and Rupert, a chipmunk. The park is closed until June, so the three become friends as they enjoy the rides together. When the park opens in summer, Wilfred refuses a job there to be with his companions.

Marilyn Hafner's illustrations enhance *That Dog!* by Nanette Newman, an author with a fine sense of humor. Young Ben's big dog, Barnum, helps his master's soccer team win by hiding the ball from opponents until suppertime. When Barnum dies, Ben does not want another dog until a puppy, Buster, follows him home. Ben thinks, "Maybe the puppy and I can remember Barnum together. He looks like he needs someone to love him and I guess I need someone to love" (45).

Helen V. Griffith shows how a gullible dog, Alex, relates to a wise cat in *Alex and the Cat*, illustrated by Joseph Low, and *More Alex and the Cat*, illustrated by Donald Carrick. In the first book, "Alex and the cat lay side by side on the warm grass. . . . The cat was purring. Alex closed his eyes and thought of nothing. It was a peaceful day" (68). In the second book, the cat offers a listening ear to the dog's complaints. Afterwards, Alex tells the cat, "Come and play" (54).

Other inseparable creatures are Penny, a penguin, and Captain Jenkins, a walrus, in *Penny and the Captain* by author-illustrator Jane Breskin Zalben. When Penny, first mate on the sailboat, *The Silverfish*, becomes homesick for Antarctica, Captain Jenkins gives her an iceberg for her birthday. After Penny goes ashore, leaving the captain alone, he misses her chatter and confesses, "It's good to be by yourself . . . but it is also fun to be with good friends" (41).

Jane Breskin Zalben is the author-illustrator of another book about friends, *Lyle and Humus*. Lyle, a monkey, and Humus, an elephant, work in the same circus. When Humus goes bicycling without telling Lyle, the two stop speaking, no longer share lunch, and sit apart on a circus bus. After Lyle gets a cramp swimming, Humus saves him, and they are best friends once more.

Louise Fatio's *The Happy Lion* and *The Happy Lion in Africa*, both illustrated by Roger Duvoisin, show a French zoo lion who later goes to Africa. The public visits the zoo lion behind bars, but when an attendant accidentally leaves the cage open and the lion roams, most people hide. Only young François is friendly as he leads the lion to his cage, saying, "Come with me, lion, let's walk back to the park together" (unp). The story continues with *The Happy Lion in Africa* which tells how the kidnapped French lion goes on a ship to Africa. He arrives at the camp of Monsieur Lentille, an animal photographer who recognizes the Happy Lion and flies him to his French home. Everyone celebrates, and the lion and his friend, François, are reunited.

Ty has an animal friend, a pelican, in *Come Again, Pelican* by author-illustrator Don Freeman. The pelican, who finds Ty's lost boot, shows the boy how to fish, and Ty rewards him with the first catch. Ty declares, "I learned about the tide, . . . how it comes and goes. . . . Just like my pelican friend" (43–44).

A toy pet, a corduroy teddy bear in green overalls, is the star of *Corduroy*, another book by author-illustrator Don Freeman. Corduroy is happy when a young black girl, Lisa, buys him in a department store and takes him to her house. After he sees his miniature bed, he proclaims, "This must be home" (30). When she sews a needed button on his overalls, he tells her, " 'You must be a friend. I've always wanted a friend.' 'Me too!' says Lisa, who gives him a big hug" (32).

Jealousy intrudes upon a bear's friendship in *Brunus and the New Bear* by author-illustrator Ellen Stoll Walsh. Brunus, a big bear, always enjoys undivided attention until Benjamin lets Heek, a small, cuddly bear, sleep between him and Brunus. Benjamin, sensitive to the problem, finds a solution: "Now when the three friends go to bed, Benjamin sleeps in the middle" (unp).

A bear that outgrows being young Johnny Orchard's pet is a character in *The Biggest Bear* by author-illustrator Lynd Ward. Johnny, a farm boy, brings a bear cub home as a pet, but the cub gets so large and eats so much that Johnny has to get rid of him. When the bear walks into a zoo trap, zoo keepers say that this is the biggest bear they have seen. They offer the bear a good home and plenty to eat, promising Johnny, "and you can come to see him whenever you want to" (82). Johnny is delighted.

Two hippopotamuses are friends in a trilogy by author-illustrator James Marshall: *George and Martha, George and Martha Encore,* and *George and Martha, One Fine Day.* In the first book, Martha praises George when he replaces his broken front tooth with a gold one. He replies:

> "That's what friends are for. . . . They always look on the bright side and they always know how to cheer you up." "But they also tell you the truth," [says] Martha with a smile. (46)

The second book shows Martha at the beach refusing suntan lotion despite George's warning. When she gets a terrible sunburn, George never says, " 'I told you so.' Because that's not what friends are for" (36). In the last book, as Martha tries tightrope walking, George shows a true friend's concern by trying to boost her confidence.

BOOKS FOR MIDDLE YEARS

There is a huge heroic mouse in Dick King-Smith's *Magnus Powermouse.* When Madeleine, a mouse, conceives, she eats a Penny-feather's Patent Porker Pill that promotes weight gain. A resultant offspring is so large his Latin-prone father, Marcus Aurelius Mouse, calls him Magnus, and his strength inspires his second name, Powermouse. The reward for feeding his gluttonous appetite comes when Magnus frees his father from a mousetrap. Eventually, Magnus and his parents enjoy being in the menagerie of a friend, a former rat catcher, Jim, and Magnus says, "I shouldn't be surprised if we didn't all live happily ever after" (117).

Barbara Dana's *Zucchini* tells about an unusual pet, Zucchini, a long thin ferret. He escapes from the Bronx Zoo and comes to a Society for the Prevention of Cruelty to Animals Shelter where he meets friendly Billy Ferguson. En route to the boy's Binghamton house, "Zucchini rode the whole way on Billy's lap. . . . He was home already" (122).

Foxes are Irina Korschunow's main subjects in *The Foundling Fox*, translated from German by James Skofield. An orphaned baby fox turns for protection to a vixen who has three young ones of her own. Soon the vixen cannot distinguish her own three from the foundling as she says, "I have given him milk, and I have warmed him. I saved him from the hound and I have carried him this far. My foundling fox belongs to me!" (27).

Jerome Kildee protects animal friends in Rutherford Montgomery's *Kildee House*. Kildee builds his house with a hinged door, so Mama and Papa Skunk and Mr. and Mrs. Grouch Raccoon are free to enter and exit, becoming part of his family when they wish. Surveying his wild life refuge on Kildee Mountain, Kildee realizes, "He had never interfered with the lives of his friends or tried to shape them; he had just lived with them" (114).

Kind folks move to Connecticut's Pine Wood in Robert Lawson's *Rabbit Hill*. Before the folks occupy the big house, Mother Rabbit worries that they may be mean, eloquent Father Rabbit sees auspicious signs, visiting Uncle Analdas seems disinterested but debonair, and young Georgie Rabbit leaps with delight. The new folks win animal approval by putting food for furry friends beside a Saint Francis of Assisi pool labeled, "There is enough for all" (123).

Tension mounts in *Mystery on Danger Road* by Florence Parry Heide and Roxanne Heide. Preadolescent Cindy Temple and her mother collect toy clowns for a craft fair, finding money inside one of them. They also discover Sam, a wounded dog whom they cure. Cindy locates Sam's owner through a newspaper advertisement. The owner, posing as a policeman, is really a robber named Bork who confines

Cindy and Sam separately in his deserted house. Sam gnaws through his tether and leads rescuers to Cindy.

George Selden's famous animal friendship series includes *The Cricket in Times Square, Tucker's Countryside, Harry Cat's Pet Puppy,* and *Chester Cricket's New Home.* The Bellini family's New York City subway station newsstand is the setting of the first book, *The Cricket in Times Square.* Chester Cricket is the pet of Bellini's son, Mario, and Chester's two friends are Harry Cat and Tucker Mouse. Referring to Tucker, Chester says, "[I] was touched that a mouse [I] had known only a few minutes would share his food with [me]" (22).

After Chester performs newsstand operas to increase sales, he plans to return to Old Meadow, Connecticut, his home, and invites Harry Cat and Tucker Mouse to join him in the second book in Selden's series, *Tucker's Countryside.* In trying to save the meadow from construction, Tucker finds a sign that leads the community to believe the town's founder, Hedley, once lived in a homestead there, so the area becomes a historic shrine. Animals honor Tucker Mouse by calling the place "Tucker's Countryside."

Harry Cat and Tucker Mouse return to their Times Square subway station drainpipe home where they befriend a stray puppy, Huppy, in Selden's *Harry Cat's Pet Puppy.* A kind musician gives Huppy a permanent home when the dog outgrows the drainpipe, and Harry Cat's farewell is "a fatherly pat on the back" (147).

For the final book in Selden's series, *Chester Cricket's New Home,* the scene shifts back to Tucker's Countryside where two overweight picnickers sit on the stump in which Chester Cricket lives and destroy his home. He accepts invitations to stay with friends, John and Dorothy Robin, Henry and Emily Chipmunk, Beatrice and Jerome Pheasant, and Donald Dragonfly, but is comfortable only in his new home that Simon Turtle and zany Walter Water Snake gnaw in a log. The snake sings, "He has a new home now—and look! He has a new friend—ME!" (143).

E. B. White's *Charlotte's Web* is about a group of farm animals: Charlotte, a clever spider; Templeton, a rat; and Wilbur, a pig destined for slaughter. Charlotte saves Wilbur's life by spinning, in her web near his pen, compliments about Wilbur that the public notices. She says to Wilbur, "You have been my friend. . . . That in itself is a tremendous thing. I wove my webs for you because I liked you" (164). He reciprocates her devotion with kindness to her babies after her death. It is a remarkably telling story of friendship and sacrifice.

BOOKS FOR LATER YEARS

Jane Wagner's *J. T.* is easy to read, but its content fits readers in their later years. Part of its appeal comes from photographs Gordon Parks, Jr. took when the story of ten-year-old J. T. Gamble was presented on television. A lonely black child, J. T., suffers because his father has deserted him and his mother. Shortly after stealing a pocket radio from a car and outfoxing two avenging young bullies, J. T. discovers Bones, an injured, one-eyed alley cat. His mother refuses to have the cat in their apartment, so the boy provides Bones with shelter in an empty lot. To feed his pet, J. T. charges cans of tuna at Mr. Rosen's grocery without his mother's permission. When bullies throw Bones into the street where he dies, J. T. mourns. His understanding grandmother says, "That cat, he somethin' real special to you, I know . . ." (53). Mr. Rosen delivers a Christmas kitten, complete with kitty litter and a pledge for free pet food. Then J. T. returns the stolen radio and gets a job with Mr. Rosen.

A story of a child who communicates better with animals than with human beings is Allan W. Eckert's *Incident at Hawk's Hill*, set in Canada in 1870. Small, shy, six-year-old Ben MacDonald, who feeds baby mice to a hurt badger, mimics animal sounds and movements. His family loves him, but they do not understand him. Ben wanders away, is caught in a storm, and, while people search for him, takes refuge in the badger's cave. He helps heal the badger's paw, and she feeds him. Two months later, Ben's older brother finds the boy in the badger's hole. The badger follows the brothers home and becomes a family pet. To save Ben from being considered a freak if the truth were known, Archbishop Peter Matheson offers a solution. Since the Indian name for badger is *mittenusk*, he advises the family to say Ben's rescuer is Mittenusk. People assume Mittenusk is a Blackfoot Chief, and Ben offers no explanations.

Girls who like horse stories enjoy Barbara Morgenroth's *Impossible Charlie*. Jackie Knapp, who wants her own horse, receives a supposedly model horse, Charlie. Fiona Jagger, a 4-H Horse Club leader, says, "I just have the feeling that you don't realize what a responsibility it is having a horse. . . . Having a horse is more than riding. . . . It's an attitude. . . ." (17). Charlie is a problem, fighting shots and shoes, and refusing jumps in a horse show. Fiona advises, "All this horse will understand is firm punishment. And if you won't do it, you'd better forget about riding because you aren't going to be able to handle this horse, or any other horse for that matter" (103). Jackie becomes firm with him, enters him as Impossible Charlie in a show, and wins two ribbons.

William Corbin's *Golden Mare* shows a bond between a twelve-year-old rheumatic fever victim, Robin Daveen, and his aged horse, Magic. Lonely Robin, who lives on a ranch, turns to his horse as a companion when his illness keeps him from activities with his brothers Barry and Wynn. Robin feels, "Here on this golden horse he was bigger than Barry or Wynn. . . . For her strength was his" (5–6). Robin summons strength in a blizzard when, atop Magic, he secures help for his mother who has broken her leg. The old mare dies from the exertion, but Robin's father comments, "It's only the boy's care and love that's kept her going this long" (101).

Fourteen-year-old Travis shows that same kind of love for Old Yeller, a stray dog, in Fred Gipson's historical fiction, *Old Yeller*, which has a sequel, *Little Arliss* (see chapter 6, "Ingenuity"). When a killer hog attacks Travis, the dog defends him. Travis notes, "Here he was trying to lick my wound, when he was bleeding from a dozen worse ones" (107). A wolf with hydrophobia bites Old Yeller after the dog rescues Travis's mother from the diseased animal. Travis must shoot his dog, knowing, "It was going to kill something inside [him] to do it" (152).

In *Where the Red Fern Grows, the Story of Two Dogs and a Boy*, Wilson Rawls describes an Ozark hillbilly, Billy Colman, of over fifty years ago. The boy is ten years old when he reads about Kentucky coonhound pups that cost fifty dollars a pair. For two years, Billy sells fish, produce, and hides, secretly saving money until his grandfather orders his pups. He names the russet animals Old Dan and Little Ann and trains them to attack coons. The pair defeat competitors in a championship coon hunt, bringing their master a gold cup plus over $300. Tragedy strikes when the dogs tree a ferocious mountain lion. Billy acknowledges, "I knew that if it hadn't been for their loyalty and unselfish courage I would have probably been killed by the slashing claws of the devil cat" (197). Before wounded Old Dan dies, Papa says

of the hound, "He only has two loves—you and hunting." (199). Little
Ann grieves until she dies on her partner's grave. Sacred red fern grows
at their burial site. The boy notices the fern when he leaves with his
parents and three sisters for a town with schools, a move made possible
by the championship money.

In Eileen Dunlop's *Fox Farm*, which is set in Scotland, Richard
Darke and a foster child in the Darke household, Adam Hewitt, are
teenagers who unite to raise young Foxy. After Mr. Darke kills a vixen,
the boys find what they believe is one of the vixen's offspring, Foxy.
Knowing a young fox is unwelcome on a farm, they hide it in
abandoned Fox Tower, spending their allowance to feed it. Adam
expresses love for the first time for Foxy. Previously aloof, Adam
changes after learning that his father and stepmother in Australia do not
want him, but that Mr. Darke will adopt him. When the boys let Mr.
Darke see Foxy, they are surprised to learn the animal is a puppy. They
are delighted to hear Mr. Darke say, "Of course you're allowed to keep
him. I was just saying to Mother the other day that it would be nice to
have a dog around the place again" (141).

In a story involving a seeing eye dog, *Follow My Leader*, James B.
Garfield shows a blind author's insight. He tells about eleven-year-old
Jimmy Carter, blinded accidentally when a friend, Mike Adams, tosses
a firecracker at him. Jimmy gets a German shepherd guide dog, Leader,
and bravely returns to school. When Jimmy and Mike attend a scout
meeting, the scoutmaster insists that the two boys shake hands, and they
resume their friendship. The scouts choose Leader as mascot of their
Dog Star Patrol. Jimmy says, "He'll make a swell mascot in his spare
time, but he knows his main job is being four-legged eyes for me!"
(191). Leader guides lost scouts, including Mike, back to camp and
rescues Mike when the boy gets a cramp swimming. Mike announces,
"He's the most wonderful dog in the world. That's twice he saved me
today" (189). Jimmy replies that Leader is "just a part of me. . . . I guess
we're Siamese twins" (190).

Dorothy Clewes's *Guide Dog* is another book that tells about a
valuable dog serving a blind youth. In England, nineteen-year-old
Roley Rolandson distrusts a dog that knocks a parcel from his hand
while he is delivering mail. When Roley retrieves the package, it
explodes, blinding him. Roley gets a Labrador retriever, Mick, to guide
him so that he can become a physiotherapist. Introducing Mick to

Susan, his former nurse and romantic interest, Roley says, "Meet the best friend a man ever had" (150).

In *The Incredible Journey—A Tale of Three Animals*, Sheila Burnford shows the devotion of three pets in Ontario, Canada to their original masters, the Hunter family. When Jim Hunter goes to England as an exchange English professor for nine months, his friend John Longridge takes the family pets to his home 250 miles away. Eight months pass, and while Longridge goes on a hunting trip, he leaves the animals behind. The three animals, lonely for the Hunters, travel through wilderness to their original home. Luath, a young yellow Labrador retriever, leads Bodger, an old bull terrier, and Tao, a Siamese cat. By sharing food and offering each other protection, they survive the 250-mile trek. After the old dog tires, his two comrades go slower. When the lost cat finds his friends, Bodger reacts as follows: "The old dog had his beloved cat, warm and purring between his paws again, and he snored in deep contentment" (101). Longridge joins the Hunters in the end to greet the three pets as they safely reach their destination.

Domesticated animals are the subjects of most of the previously noted books, but a wild rare whooping crane, Whooper, is important in Larry Callen's *Sorrow's Song*. The story is set in rural Four Corners, where a gentle young mute, Sorrow Nix, and her friend Pinch Grimball catch an injured crane and Sorrow heals its broken wing. After Whooper, the crane, kills an attacking copperhead, Pinch feels the brave animal is protecting Sorrow. She and Pinch finally give the endangered bird his freedom.

SUMMARY

A variety of animals are the subjects of the fifty-one books discussed—from a whooping crane to a ferret to hippopotamuses, though dogs slightly predominate. Of the twenty-nine books for early years, seventeen show the value of friendship among animals themselves; in twelve, there is a relationship between animals and people. Of the eleven books for middle years, three show friendship among animals alone and nine depict their ties with people. All eleven books for later years show the value of friendship between animals and people. Obviously friendship with and among animals is a favorite topic for children.

References

Burnford, Sheila. *The Incredible Journey—A Tale of Three Animals.* Illustrated by Carl Burger. Little, Brown & Company, 1961. 145 p. (L) (Loyalty)

Callen, Larry. *Sorrow's Song.* Illustrated by Marvin Friedman. Little, Brown & Company, 1979. 150 p. (L) (Cooperation)

Caudill, Rebecca. *A Pocketful of Cricket.* Illustrated by Evaline Ness. Holt, Rinehart & Winston, 1962. Unpaged. (E)

Clewes, Dorothy. *Guide Dog.* Illustrated by Peter Burchard. Coward-McCann, 1965. 159 p. (L) (Cooperation)

Corbin, William. *Golden Mare.* Illustrated by Pers Crowell. Coward-McCann, 1955. 122 p. (L) (Cooperation)

Dana, Barbara. *Zucchini.* Illustrated by Eileen Christlow. Harper & Row, Publishers, 1982. 122 p. (M) (Ingenuity)

Dunlop, Eileen. *Fox Farm.* Illustrated by Mary Binsdale. Holt, Rinehart & Winston, 1978. 149 p. (L) (Responsibility)

Duvoisin, Roger. *The Happy Hunter.* Illustrated. Lothrop, Lee & Shepard, Company, 1961. Unpaged. (E)

Eckert, Allan W. *Incident at Hawk's Hill.* Illustrated by John Schoenherr. Little, Brown & Company, 1971. 173 p. (L) (Courage, Self-respect)

Ets, Marie Hall. *Play with Me.* Illustrated. The Viking Press, 1955. 31 p. (E)

———. *Mr. T. W. Anthony Woo.* Illustrated. The Viking Press, 1951. 55 p. (E) (Ingenuity)

Fatio, Louise. *The Happy Lion.* Illustrated by Roger Duvoisin. McGraw-Hill Company, 1954. Unpaged. (E)

———. *The Happy Lion in Africa.* Illustrated by Roger Duvoisin. McGraw-Hill Book Company, 1955. 30 p. (E)

Freeman, Don. *Come Again, Pelican.* Illustrated. The Viking Press, 1961. 44 p. (E) (Ingenuity)

———. *Corduroy.* Illustrated. The Viking Press, 1968. 32 p. (E)

Garfield, James B. *Follow My Leader.* Illustrated by Robert Greimer. The Viking Press, 1957. 191 p. (L) (Cooperation, Ingenuity)

Gipson, Fred. *Old Yeller.* Illustrated by Carl Burger. Harper & Brothers, 1956. 158 p. (L) (Courage)

Griffith, Helen V. *Alex and the Cat.* Illustrated by Joseph Low. Greenwillow Books, 1983. 55 p. (E)

———. *More Alex and the Cat*. Illustrated by Donald Carrick. Greenwillow Books, 1983. 55 p. (E)

Heide, Florence Parry and Heide, Roxanne. *Mystery on Danger Road*. Illustrated by Seymour Fleishman. Albert Whitman & Company, 1983. 128 p. (M) (Loyalty, Ingenuity)

Hoban, Russell. *Best Friends for Frances*. Illustrated by Lillian Hoban. Harper & Row, Publishers, 1969. 31 p. (E)

———. *Emmet Otter's Jug-band Christmas*. Illustrated by Lillian Hoban. Parents' Magazine Press, 1971. Unpaged. (E)

King-Smith, Dick. *Magnus Powermouse*. Illustrated by Mary Rayner. Harper & Row, Publishers, 1984. 120 p. (M) (Maturing)

Korschanow, Irina. *The Foundling Fox*. Translated from German by James Skofield. Illustrated by Reinhard Michl. Harper & Row, 1984. 48 p. (M) (Responsibility)

Lawson, Robert. *Rabbit Hill*. Illustrated. The Viking Press, 1944. 128 p. (M)

Lionni, Leo. *Alexander and the Wind-up Mouse*. Illustrated. Pantheon, 1969. Unpaged. (E)

Lobel, Arnold. *Frog and Toad All Year*. Illustrated. Harper & Row, Publishers, 1976. 64 p. (E)

———. *Frog and Toad Are Friends*. Illustrated. Harper & Row, Publishers, 1970. 64 p. (E)

———. *Frog and Toad Together*. Illustrated. Harper & Row, Publishers, 1972. 64 p. (E)

Marshall, James. *George and Martha*. Illustrated. Houghton Mifflin Company, 1972. 46 p. (E)

———. *George and Martha Encore*. Illustrated. Houghton Mifflin Company, 1973. 46 p. (E)

———. *George and Martha, One Fine Day*. Illustrated. Houghton Mifflin Company, 1978. 46 p. (E)

Montgomery, Rutherford. *Kildee House*. Illustrated by Barbara Cooney. Doubleday & Company, 1949. 209 p. (M) (Cooperation)

Morgenroth, Barbara. *Impossible Charlie*. Illustrated by Velma Ilsley. Atheneum, 1979. 153 p. (L)

Newman, Nanette. *That Dog!* Illustrated by Marylin Hafner. Crowell, 1983. 47 p. (E) (Ingenuity)

Rawls, Wilson. *Where the Red Fern Grows, the Story of Two Dogs and a Boy*. Doubleday & Company, 1974. (L) (Courage, Loyalty, Responsibility)

Selden, George. *Chester Cricket's New Home*. Illustrated by Garth Williams. Farrar, Straus & Giroux, 1983. 144 p. (M)

————. *The Cricket in Times Square*. Illustrated by Garth Williams. Farrar, Straus & Giroux, 1960. 160 p. (M) (Ingenuity)

————. *Harry Cat's Pet Puppy*. Illustrated by Garth Williams. Farrar, Straus & Giroux, 1974. 160 p. (M)

————. *Tucker's Countryside*. Illustrated by Garth Williams. Farrar, Straus & Giroux, 1969. 176 p. (M) (Ingenuity)

Sharmat, Marjorie Weinman. *Bartholomew, the Bossy*. Illustrated by Normand Chartier. Macmillan Publishing Company, 1984. 32 p. (E)

————. *Burton and Dudley*. Illustrated by Barbara Cooney. Holiday House, 1975. Unpaged. (E)

Steig, William. *Amos & Boris*. Illustrated. Farrar, Straus and Giroux, 1971. 32 p. (E) (Ingenuity)

Stevenson, James. *Wilfred the Rat*. Illustrated. Greenwillow Books, 1977. 32 p. (E)

Wagner, Jane. *J. T.* Photographs by Gordon Parks, Jr. Van Nostrand-Reinhold Company, 1969. 63 p. (L) (Responsibility)

Walsh, Ellen Stoll. *Brunus and the New Bear*. Illustrated. Doubleday & Company, 1979. Unpaged. (E)

Ward, Lynd. *The Biggest Bear*. Illustrated. Houghton Mifflin Company, 1952. 84 p. (E) (Ingenuity, Responsibility)

Wells, Rosemary. *Benjamin and Tulip*. Illustrated. Dial Press, 1973. 30 p. (E)

White, E. B. *Charlotte's Web*. Illustrated by Garth Williams. Harper & Row, Publishers, 1952. 184 p. (M) (Loyalty, Ingenuity, Responsibility)

Zalben, Jane Breskin. *Lyle and Humus*. Illustrated. World's Work, 1976. Unpaged. (E)

————. *Penny and the Captain*. Collins/World, 1978. 60 p. (E)

IV

Friendship and Love of People

Bonding between individuals may be in terms of friendship or, if more intense, love. Fortunately, literature for young people stresses this value. The bonding may be with relatives, running the gamut from a tie with a great-great-aunt to one with a stepsister. The link between nonfamily members may be romantic or platonic, and may include friendships that cut across racial, cultural, economic, or religious lines and those that involve individuals of varying degrees of intelligence and health.

BOOKS FOR EARLY YEARS

Author-illustrator Aliki shows the love between a gentle Greek grandfather and granddaughter in *The Two of Them*, stating, "He made a cradle for her doll, and a flute of bamboo, and they sat under the trees and played music together. And every year she loved him even more than the things he made for her" (unp). Before his death, she says, " 'Good night, Papouli,' and he answer[s] with a kiss" (unp).

Jeannette Caines shows a daughter's relationship with her father in *Daddy*, illustrated by Roger Himler. In a black urban family, the parents seem to be separated, and Daddy, who lives with his friend Paula, calls for his young daughter Windy every Saturday. He always brings two boxes of chocolate pudding to make with Windy as their final activity. Windy plays hide-and-seek under the kitchen table in Daddy's apartment and in a supermarket aisle. When Daddy pretends to lose his eyeglasses, Windy always find them. Windy looks forward to next

Saturday. "We're going to fly a kite on his roof. I know he won't forget because he wrote our date on his calendar and in his head" (29).

Lois Osborn's *My Dad Is Really Something*, illustrated by Rodney Pate, stresses Dad's ties to his son and his son's friend. When Harry George praises Dad, Ron, a new boy in class, brags more about *his* father although, Harry learns, Ron's father is dead. Harry invites Ron to fish with him and Dad. After they enjoy themselves, Ron brags about Harry's father. Harry says, "I'm glad my Dad is real" (unp).

Martha Whitmore Hickman's *When Can Daddy Come Home?* has Francis Livingston's illustrations. It shows second grader Anderson Smith, his mother, and sister Angela. They move to Nashville to be near Daddy, who is in prison for stealing. Anderson avoids questions about Daddy in school. The boy befriends a new black pupil, Joel, whose father is in a hospital. Joel's father loses one leg and may lose the other, so Anderson feels lucky by comparison, especially when he learns Daddy will be paroled.

Author-illustrator William Steig depicts a married couple in *Caleb & Kate*. After a lover's quarrel, Caleb naps in a forest. He is asleep when witch Yedida tests a new spell by touching her thumb to the tip of Caleb's left forefinger. In place of a snoring carpenter, she leaves a snoozing dog. The dog can only growl after he returns to Kate, who searches in vain for her "dear husband." When burglars enter Kate's home, one slices skin off a toe on the dog's front paw to disable the animal. The thief cuts the very spot witch Yedida had touched, undoing the spell. Restored as a man, Caleb lets the burglars escape while kissing Kate. Caleb and Kate "leaped into each other's arms and cleaved together for a long time" (unp).

In *Sisters*, author-illustrator David McPhail presents two unlike siblings. One is big while the other is little, and one prefers pizza while the other likes corn on the cob. Although both enjoy baking cookies and dancing, they are most alike because "they loved each other very much" (unp).

Author-illustrator Tomi Ungerer shows how a child can change evil men in *The Three Robbers*. After three robbers in tall hats rob a carriage carrying orphaned Tiffany, they take her to their cave where she questions them about how they intend to use their wealth. Influenced by her, the robbers "gathered up all the lost, unhappy, and abandoned children they could find. They bought a beautiful castle where all of them could live" (27–28). When the children are grown, they build a village around the castle and in "memory of their kind foster fathers, buil[d] three tall, high-roofed towers. One for each of the three robbers" (33).

It is as though old Bartholomew is Nelly's foster father in Sally Wittman's A *Special Trade*, illustrated by Karen Gundersheimer. When Bartholomew first meets Nelly, she is a next-door baby, so he takes her for daily walks in her stroller, stopping to pat friendly dogs. Bartholomew assists Nelly only when she needs it as she learns to walk. "The neighbors call them ham and eggs because they [are] always together" (unp). When Nelly goes to school, she helps aging Bartholomew cross the street. While out alone, he falls, and returns from a hospital in a wheelchair. Nelly pushes him, now that there is a special trade of caretaker roles.

Neighbors are also characters in Eve Bunting's *Clancy's Coat*, illustrated by Lorinda Bryan Cauley. After Bridget, the cow of a tailor, Tippitt, tramples Clancy's nearby garden, Clancy is no longer Tippitt's friend. When Clancy brings the tailor an old coat to turn inside out, Tippitt promises it for Saturday, but weeks go by and it is not ready. Each time Clancy comes for the coat, the two talk. While Clancy waits, he and Tippitt become friends again. Tippitt thinks, "A garden comes back with time and attention; I thought maybe a friendship could too" (unp).

Cynthia Rylant's *Miss Maggie* describes another neighbor, poor, tobacco-chewing Maggie Ziegler who lives alone near an Appalachian farm boy, Nat Crawford. One winter day, when no smoke comes from her chimney, Nat enters her house for the first time and finds her distraught because her bird, Henry, is dead. After he takes her temporarily to his home with the dead bird, she gives him empty tobacco tins for his collections, and he gives her empty coffee cans as spittoons.

Thomas Di Grazia illustrated both *Miss Maggie* and Lucille Clifton's *My Friend Jacob*. In Clifton's book, Sam celebrates his eighth birthday at the same time as his seventeen-year-old neighbor, Jacob. Illustrations show Sam to be black and Jacob, white. Jacob teaches Sam basketball and the names of cars while Sam helps Jacob remember, which is hard for Jacob. Sam teaches him to remember to knock before entering Sam's house. Sam says, "He [Jacob] is my very very very best friend in the whole wide world!" (unp).

Roberta Greene also features interracial friends in *Two and Me Makes Three*, illustrated by Paul Galdone. In New York City, Joey enjoys follow-the-leader and kick-the-can with a black friend, Willie, and a Puerto Rican pal, Juan. When the three are sad, they find a softball, fight over it until it rolls into a sewer, and angrily part. A week later, the three meet at a traffic light, shouting together, "I'm sorry" (unp). Then Joey puts his arms around his two chums and Willie says, "Come on or we'll be late for school" (unp).

Maude and Sally, created by author-illustrator Nicky Weiss, presents two best friends. Maude tells Sally, "If you were a little taller and I was a little shorter, . . . we could be twins" (unp). When only Sally goes to summer camp for six weeks, Maude plays with Emmylou, who teaches her "Heart and Soul" on the piano. After Sally returns, school begins and in music class, Emmylou sits on one side of Maude and Sally on the other. On Hallowe'en, the three dress like bumble-bees. " 'If your wings were a little bigger,' Maude said to Emmylou, 'and your antennae were a little longer,' she said to Sally, 'we could be triplets' " (unp).

In a similar vein is Pat Ross's *Meet M and M*, illustrated by Marylin Hafner. The book begins, "Mandy and Mimi were friends. They were such good friends that sometimes they pretended to be twins" (5). Mandy from apartment 2B and Mimi from apartment 3B have a bad fight. It is not until a rainy day that a yellow pail drops from the third floor outside Mandy's 2B window with a promptly answered message. After an exchange of notes and items, Mandy writes, "Meet me on the stairs" (39). The story ends, "They met halfway, where they sat and talked about what to do tomorrow" (41).

Lee Henry learns to have more than one friend in Judy Delton's *Lee Henry's Best Friend*. Blair Andrew sees that Lee Henry gets first turn to bat in baseball, and Blair Andrew never takes all the blankets when he sleeps overnight. After Lee Henry gives a talk on spiders at school, only Blair Andrew claps. Lee Henry relates, "Blair Andrew said he likes me best of all the kids at school, and I said I like him best" (unp). Then Blair Andrew moves to Cincinnati but writes Lee Henry that he misses him. When a new boy from California moves nearby, Lee Henry says to him, "I already have a best friend" (unp). The boy replies, "I already have a best friend, too" (unp). Lee Henry decides, "This new kid is okay, too" (unp).

Moving is also a problem for Inatuk, a little Eskimo boy, in Suzanne Stark Morrow's *Inatuk's Friend*, illustrated by Ellen Raskin.

Inatuk is unhappy because his family is moving to find game. Inatuk is sad, knowing that he must leave his best carving friend, Soloquay. As a farewell gift, Soloquay presents a small walrus tusk carving, claiming it is a good luck symbol that leads to a friend. Sure enough, Inatuk finds that pal is his little brother, Swenik.

A picture storybook showing friends' loyalty is Judith Viorst's *Rosie and Michael* with cartoon-like illustrations by Lorna Tomei. Rosie likes Michael even when he puts Kool Whip in her sneakers. She comforts him when his parakeet dies. Michael likes Rosie even when she is grouchy and lets air out of his basketball. He consoles her when her dog runs away and when someone steals her bicycle.

Another book about loyal friendship is Marjorie Weinman Sharmat's *Gladys Told Me to Meet Her Here,* illustrated by Edward Frascino. As little Irving waits for his best friend, Gladys, he worries that she might be lost and searches for her, recalling incidents, such as when she whispered lines he forgot in a school play. When they exchanged Valentines, Irving wrote Gladys, "I HATE YOU LIKE I HATE CANDY AND ICE-CREAM SODAS" (11). Once Irving tied her shoelaces because she had a sore thumb. He even let Gladys name his male goldfish Barbara. After Irving returns to their meeting place, he finds Gladys waiting with a popsicle.

Besides Sharmat's book, Edward Frascino also illustrated Shirley Gordon's *Crystal Is the New Girl* and its sequel, *Crystal Is My Friend.* In the first book, Susan helps a new pupil, Crystal, adjust to school. They talk to each other so much in class that the teacher sends them to the principal's office. Susan declares, "Crystal and I are going to be friends forever" (83), and Crystal cautions Susan before vacation, "Don't catch amnesia and forget me!" (31).

In Gordon's *Crystal Is My Friend,* Crystal stays overnight, and Susan's mother insists that the guest choose activities. Susan loses when Crystal picks Yahtzee rather than Monopoly. Susan hates raisins and Crystal secretly puts them in the brownies they make. Crystal even chooses to sleep in Susan's bed, and the young hostess is so angry that she has fun only after Crystal agrees not to have first choice. Crystal declares, "First dibs is more fun" (25). In a positive ending, Susan asks Mother, "When can Crystal come and sleep over again?" (32).

Barbara Rinkoff's *Rutherford T. Finds 21B,* illustrated by Tomie dePaola, shows six-year-old Rutherford Turner, a newcomer in his neighborhood, on his first day in school. He asks a pupil where room 21B is, and they search together. They enlist help from so many others that when they eventually find the room, Rutherford has friends.

School is again the setting for Miriam Cohen's *Best Friends*, illustrated by Lillian Hoban. Paul, anxious to watch incubator eggs hatch, rushes into class without greeting his best friend, Jim. Nothing goes well for Jim, including a picture he tries to draw. When Sammy announces that he is Jim's best friend, Paul refuses to sit next to Jim for milk and cookies because he says, "Everybody is your best friend except me!" (unp). At recess, Jim and Paul go to their room for balls. Noticing the incubator light out, Jim keeps the eggs warm while Paul gets the janitor to replace the light bulb, and the friends are reunited.

Carrie is a shy, five-year-old Manhattan girl, afraid to visit another child, in Norma Klein's *Visiting Pamela*, illustrated by Kay Chorao. At Mother's insistence, Carrie accepts Pamela's invitation to visit her and travels on a crowded school bus with Pamela. After a smelly baby brother and a growling dog greet her, Carrie calls Mother to come for her soon. Mother delays thirty minutes, time for the girls to fashion pop beads and watch "Batman" on television. Carrie concludes, "I might even like to go to her house again. . . . I don't think I mind visiting people anymore" (30).

Two frequent visitors are the narrator and John in Charlotte Zolotow's *My Friend John*, illustrated by Ben Shecter. The young narrator suggests that he and John pool information, including what is in each other's refrigerator, secret fears, favorite girl friends, and hiding places. The story ends, "John is my best friend and I'm his and everything that is important about each other we like" (32).

In *5A and 7B* by author-illustrator Eleanor Schick, Toby lives in 5A and Sandy, in 7B of the same building, but it takes time before they meet. Sandy awakens early while Toby is still asleep, and they use different elevators. When Sandy's sister is ill, Sandy and her mother, late on errands, pass Toby and her mother at stores and in the apartment entrance. After they introduce themselves, Toby's mother invites Sandy to visit. "That night, before they went to sleep, Sandy and Toby both wished on the very same star that they would be friends forever" (unp).

In Beverly Keller's *Fiona's Bee*, illustrated by Diane Paterson, young Fiona makes friends ingeniously. Fiona has no dog but buys a dog dish, fills it with water, and attracts a bee who almost drowns. Saving the bee that perches on her shoulder, Fiona goes to a park, the bee's new home, and meets seven children who befriend her because of her courage with the insect. She tells Mother, "I saved a bee, and I got famous. I don't know if I'll still be famous tomorrow, but I sure have a lot of friends" (44).

Young friendships are fragile, as Marjorie Weinman Sharmat shows in *I'm Not Oscar's Friend Anymore*, illustrated by Tony DeLuna. The young narrator relates why he and Oscar, his "former friend," have parted. Then he phones Oscar, telling him they can be friends again. Apparently Oscar is not aware of a break in their ties and plans to play with him again on five-minutes notice.

A *Friend Is Someone Who Likes You* by author-illustrator Joan Walsh Anglund speaks simply about friends, stating, "It [a friend] can be a boy. It can be a girl or a cat or a dog or even a white mouse" (unp). A different kind of friend can be a tree which gives fruit or a place to swing. A gurgling brook that cools toes can be a friend. The pushing wind can be a friend that sings soft songs at night. If you are friendless, "look around carefully, to see someone who smiles at you in a special way" (unp).

BOOKS FOR MIDDLE YEARS

Sharon Bell Mathis's *The Hundred Penny Box* shows love between a young black boy, Michael ("Mike") Jefferson, and Great-great-aunt Dewbet ("Dew") Thomas. Aunt Dew projects warmth to Mike. "Come here, boy. Come here close. Let me look at you. . . . Get closer," she says (42). Mike's mother, Ruth, wants to replace Aunt Dew's old broken box that holds a penny for each of her hundred years. Mike enjoys counting pennies while Aunt Dew tells him a tale behind each cent. She says her dead husband, Henry, put in the first fifty-six pennies when they lived in Atlanta and she put in the rest. She declares, "It's *my* old cracked-up, wacky-dacky box with the top broken. Them's my years in that box. That's me in that box" (19). Mike shows his devotion by persuading Mother to save Aunt Dew's treasured box.

Peter Härtling tells a tale set in Germany about the growing love between Kalle and his grandmother, Frau Erna Bittel, in *Oma* (the German word for grandmother). The story covers five years from the time Kalle, at age five, becomes her ward after his parents' car-crash deaths. Oma confides, "Maybe I can't do much at times, but Kalle means a second lease on life for me" (92), and he reciprocates her affection. When she is in a hospital, he tells her, "It's terrible without you, Oma" (90). In the end, she is seventy years old and he is ten, but when he worries, she says, "I've made up my mind to live as long as I possibly can, Kalle" (94).

In Doris Gates's *A Morgan for Melinda: A Novel*, which takes place in California's Monterey Peninsula, ten-year-old Melinda Ross is afraid of horses. She shows her love for her father by learning to ride his gift horse, Ethan, a Morgan stallion. Melinda feels that she is substituting for her brother Martin, who had been five years older than she when he died of leukemia. She tells a friend, "I know it means an awful lot to Dad to have me become a good horsewoman. Losing Martin was very hard on him. I feel I want to make it up to him if I can. You see, I really love him" (135–136). Father tells the friend, "I was a lot luckier than many men who lose their sons. I had a most wonderful little daughter. I had Melinda" (163).

Rachel Vellars, How Could You? by Lois I. Fisher shows bonds between a father and daughter and between friends. Eleven-year-old Cory Matthewson and her best friend Rachel Vellars live in the same Port Hudson, New York condominium building with divorced fathers because their mothers do not want custody of them. Cory, realizing Mother's Manhattan dress-designing business is more important to her than child rearing, still spends some weekends with Mother. Although Rachel has had four stepmothers, Cory's father has not remarried. When he leaves her school lunch at the vice-principal's office and Cory retrieves it, Rachel Vellars tells the sixth grade that Cory is being disciplined for putting a mash note on the vice-principal's Datsun. Cory moans, "Rachel Vellars, how could you?" (16). Cory makes other friends but is still loyal to Rachel, becoming her kite teammate in a contest. Cory's father witnesses the pair's success, and Cory tells him, "Daddy! We won! My best friend and I won it together!" (154–155).

Beverly Cleary depicts parent-daughter relationships in separate books: *Ramona and Her Father* and *Ramona and Her Mother*. In the first book, Ramona Quimby is seven years old and her sister, Beatrice ("Beezus"), is eleven. When Mr. Quimby, who is a heavy smoker, loses his job, his daughters start an antismoking campaign that angers him. Ramona reflects, "Nobody ever paid attention to second graders except to scold them. No matter how hard she tried to save [her father's] life, he was not going to let her save it" (101). To avoid depression, she becomes a sheep in a Sunday school play, getting a thumbs-up signal from her father while she is on stage.

Cleary's *Ramona and Her Mother* takes place six months later. Father gets a cashier's job, but Mother continues to work to pay bills, and Ramona tells her, "I like it when you stay home" (38). After Ramona decides to run away, Mother helps her pack her heaviest things. Ramona interprets this as proof of Mother's love, announcing:

> "You tricked me! . . . You made the suitcase too heavy on purpose. You don't want me to run away!"
>
> "I couldn't get along without my Ramona," said Ramona's mother. She held out her arms. Ramona ran into them. Her mother had said the words she longed to hear. (200–201)

Eleven-year-old Margot Green tries to help her mother in Johanna Hurwitz's *The Law of Gravity: A Story*, set in New York City. While her flutist father is on a concert tour, Margot decides her summer project for sixth grade is to get Mother downstairs. For nine years, Mother has had a psychological block about leaving their fifth-floor walk-up apartment and rooftop garden. Margot's campaign assistant is a twelve-year-old bookworm, Joseph ("Bernie") Bernazzoli, who reminds her about Newton's law of gravity: What goes up must come down. Margot has no long-term success with Mother though their relationship improves. Her major accomplishment is cementing her friendship with Bernie.

Constance C. Greene's *I and Sproggy* focuses on the ties between ten-year-old Adam and his stepsister Sproggy in another New York City tale. Adam lives with his mother, a divorcee. His father returns from England with his English bride, Arabella, and her daughter Sproggy, who is two months older than Adam and taller. Father tells Adam, "I'd like you to more or less take [Sproggy] under your wing, show her the ropes, be kind to her. . . . I think she could use a friend" (25–26). It is Sproggy, however, who saves Adam from a mugger. Only later does he assist her when a girl jokes about her formal name, Evangeline. In the end, Father proposes an outing just with his son, but Adam says, "Let's take Sproggy along too" (149).

In Kristi Holl's *Just Like a Real Family*, twelve-year-old June Finch goes with her sixth-grade class to Reed's Retirement Ranch for a foster-grandparent program. June's partner, terse Franklin Cooper, prefers his own home but has to live at the ranch for hot food and medication. Eventually June and her mother, Anne, become his friends. After Mother's hospitalization, she must sell their home to pay bills and can only work part-time. When June suggests that the three move to Franklin's old home, he agrees, telling Anne, "You know I'm not the grandfatherly type. I never had children, and frankly, I never wanted any. But after seeing June week after week, and getting to know you, I began to think of you as family" (119).

Robert Burch's *Ida Early Comes over the Mountain* and *Christmas with Ida Early*, set in rural Georgia, tell how four children, whose mother is dead, welcome a "mountain Mary Poppins" as cook and housekeeper. Mr. Sutton, a widower, lives on a farm with his children: twelve-year-old Ellen, eleven-year-old Randall, and five-year-old twins, Clay and Dewey. In *Ida Early Comes over the Mountain*, the children, anxious to be rid of bossy Aunt Ernestine, adore Ida Early, a tall, scarecrow-like woman in overalls and clodhopper shoes who asks to work for them. She yodels when she sings the twins to sleep, plays tiddelywinks, and does rope tricks in school assembly. She disappears but returns before Thanksgiving, saying, "I missed my *true friends*" (144).

In the Robert Burch sequel, *Christmas with Ida Early*, the twins consider the Thanksgiving turkey a pet, so Ida prevents it from being killed by acting as a ventriloquist. The turkey seems to speak. At church, Ida encourages unconventional reenactment of the Christmas story, supported by her adopted family. The twins tell her, "We love you, Ida, just the way we loved Mama" (64). She replies, "All the same, you must remember her as your rightful mamma. I'm just filling in for a little while" (64).

An adult is a shy child's first friend in Ruth Hooker's *Gertrude Kloppenberg (Private)*. In her private diary entries, Gertrude Kloppenberg, who is about eleven years old, tells how she uses candy as a bribe, trying unsuccessfully to make friends. The lonely girl looks so often at a special garden that its owner, Mrs. Blonski, invites her to visit and help. She decides, "A person doesn't have to be your age to be a friend" (42). Mrs. Blonski with her son, a hospital intern, assist Gertrude when she learns to jump rope. Gertrude brings to the garden a classmate, Sandy, who invites her at recess to jump rope. Mrs. Blonski gives the classmates marigold seedlings, and Gertrude realizes that her interest in plants has led her to friends.

Another shy child, ten-year-old Jamie Johnson, becomes a friend and "part-time boy" of an adult neighbor, Mattie Swenson, director of a natural science center, in Elizabeth T. Billington's *Part-time Boy* When his adolescent brothers, Paul and Carl, exclude him from playing with them, Jamie helps Mattie with plants and pets, even spending a summer in the country with her. After he returns home, his brothers include him in sports. Paul shouts, "Jamie, you're on my team. Play center forward" (88). Then the three play together.

In Patricia Wrightson's *A Racecourse for Andy*, set in Sydney, Australia, Andy Hoddell is retarded. He started school with twelve-year-old Mike O'Day and three other buddies but now attends a separate school, realizing himself that he is different. Since he is "always warm and admiring, always glad to see them and careful not to be a nuisance, the others [are] still his friends" (16). His chums make a game of claiming ownership of public property, so Andy, not understanding the joke, pays three dollars to a tramp who "sells" him a racecourse. The owners grow angry when Andy begins to decorate stands and paint benches at "his" Beecham Park Trotting Course. Luckily Andy tells a kind groundskeeper about strangers offering money if he gives special food to horses, and authorities arrest men with drugged fodder. The owners pay Andy ten dollars to "buy back" the track, and with it, he purchases a model airplane. Mike O'Day says, "He's got to have things sometimes, even if he does bust them" (155).

An eighteen-year-old girl with Down's Syndrome, Dede Atkins, pals with a sixth grader, Jill Harvey, in Sheila Garrigue's *Between Friends*. Jill, who recently moved from California to Massachusetts, continues to be Dede's friend when neighborhood girls return from vacation and shun Dede. Jill's own pregnant mother avoids Dede, who reminds her of a short-lived, deformed baby she once had. Jill accepts a Christmas party invitation to Dede's special school despite a conflicting engagement with her own classmates. She is sorry to learn later that Dede is moving to Arizona. Jill realizes she will miss this girl who "knows more about being a friend than anyone else I know" (160).

An eleven-year-old boy tells about his best friend, Jamie, in Doris Buchanan Smith's *A Taste of Blackberries*. It is Jamie who disregards warnings, arousing bees by poking into a bee hole while children are picking grapes nearby. His pal realizes Jamie's acting ability when he says, "For my best friend he surely did aggravate me sometimes. I mean, if we got to pretending, . . . he didn't know when to quit" (2). Thinking Jamie is acting again, the pal feels guilty for not helping Jamie after bees sting his allergic chum and cause his death. In the end, the narrator picks blackberries for Jamie's mother who invites him to "come slam the door for me now and then" (73).

In Mary Stolz's *The Noonday Friends,* eleven-year-old Franny Davis and Simone Orgella are best friends who see each other mainly during the lunch hour in a New York City school. Franny cannot be with Simone after classes because she cares for her four-year-old brother Marshall while Mother works. Her twin, Jim, seldom helps with Marshall. Artistic Mr. Davis, who is often unemployed, gets fired as a shoe clerk but secures that job for Francisco Orgella, Simone's cousin from Puerto Rico. The shoe shop owner is so proud of his portrait painted by Davis that he puts it in the store window with an announcement about the artist, and Davis gets advertising work as a result. After a tiff, Franny and Simone renew their friendship, supported by families that appreciate each other.

Two other New York City schoolmates are in LouAnn Gaeddert's *Your Former Friend, Matthew.* Gail Walden and Matthew Morrison are such good friends; they are always together after school, and she accepts his idea of a rock collection for next year's school project. When he returns from summer vacation, however, he avoids Gail, plays basketball with boys, and has a new friend, Jay. She begins to enjoy the company of Amanda, who lives in her building, and that of Joyce with whom she sees the Museum of Natural History. Still coveting Matthew's friendship, she tells his buddies private information, later apologizes, and receives a reply signed, "Your former friend, Matthew" (58). When she gives him rock specimens for a science project, Matthew whispers, "Thanks, old pal," (73) and invites her to play Diplomacy. He says, "It's Jay's game. He's coming over with it, but we need more than two. You and Amanda? Mom says we can send out for pizza and play all day" (75).

Two eleven-year-old loners enjoy each other's company in E. L. Konigsburg's *Jennifer, Hecate, Macbeth, William McKinley, and Me, Elizabeth.* On Hallowe'en, Elizabeth, dressed like a pilgrim, and Jennifer, like a witch, meet on the way home from William McKinley

School. Jennifer trains Elizabeth to be an apprentice witch and later, a journeyman witch. On Saturdays, they meet in the park where Jennifer acts like a "Macbeth" witch, Hecate. Elizabeth prevents Jennifer from putting her toad, Hilary Ezra, in an ointment she is making. When Elizabeth learns Jennifer is not a witch but a neighbor in her same building, she is thrilled. Elizabeth concludes, "Neither of us pretends to be a witch anymore. Now we mostly enjoy being what we really are, just Jennifer, and just Me, just good friends!" (117).

Eleven-year-old Jenny finds a fickle companion in Shirley Simon's *Best Friend*. Jenny worries when her inseparable pal, Dot, moves from their apartment building, even though they will still be together in school. Dot meets Edythe and joins a charm school club run by Edythe's mother for their building's residents only. Dot and Edythe become best friends, excluding Jenny. After Jenny's nonconformist grandmother stays with them, Dot and Edythe ridicule Grandma for riding a bicycle, repairing roller skates, and working in shops. Two other classmates, Ruthie and Betty, appreciate Grandma. When Dot wants to be Jenny's best friend again, Jenny prefers to have more than one chum and thereby benefits from their varied interests.

Eleven-year-old girls form a club to exclude the unidentified narrator of Phyllis Krasilovsky's *The Popular Girls Club*. As the snubbed girl walks home from school, club members avoid her. To hide hurt feelings, she feigns interest in autumn leaves with intelligent Clara who wants the two to preserve leaves together. The girl refuses, fearing ostracism if she visits "Cyclops Clara." As days pass, only shy Amy eats lunch with the girl, upset because the club is giving a Hallowe'en party. On the holiday, she joins Amy in costume to trick-or-treat, and the next day visits Clara, finding her new pals more stimulating than the old ones. She thinks, "When I learned a few weeks later that the popular girls—or rather, the *un*popular girls—club was breaking up, it didn't matter to me one way or the other. . . . Rotten clubs don't usually last and neither do false friendships" (47).

Eleven-year-old girls refuse to allow a boy in their club in Margaret Hodges's *A Club Against Keats*. Sarah Carter and her pals— Dot, Abby, Babby, and Mary Jo—realize Keats Connelly, the boy next door, is spying when they have their first club meeting at Sarah's. In a room over Sarah's garage, the girls practice a "Cinderella" play. Keats hangs a stage curtain, paints boxes into a fireplace-throne, makes a

pumpkin-coach, and acts the role of prince. When the neighborhood
enjoys the play, the girls invite Keats to be a club member, but he
refuses, preferring to work behind the scenes.

Other sixth graders are involved in a play in Dori White's *Sarah
and Katie*. If their teacher chooses the Thanksgiving play they write,
Sarah is to direct it and Katie is to be its star. After the teacher picks their
play, director Sarah, impressed by the wealth of a new pupil, Melanie,
gives her the lead. Katie stops speaking to Sarah. The play is a success,
despite Melanie's threats not to perform. When the teacher accuses
Danny of stealing her diamond ring, Sarah finds the ring on her
teacher's desk and clears his name. Katie and Sarah resume being
friends, glad that Melanie is moving.

Mary, a U.S. girl, and Helen, a Canadian, both in Canada and
eleven years old, help each other in Jessie Corrigan Pegis's *Best Friends:
A Canadian Story*. Lonely Helen has lived with her mother since her
father died eight years before. Outspoken Mary, whose mother has just
died, stays with her aged grandmother while her father regains his
health. After the girls become close, Mary's grandmother dies, so Mary
moves in with Helen until Mary's father announces plans to remarry.
When Mary leaves to join him, Helen knows how to make friends and
Mary is less selfish.

In Canada, the Winston sisters entertain week-long U.S. visitors,
the Swann sisters, in Jean Little's *Stand in the Wind*. At the Winston
beach cottage, preteener Martha Winston pairs with Christine ("Kit")
Swann, and Ellen Winston, who is in her early teens, with Rosemary
Swann. At first, Rosemary dominates her younger sister, timid Kit. It is
Martha who helps Kit overcome fears, especially of storms. When the
two are in a summer gale, Martha teaches Kit not to fall down but to
face high winds and sing, "I stand in the wind and eat peanut brittle"
(138). Before leaving, Kit shows her gratitude to Martha:

> Marth, thanks a lot for everything. I mean, I think Rosemary
> and I will have a lot more fun together now. We're still
> different and everything, but I feel more like her sister, and
> she does too. Something like you and Ellen. And . . . my
> report card always says I'm "Withdrawn," but nobody could
> stay withdrawn with a friend like you around (240).

Natalie Savage Carlson's *Ann Aurelia and Dorothy* focuses on a
pair of ten-year-old classmates. Ann Aurelia, a white girl, has been in

three foster homes since her widowed mother married a man who refuses to keep her daughter. Dorothy, a black girl from a secure home, invites Ann Aurelia to make lemonade and work on the safety patrol with her. Together they save their teacher from drowning. Ann Aurelia relates well to her present foster mother, Mrs. Hicken, so she reluctantly moves when her mother leaves her husband and wants her daughter. Since her mother rents an apartment for them near school, Ann Aurelia continues her friendship with Dorothy.

Another pair of ten-year-old girls are New York City friends in Doris Orgel's *Next Door to Xanadu*. Overweight Patricia Malone sings her wish, "A girl my age will move next door" (17). A dream fulfilled is her new neighbor, Dorothy Rappaport. Dorothy's mother is dead, so she lives with a housekeeper and her father, a Brooklyn College professor. When boys call Patricia "Patsy Fats," Dorothy threatens, "You're never going to call her that dumb name again!" (39). Patricia and Dorothy become "family members" in each other's apartment, and it is when she is at Dorothy's home that Patricia begins to diet. Dorothy teases Patricia that she might move to Kubla Khan's beautiful Xanadu, but later, Dorothy announces real moving plans. Patricia is so hurt, she abandons her diet but then recovers enough to give her friend a going-away party. After Dorothy settles in her new home, she invites Patricia to visit.

Christine McDonnell's *Lucky Charms & Birthday Wishes* tells how shy Emily Mott forms the Lucky Stones Club by giving lucky stones to classmates who sit beside her. Next, she copes with Johnny Ringer, a class bully jealous of her good grades. After she praises his origami work, he gives her a paper crane in friendship, and she puts her sumi ink painting and haiku in his desk signed, "For Johnny from your friend, Emily" (31). She enjoys Lydia, a Christmas visitor at her neighbor's home. On her birthday, Emily says, "That's what's been nice about this year. Making friends. I didn't even wish for them, either. They just happened" (83–84).

In Catherine Woolley's *Cathy's Little Sister*, nine-year-old Chris regards her eleven-year-old sister Cathy as the one with whom she is most intimate, but the feeling is no longer reciprocated. After the owner reclaims a dog Chris is sheltering, Father gives her a special treat. He takes her by train to visit Ellen, a girl her age. Ellen and her mother show Chris the city and celebrate her birthday with a party. When she sees Ellen's tag-along young sister, she understands how Cathy must feel about her. On a plane ride home, Chris plans to make her own friends.

Nine-year-old Lotty McDaniel copes with an I Hate Lotty Club in Susan Shreve's *The Bad Dreams of a Good Girl*. The club organizer, Kathy Sanders, is jealous because Lotty attends Beech Tree, an elementary school for gifted children. Lotty follows an older brother's suggestion to join the club, but after she pays dues, the club disbands. Lotty observes:

> Girls in fourth grade can change their mind about friendship—that is, go from love to hate—in a matter of seconds. So I was never sure whether I was going to have the same friends at the end of language arts class as I had at the beginning. It can make you a little nervous. (34)

In Ellen Conford's *Felicia the Critic*, another fourth grader, Felicia Kershinbaum, annoys others with critical comments. After Mother recommends constructive criticism, Felicia gives a school crossing guard her list of ways to improve traffic flow. There is a traffic jam while the guard forgets his duties to read her list. Four classmates invite Felicia to join their club on condition she not criticize ideas, and she reluctantly agrees. When the girls decide on an outdoor winter carnival, Felicia thinks it risky but feels she cannot criticize. Snow ruins the event, so the girls accuse Felicia of not warning them. Felicia's best friend, Cheryl, defends her, restoring her future right to criticize.

Because Mother's work often takes her out of town, eight-year-old homesick Victoria starts boarding school in Ursula Nordstrom's *The Secret Language*. Miss Mossman, a strict housemother, is unkind, letting the lonesome girl cry for ten days. Then Victoria meets rebellious Martha who becomes her roommate and who teaches her a three-word secret language. When the dreaded housemother leaves, her replacement, Miss Denton, tempers discipline with love and makes it bearable for Victoria to stay at school during holidays. After school ends, Victoria worries because Martha threatens not to return, but Miss Denton says Victoria will be special next year because she will be an "old" girl.

Another shy new third grader is Janice who thinks she will not get any valentines in Maud H. Lovelace's *The Valentine Box*. During a holiday snowstorm, Janice, en route back to school after lunch, puts her own valentines down to help a popular classmate, Margaret, chase valentines blown from her hands by the wind. They have fun together, but when Janice gets to school, she realizes where she left her own valentines, and another classmate, Bobby, retrieves them with her. That afternoon, Janice gets three valentines, and the one she values most is handmade by her new friend, Margaret.

Anne Lindbergh's *The People in Pineapple Place* is a fantasy. After his parents' divorce, ten-year-old August Brown moves with his mother from Vermont to Georgetown in Washington, D.C. In the ten days before entering fourth grade, friendless August follows a rag-bag lady, Mrs. Pettylittle, down an alley, Pineapple Place, where he meets seven children who are invisible to almost everyone but him. No one in the alley ages, though for forty-three years, they have moved in the United States and Europe if their leader, Mr. Sweeny, felt ill. The children, guided by ten-year-old April Anderson, take August when they roller skate in the National Gallery or ride old-fashioned streetcars and carousels. April tells August, "You're the nicest person I've met in my whole life . . . and I've been alive for a long, long time!" (138). Since Mr. Sweeney feels ill again, the group is leaving for Chicago, so April helps August meet Peter Snyder-Smith who will be in his school class, a neighbor he considers "terrific."

BOOKS FOR LATER YEARS

The power of love for a father and brother are dominant in Madeleine L'Engle's science fiction, *A Wrinkle in Time*. When Mr. Murry, a physicist, disappears for a year while working on a governmental project, twelve-year-old Meg, her five-year-old brother Charles Wallace, and her fourteen-year-old friend Calvin O'Keefe, find him imprisoned on an evil planet, Camazotz. Three good witches, Mrs. Whatsit, Mrs. Who, and Mrs. Which, help them *tesseract*, or travel via a wrinkle in time, to the planet and rescue Mr. Murry from IT, a terrible human brain. IT controls Charles Wallace's mind, but Meg wins him back by declaring, "Charles, I love you" (187). She realizes, "Love. That was what she had that IT did not have" (187). In the end, all four characters, united by love, successfully *tesseract* home.

In realistic fiction, Norma Fox Mazer's *A Figure of Speech* tells about the love of an eighty-three-year-old grandfather and his thirteen-year-old granddaughter, Jenny Pennoyer. Jenny is the only family member who treats Grandpa like a sensitive person, not as an old man, a cliché, or figure of speech. When her brother Vince marries, her parents give Grandpa's basement apartment to the couple, forcing the elderly man to share an upstairs bedroom with Jenny's young brother. They do not consult Grandpa. Jenny is incensed that Grandpa cannot even talk about his boyhood without being reminded that everyone knows his tales. She tells Mother, "You and Dad talk to Grandpa like he's dumb. Or a kid. You make him feel awful" (33). After Jenny reports to Grandpa that her folks are going to put him in a home for the aged, he and Jenny move to his run-down boyhood farmhouse, but they cannot survive there. He goes out one cold night and Jenny, who finds him dead from exposure, believes he picked death over placement in a home.

Louisa R. Shotwell's *Magdalena* opposes a Puerto Rican grandmother, who represents tradition, and her modern granddaughter. Magdalena Mendez's mother has been dead for two years, and during that time, her seaman father brought her grandmother, Nani, from Puerto Rico to Brooklyn to raise his daughter. When boys in her sixth-grade class for the gifted call Magdalena "Miss Two Ropes," the eleven-year-old girl wants to cut her braids, but Nani favors the hair style of Puerto Rico. The school principal, Mrs. Rostock, gets Magdalena to befriend a neglected, dirty troublemaker, Daisy ("Spook") Gonzales. At the library, Spook makes a friend of poor old Miss Esmeralda Lilley. Miss Lilley persuades Magdalena to have a barber cut her hair and raises money to pay for it though she herself is "plain hungry" (55). Nani, thinking Miss Lilley is a witch, ritually cleanses the girl of her influence. Nani, however, understands Spook, scrubs her, and gives her a dress. Spook spends her last dime in a booth phoning Magdalena to ask, "Are you still my friend? . . . I wish I wasn't such a stinker" (91). Nani realizes Miss Lilley is not a witch when she and Spook are her dinner guests. Then Nani pays for Magdalena's second haircut.

Sixteen-year-old Sandy, the youngest of three daughters, doubts her father's love for his family in Lynn Hall's *Denison's Daughter*. After her father is affectionate with his grandson, Brian, Sandy realizes love is what she craves. Her father, whose parents were not demonstrative, is less attentive than her mother. When Sandy drives the tractor without permission on their Iowa dairy farm, she accidently runs over Brian. Then her father shows his love for her clearly by shouldering the blame. "The solidity of her father's support made Sandy's nose sting with the threat of tears that had been near the surface all day" (109).

Michelle Magorian's *Good Night, Mr. Tom* tells about the love an abused eight-year-old boy, William ("Willie") Beech, gets from Thomas ("Tom") Oakley. Willie's mother, a religious fanatic, batters the boy, and when authorities force his evacuation from London during World War II, she sends him with a note saying, "Like most boys he's full of sin" (23). Willie lives in the country with Tom, a recluse since his wife and baby died. Tom, the townsfolk, and another evacuee, nine-year-old Zach Wrench, help Willie become a normal child. Willie "could hardly believe Zach was his special friend. Zach said he was a good listener and that he was a sensitive being" (128). When bombs kill Zach, Willie learns to accept his loss without forgetting. Willie's mother, who has a baby, calls her older child back to London, and Tom follows when he dreams of the boy shouting for him from an enclosed place. He finds the boy locked in a stairway closet with his dead baby brother in his arms and his mother gone. Tom eventually takes Willie home and adopts him after he learns the boy's mother has committed suicide.

When thirty-eight-year-old Janet Bernstein suddenly dies of a cerebral hemorrhage in Barbara Girion's *A Tangle of Roots*, her surviving sixteen-year-old daughter, Beth, and forty-year-old husband, Steve, have to untangle their roots of love for her and each other. Beth, a high school junior in Millburn, New Jersey, loses her boyfriend when she breaks two dates to be with her lonesome father. After the mourning month, she goes with her father to Florida for Thanksgiving weekend. There they meet twenty-eight-year-old Stacy Arnold, who becomes Father's romantic interest. Beth is involved with her grandmother, who tries to be a substitute mother; her mother's younger sister, Aunt Nina, a model; and her best friend, Joyce. However, her main concern is that her father in a flurry of dating may forget her mother. When she finds his annual gift to his wife, yellow roses on New Year's Eve, on Mother's snowy grave, she knows where his heart is even if he is in Vermont with Stacy. She thinks, "If the skiing was good, I would tell him to take some extra time in Vermont" (154).

Another book by Barbara Girion, *In the Middle of a Rainbow*, tells about an Irvington, New Jersey high school senior—pretty, studious Corrie Dickerson. Despite her two part-time jobs and her mother's job, Corrie, a widow's daughter, cannot go to college without a scholarship. She feels lucky to be going steady with school soccer star, handsome, wealthy Todd Marcus. She thinks, "Love is a four letter word and so is

Todd, and to me they're practically interchangeable" (1). He makes her feel as if she were in the middle of a rainbow. However, when Corrie wins scholarships to Briarwood College in Vermont, she accepts Todd's going to a California college. Unsure of their future, she believes, "If it was meant to be, it would be" (196), because she does not want all her college plans "to revolve around him, revolve around us" (196).

Him She Loves? by M. E. Kerr is a humorous account of a high school junior, seventeen-year-old Henry Schiller, who falls in love with a senior, Valerie Kissenwiser, wins over the girl's reluctant father, and then loses the girl. A six-foot blonde newcomer to Long Island, Henry works in his family's restaurant. Valerie is the beautiful, pampered daughter of a famous Jewish comedian, Al Kiss. On national television, Kiss ridicules his daughter's date, Henry, as Heinrich, saying, "Heinrich's got ears so big he could play Ping-Pong without a paddle" (81). At the end of each act he asks the audience, "*Him* she loves?" (81). When Kiss jokes about Heinrich's restaurant, business flourishes. After Valerie goads Henry to change her father's opinion of him, the lad advertises in the mail, "Watch for the sneeze of Al Kiss" (175). Grateful for publicity, the comedian changes his mind about Henry, but so does Valerie, and the six-month torrid romance ends.

Equally star-crossed are two love-starved seventeen-year-olds in *If I Asked You, Would You Stay?* by Eve Bunting. Charles Robert O'Neill, known by his acronym, Crow, leaves a foster home, works in a sports clothing shop, and lives in a secret room over a seaside carousel. He sees a young woman attempting to drown herself and rescues her. She is Valentine Love who has left an unhappy home before graduating from high school to run away with Marty, a pimp. Lonely Crow questions, "If I asked you, would you stay?" (148). She plans to go to her aunt in Oregon and he, to return to his foster home in Illinois. She says, "Isn't it strange, Crow, that we're two of a kind? We're just turned around, that's all. I ran away to find love. You ran away from love. Crazy" (149).

San Francisco is the setting of Marilyn Sachs's *Class Pictures*. Annual school photographs are reminders of the friendship of two girls from kindergarten through high school. A waitress's daughter, thin, dark, gifted Patricia ("Pat") Maddox differs from diplomatic, fair-haired Lorraine ("Lolly") Scheiner, a physician's child. When they are five years old, Pat bites one of Lolly's fat, apple-like cheeks but later is kind when Lolly urinates during a Hallowe'en dance rehearsal. Pat says, " 'I'll show you where the girls' room is.' . . . That's how we became friends" (7). When Lolly has her six-year-old birthday party, popular Pat gets others to attend by promising to invite them to her own party. In the early grades, Pat is Lolly's protector, but in junior high, Lolly becomes beautiful and boys like her. Still pals after high school graduation, Pat accepts a scholarship to MIT and Lolly works on anti-nuke campaigns.

Another Marilyn Sachs book, *Bus Ride*, describes how two sixteen-year-old high school students, Judy Koppelmacker and Ernie Russo, relate on bus rides to and from high school. He discusses his Italian culture and his widowed mother while she speaks of her German background and her domineering father. Her hair covers part of her face to conceal acne. He wants her to arrange a date for him with popular Karen Shepherd, and he will ask Alex Zimmer to escort her, so they can double date. He even invites himself to Judy's house to suggest what she should wear and comments, "The sacrifices one makes in the name of friendship" (79). Finally, Ernie shows interest in dating Judy when he asks, "Do you think two loners can make one winning combination?" (107)

A third book by Marilyn Sachs, *Hello . . . Wrong Number*, is an account of two sixteen-year-old Washington High students. Petite Angie Rogers, who sounds like Minnie Mouse, tries to call Jim McCone, the school's best-looking male, when she dials the wrong number and reaches another Jim, later discovered to be Jim Holman. She calls Jim Holman many times and he says, "No, Angie. You don't bother me. I like hearing from you. Keep on calling" (40). He tells her he is six feet tall and performs as a rock singer. On the phone he sings his original composition, "Angie's Song," ending, "I love only one girl and her name is Angie" (72). He is reluctant to meet her, however, and when she learns he has deceived her, she is bitter. She identifies him as a short student with a big nose who lacks the confidence to sing professionally. After they spend hours together, she looks beyond surface appearance, confessing when he phones her, "I think I love you, Jim" (104).

Another book about a telephone friendship is Judie Angell's *Secret Selves*. In this novel, thirteen-year-old Julie Ann Novick and fourteen-year-old Russell ("Rusty") Parmette get along best on the telephone as imaginary Barbara Birdsong and Wendell Farnham. In actuality, Julie, a physician's daughter, is horrified at the male chauvinism of the soccer hero, Rusty, who works in the family sporting goods store. Julie argues against Rusty in a school debate on sexual equality. He seems to agree with her, implying that his family, not he, is sexist. He is broad-minded enough to express no anger after the debate when Julie's grandmother, playing Cupid, asks him to make a home delivery from his store. Grandma tells Rusty, "She [Julie] makes believe she's someone else because she thinks somebody doesn't like her the way she is. . . . You think she'd go through that because she didn't care for you?" (173–174). That night, for the first time, Rusty calls Julie.

Ninth-grade neighbors in Sweden are Christine Nöstlinger's subjects in *Luke and Angela*. Luke Dostal, previously a quiet follower, is an outgoing, dramatic person when he returns from six weeks in England. He changes his appearance, wearing weird clothes and falling for an older woman. When others criticize him, Angela Ammerling defends him, saying, "Luke and I have always been best friends, as well as living next door" (9). She adds, "It used to be other people came up to me in the corridor to ask how I was, and I was the one who got asked to parties, and I'd always say, 'Can Luke come too?' " (50). Now he arrives at a party and is disappointed if she is not there.

Another book set in Europe is Doris Orgel's *The Devil in Vienna*. It shows how two thirteen-year-old girls of different religions maintain a life-threatening friendship in Vienna during World War II. Inge Dornenwald, who is Jewish, and Lieselotte Vessely, a Catholic Nazi's daughter, have been companions since first grade. At one point, they place a bit of each other's blood in wine and drink it. Lieselotte says, "Blood sisters forever! . . . And if we ever need each other, we'll be there" (32). Lieselotte moves to Munich but eventually returns to Vienna, handing the Dornenwald maid, Mitzi, letters she wrote Inge but could not mail. In school, Lieselotte reveals her true feelings by sitting in the last row where Jewish girls must sit. Before Inge's family leaves the country, the two girls meet at an amusement park. Inge confesses, "Our friendship is in a book now . . . mostly it's about how I 'really and truly' feel about you. And about things we've done together. It has your letters in it also" (240).

After his mother dies, Luis leaves Puerto Rico, and Mary Anderson's *Just the Two of Them* describes how lonely Luis feels in his uncle's basement New York City apartment. In the summer, Luis goes to nearby Central Park where an operator invites him to ride a merry-go-round. Afterwards, the operator says that the person who paid for the ride is Mad Mags, an old woman rumored to live in the park. Luis thanks her and later joins her on zoo excursions after closing time or in hunting through trash for rejected Christmas treasures. When they find a solitary Puerto Rican bully, Carlos, crying, they befriend him.

Bernice Grohskopf's *Shadow in the Sun* focuses on thirteen-year-old Fran Phillips who, during a month-long Cape Cod summer visit with her Aunt Louise, voluntarily becomes disabled Wilma's companion. Wilma lives most of the year with her mother, but in the summer, she stays with her divorced father, Ralph Byner, a musician whose young wife, Gretchen, is pregnant. Ralph babies sarcastic Wilma, who is jealous of her stepmother and who rudely gives everyone orders. When Fran refuses Wilma's order to be taken to the library, Wilma says Aunt Louise is a lesbian, and Fran runs home. Then Wilma starts for the library alone in her wheelchair and has an accident. Fran tries to be Wilma's friend, explaining, "She just wants people to treat her like an ordinary person, not like some freak" (104). Wilma, however, does not know how to reciprocate friendship.

Rob, who is about thirteen in Mary Towne's *The Glass Room*, prefers the quiet family of a new pal, Simon, to his own loud one, until there is a crisis. The boys meet one day when Rob escapes his mother singing in the kitchen, his younger brother practicing the clarinet, his older brother playing with his band, and his father and sister doing Mozart duets on the piano. He goes to the country where he meets Simon Fowler who invites him home for lunch. There he sees hushed, orderly Mr. Fowler working in a soundproofed glass room. The boys' friendship grows, but there is a crisis when Rob's dog falls into a stream. Simon, trying to rescue the dog, breaks his ankle after he wedges his foot under a rock. With great effort, Rob arouses Mr. Fowler to save Simon. Then Rob realizes he prefers his own noisy family members who really want to hear him.

More humorous are two thirteen-year-old boys in Syd Hoff's *Irving and Me*. Artie Granick from Brooklyn, a newcomer in Sunny Beach, Florida, meets Irving Winkleman. When Artie joins Irving's Community Center, the two act in a play, both falling for the blonde lead, Arlene Morgan. After the boys' first guitar lesson, Irving volunteers for them to do guitar duets at Arlene's party, but Irving arrives very late. Charlie, the town bully, joins the Community Center, taking Artie's part in the play, his place on the baseball team, and even Arlene. Artie half-heartedly tries to run away, but his best friend, Irving, persuades him to return.

Jane O'Connor's *Just Good Friends*, set in Hingham, Massachusetts, shows a strain on friendship if one person is more mature than the
other. Thirteen-year-old Jocelyn ("Joss") Longman, who is 5′ 9″ tall,
acts younger than Fletcher Dwoskin and finds his obsession with sex
annoying, justifying the nametag, "Overactive Gland." Though Joss
seems to be Fletcher's convenient sidekick, she likes him as a boyfriend.
When a new girl from California, Laura Weiss, becomes her best
friend, Joss prefers that Fletcher not date Laura. Joss thinks, "If Fletcher
and Laura were a couple, where would that leave her? . . . Deep down,
Joss wanted to keep them both for herself" (117), and she succeeds.

In *All Together Now*, Sue Ellen Bridgers tells how twelve-year-old
Casey Flanagan, spending the summer in North Carolina with her
grandparents during the Korean War, becomes the protector of Dwayne
Pickens, a thirty-three-year-old retarded man with a twelve-year-old
mental age. At first, Dwayne, who rejects girls, thinks Casey with her
short-cropped hair is a boy, but even after he learns her sex, they play
baseball and go to stock car races or movies. When Alva Pickens jails
Dwayne while trying to place him in a home, the Flanagans get him
out. As summer ends, "Casey knew there was something to be said for
having someone depend on you. She'd learned that from Dwayne. . . .
Having someone to love gave you a chance to be loved yourself" (229).
Besides Dwayne, Casey relates to her grandparents. Grandmother
counsels, "Loving is truly the biggest risk a person can take, and the one
that is most worth it" (73).

Twelve-year-old Arden Gifford, in Suzanne Newton's *An End to
Perfect*, thinks life in quiet Haverlee is perfect until her seventeen-year-
old brother Hill leaves and her best friend DorJo Huggins has domestic
problems. Hill moves with his grandparents to attend a superior high
school. DorJo's mother returns to her two daughters after abandoning
them for three years. Mrs. Huggins tells big DorJo that Arden must be
using her for protection or feeling sorry for her, but Arden assures
DorJo, "You're the best friend I ever had. I never felt sorry for you a
single minute, and I guess if I need protection I have a perfectly good
dad, not to mention a brother in high school and a mother who knows
karate!" (10). After fighting with her mother, DorJo runs away, starving
for three days in the woods. When she seeks refuge with Arden, it is
Arden's mother who buys her a wardrobe, arranges her return to school,
and visits her older sister, Jessie, who has also left home. Jessie had to
drop out of school to support herself and her sister, paying three months

of Mrs. Huggins's overdue rent. Jessie does not return to her mother but DorJo does. Arden realizes she can keep DorJo's friendship by helping the struggling girl adjust to her own mother.

Martha Abbott tells the story of her ties with Ivy Carson in *The Changeling* by Zilpha Keatley Snyder. At seven, Martha is fat, clumsy, and known as a crybaby. She becomes a pal of wispy, imaginative Ivy Carson whose large family is always in trouble with the law. Ivy thinks of herself as a "changeling," a child fairies put into her family. Martha and Ivy express their fantasies at Bent Oaks, a secret place near their homes. In junior high, after a new drama teacher casts them in a play, they discover the stage is a place to enact their fantasies. The Carsons leave town, but Martha continues to act in plays. Ivy, studying dance in New York City, writes in a letter, "I know I was right about being a changeling. I had to be. But lots of people are changelings, really. You might be one yourself, Martha Abbott. I wouldn't be surprised" (219).

Two scoliosis patients learn to relate in *Just Like Always* and *Where Are You, Cow Patty?* by Elizabeth-Ann Sachs. In *Just Like Always*, twelve-year-old Janie Tannenbaum and Courtney-Ann Schaeffer become friends when they share a hospital room. Both have operations and body casts to treat scoliosis (spinal curvature). Janie is a baseball enthusiast and Courtney lives in a fantasy world, but each appreciates the other. They leave with reluctance as they follow Nurse Rogers's advice, "If you don't actually use the word goodbye, then you'll never really have parted. And when you see one another again, it'll be just like always" (157). *Where Are You, Cow Patty!* is the sequel which shows the two girls meeting again a year later. (Cow Patty is the name Janie gives to a calf whose birth she witnesses). Janie is jealous when Courtney-Ann visits and Janie's friend, Harold, seems fascinated with her. Janie eventually dates Harold herself, so the girls remain close.

Constance C. Greene's *A Girl Called Al* and its sequel, *I Know You, Al*, are humorous accounts of twelve-year-old Al (a nickname for Alexandra) and an unidentified narrator, her best girl friend. In the first book, heavy Al wears pigtails, but she loses weight and cuts her hair. Mr. Richards, assistant superintendent of the apartment building, lets the girls strap rags to their shoes and skate on his kitchen floor to polish it. They find him after he has a heart attack, see that he gets to a hospital, and visit him before he dies.

Greene continues her story in *I Know You, Al*. Al's parents are divorced, so Al is surprised when Father, whom she has not seen in six years, asks her to his wedding. Advising her to attend, her friend prefaces some remarks with "I know you, Al" (38). After the wedding, Al makes a long-distance call to assure her pal back home that she likes Father's new family, they like her, and that she has met an interesting boy.

C. S. Adler shows how two imaginative children relate in *The Magic of the Glits*. Twelve-year-old Jeremy, whose broken leg is in a cast, is the Cape Cod companion of a family friend, seven-year-old Lynette, the summer after her mother drowned. To amuse her, he fashions a tale about "Glits," small, fun-loving creatures who nestle among wave tips and beach debris. The two children become close, sharing this fantasy. Jeremy worries that Lynette may live in an orphanage, and the boy is relieved when a kind uncle in New Mexico offers her a home. As summer ends, Jeremy realizes, "He'd never cared as much about another person. . . . He probably would never forget Lynette . . . even if he tried. . . . He also learned the magic of the Glits was real after all" (112).

Another book about summer friendship and magic is Judie Angell's *In Summertime It's Tuffy*. Eleven-year-old Elizabeth ("Tuffy") Kandell is in Pennsylvania for her fourth year of summer camp. She and two of the six other girls in her bunk were at the same camp, MA-SHA-NA, last year. She is fond of a guitar-playing bunkmate, Iris, a reserved girl compared to Tuffy, who speaks before she thinks. Prompted by Iris's book on magic spells, the two make a voodoo doll of the camp manager, Uncle Otto, who unfairly fires a camp counselor. The girls stick a pin in their doll's foot, and the next day, Uncle Otto sprains that very ankle. Tuffy refuses to cast a spell for boy-crazy Natalie, thinking, "Maybe it was a *freak* coincidence. . . . But what if somebody got hurt?" (223). She prefers safer summer fun.

In Barbara Rinkoff's *The Watchers*, eleven-year-old Chris Blake, suffering from his parents' constant quarrels, forgets his problems when he befriends an uncoordinated ten-year-old new boy in his building, Stanford ("Sandy") Townsend. Chris defends Sandy, who is belittled for his nervous twitches, but he has his own problems when he must pay for a paperweight he steals at a candy store. Unable to earn the price, Chris turns to Sandy who gives him the money. Chris teaches Sandy to run, row a boat, and throw a ball, adding to his self-confidence. Chris suffers severe depression when his father chooses to leave home rather than cease gambling. Then Sandy helps Chris's "injured" mind as much as Chris helps Sandy's injured body.

Two ten-year-old pupils, Jess Aarons, born in rural Lark Creek, and Leslie Burke, a newcomer, become close friends after competing to be the fifth grade's fastest runner in Katherine Paterson's *Bridge to Terabithia*. Jess has to hide his artistic abilities from his father, a farmer, and his four sisters, but Leslie's literary parents encourage the development of her talents. It is imaginative Leslie's idea to create Terabithia in the woods, "a whole secret country, and you and I would be the rulers of it" (39). The only way to enter is by swinging across a creek on a rope. One rainy day while Jess is at the art museum, Leslie goes to Terabithia alone, falls off the rope, hits her head, and drowns. Lonely Jess continues to mourn when Leslie's father tells him, "She loved you, you know. . . . Thank you for being such a wonderful friend to her" (113). Even the teacher, Mrs. Myers, says, "If it's hard for me, how much harder it must be for you. Let's try to help each other, shall we?" (125).

SUMMARY

Of ninety-three selected books on the value, friendship and love with human beings, twenty-eight are for early years, thirty-four are for middle years, and thirty-one are for later years. Books range from those showing friends so fickle that they organize clubs to reject a former chum, to those so loyal that they stick together even in life-threatening situations.

References

Adler, C. S. *The Magic of the Glits*. Illustrated by Ati Forberg. Macmillan Publishing Company, 1979. 112 p. (L) (Responsibility)

Aliki. *The Two of Them*. Illustrated. Greenwillow Books, 1979. Unpaged. (E)

Anderson, Mary. *Just the Two of Them*. Illustrated by Carl Anderson. Atheneum, 1974. 178 p. (L)

Angell, Judie. *In Summertime It's Tuffy*. Bradbury Press, 1977. 230 p. (L)

———. *Secret Selves*. Bradbury Press, 1979. 177 p. (L) (Maturing)

Anglund, Joan Walsh. *A Friend Is Someone Who Likes You.* Illustrated. Harcourt, Brace & Company, 1958. Unpaged. (E)

Billington, Elizabeth T. *Part-time Boy.* Illustrated by Diane de Groat. Frederick Warne, 1980. 88 p. (M)

Bridgers, Sue Ellen. *All Together Now.* Alfred A. Knopf, 1979. 238 p. (L) (Humaneness)

Bunting, Eve. *Clancy's Coat.* Illustrated by Lorinda Bryan Cauley. Frederick Warne, 1984. Unpaged. (E) (Ingenuity)

———. *If I Asked You, Would You Stay?* J. B. Lippincott, 1984. 151 p. (L)

Burch, Robert. *Ida Early Comes over the Mountain.* The Viking Press, 1980. 145 p. (M) (Humaneness)

———. *Christmas with Ida Early.* The Viking Press, 1983. 157 p. (M) (Cooperation)

Caines, Jeannette. *Daddy.* Illustrated by Ronald Himler. Harper & Row, Publishers, 1977. 32 p. (E)

Carlson, Natalie Savage. *Ann Aurelia and Dorothy.* Illustrated by Dale Payson. Harper & Row, Publishers, 1968. 130 p. (M) (Humaneness)

Cleary, Beverly. *Ramona and Her Father.* Illustrated by Alan Tiegreen. William Morrow & Company, 1977. 186 p. (M)

———. *Ramona and Her Mother.* Illustrated by Alan Tiegreen. William Morrow & Company, 1979. 208 p. (M)

Clifton, Lucille. *My Friend Jacob.* Illustrated by Thomas Di Grazia. Elsvier-E. P. Dutton Publishers, 1980. Unpaged. (E) (Humaneness)

Cohen, Miriam. *Best Friends.* Illustrated by Lillian Hoban. Macmillan, 1971. 32 p. (E)

Conford, Ellen. *Felicia the Critic.* Illustrated by Arvis Stewart. Little, Brown & Company, 1973. 145 p. (M)

Delton, Judy. *Lee Henry's Best Friend.* Illustrated by John Faulkner. Albert Whitman & Company, 1980. Unpaged. (E)

Fisher, Lois I. *Rachel Vellars, How Could You?* Dodd, Mead & Company, 1984. 155 p. (M)

Gaeddert, LouAnn. *Your Former Friend, Matthew.* Illustrated by Mary Beth Schwark. E. P. Dutton, 1984. 75 p. (M)

Garrigue, Sheila. *Between Friends.* Bradbury Press, 1978. 160 p. (M)

Gates, Doris. *A Morgan for Melinda: A Novel.* The Viking Press, 1980. 189 p. (M) (Self-respect)

Girion, Barbara. *In the Middle of a Rainbow*. Charles Scribner's Sons, 1983. 197 p. (L) (Maturing)

———. *A Tangle of Roots*. Charles Scribner's Sons, 1979. 154 p. (L) (Maturing, Responsibility)

Gordon, Shirley. *Crystal Is My Friend*. Illustrated by Edward Frascino. Harper & Row, Publishers, 1978. 32 p. (E)

———. *Crystal Is the New Girl*. Illustrated by Edward Frascino. Harper & Row, Publishers, 1975. 31 p. (E)

Greene, Constance C. *I and Sproggy*. Illustrated by Emily McCully. The Viking Press, 1978. 155 p. (M)

———. *A Girl Called Al*. Illustrated by Byron Barton. The Viking Press, 1969. 127 p. (L)

———. *I Know You, Al*. Illustrated by Byron Barton. The Viking Press, 1975. 126 p. (L)

Greene, Roberta. *Two and Me Makes Three*. Illustrated by Paul Galdone. Coward-McCann, 1970. Unpaged. (E)

Grohskopf, Bernice. *Shadow in the Sun*. Atheneum, 1975. 182 p. (L)

Hall, Lynn. *Denison's Daughter*. Charles Scribner's Sons, 1983. 115 p. (L) (Responsibility)

Härtling, Peter. *Oma*. Translated from German by Anthea Bell. Illustrated by Jutta Ash. Harper & Row, Publishers, 1977. 96 p. (M) (Maturing)

Hickman, Martha Whitmore. *When Can Daddy Come Home?*. Illustrated by Francis Livingston. Abingdon Press, 1983. Unpaged. (E)

Hodges, Margaret. *A Club Against Keats*. Illustrated by Rick Schreiter. Dial Press, 1962. 64 p. (M)

Hoff, Syd. *Irving and Me*. Harper & Row, Publishers, 1967. 226 p. (L)

Holl, Kristi. *Just Like a Real Family*. Atheneum, 1983. 122 p. (M) (Humaneness)

Hooker, Ruth. *Gertrude Kloppenberg (Private)*. Illustrated by Gloria Kamen. Abingdon Press, 1970. 96 p. (M)

Hurwitz, Johanna. *The Law of Gravity: A Story*. Illustrated by Ingrid Fetz. William Morrow & Company, 1978. 192 p. (M)

Keller, Beverly. *Fiona's Bee*. Illustrated by Diane Paterson. Coward, McCann & Geoghegan, 1975. 47 p. (E)

Kerr, M. E. *Him She Loves?* Harper & Row, Publishers, 1984. 215 p. (L) (Ingenuity)

Klein, Norma. *Visiting Pamela*. Illustrated by Kay Chorao. The Dial Press, 1979. Unpaged. (E)

Konigsburg, E. L. *Jennifer, Hecate, Macbeth, William McKinley, and Me, Elizabeth.* Illustrated. Atheneum, 1967. 117 p. (M) (Maturing)

Krasilovsky, Phyllis. *The Popular Girls Club.* Illustrated by Trina Schart Hyman. Simon & Schuster, 1972. 47 p. (M)

L'Engle, Madeleine. *A Wrinkle in Time.* Farrar, Straus & Giroux, 1962. 211 p. (L) (Courage)

Lindberg, Anne. *The People in Pineapple Place.* Harcourt Brace Jovanovich, 1982. 153 p. (M)

Little, Jean. *Stand in the Wind.* Illustrated by Emily McCully. Harper & Row, Publishers, 1975. 247 p. (M) (Maturing)

Lovelace, Maud Hart. *The Valentine Box.* Illustrated by Ingrid Fetz. Thomas Y. Crowell, 1966. Unpaged. (M)

McDonnell, Christine. *Lucky Charms & Birthday Wishes.* Illustrated by Diane deGroat. The Viking Press, 1984. 84 p. (M)

McPhail, David. *Sisters.* Illustrated. Harcourt Brace Jovanovich, 1984. Unpaged. (E)

Magorian, Michelle. *Good Night, Mr. Tom.* Harper & Row, 1981. 318 p. (L) (Humaneness)

Mathis, Sharon Bell. *The Hundred Penny Box.* Illustrated by Diane Dillon. The Viking Press, 1975. 47 p. (M) (Humaneness)

Mazer, Norma Fox. *A Figure of Speech.* Delacorte Press, 1973. 197 p. (L) (Humaneness)

Morrow, Suzanne Stark. *Inatuk's Friend.* Illustrated by Ellen Raskin. Little, Brown & Company, 1968. 48 p. (E)

Newton, Suzanne. *An End to Perfect.* Viking Kestrel, 1984. 212 p. (L)

Nordstrom, Ursula. *The Secret Language.* Illustrated by Mary Chalmers. Harper & Row, Publishers, 1960. 167 p. (M)

Nöstlinger, Christine. *Luke and Angela.* Translated by Anthea Bell. Harcourt Brace Jovanovich, 1979. 144 p. (L)

O'Connor, Jane. *Just Good Friends.* Harper & Row, Publishers, 1983. 216 p. (L)

Orgel, Doris. *The Devil in Vienna.* The Dial Press, 1978. 246 p. (L) (Courage)

————. *Next Door to Xanadu.* Illustrated by Dale Payson. Harper & Row, Publishers, 1969. 160 p. (M)

Osborn, Lois. *My Dad Is Really Something.* Illustrated by Rodney Pate. Albert Whitman, 1983. Unpaged. (E)

Paterson, Katherine. *Bridge to Terabithia*. Illustrated by Donna Diamond. Thomas Y. Crowell, 1977. 128 p. (L) (Maturing)

Pegis, Jessie Corrigan. *Best Friends: A Canadian Story*. Hastings House, 1964. 128 p. (M)

Rinkoff, Barbara. *Rutherford T. Finds 21B*. Illustrated by Tomie de Paola. G. P. Putnam's Sons, 1970. Unpaged. (E)

————. *The Watchers*. Alfred A. Knopf, 1972. 130 p. (L) (Humaneness)

Ross, Pat. *Meet M and M*. Illustrated by Marylin Hafner. Pantheon, 1980. 41 p. (E)

Rylant, Cynthia. *Miss Maggie*. Illustrated by Thomas Di Grazia. E. P. Dutton, 1983. 32 p. (E) (Humaneness)

Sachs, Elizabeth-Ann. *Just Like Always*. Atheneum, 1981. 160 p. (L) (Humaneness)

————. *Where Are You, Cow Patty?* Atheneum, 1984. 146 p. (L) (Humaneness)

Sachs, Marilyn. *Bus Ride*. Illustrated by Amy Rowen. Elsevier-Dutton Publishers, 1980. 107 p. (L)

————. *Class Pictures*. E. P. Dutton, 1980. 138 p. (L)

————. *Hello . . . Wrong Number*. Illustrated by Pamela Johnson. E. P. Dutton, 1981. 112 p. (L)

Schick, Eleanor. *5A and 7B*. Illustrated. Macmillan Publishers, 1967. Unpaged. (E)

Sharmat, Marjorie Weinman. *Gladys Told Me to Meet Her Here*. Illustrated by Edward Frascino. Harper & Row, Publishers, 1970. 32 p. (E)

————. *I'm Not Oscar's Friend Anymore*. Illustrated by Tony DeLuna. E. P. Dutton, 1975. Unpaged. (E)

Shotwell, Louisa R. *Magdalena*. Illustrated by Lilian Obligado. The Viking Press, 1971. 124 p. (L)

Shreve, Susan. *The Bad Dreams of a Good Girl*. Illustrated by Diane deGroat. Alfred A. Knopf, 1982. 92 p. (M)

Simon, Shirley. *Best Friend*. Illustrated by Reisie Lonette. Lothrop, Lee & Shepard, 1964. 191 p. (M)

Smith, Doris Buchanan. *A Taste of Blackberries*. Illustrated by Charles Robinson. Thomas Y. Crowell, 1973. 58 p. (M) (Maturing)

Snyder, Zilpha Keatley. *The Changeling*. Illustrated by Alton Raible. Atheneum, 1970. 220 p. (L)

Steig, William. *Caleb & Kate*. Illustrated. Farrar, Straus & Giroux, 1977. Unpaged. (E)

Stolz, Mary. *The Noonday Friends*. Illustrated by Louis S. Glanzman. Harper & Row, Publishers, 1965. 182 p. (M)

Towne, Mary. *The Glass Room*. Illustrated by Richard Cuffari. Farrar, Straus & Giroux, 1971. 121 p. (L) (Maturing)

Ungerer, Tomi. *The Three Robbers*. Illustrated. Atheneum, 1962. Unpaged. (E)

Viorst, Judith. *Rosie and Michael*. Illustrated by Lorna Tomei. Atheneum, 1974. Unpaged. (E) (Loyalty)

Weiss, Nicki. *Maude and Sally*. Illustrated. Greenwillow Books, 1983. Unpaged. (E)

White, Dori. *Sarah and Katie*. Illustrated by Trina Schart Hyman. Harper & Row, Publishers, 1972. 168 p. (M) (Loyalty)

Wittman, Sally. *A Special Trade*. Illustrated by Karen Gundersheimer. Harper & Row, Publishers, 1978. Unpaged. (E) (Humaneness)

Woolley, Catherine. *Cathy's Little Sister*. Illustrated by Liz Dauber. William Morrow & Company, 1964. 190 p. (M)

Wrightson, Patricia. *A Racecourse for Andy*. Illustrated by Margaret Horder. Harcourt, Brace & World, 1968. 156 p. (M) (Humaneness)

Zolotow, Charlotte. *My Friend John*. Illustrated by Ben Shecter. Harper & Row, Publishers, 1968. 32 p. (E)

V

Humaneness

Since children's values determine their attitude and behavior towards others, and fear of the unknown affects such attitudes, prejudice and intolerance are easy to acquire and difficult to erase. Boys and girls are influenced by personal experiences, beginning in the home. Through books, they can vicariously relate to those who are different in cultural, ethnic, and religious backgrounds; social or economic classes; and physical or mental disabilities. Humaneness implies kindness, mercy, or compassion for all creatures.

BOOKS FOR EARLY YEARS

A wise teacher changes third graders' attitudes toward a little Jewish girl whose family emigrated from Russia a year before in *Molly's Pilgrim*, written by Barbara Cohen and illustrated by Michael J. Doraney. The children tease Molly because of her Yiddish accent, her clothes, and the fact that she does not know about Thanksgiving. After the teacher asks girls to clothe dolls like Pilgrims for a Thanksgiving sand table, Mama dresses a clothes pin doll in garments similar to hers as a Russian emigrant. When pupils laugh, the teacher says:

> Molly's Mother is a Pilgrim. She's a modern Pilgrim. She came here just like the Pilgrims long ago, so she could worship God in her own way, in peace and freedom. The Pilgrims got the idea from the Bible about the Jewish harvest holiday of Tabernacles, called Sukos today. (unp)

A picture storybook in which a blind boy hears distinguishing sounds is Florence Parry Heide's *Sound of Sunshine, Sound of Rain*, illustrated by Kenneth Longtemps. The little boy notices, "Mother's voice is warm and soft as a pillow. His sister's voice is sharp and high" (unp). After his sister leaves him alone in the park, he counts steps from his bench to a bubbler, a phone booth, or the curb where Abram gives him free ice cream. As he walks the boy back to the bench, Abram explains, "The park is for lucky people who can see things inside themselves, instead of just what their eyes tell them" (unp). On the way home, his sister is upset because a customer in a store tells the clerk, "Better wait on this here colored lady first, so she can keep on going out of here and back where she belongs" (unp). The boy, who does not know if Abram is black or white, tells his sister, "Abram says color don't mean anything" (unp). Then his sister cries, "I wish everyone in the whole world was blind" (unp).

A simple story of accepting someone who is different is *See You Tomorrow, Charles* by author-illustrator Miriam Cohen. After blind Charles enrolls in first grade, classmates are too helpful and treat him like a unique person. One day, after the children get locked in a dark basement, Charles finds and opens a door for them. When they leave for home, the pupils say, "So long, Charles. See you tomorrow" (unp).

It is still difficult for many boys to engage in activities that were once considered to be for girls, as author-illustrator Tomie dePaola shows in *Oliver Button Is a Sissy*. Boys scribble on the school wall, "OLIVER BUTTON IS A SISSY" (unp), because Oliver likes to read, draw, dance, and dress up, rather than play ball. After attending dancing school, he performs in a talent contest while many classmates watch in the audience. Though he does not win a prize, the next day he discovers a line drawn through the word *SISSY* on the school wall and the word *STAR* in its place.

BOOKS FOR MIDDLE YEARS

An early form of prejudice derives from superstition. Natalie Babbitt's fantasy, *Knee-Knock Rise*, discusses the difficulty of changing persons' attitudes and opinions. During stormy weather, people believe they hear the voice of a monster, called the Megrimum, from a cave, Knee-Knock Rise, in the Mammoth Mountains. At the foot of a mountain is a village where Egan visits his aunt and uncle. When he attends the annual Instep Fair, villagers shout, "Come and eat and dance; be entertained and spend your money; and—hear the Megrimum for yourselves" (7). Villagers claim the monster ate Egan's Uncle Ott, so Egan and Uncle Anson follow his trail up Knee-Knock Rise. They discover there is no monster, but the noise comes from rain seeping into a hole where there is a hot mineral spring. When Egan tries to tell people the truth, they do not believe him. Uncle Anson says, "If your mind is made up, all the facts in the world won't make the slightest difference" (111).

To be humane implies flexibility, a trait Grandfather finally acquires in Mary Stolz's *The Mystery of the Woods*. Will asks Grandfather why they always do the same things, so Grandfather replies, "To do something different from what you've always done means you must *change*" (15). After their pet, Tom Kitten, escapes into nearby woods, they follow but get lost until Tom Kitten leads them home. Then Grandfather concedes, "As I was going to say when Tom Kitten came along to guide us home, maybe it's a good idea for us to go by some rules and see that some rules go by us" (46).

Prejudice against blacks, orientals, and American Indians is particularly difficult to erase. In Rose Blue's *The Preacher's Kid*, when the school district buses thirty-two black pupils to her building, ten-year-old Linda Maynard, a minister's daughter, decides if she should attend classes. Most parents boycott the school. Asked on television who is right and who is wrong, Reverend Maynard replies, "Society just isn't that simple. There's right and wrong on both sides" (2). Though there already were a few black pupils enrolled, one man says, "But the minute we let kids from poor families in here, down go our property values" (9). There are only seven present in Linda's class, including three who are bused, when she concludes, "If everything's quiet and everyone wants to learn, it doesn't matter how many kids there are in your class or what color they are. You can learn just the same" (33–34). Linda and her father feel some adults use children as a cause after militant blacks protest just as school is becoming calm. Asked to resign, Reverend Maynard finds a new church nearby where the congregation admires him.

Bright April, written and illustrated by Marguerite deAngeli, helps children understand discrimination. A nine-year-old Philadelphian, April Bright, is a postman's daughter and a nurse's sister. Bright April is her nickname because her skin is "the color of coffee with good cream in it" (9). She loves her Brownie troop with its DYB (Do Your Best) code. She first feels discrimination when she projects being a hat designer in the future and a child says, " 'You? Why they never let . . .,' as the leader puts a hand over the child's mouth" (41). Mother, talking about the future, says to April, "You are going to learn to do what you want to do so well that you will find a place for yourself wherever you want to go" (46). On a Brownie overnight trip, a southern girl, Phyllis, shies away from April at first but later creeps into her cot during a storm. Both discover they like to read and study nature. April tells Mother, "I guess if she had known the truth about me, she would have liked me at first" (88).

Audree Distad's *Dakota Sons* depicts attitudinal change through association. Tad Brokow, bored playing only with Clifford Potts during the summer, befriends Ronnie White Cloud, the only boy left at the mission school. Tad and Clifford are embarrassed at the way Indians, like Ronnie, are treated. At the rodeo, after his older brother insults Ronnie, Clifford defends him. When Ronnie tries to decide if he should be a pow wow dance contestant, he dances for the two boys. Impressed by Ronnie's face, Tad notes:

> For, while his feet followed the remembered patterns, his face was no longer remote or distressed. It showed eagerness and pride. . . . In the spattered shadows of the yard, the dancing figure spun as free as a leaf on the wind whirling this way and that, rising and dipping. This is how it should be for Ronnie, thought Tad—this free. (108)

Learning that his father, whom he has been awaiting all summer, is not coming for him, Ronnie runs away. Tad finds him and eases Ronnie's disappointment by helping him rekindle pride in his heritage.

Helen Coutant's *The Gift* is about Anna, a sensitive Vietnamese child, but it is also a tale of friendship between generations. Every day, Anna stops to talk to elderly Nana Marie on her way home from school. When Nana Marie becomes blind, Anna promises her this special gift:

> You didn't have a last day to look at the world. So I brought it to you. Everything I saw today, just as if you saw it with me. . . . And tomorrow I'll bring you another—and the next day another. I'll bring you enough seeing to last forever." (unp)

Children can be cruel to a peer who seems different due to an invisible physical or mental disability. In Elizabeth Rider Montgomery's *The Mystery of the Boy Next Door,* a newcomer, Joe Gold, does not hear other children call him to play. He does not answer the door when neighbors request their ball that is in his yard. After May asks him for the ball, he makes gestures and strange sounds before returning it. May recognizes the American Manual Alphabet on his T-shirt and realizes he is deaf. His mother signs that she is also deaf. Neighbors, glad to end the mystery, accept Joe and decide to "learn how to talk to him" (47).

Solving another mystery and accepting her retarded sister Louann are challenges for twelve-year-old Amy Treloar in Betty Ren Wright's *The Dollhouse Murders.* Amy tells her parents she is "sick of baby-sitting and losing my friends and having everyone stare when we go by. I don't want to protect her anymore" (10). Aunt Clare, who believes Louann needs to be independent of the family, says to visiting Amy, "Your mother feels guilty in her way. She blames herself because Louann is brain-damaged. You and your father feel guilty too" (144). Louann comes to stay with Amy and Aunt Clare and helps solve a mystery of murdered grandparents through Aunt Clare's childhood dollhouse. Unraveling the dollhouse murders unites Amy and Louann because "They'd been partners, holding on to each other when they were too frightened to stand alone" (146).

Jews have suffered much discrimination internationally, culminating in Nazi atrocities before and during World War II. A book set in Berlin in 1933 is Judith Kerr's *When Hitler Stole Pink Rabbit,* which precedes *The Other Way Round* (see chapter 8, "Maturing"). The father of nine-year-old Anna is a famous Jewish writer who moves his family from Germany to Switzerland. Mother explains, "Not only because we are Jews. Papa thinks no one would be allowed to say what they thought anymore, and he wouldn't be able to write. The Nazis don't like people to disagree with them" (18). Anna regrets taking into exile a new woolly dog instead of her old, worn Pink Rabbit. Before Papa looks for a job in France, he tells Anna:

> There are Jews scattered all over the world, and the Nazis are telling terrible lies about them. So it's very important for people like us to prove them wrong . . . We have to be more honest. . . . We have to be more hard-working than other people." (85–86)

When Papa eventually decides to go to England, he urges Anna and her brother Max to stay with their grandparents, but Anna says, "I think we should stay together. I've never minded being a refugee before. . . . But if you send us away now I'm so terribly frightened . . . that I might really feel like one" (179).

A tale to counter discrimination is Susan Sussman's *There's No Such Thing as a Chanukah Bush, Sandy Goldstein*. Though both Robin and Sandy are Jewish, only Sandy has a Christmas tree, which she calls a Chanukah bush. At a union party, Robin's grandfather explains the difference between celebrating something because you believe in it and helping friends observe what is important to them. Robin invites a Christian friend, Heather, to dinner on the last night of Chanukah, and Heather invites Robin to her house for Christmas dinner. Robin tells her parents, "On my way home I decided it wasn't so tough to be Jewish if you had friends who shared with you, and maybe Sandy Goldstein didn't . . . which was why she needed a Chanukah Bush" (48).

The Hundred Dresses by Eleanor Estes is a popular book that shows prejudice toward a poor, motherless child with a foreign name. Wanda Petronski lives with her father and brother in a run-down shack and always wears the same faded blue dress to school. One day, when girls exclaim about a pupil's new outfit, Wanda says, "I got a hundred dresses home" (29). Then girls tease Wanda and have her describe what she imagines. When it is time to choose a winner of a fourth-grade drawing contest, children discover the classroom walls covered with a hundred pictures of dresses, but Wanda is gone. The teacher, Miss Mason, declares Wanda the winner, and she reads this letter from Mr. Petronski:

> Dear Teacher:
>   My Wanda will not come to your school anymore. Jake also. Now we move away to big city. No more holler Polack. No more ask why funny name. Plenty of funny names in the big city.
>
> Yours truly, Jan Petronski. (47)

Two classmates, Peggy and Maddie, ashamed of their behavior, go to Wanda's house to apologize, but the Petronskis have moved. The girls write Wanda, and at Christmas, Miss Mason gets Wanda's reply, giving Peggy and Maddie pictures of the dresses they like.

The Best Christmas Pageant Ever by Barbara Robinson is a humorous account of the terrible Herdman brood. They may lie, steal, smoke cigars, hit young children, curse teachers, and take the name of the Lord in vain, "but they never, never [get] kept back a grade" (7), because another sibling is coming along. After they hear about refreshments at Sunday school, they all appear. At tryouts for the Christmas pageant, the Herdmans volunteer for major roles. They want to know about Jesus and go to the library to do research on Herod. The night of the pageant, the church is packed. As one of the three kings, Leroy Herdman gives the Christ child a ham that the church presented to his family. Everyone agrees, "It was the best Christmas pageant we ever had" (78).

Migrants suffer from being in the lowest socio-economic class. Louisa R. Shotwell's *Roosevelt Grady* portrays a nine-year-old boy, Roosevelt Grady, who is identified as being black only on the book jacket. Roosevelt dreams of living in one place and going to school long enough to learn how to divide. His mother tells him her secret wish, "My children are going to grow up to be something else besides stooping, crawling beanpickers" (59). Roosevelt befriends an orphan, Manowar, and the two plan how to get to Ellcott Bus Camp where there may be year-round work for Roosevelt's father. Their plan has three steps: (1) learn where the bus camp is, (2) find a way to get their crew there, and (3) get a winter job for Papa Grady. After their success, Manowar joins the Grady family.

A feminist mother who tries to prevent her daughter from playing with dolls causes a problem in Sheila Greenwald's *The Secret in Miranda's Closet*. Fat, friendless Miranda Alexis Perry receives from her baby-sitter, Mrs. Nelson, an old doll and a trunk with doll clothes which she hides in her closet. While shopping for items to convert her closet into a dollhouse, Miranda befriends Mildred Manson, a loner like herself. She thinks, "A friend. She had made a friend on her own without help or assistance" (87). When her mother loses her job, Miranda offers to sell her antique doll, but her mother declines, admitting, "I guess that I was forcing you into a way of behaving just as I had once been" (131).

Feminist issues dominate the miserable month of April for eleven-year-old Cress Richardson in Lila Perl's *That Crazy April*. Mrs. Richardson, a women's rights advocate, is not happy when Cress participates in a bridal show. Forced to be a male ring bearer rather than a flower girl, Cress is upset when a flower girl trips her; she falls, splits her pants, and loses the ring. Her mother, who is present, tells the woman in charge, "She's been very humiliated by what's happened. Cress is used to being treated like a person. She's not accustomed to playing the role of a court jester" (149). Later, when her school metalwork shop club rejects Cress, she cries:

> I hadn't told Mr. Grinnell what I really wanted to tell him;
> that *he* might not want me in his club because I was a girl but
> I didn't want to be in the club because he was a prejudiced,
> narrow-minded horrible old man. (160)

All ends well as Cress anticipates summer camp. She thinks, "It was a camp for learning survival techniques in the raw. From the ground up. And it was for both girls *and* boys" (188).

Stereotyping sexes is not limited to the United States. In *Taiwo and Her Twin* by Letta Schatz, Taiwo lives in a Nigerian village where the government is building a school. Father decides that only his male children can go to school. A brother, Babatune, says, "What can a girl do? Schooling is not for girls. A girl cannot be a big somebody" (29). When the headmaster suggests that Taiwo attend, Father protests, "We cannot send them all. And she is a girl. What need has a girl for schooling? Will it teach her to be a proper wife? All she needs to know, the women of the household can teach her" (35). Taiwo wants to attend so desperately that she gets her brothers to share what they learn. Seeing her zest for knowledge, Father buys her needed books, slate, and chalk. She thinks:

> The books even had a special strange, wonderful new book
> smell, not like any other smell she knew. And they had
> words. Some words she could not read. Others were new. But
> soon she would know all the words. Tomorrow the new
> school was opening, and she would attend. (113)

BOOKS FOR LATER YEARS

A fantasy of appreciation for those who are different is Randall Jarrell's *The Animal Family*. A hunter falls in love with a mermaid who leaves her home in the sea to live with him on land. "The hunter and the mermaid were so different from each other that it seemed to them, finally, that they were exactly alike. And they lived together and were happy." (54) Gradually, the family enlarges with a bear cub, a lynx kitten, and a little boy found in a boat with his dead mother. Sometimes they tell the boy that the lynx found him but

> he knew that the hunter was his father and the mermaid his mother and always had been. (The two of them were different from him, different from each other, but aren't a boy's mother and father always different from him, different from each other?) (156–157)

An illegitimate child today suffers less than in the past. In 1917 in Oregon, illegitimate persons were disgraced in their home towns. In *Three Knocks on the Wall* by Evelyn Sibley Lampman, a child, Antoinette Hutchinson, and a woman, Edna Pope, were born out of wedlock. A twelve-year-old girl, Marty Burnham, lives next to the ten-foot wall that surrounds the home of reclusive Mrs. Hutchinson and her daughter, Miss Rebecca Hutchinson. Marty makes a pet cemetery next to the wall at the foot of the garden. One day, when the Hutchinsons are at church, Marty hears knocking on the wall and talks through the barrier to Miss Hutchinson's daughter, Antoinette. When Marty asks why the girl is hiding, she replies, "But my m——Rebecca wasn't married. That's why Mrs. Hutchinson calls me Sinette. (The name is based on "sin.") It's a great disgrace. We have to spend the rest of our lives making up for it" (78). Marty answers, "It's not your fault. It doesn't matter to me a whiffle. You're not to blame for what happened" (78). Marty also befriends seamstress Edna Pope, who has overcome her illegitimacy, staying in her home town with her head held high. After Mrs. Hutchinson dies, Marty's father and Edna Pope arrange a way to release Antoinette and Rebecca and help them save face.

Child abuse is a serious social problem today. *Don't Hurt Laurie!* by Willo Davis Roberts tells the story of eleven-year-old Laurie Kolman who is physically abused by her mother, Annabelle. Annabelle is now married to Jack Summers, who has two children, eight-year-old Tim and four-year-old Shelly. Annabelle had previously moved often to prevent investigations by hospital workers of Laurie's constant "accidents." Laurie "didn't really understand why she felt it must be a secret that her mother mistreated her; but she did know she was ashamed of it, as if in some way, it were her fault" (33). Laurie finally tells her neighbor George, "She hates me because I'm like my father. He deserted us when I was little" (85). When Laurie breaks a plate,

Annabelle says, "The older you get, the more you're like Harry Kolman. Sometimes you're so much like him I could kill you" (93). After Annabelle does nearly kill her with a broom and poker, Tim takes Laurie and Shelly with him to his grandmother's. Jack explains to Laurie that her mother had herself been an abused child and then was deserted by her husband. He adds, "It doesn't mean that she hates you, or that she doesn't care what happens to you. It just means she's unhappy and she can't help the things she does" (161). Annabelle gets help while the children stay with Jack's mother.

In Louise Dickinson Rich's *Summer at High Kingdom*, working together changes the attitude of a Maine community toward hippies who rent High Kingdom farm. A hippie explains:

> We consider ourselves a family. We trust each other and accept each other just as we are. We share and share alike. We're committed to each other and to the same ideas. Isn't that what's supposed to make a family, even if we're not blood relatives? Truly loving each other? (15)

Thirteen-year-old Dana Chadwick cannot understand why his grandfather is with the hippies often and gives them his pet cow, Blossom. Even Dan's brother, Whit, befriends them. During a Chadwick farm crisis, the hippies come to pick beans. When a neighbor, Tom Akers, wants to join the commune in the winter, Pa says, "I'll give odds that about everyone in the Valley is more tolerant of odd-balls than they were last spring, because of those people" (104). Gramp asks Tom's mother, "Look, do you figure you've given Tom a good bringing up, taught him right from wrong? In all his twenty-two years, has he ever been in trouble here in the Valley?" (107) Gramp, who does not regret working at High Kingdom, explains, "It wasn't wasted, not by a long shot. For one thing I had a good time harking back to the old days. Chiefly, though, it shook me out of my rut. I learned something. I learned that you can't turn back the clock" (111)

Among books portraying American Indian problems is Weyman Jones's *Edge of Two Worlds*, a story of the last days of Sequoyah, who developed the Cherokee alphabet. Fifteen-year-old Calvin Harper, en route from Texas to his Boston school, is the sole survivor of a Comanche wagon train massacre. His rescuer is Sequoyah, himself near death but searching for his people's origins. Sequoyah says, "Where two worlds meet, they make a lonely place. . . . There's a boy's world and a man's world. In a boy's world it's always someone else's fault" (84). Eventually, Sequoyah's son and a friend find them. They give Calvin a horse, food, a rifle, and directions to the nearest town where he can decide whether to return home or go to school.

An unusual twist on the subject of prejudice is *Season of the Two-Heart* by Lois Duncan. Martha (Natachu) Weekoty leaves her Pueblo village to spend her senior year in an Albuquerque high school, living as an *au pair* girl, or student helper, with a white family, the Boyntons. She thinks, "Sometimes I feel as though my mind were a tiny seed in a jar. All withered up, waiting for the storage room. I want to take it out and plant it and let it grow" (5). Her teacher tells her, "We never stop learning. Take advantage of every opportunity" (48). Martha is horrified to discover her own prejudice when she objects to sharing a locker with a Navaho girl. Torn between American Indian and white cultures, Martha returns to the Pueblos, admitting, "I am forgetting things which are my birthright. It is not good, being a two-heart" (84). Her uncle and a classmate, Alan Wallace, show her how she can have the best of both worlds. She believes, "I am not a two-heart. My skin may be that of an Indian, but my mind and heart are those of a Bahana [white person]" (108).

In *This Is a Recording* by Barbara Corcoran, a white girl tries to help American Indians to develop red power. While her parents are traveling, fourteen-year-old Marianne Temple goes to Montana and struggles to relate to her grandmother, a former actress. Instead of writing personal letters, Marianne talks into a tape recorder. She befriends Oliver Everybodylooksat, a Kootenai Indian classmate and her grandmother's part-time employee. Marianne wants to live on a reservation to help Indian people unite, but Oliver says, "Me, I don't like power—white or red or black or whatever. People use power to grind down other people. . . . What you don't see is that a Navajo for instance is just as different from a Blackfeet as an Irishman is different from a Jew" (90). Marianne writes strong letters to the local newspaper editor on the environment and maltreatment of the Indians, but the editor refuses to publish one letter, explaining, "I was afraid it might exacerbate their troubles . . . by stirring up an anti-Indian backlash. . . . Goading people won't help" (148). In the end, Marianne returns to Boston with her newly divorced mother.

Many of Evelyn Sibley Lampman's books, such as *The Year of Small Shadow*, concern American Indians in Oregon's early days. In

1880, the chief brings Small Shadow, or Shad, from his reservation to live with his father's lawyer, Dan'l Foster, until his father's prison term ends. When the lawyer, a single man living in a boarding house, refuses, Shad begs, "Do not send me back, Dan'l Foster. The others will laugh because you did not want me" (23). Dan'l charms his landlady, Mrs. Hicks, into accepting and helping Shad. A church woman, while fitting new clothes for Shad, says the house is contaminated, and Shad understands that "he was the contaminator" (50). Shad notices that Mrs. Hick's employee, Bertha, is not welcome at a party, so he realizes, "Whites were not all equal just because their skin color was the same" (58). At the party, guests shake Shad's hand, apologetic for accusing him of stealing a brooch, which they find in a coffee pot. He realizes, "Their touch proved that he was no longer contaminated" (69). A printer's apprentice teaches the boy to read and write while Shad works for the printer. After Shad rides alone to an Indian village for Maggy, whose husband upsets the town, people treat Shad like a hero and want him to stay. But when his father is free, he returns to the reservation, explaining, "I can't stay. They're trying to make me into a [w]hite, but I'm not a [w]hite. I'm an Indian. I belong with my own people" (188).

In another Evelyn Sibley Lampman book, *Go Up the Road*, twelve-year-old Yolanda Ruiz finds that Hispanic migrant workers have two strikes against them. After her father loses his farm and his family joins the crew of unscrupulous Juan Sanchez, Yolanda learns that constant moving is difficult. Prejudice creeps into remarks, even from a child like Kim, who says to Yolanda that whites must stop picking strawberries because of the heat, but "You don't feel it the way we do on account of your skin. Mrs. Pepper says that's why dark-skinned people always work in the fields" (45). Conditions improve when Papa takes his family to Oregon to see recently widowed Aunt Connie. After she helps Papa get a local job so the children can attend school regularly, the aunt says:

> Today we live in an Anglo world. But it will not always be that way. Some day the brown, the black, the red men will have equal voices, but only if the words they speak are worth listening to. They cannot be words of hate and anger. They must be calm and filled with wisdom. Learning comes from education. (179)

Another Hispanic is twelve-year-old Maria Louisa Santos in *Maria Louisa* by Winifred Madison. After her mother is hospitalized with tuberculosis, Maria Louisa and her six-year-old brother Juan go from a small Arizona town to San Francisco to stay with relatives. On her first day in a new school, Maria Louisa suffers when another pupil, Carol Kraus, remarks, "Brother, this school is something else. Talk about pollution. This really stinks" (51). The Hispanic girl asks herself, "Was this the racial prejudice she'd read about and seen on TV?" (52) Since Maria Louisa's dominant language is Spanish and most of her courses are in English, she enters a special class whose teacher, Ms. Stein, makes non-English speakers feel at ease. Ms. Stein tells the girl, "Whatever happens to you, whatever is your experience, is what you have to say. It will be different from what anyone else has to say. There is only one Maria Louisa Santos" (154).

Many books for teenagers discuss discrimination against blacks or show a black sports star. *Life. Is. Not. Fair.* by Gary W. Bargar has a different twist. Louis Lamb, a seventh grader determined to be a "cool," not a "dip," wears the right clothes and carries a clipboard instead of a notebook. Louis's new black next-door neighbors are Mrs. Clausen and her nonathletic son, DeWitt, who is studying to be a concert pianist. Unable to accept the "cools' " treatment of DeWitt, Louis finds he likes the pianist better than "cool" Paul, his former best friend. Louis thinks, "DeWitt looked at me and I looked at DeWitt. Then we both smiled shyly. Something had changed between us since this morning. We had crossed some kind of line" (50). When an opponent becomes student council president by stealing Louis's speech, Louis and DeWitt seek revenge. They get Ellie Siegel, another misfit, to join them in an assembly skit to embarrass the "cools," but their opposition enjoys it. DeWitt reminds Louis, "Life. Is. Not. Fair." (173)

John Neufeld's *Edgar Allan* tells about a white community that becomes anti-black when Reverend Robert Fickett takes in a three-year-old black boy, E. A. (Edgar Allan), with the option of adopting him. His children, church members, and the community are horrified. Fourteen-year-old Mary Nell Fickett relates, "It is hard enough being a preacher's kid, but can you imagine the look on my friends' faces when I introduce him as my *brother*? . . . He's visible and he's different and he *is not ours*" (22). Her mother replies, "Still we are determined to give something to E. A. and I suspect that by doing so, we can give you something . . . Integrity" (23). After the minister concedes to outside pressures and returns E. A., Michael Fickett expresses disappointment with his father, "He told us what was important, and what wasn't, and then he went ahead and mixed them up" (90). Even church members switch positions and ask the minister to leave because he does not support his principles.

In *Go Well, Stay Well* by Toeckey Jones, fifteen-year-old Candy sprains her ankle while shopping in Johannesburg, South Africa and accepts help from fifteen-year-old Becky, a Zulu from the black area of Soweto. Candy takes Zulu lessons from Becky, so the two friends have an excuse to meet. While studying Hamlet, Candy realizes what it means to be black in South Africa. She "was afraid for herself as well as for Becky and Tomi [their house servant], seeing them all as Hamlets in their separate ways, caught up in a sinful system of suffering which they all seemed incapable of changing" (49). Candy believes, "A sense of the ridiculous helped Becky to remain human under an inhuman system" (58). Candy "was continually having to choose between Becky and her own inclinations and interests because Becky's blackness barred her from sharing any of them" (101). With help from Dirk deVilliers, an Afrikaner, Candy changes her family's attitude toward Becky, and her parents let her go with Becky to visit Becky's Swaziland relatives.

Blacks suffer discrimination in England too, as Reginald Maddox shows in *Danny Rowley*. When Danny's mother tells him her plans to remarry, he gets so angry, he goes out and smashes gas lamps. Two black boys with whom he becomes friends, Hector Robinson and Lefty Bates, save him from the police. His mother criticizes the new friends, saying, "They're different! It can't be long since they were savages. . . . They aren't like us. One of these days they will be, but it'll take time" (5). She marries Walter Higgins, and he brings his daughter, Lorna, to live with them. Lorna hates the marriage as much as Danny, but when the girl treats his mother cruelly, he finds, "All my bitterness had to be used against her and I had none left for Walter Higgins" (106). After two white delinquents ransack Walter's workshop, it is Danny and Walter who prove the innocence of the two accused blacks, Hector and Lefty. Danny accepts Walter and feels self-pride in receiving this soccer compliment from night watchman Joe: "That was a grand goal you scored Saturday. . . . You had to work for your goal, lad, and you took it well. Keep on being that way and you'll never go far wrong" (176).

Yoshiko Uchida depicts shameful treatment of the Japanese in the United States during World War II. In *Journey to Topaz*, sensitive, kind, eleven-year-old Yuki Sakane and her family live in Berkeley, California. Yuki says, "Mother and Father were ISSEI [first generation Japanese]. They were law abiding and loyal as any American, but they had never become citizens because of a law that wouldn't permit them to" (14). After the attack on Pearl Harbor, the United States confines 110,000 people of Japanese ancestry in inland camps. Yuki's father, Mr. Sakane, a samurai's grandson, is brave and dignified with a gentle heart, but authorities send him to a Montana internment camp. The rest of his family go to a camp called Topaz in the Utah desert. When a friend speaks bitterly of Americans imprisoning their own residents, Mother says, "Fear has made this country do something she will one day regret, but we cannot let this terrible mistake poison our hearts. If we do, then we will be the ones to destroy ourselves and our children as well" (90). Father joins them at Topaz, and when they secure their freedom, the family moves to Salt Lake City.

In Yoshiko Uchida's sequel, *Journey Home*, the Sakanes, anxious to return to California, reflect, "But Salt Lake City was a lot better than California. Even if you were scared, it was better to be free than to be kept inside a barbed wire fence" (18). After the family moves back to Berkeley, Yuki's brother, Ken, joins them; he is bitter and withdrawn. Ken, a discharged American soldier wounded in France, mourns his best friend who died saving him and others. Many still resent the Japanese, but white neighbors help the Sakanes. Yuki feels every time she moves that she leaves behind a small piece of herself and soon there'll "be nothing left of her old self" (41). After Ken visits his best friend's family and decides to go to college, Yuki realizes that "everything was going to be all right. She'd finally come home, too" (131).

Mixed marriages can cause problems in family relations, as Betty Cavanna shows in *Jenny Kimura*. After World War II, Jenny Kimura's American father marries her Japanese mother and stays in Japan, though her Japanese grandparents never accept the marriage. Her father comments about his Japanese and American household, "We're very lucky people, actually. We have the best of two worlds" (27). When she is sixteen years old, Jenny nervously plans a visit with her American grandmother in Kansas City. Her father, describing his mother as a woman of high principles and strong prejudices, advises, "Just be yourself and she'll grow to love you, but it may take a while" (59). After Jenny nearly drowns while on a Cape Cod vacation, her grandmother says, "For nearly an hour I didn't think you'd make it, and I promised myself, if you pulled through, that I'd try to be a bigger person, a better grandmother. . . . I've been a bitter old woman, Jenny, but you've made me love you" (210).

For centuries in many countries, gypsies have endured discrimination. In *The Diddakoi* by Rumer Godden, seven-year-old Kizzy Lovell lives with her great-great grandmother in a caravan on Admiral Cunningham Twiss's estate. Classmates treat Kizzy cruelly and call her Diddakoi, meaning half-breed. When Gran dies, Admiral Twiss, an eccentric with two male servants, lets Kizzy live with him. But the community questions how well three men can raise a girl. Olivia Brooke, a magistrate, defends Kizzy's clothes and attitude when she says, "Try to remember we are dealing with different standards, and different doesn't mean bad" (88). Through the kindness of Miss Brooke and Admiral Twiss, Kizzy relaxes. In the end, the community accepts her, she and her classmates become friends, and the Admiral and Miss Brooke adopt her after they marry.

A story of wartime love and hate among various nationalities is Kate Seredy's *The Singing Tree*, a sequel to *The Good Master* (see chapter 8, "Maturing"). In Hungary during World War II, twelve-year-old Kate, a tomboy, is living on her Uncle Morton Nagy's farm. Moses and Sarah Mandelbaum, Jewish storekeepers, are her uncle's friends. Following a declaration of war, Uncle Morton enlists, leaving his thirteen-year-old son Jancsi to operate the farm. When Old Arpad, a farm hand, calls Jancsi the Young Master, the boy thinks, "I will be. . . . I will be . . . like father" (59). During the war, after Jancsi lets six Russian prisoners help on the farm and accepts six German children, the Russians, Hungarians, and Germans become friends. A German child writes to his mother:

> I do not hate Russians now, Mother, and I think that Jews are very kind and good. When I grow up I want to teach what Gregori [a Russian prisoner] is always saying. He says that people are all the same in Russia and Germany and Hungary and that we are all brothers. (222)

Upon his return, Uncle Morton tells about the night his men advanced on Russians through a devastated forest and came upon a single apple tree alive with birds singing to the dawn. He reflects, "Small orphans, . . . large ones, . . . for a while found shelter on its sturdy limbs" (237). Jancsi thinks their sheltering farm is similar to the apple tree.

An unusual story of fear, courage, and caring for someone who is mentally disabled is *Willie Bea and the Time the Martians Landed* by Virginia Hamilton. In October 1938 in a small Ohio town, Willie Bea's family gathers for Sunday dinner with Big, a large, mentally slow cousin, as a guest. When Mother smacks Big for endangering her baby son, Willie Bea sees "Big's face break up in pieces as tears filled his eyes. She knew the smack from her Mama could never hurt old Big. What had broken down was his pride" (44). The family is upset after the Orson Welles radio broadcast, "The Martians Have Landed," and Willie Bea imagines the night harvesters at the Kelly farm to be Martians. After she and Big go to that farm, she sustains a minor injury from a combine. Her parents make Willie Bea stay in bed, and it is Big who visits, restoring her self-confidence.

A mentally disabled man changes Will's attitude in *The Hayburners* by Gene Smith. Will is unhappy when his parents bring thirty-year-old Joey from a state institution to do summer work on their farm. Mother is furious when Will asks in French in front of Joey, "How did our moron do today?" (25). In a 4-H drawing, Will picks a high number and must be among the last to choose a steer for summer breeding. As expected, his steer is a hayburner, or second rate. Joey, who adores the steer, calls it Mickey. Will begins to appreciate Joey and says, "But it's different with Joey. . . . There's gaps in Joey. That's the way my father puts it. But that doesn't mean he doesn't understand things" (46). Joey's employment ends following the auction. After Mickey is one of the top ten, Will wonders if Joey knows it will be slaughtered. Before leaving the fair grounds, Joey gives Mickey a container of salt and mutters, "I guess I won't be seeing you anymore. . . . You were great, Mickey" (59)

Being too tall or too short can be a disability, but many overcome embarrassment to lead productive lives. In *Little Little* by M. E. Kerr, after orphaned Sidney Cinnamon, a dwarf, performs at a surprise eighteenth birthday party for a female dwarf, Little Little, he falls in love with her. While her wealthy, normal-sized family hosts the party, her mother cautions, "Don't say 'dwarf'! Call yourself a little person or a midget or diminutive" (12). When Sidney grew up at Twin Oaks Orphans' Home, his friend was Little Lion, now a famous evangelist, who told him, "When you go on a job, make sure your little ass goes first class. Make sure ahead you've got first class accommodations" (4–5). Sidney does go first class after he becomes a television star as Roach in Palmer Pest Control commercials. Little Lion plans to marry Little

Little until he meets Eloise Ficklin, a television commercial star, at a convention of Tadpoles (Children of American Diminutives) and PODS (Parents of Diminutives). At the end of this story, written in alternate chapters by Sidney and Little Little, the two narrators are friends, but their relationship does not become romantic.

In *Madeline and the Great (Old) Escape Artist* by Rebecca C. Jones, twelve-year-old Madeline has her first epileptic seizure in class shortly after she and her mother move to Mother's home town. No one is more horrified than her class project partner, Jennifer Springer. In the hospital, Madeline meets ninety-four-year-old Mary Gibson from Happy Harvest Rest Home. Madeline worries, "Why was I having these convulsions or fits or seizures or whatever they're called? Maybe I was being punished for something I've done?" (20). After Madeline is nasty to Mary, the old lady says, "It's a wonder you don't fall down. . . . That chip on your shoulder must be awfully heavy. . . . Everybody's got problems, child. That's what life is all about" (27). The old lady and Madeline fail in their attempt to run away, and realizing that she must return to the home, Mary states philosophically, "I suppose we all have a dragon to face" (76). These words inspire Madeline when she returns to school and helps a classmate face her own dragon.

Deafness is a difficult disability because it is invisible. In Veronica Robinson's *David in Silence*, thirteen-year-old Michael Guest befriends his next-door neighbor, David, who is deaf. Michael's older sister, Eileen, says, "If he really is deaf and dumb . . . you shouldn't laugh at him. . . . He can't help being like that" (7). David teaches Michael sign language and they go to movies together. After David overreacts while playing ball, teammates chase him. He hides in a tunnel, escaping dirty and tired with frightening feelings:

> Suddenly he was swept by a wave of terror and desolation, people everywhere who could help him so easily if they were able to . . . until the moment they realized he was deaf, and then they would become frightened by their own ignorance of how to talk to him." (86)

Finally, Michael sees him and takes David home.

Jews have been persecuted in every country and in every century. Children are not immune to such persecution, as Johanna Hurwitz shows in *The Rabbi's Girl*. The story takes place in 1923 in Lorain, Ohio, a town of 50,000 with only 300 Jews when eleven-year-old

Carrie Levin moves there. Papa antagonizes an important Jewish doctor when he calls a gentile physician to save the life of his youngest child. Selena Edwards, who lives behind the Levin's, taunts Carrie, "My grandma says that I can't play with you. You're dirty Jews" (26). But Selena wants to be friendly, so she suggests going to Saturday movies. When Carrie refuses because it is Sabbath, Selena is angry again. After a tornado strikes on Saturday, Papa helps others even though he is ill. The tornado collapses a theater and two Jewish girls are among the dead, so some say they suffered for violating the Sabbath. Papa preaches, "Don't blame God and don't blame yourselves. When there is a calamity in nature, everyone is a victim, Jews and Christians, good people and bad. We can only continue to live our lives and hold on to our values" (142). After Papa's death, the family prepares to move to New York.

An unprejudiced person may find it difficult to understand one who is biased. In *Look Through My Window* by Jean Little, Emily discovers that people often hide inner sentiments. Emily's family moves to a large house to accommodate four cousins whose mother is hospitalized with tuberculosis. Then Emily makes friends with neighbors, Kate and Lindsay. When planning a play, Kate says, "I guess I shouldn't help with a Christmas play anyway, I'm part Jewish, you know" (79). Lindsay is horrified to learn the cousins are Catholic. Emily believes, "It doesn't make one bit of difference. It didn't before we knew—so why should it now. We're the same people we were ten minutes ago" (182–183). Emily's mother explains Kate's reluctance to tell Emily that she is Jewish. The mother realizes, "Many people have deep and terrible prejudices against Jews. Kate has to live in that world" (199). Emily "looked through Kate's window" (202). It's like trying to "walk in her shoes or try seeing it through her eyes" (202).

There is an ironic ending to *Berries Goodman* by Emily Cheney Neville. The Goodman family moves from New York City to Olcott, Acres, a New Jersey suburb. A realtor takes them only to certain neighborhoods, influenced by the presence of their Jewish guest, Izzy Weinstein. Mrs. Goodman says, "That's what Miss Real Estate was doing when we first came out, and Izzy Weinstein and his bag of bagels was with us. She only showed us houses in Olcott Acres and Indian Road" (105). Mrs. Goodman learns more about segregated housing patterns when she becomes a real estate agent. Although he befriends Sydney Fine, a Jewish boy who lives in a special section of town, Berries dislikes his neighbor Sandra who repeats her mother's prejudices toward Jews. Hal, Berries's seventeen-year-old brother, calls Sandra a Nazi. Hal asks, "Don't you know the Nazis rounded up the Jewish people and put them in one part of town, and then they put them in concentration camps, and then they killed them?" (45). Before the Goodmans return to New York City, they sell their house to a Jewish family named Goodman because a real estate agent probably thinks they are Mormons, like Berries' father.

In *Peter and Veronica* by Marilyn Sachs, Peter is getting ready for his Bar Mitzvah. He and Veronica enjoy biking and skating together although his mother objects to his special friend. He asks, "It's because she's not Jewish isn't it? You're prejudiced" (47). When he tells Veronica, she says, "My mother does mind that you're Jewish. I'm so glad. I was so ashamed. I wasn't going to tell you" (83). Unless Veronica receives an invitation, Peter refuses to be a bar mitzvah participant. In his ceremonial speech, he declares:

> All over the world, people are fighting and killing each other because their hearts are filled with hatred. I pledge myself to work for better understanding among all men so that one day the word of God as shown to Isaiah will be fulfilled. (137)

Peter is furious when Veronica does not come to his bar mitzvah but forgives her when he learns she is scared of parties.

International children are characters in Sally Watson's *To Build a Land*, which precedes *Other Sandals* (see chapter 8, "Maturing"). Fifteen-year-old Leo Morelli and his twelve-year-old sister, Mia, are Naples scavengers in 1947. When Mia tries to steal from two American soldiers, she breaks her arm. The soldiers take Mia and Leo to the Red Cross, which sends them to Marseilles. Then Youth Aliyah brings them to an Israeli kibbutz, Gan Shalom, where Mia adjusts but Leo does not. He "resented the fact that men from other countries should be able to decide their future. Leo hated any kind of authority or control" (126). Leo cannot understand Dan, a Dutch pacifist. Dan has his own problems, debating if he should be inactive or fight for Israel:

> What if he had shot the Arab and Joshua had lived? What right had he to judge who should live and who should die? He was the member of a new state, and yet he was unwilling to fight for it. Was he shirking his duty? Was citizenship in a state an obligation to fight for it? (203)

After Arabs capture Leo, another maverick, Shari, rescues him, and they become friends as they join those who build a new land.

A tragic religious war is the continuous one between Catholics and Protestants in Northern Ireland. Joan Lingard's four books depict hatred and prejudice on both sides and what it does to people. In *The Twelfth of July: A Novel of Modern Ireland*, modern Protestants prepare to celebrate William of Orange's conquest of James II in 1690. At night, a hot-tempered, fourteen-year-old Catholic, Kevin McCoy, and his friend paint on the wall behind the house of a Protestant, Sadie Jackson, "DOWN WITH KING BILLY" (31). Sadie hears them, chases them, and catches Kevin when he falls. Catholics discover Sadie and her brother Tommy after they retaliate and paint in orange, "KING BILLY. NO POPE HERE" (59), over the words, "GOD BLESS THE POPE" (59), in the Catholic section. During the night, Sadie sneaks into Kevin's house and prints in ink on the kitchen table, "KING BILLY WAS HERE. LONG LIVE KING BILLY" (92). Kevin catches her but she escapes. On the night of July 11, Catholic and Protestant children throw rocks at each other, and Kevin's sister Brede is hurt. Tommy and Sadie go with Kevin to the hospital to see Brede. The next day, instead of marching in a Protestant parade, Sadie and Tommy spend the time with Kevin at the seashore. Kevin jokes, "I never expected to spend the 'Twelfth' with a couple of Prods" (157).

In Lingard's *Across the Barricades*, Kevin and Sadie meet three years later and begin dating. "They had started as enemies, had even fought with stones and fists; then for awhile they had been friends but eventually drifted apart because of the difficulties of meeting" (6). A neighbor tattles about Sadie's secret dates with Kevin, and Catholics beat the lad because of his Protestant girlfriend. A former teacher, Mr. Blake, befriends them, but he pays with his life when opponents set his house afire while he is inside. Kevin decides to go to Liverpool, explaining, "Sadie, I've got to go away. I can't stand it any longer. I haven't a job and I'm sick of bombs and people getting killed. And now this has happened to Mr. Blake" (54). At the dock before Kevin boards his ship, Sadie appears and says, "I haven't come to see you off. I'm coming with you" (160).

In Lingard's third book, *Into Exile*, Kevin and Sadie marry and live in a London slum. Kevin, who misses Belfast, "longed to be there, for it was not all bombs and blood and suffering. People laughed a lot and enjoyed themselves, when they were allowed to, and they were friendly" (32). Sadie hates being poor and quarreling before reconciling with

Kevin. She reflects, "She did not understand how it was so easy one minute to love someone so much that it almost hurt, and the next hate him more than anyone in her life" (89). They both question if it is right to let their happiness cause misery to others but think that "if they had given in, it would have been giving in to all of it, the prejudice and hate, the violence and stupidity" (101). After his father's death, Kevin returns to Belfast to help his mother, settling her in the country with her married daughter Brede. Torn between his duties as a son and husband, Kevin decides to return to Sadie because she cannot live with his family in Ireland. Before he leaves, Sadie arrives, and Kevin tells her, "Yes, it's peaceful. But that's not everything. And there are other peaceful places, Sadie. We'll find one of our own" (176).

In Lingard's *A Proper Place*, Kevin and Sadie live in a Liverpool slum. Kevin, a day laborer, sends money home to his mother. When Sadie's mother visits, she argues with Sadie, especially about the Loyal Orange Lodges. Sadie claims, "They were breeding grounds of prejudice" (25). Her mother calls them "an institution that had existed for nearly three hundred years to protect all they held dear from Catholics" (25). After Mrs. Jackson returns home, Kevin's seventeen-year-old brother—bitter, lazy Gerald—comes to live with them. While Kevin washes dishes, Gerald complains, "That's a fine sight, me brother Kevin with his hands in the sink like a woman" (55). Kevin and Gerald get farm jobs and move to the country with Sadie, who enjoys being there. Kevin becomes head cowman and Gerald works with horses until Gerald returns to Ireland to work in a stable. After Kevin copes with a threatening gang during his and Sadie's visit to Liverpool, he philosophizes about blame for urban crimes. "Blame was something that got more difficult to dish out, Kevin found, the older he got" (153).

Socio-economic differences do not interfere with friendship in Karin Anckarsvärd's *Doctor's Boy*, a story set in Sweden before the advent of the automobile. One day, ten-year-old Jon accompanies his doctor father on rounds and stays with the horse while his father visits patients in a slum area. Jon, who recognizes his classmate Rickard, is surprised to learn that his father is paying for Rickard's schooling and plans to help the boy go to Latin school. En route with Jon to see an old, ill man who lives alone on an island, the doctor sees Rickard and invites him to join them. The boys assist in an emergency operation, and the doctor arranges for orphaned Rickard to stay with his old patient. While the two boys do chores, they discover that they share similar goals, interests, and values despite a difference in socio-economic backgrounds.

From France comes a story of friendship between boys of different backgrounds. In Michel-Aimé Baudouy's *More than Courage*, fourteen-year-old Michael ("Mick") Martel disappoints his parents because he prefers working on machines to attending school. His parents are rich although his maternal grandfather had been a blacksmith. When Mick tells his mother he wants to hammer iron rather than study, she says:

> My father swung a hammer all his life. . . . He served a long
> apprenticeship with his father and that can be the hardest of
> schools. . . . The school you go to now takes the place of
> apprenticeship. . . . Learn everything you can there and one
> day you'll be free to use what you learn in your own way." (37)

When a railroad worker's son, Paulo, finds his father's old motorcycle, Mick and other friends help him prepare the cycle for races, hiding it in the former smithy of Mick's grandfather. After Mick visits a new friend's home, he thinks, "He was in a world where things had different values from the one he knew" (48). Mick, the chosen driver in the first race, is afraid of his father's reaction. The lad wins the race but breaks his ankle afterwards. Later, he hears one of his father's important customers say, "I wonder if you fully realize what that boy of yours has done. . . . He's off to a fine start in life. . . . You have something to be proud of in that boy" (159).

An unusual story of a relationship between two social classes is *The Battle Horse* by Harry Kullman. In the 1930s in Stockholm, Sweden, there is wide division between preppies, or private school students, and public school children, although they live in the same apartment complex. A young entrepreneur, who calls himself Buffalo Bill, organizes feudal jousting of knights with preppies as knights and public school pupils as horses. A mysterious masked Black Knight, riding on a mute boy, appears at times and defeats each contestant. Two public school pupils, Roland and a girl named Kossan, live in the same courtyard with Henning, a top private school athlete. Peers force Henning to challenge the Black Knight. Henning's horse is strong Kossan, dressed with a horse's head. In the first joust, the Black Knight wins. In the second, lances shatter and Henning wins, unmasking the Black Knight, who is Rebecca, a private school student. When lances shatter, a splinter under Kossan's collar kills her. Devastated, Roland remembers Kossan's desire to become a teacher and what she said when discussing *Gulliver's Travels*:

> The Kingdom of the Horses! One day we horses are going to go over the ocean the way Gulliver did and leave the land of the Yahoos. And we'll get them to stop fighting, we'll abolish war, and nobody will have to be at the bottom of the heap. We'll take control and there won't be any words for lying, for rich or poor. (163)

In the United States, too, there is discrimination against people of low economic level. In Frieda Friedman's *The Janitor's Girl*, twelve-year-old Sue Langer and her fourteen-year-old sister Laura are daughters of a New York City apartment house superintendent. Laura hates being a janitor's girl, but Sue figures that among seventy-four families, everyone will not be snobs, so she suggests to Laura, "Be sensible. . . . Probably some of the girls will like you and some won't. You'll have to wait and see" (22). When Sue shows an apartment to Rosalie Duke and her mother, Rosalie says, "It's too bad you're so tall and skinny. Or I could give you my dresses when I outgrow them, the way I do with the janitor's girl where we are now" (48). While she is a tenant, aloof Rosalie temporarily severs Sue's friendship with Cathy, another tenant. Sue befriends the handyman's daughter, Magda, a recent immigrant whose accent and clothes at first embarrass Sue. Later, Magda's cousin, Anton, shares her home, and the three become Saturday sightseeing chums. After Cathy joins them, Anton asks if three boys can come even if "one of the boys is foreign. He can hardly talk English. But he is smart and learning fast" (155). Sue asks, "What difference in the world does it make?" (155). Suddenly she realizes how she has changed in five months.

SUMMARY

It takes relatively mature readers to comprehend books dealing with humaneness, appreciation of differences, tolerance, and lack of prejudice; so it is not surprising that this chapter contains only four books for the early years. There are sixteen books recommended for the middle years and thirty-seven for the later years, or a total of fifty-seven books.

References

Anckarsvärd, Karin. *Doctor's Boy*. Translated from Swedish by Annabelle. Illustrated by Fermin Rocker. Harcourt, Brace & World, 1965. 156 p. (M) (Friendship)

Babbitt, Natalie. *Knee-Knock Rise*. Illustrated. Farrar, Straus & Giroux, 1970. 117 p. (M)

Bargar, Gary W. *Life . Is . Not . Fair* . Clarion Books, 1984. 174 p. (L)

Baudouy, Michel-Aimé. *More than Courage*. Translated from French by Marie Ponsot. Harcourt, Brace & World, 1961. 159 p. (L) (Cooperation, Friendship, Ingenuity)

Blue, Rose. *The Preacher's Kid*. Illustrated by Ted Lewin. Franklin Watts, 1975. 52 p. (M)

Cavanna, Betty. *Jenny Kimura*. William Morrow & Company, 1964. 217 p. (L)

Cohen, Barbara. *Molly's Pilgrim*. Illustrated by Michael J. Deraney. Lothrop, Lee & Shepard Books, 1983. 32 p. (E)

Cohen, Miriam. *See You Tomorrow, Charles*. Illustrated by Lillian Hoban. Greenwillow Books, 1983. Unpaged. (E)

Corcoran, Barbara. *This Is a Recording*. Illustrated by Richard Cuffari. Atheneum, 1971. 168 p. (L) (Maturing)

Coutant, Helen. *The Gift*. Illustrated by Vo-Dinh Mai. Alfred A. Knopf, 1983. Unpaged. (M) (Friendship)

deAngeli, Marguerite. *Bright April*. Illustrated. Doubleday & Company, 1946. 88 p. (M)

dePaola, Tomie. *Oliver Button Is a Sissy*. Illustrated. Harcourt Brace Jovanovich, 1979. Unpaged. (E)

Distad, Audree. *Dakota Sons*. Illustrated by Toby Chen. Harper & Row, Publishers, 1972. 159 p. (M) (Friendship)

Duncan, Lois. *Season of the Two-Heart*. Dodd, Mead & Company, 1964. 213 p. (L)

Estes, Eleanor. *The Hundred Dresses*. Illustrated by Louis Slobodkin. Harcourt, Brace & World, 1944. 81 p. (M)

Friedman, Frieda. *The Janitor's Girl*. Illustrated by Mary Stevens. William Morrow & Company, 1956. 157 p. (L) (Friendship)

Godden, Rumer. *The Diddakoi*. The Viking Press, 1972. 149 p. (L)

Greenwald, Sheila. *The Secret in Miranda's Closet*. Illustrated. Houghton Mifflin Company, 1977. 138 p. (M) (Friendship, Self-respect)

Hamilton, Virginia. *Willie Bea and the Time the Martians Landed*. Greenwillow Books, 1983. 208 p. (L) (Friendship)

Heide, Florence Parry. *Sound of Sunshine, Sound of Rain*. Illustrated by Kenneth Longtemp. Parents' Magazine Press, 1970. Unpaged. (E)

Hurwitz, Johanna. *The Rabbi's Girls*. Illustrated by Pamela Johnson. William Morrow & Company, 1982. 158 p. (L)

Jarrell, Randell. *The Animal Family*. Illustrated by Maurice Sendak. Pantheon Books, 1965. 180 p. (L) (Friendship)

Jones, Rebecca C. *Madeline and the Great (Old) Escape Artist*. E. P. Dutton, 1983. 88 p. (L)

Jones, Toeckey. *Go Well, Stay Well*. Harper & Row, Publishers, 1979. 202 p. (L) (Friendship)

Jones, Weyman. *Edge of Two Worlds*. Illustrated by J. C. Kocsis. The Dial Press, 1968. 143 p. (L) (Friendship, Maturing)

Kerr, Judith. *When Hitler Stole Pink Rabbit*. Coward, McCann & Geoghegan, 1972. 191 p. (L)

Kerr, M. E. *Little Little*. Harper & Row, Publishers, 1981. 183 p. (L)

Kullman, Harry. *The Battle Horse*. Translated from Swedish by George Blecher and Lone Thygesen-Blecher. Bradbury Press, 1981. 183 p. (L)

Lampman, Evelyn Sibley. *Go Up the Road*. Illustrated by Charles Robinson. Atheneum, 1972. 187 p. (L)

———. *Three Knocks on the Wall*. Atheneum Publishers, 1980. 182 p. (L)

———. *The Year of Small Shadow*. Harcourt Brace Jovanovich, 1971. 190 p. (L) (Friendship)

Lingard, Joan. *Across the Barricades*. Thomas Nelson, 1972. 160 p. (L)

———. *Into Exile*. Thomas Nelson, 1973. 176 p. (L)

———. *A Proper Place*. Thomas Nelson, 1975. 159 p. (L)

———. *The Twelfth Day of July: A Novel of Modern Ireland*. Thomas Nelson, 1970. 158 p. (L)

Little, Jean. *Look Through My Window*. Illustrated by Joan Sandin. Harper & Row, Publishers, 1970. 258 p. (L) (Friendship)

Maddock, Reginald. *Danny Rowley*. Little, Brown & Company, 1969. 183 p. (L)

Madison, Winifred. *Maria Luisa*. J. B. Lippincott Company, 1971. 187 p. (L) (Friendship)

Montgomery, Elizabeth Rider. *The Mystery of the Boy Next Door*. Illustrated by Ethel Gold. Garrard Publishing Company, 1978. 48 p. (M)

Neufeld, John. *Edgar Allan.* S. G. Phillips, 1968. 95 p. (L)

Neville, Emily Cheney. *Berries Goodman.* Harper & Row, Publishers, 1965. 178 p. (L) (Friendship)

Perl, Lila. *That Crazy April.* The Seabury Press, 1974. 188 p. (M)

Rich, Louise Dickinson. *Summer at High Kingdom.* Franklin Watts, 1975. 112 p. (L)

Roberts, Willo Davis. *Don't Hurt Laurie!* Illustrated by Ruth Sanderson. Atheneum, 1977. 166 p. (L)

Robinson, Barbara. *The Best Christmas Pageant Ever.* Illustrated by Judith Gwyn Brown. Harper & Row, 1972. 80 p. (M)

Robinson, Veronica. *David in Silence.* Illustrated by Victor Ambrus. J. B. Lippincott Company, 1965. 126 p. (L) (Friendship)

Sachs, Marilyn. *Peter and Veronica.* Illustrated by Louis Glanzman. Doubleday & Company, 1969. 174 p. (L) (Friendship)

Schatz, Letta. *Taiwo and Her Twin.* Illustrated by Elton Fax. McGraw-Hill, Inc., 1964. 128 p. (M) (Ingenuity)

Seredy, Kate. *The Singing Tree.* Illustrated. The Viking Press, 1967. 247 p. (L) (Friendship, Maturing)

Shotwell, Louisa R. *Roosevelt Grady.* Illustrated by Peter Burchard. The World Publishing Company, 1963. 151 p. (M) (Responsibility, Self-Respect)

Smith, Gene. *The Hayburners.* Illustrated by Ted Lewin. Delacorte Press, 1974. 64 p. (L)

Stolz, Mary. *The Mystery of the Woods.* Illustrated by Uri Shulevitz. Harper & Row, Publishers, 1964. 47 p. (M)

Sussman, Susan. *There's No Such Thing as a Chanukah Bush, Sandy Goldstein.* Illustrated by Charles Robinson. Albert Whitman & Company, 1983. 48 p. (M)

Uchida, Yoshiko. *Journey Home.* Illustrated by Charles Robinson. Atheneum, 1978. 131 p. (L) (Loyalty, Maturing)

———. *Journey to Topaz: A Story of the Japanese-American Evacuation.* Illustrated by Donald Carrick. Charles Scribner's Sons, 1971. 149 p. (L) (Courage, Loyalty)

Watson, Sally. *To Build a Land.* Illustrated by Lili Cassel. Holt, Rinehart & Winston, 1957. 255 p. (L) (Courage, Friendship, Maturing)

Wright, Betty Ren. *The Dollhouse Murders.* Holiday House, 1983. 149 p. (M)

VI

Ingenuity

Children's books emphasize the value ingenuity, through problem solving; creativity; unraveling of a mystery; exposing trickery; magic; and the trying of new techniques, products, locations, or languages. Varied approaches are apparent in a range of situations—from surviving danger to protesting fraud and from earning money to electioneering. Readers of all ages appreciate imaginative, adventurous characters who are resourceful and full of surprises.

BOOKS FOR EARLY YEARS

Janice May Udry's *The Sunflower Garden*, illustrated by Beatrice Darwin, shows how Pipsa, a young Algonkian girl in the premodern era, is enterprising enough to try something new. Father praises his four older sons but not her as she watches her little brother, Grey Squirrel. While visiting another village, Pipsa gathers sunflower seeds and learns how to use them, becoming the first at home to cultivate the flowers. She is hoeing her plants when she kills a rattlesnake that slithers toward her young brother. Afterwards, Father appreciates her enough to get her older brothers to guard her plants. Everyone calls her Sunflower Girl because, when the seeds are ripe, she bakes them in cakes and uses them to extract a fine hair oil.

Frederick by author-illustrator Leo Lionni shows how Frederick, a field mouse, works in a unique way while family members collect food. He gathers sun rays, colors, and words. Late in winter when supplies are low, other mice ask Frederick for his gatherings. "And as Frederick spoke of the sun, the four little mice began to feel warmer. . . . They saw the colors as clearly as if they had been painted in their minds" (21–23). Then Frederick recites a poem with expert use of language, alleviating winter's bitterness.

Creativity is evident in *Lion* by author-illustrator William Pène duBois. This fantasy says that long ago, heavenly artists would design each beast and send a pair to Planet Earth. In the sky, 104 artistic angels dip ermine brushes in gold paint, drawing in the animal factory, determining the sight and sound of each animal. It is the boss, Artist Foreman, who thinks of a new work, "lion." With colleagues' help, he paints the King of the Beasts, finally deciding the lion should roar, not say, "Peep peep!"

Readers find ingenuity through creativity in Elizabeth Coatsworth's *Lonely Maria,* illustrated by Evaline Ness. Little Maria lives with her parents and grandfather on a small West Indies island with the sea as her only playmate. When she tells Grandfather that she is lonely, he suggests she "make things happen" (unp). Using his advice, she sketches on the beach a house and garden, but when the sea washes her pictures away, she draws an elephant. If it is washed away, she plans to draw a giraffe and then a dragon, endless possibilities for make-believe companions.

Similarly, young Christina Katerina is imaginative with a discarded refrigerator box in Patricia Lee Gauch's *Christina Katerina & the Box,* illustrated by Doris Burn. Christina paints the box to look like a castle and when her friend Fats knocks it over, she converts it into a clubhouse. Fats collapses the roof, so Christina uses it as a racing car and after it flattens more, as a mansion floor. Her mother throws out the box just as Fats delivers two more from a washer and dryer.

Author-illustrator Holly Keller shows multiple ways of using a favorite blanket in *Geraldine's Blanket.* Geraldine, a young personified pig, loves a blanket Aunt Bessie gave her as a baby. As Geraldine gets older, so does the blanket, now in fragments from being dragged everywhere. When Aunt Bessie sends a new present, a pig doll named Rosa, Geraldine resourcefully makes a doll dress from the remains of the blanket. She says, "Now Rosa has the blanket and I have Rosa" (unp). Since she keeps the doll with her always, this is an acceptable way of constantly holding her favorite blanket.

In Charlotte Pomerantz's *The Half-Birthday Party,* illustrated by Dy Anne DiSalvo-Ryan, Daniel inspires creativity from his guests when he gives a half-birthday party for Katie, his six-month-old sister.

Impressed because Katie is standing alone for the first time, Daniel sends invitations to Mom, Dad, Grandma, her escort, Mr. Bangs, and Lily, a neighbor, asking half a present for the party and requesting, "You have to tell a whole story about the half present" (unp). Lily brings a slipper her dog chewed when he ruined her pair, Dad reads an original half-poem, and Mom presents an earring she did not lose when she met Dad. Grandma and Mr. Bangs give two halves of a birthday cake, and Daniel waits until it is dark to show his gift, a half-moon.

Young Adam is a problem solver in *We Never Get to Do Anything* by author-illustrator Martha Alexander. The boy begs Mother to take him swimming, but she replies, "Not today, I'm busy" (unp). After he tries to go on his own, she ties one end of a rope to his clothes and fastens the other end to a clothesline. He wriggles out of his clothes and walks downtown nude, looking for a place to swim before she finds him. Father builds him a sandbox, so when it rains, he converts it into a pool, swimming at last.

A jester solves problems by outwitting a king in Alice Schertle's *The April Fool*, illustrated by Emily Arnold McCully. The king has to be carried because he cannot find comfortable shoes, although he owns 159 pairs and has a mountain of discards. To forget sore feet and be amused, he hires a new jester each month but dismisses all except the one on duty in April. The April Fool promises the king the world's most comfortable shoes in exchange for his discarded pairs and gold, provided the king follows him alone. The king starts by wearing stiff new shoes that pinch his feet as he follows over rough cobblestones and climbs a tree. While the king naps, the April Fool removes the monarch's shoes and claims his prize with this scuffed pair. The king rewards him because now the shoes are "as comfortable as old friends" (unp). Then the April Fool goes to a new kingdom to open a shoe store.

Another king encourages problem solving in Benjamin Elkin's *Gillespie and the Guards*, illustrated by James Daugherty. A king is so proud of his three guards' superior vision that he promises a gold and diamond medal to anyone who tricks them. A little boy, Gillespie, enters the contest and daily brings from the palace past the guards wagonloads of worthless materials like leaves, sand, stones, grass, weeds, old cans, and bottles. The guards think he is foolish to take such things from the palace "when you can find all you want right on your own block" (25). After Gillespie claims his prize, he takes the king home with him and says, "Your Majesty, you remember that palace storeroom for all the toys? Well, I borrowed all these things from that storeroom and took them right past the Royal Guards!" (48–49). Gillespie wins the medal since the guards only consider the wagon contents and not the wagons themselves. In his garage are different shapes and designs of "dozens and dozens and dozens of little red wagons!" (52).

An emperor promises jewels for a solution to a problem in Jane Yolen's *The Seeing Stick*, illustrated by Remy Charlip and Demetra Maraslis. In ancient Peking, an emperor is sad because his only daughter, Princess Hwei Ming, who is blind and self-centered, cannot see beauty. A tattered old man helps her with his "seeing stick." As she begins to "see," illustrations appear in color (earlier ones are in black and white). The old man tells about his journey to Peking, carving each character and object on his stick and teaching the princess to "see" with her hands and heart. After she "feels the lines in the old man's face" (unp), she traces her father's tear-stained face. She explores, growing "eyes on the tips of her fingers" (unp), and assists others without eyesight, as the blind old man helped her.

Scotland is the setting for Munro Leaf's *Wee Gillis*, illustrated by Robert Lawson. Twelve-year-old Wee Gillis needs to plan his future occupation and home, so he tries living one year with Mother's relatives in the Lowlands and one year with Father's family in the Highlands. His lungs grow strong as he calls Lowland cows and holds his breath stalking Highland stags. He decides to use his lung power as a bagpiper while he "stays in his house half-way up the side of a medium-sized hill and plays the biggest bagpipes in all Scotland" (64).

Joan Lexau's *Benjie* and *Benjie on His Own*, both illustrated by Don Bolognese, show how a young black boy solves problems for Granny. In *Benjie*, before church and at a bakery later, Benjie and Granny pass friends with whom Granny converses. They are almost home when Granny misses an earring. They search the sidewalk before discouraged Granny goes home. Benjie checks the bakery and, sure enough, the earring is in their trash barrel. A bigger problem awaits the boy in *Benjie on His Own*. When he does not see Granny waiting for him after school, Benjie worries about her and walks home on his own. Finding Granny ill, he goes to a phone and gets Ray, a tall boy who can reach the phone, to call an ambulance. While Granny is in the hospital, Benjie stays with Ray.

Similarly, in Janice May Udry's *Mary Jo's Grandmother*, illustrated by Eleanor Mill, a grandchild, Mary Jo, resourcefully gets help for her ailing grandmother. While the girl visits Grandmother in the country, there is a big snowstorm. As she fixes breakfast, Grandmother hurts herself so badly she cannot stand, even with Mary Jo's help. The girl makes Grandmother comfortable, giving her a blanket, pillow, and cup of coffee. Since there is no telephone, Mary Jo walks to a main road, sees a snowplow, and asks the driver to give her father a message. Father arrives with a doctor, so Grandmother is safe.

Author-illustrator Martha Alexander shows in *Sabrina* how a girl on her first day in school tries to solve the problem of an unusual name, Sabrina. She tells her teacher to call her Susan and give her name away. Surprised at the number of girls who want to accept her offer, she concludes, "Who would be dumb enough to give away a beautiful name like Sabrina!" (unp).

In Osmond Molarsky's *Right Thumb, Left Thumb*, illustrated by John E. Johnson, young Victor learns to distinguish between left and right hands in an ingenious way. While she feeds her baby, Mother tells hungry Victor to go to the store alone for the first time to buy lunch food. She gives him directions, and since he will always turn right, she cleverly ties a string to his right thumb. At the store, the grocer fills Victor's order, gives him change, and moves the string to the boy's left thumb, explaining he will make left turns on his return. At home, Victor is proud of the solution to his problem.

Katie, who is about seven, also solves a directional problem in Muriel Stanek's *Left, Right, Left, Right*, illustrated by Lucy Hawkinson. Katie causes a traffic jam when she climbs the wrong side of the school steps. Asked to lead a parade and turn left, she turns right and marches alone while spectators laugh. Ashamed, she runs home to Grandma who gives her the same ring Mother wore on her right hand when she was young and had the identical need. Soon Katie can get along without the ring.

Taro Yashima's illustrations enhance June York Behrens's *Soo Ling Finds a Way*, a book whose very title indicates ingenuity. Young Soo Ling is disappointed when men announce a laundromat will occupy the building across from Grandfather Soo's hand laundry. Grandfather sadly affirms, "It is the new way, my child. We may have to close the Golden Lotus Hand Laundry" (unp). With determination, Soo Ling thinks, "There must be some way to help Grandfather Soo" (unp). She suggests Grandfather move his ironing board and magical iron to the big window in front of the laundry. Fascinated passersby include the owner of the new laundromat, who offers Grandfather a business partnership.

Nathan Zimelman's humorous *Mean Murgatroyd and the Ten Cats*, illustrated by Tony Auth, shows how young Arabella solves a problem. The neighbor's dog, Mean Murgatroyd, and other hounds he attracts, chase her ten cats when Arabella takes them for a walk. The girl wants a protective lion but cannot get one at a pet shop or the zoo, so she buys a lion costume which she wears, noting "The dogs never bothered Arabella's cats again" (unp).

Author-illustrator Gene Zion shows a clever way to earn money in *The Plant Sitter*. Young Tommy's father invites him to choose a local summer activity, so the boy brings plants home from neighbors leaving on vacations. He tells Father, "I'm a plant sitter and I get two cents a day for each plant I take care of" (unp). Father complains about living in a jungle because there is foliage in every room, growing fast with Tommy's good care. After dreaming about plants overgrowing the house, Tommy solves his problem by following directions in a library botany book. He trims plants, nurturing cuttings in small flower pots. Returning neighbors are glad their plants look well and are happy when Tommy gives their children rooted cuttings.

Personified animals solve problems too. In *Inch by Inch* by author-illustrator Leo Lionni, a small inchworm saves himself from being eaten by a bird. He does this by convincing his predator that he is useful for measuring things. He almost becomes the prey of a nightingale who says, "Measure my song or I'll eat you for breakfast" (19). The inchworm's solution is to urge the nightingale to sing while he "measured and measured until he inched out of sight" (23).

Doctor De Soto by author-illustrator William Steig features a mouse dentist, Doctor De Soto. Although a small creature, Doctor De Soto finds a unique way to work on larger animals' teeth. While his patients sit on the floor, Doctor De Soto uses a ladder or hoist to reach their mouths. He advertises, "Cats and other dangerous animals not accepted for treatment" (unp). When a sly fox is his patient, Doctor De Soto puts in a new tooth but glues the threatening animal's jaws together with a formula that will wear off after the fox's departure.

A Parisian mouse, Anatole, spurred by his wife, Doucette, engages in problem solving in Eve Titus's *Anatole* and *Anatole and the Cat*. In *Anatole*, the mouse is depressed to know he is unpopular with most people. Doucette says, "If only we could give people something in return" (16). That thought spurs Anatole to work in a cheese factory where he leaves notes on cheeses, recommending ingredients to perfect them. In *Anatole and the Cat*, a cat threatens the mouse's position as vice-president in charge of cheese tasting. The cat is so frightening that Anatole puts wrong suggestions on cheese, but his confusion causes a popular new cheese. Thinking about the cat, he says, "*Voila*! If a man may build a mouse-trap, then a mouse may build a cat-trap!" (23) He bells the cat, avoiding its warning sound.

In Russell Hoban's *A Bargain for Frances*, illustrated by Lillian Hoban, a badger, Frances, retaliates for the trickery of a playmate, Thelma. Frances is the loser when she agrees to no "backsies" or refunds as she buys Thelma's plastic tea dishes with money saved for a china set. After Thelma buys a china set, Frances phones her, asking if she can keep what is in her plastic sugar bowl. Believing that is where she put her birthday money, Thelma agrees to trade back. Although the two complain about being deceived, they continue to be friends.

A second book written and illustrated by Lillian Hoban, *Arthur's Honey Bear*, repeats the idea of trickery in a trade. Arthur and his younger sister Violet, personified monkeys, offer old toys in a tag sale. Arthur reluctantly discards his teddy, Honey Bear, and Violet purchases it for thirty-one cents, a coloring book with crayons, and a half-eaten box of Cracker Jacks. With ingenuity, Arthur keeps control over the bear, declaring, "I am your uncle, Honey Bear. . . . And do you know what uncles do? . . . Uncles play with their nephews, and they take them out for treats" (59–60). Then he spends the money from Violet on ice cream cones for the three, knowing his sister and he will eat Honey Bear's.

Stanley, a mouse-like animal, influences his sister Rhoda in *Stanley & Rhoda* by author-illustrator Rosemary Wells. When Rhoda pretends to be stung by a bee, Stanley cleverly describes how Daddy will fix it with a needle, tweezers, or boiling butter. After he suggests Dr. Zuckerman's new splinter drills as a remedy, Rhoda declares, "It's better now, Stanley. . . . It will be perfect if you kiss it" (27–28).

Curley Cat uses ingenuity to control Baby, his brother, in Pauline Watson's *Curley Cat Baby-sits*, illustrated by Lorinda Bryan Cauley. Curley gets Baby down from a tree by promising a surprise. When Baby jumps into a lake but cannot swim, Curley calls, "Catch the vine and get a free ride!" (unp). Then the older cat throws a vine to Baby, bringing his brother to the shore. Finally, Curley entices Baby to return home by playing tag with him.

In A *Holiday for Mister Muster*, author-illustrator Arnold Lobel shows the way wise Mister Muster, a loving zoo keeper, gets animals he has driven to the seashore to board a homeward-bound bus. The beasts are having so much fun, they do not want to leave. Mister Muster puts on a disguise and successfully baits the animals into thinking the bus is another amusement park ride. "They [the animals] all wanted to try the most exciting ride in the whole amusement park and quickly climbed on the bus" (26).

Dragons highlight the last two picture storybooks, beginning with *Faint George* by author-illustrator Robert E. Barry. Through hard work, Faint George gets the armor and castle he believes he must have to be a brave knight. The last requisite he thinks is to slay a dragon. After his first attempt with a small dragon fails, he finds a bigger dragon but cannot kill him. Instead, he leashes him and rides him as he seeks adventure.

The second dragon story is *How Droofus the Dragon Lost His Head* by author-illustrator Bill Peet. Droofus, a four-year-old sensitive dragon, worries when a king, wanting to mount a dragon head on his castle wall, offers a reward of a hundred golden quadrooples for the beast's capture. Droofus, hiding from pursuers, finds a stray lamb, Flossie, and sleeps beside it. After discovering them, a young shepherd does not seek the reward, thinking, "If he wouldn't hurt my lamb then he must be a good dragon. So I'll never tell anyone where he lives" (19). When the shepherd's family uses Droofus to move boulders, plow fields, weed, sow seeds, cut firewood, and act as a scarecrow on their farm, they conclude, "He's worth a lot more than a hundred quadrooples" (35). There is a creative ending which satisfies everyone because the shepherd's father collects thirty quadrooples every time the king projects Droofus's neck through an opening, displaying a live dragon head on his wall.

BOOKS FOR MIDDLE YEARS

Elmer Elevator's son tells how his father, as a young boy, outwitted jungle animals to free a baby dragon in Ruth Stiles Gannett's "*My Father's Dragon*." On Wild Island, other animals enslave a dragon to transport them across a river. Elmer distracts the tigers with chewing gum; the rhinoceros with a toothbrush and paste; the lion with a comb, brush, and ribbon for his mane; the gorilla with magnifying glasses; and the crocodiles with lollipops. He ties lollipops on the crocodile tail tips, creating a single-file formation, or crocodile bridge, on which he crosses the river to rescue the dragon. Elmer escapes by obeying the dragon's command, "Hurry and cut my ropes, and I will fly you to safety" (85).

In Joan Carris's *Witch-cat*, Rosetta, the cat of the Greymalkins' Order, follows witch Gwynellan's instructions to go to a small Ohio town and tell Gwenyth Jean Markham she has witch powers. The cat cannot speak but communicates with human beings in a cat-like way. When Gwenyth understands, she tests her witchcraft and learns that if her powers are not wisely used, she can harm others, like turning off lights at a busy intersection. Gwenyth sees a letter from ancestor Gwynellan which advises, "Never waste yourself on small magic" (153). Guided by the cat, Gwenyth performs large magic by saving a drowning girl.

James Thurber's *Many Moons*, illustrated by Louis Slobodkin, portrays a person clever enough to ask a girl how she perceives the moon when she demands it. Ten-year-old Princess Lenore, ill from overeating, tells the king she will be well if she can have the moon. The king's wise men cannot grant her request, but the court jester asks how the moon appears to her. She says, "It is just a little smaller than my thumbnail for when I hold my thumbnail up at the moon, it just covers it. . . . It's made of gold, of course, silly" (unp). The court jester brings a tiny gilded moon and chain from the royal goldsmith to the princess and she recovers. That night, the court jester asks the princess how the moon can be around her neck and also in the sky. Princess Lenore replies, "When I lose a tooth, a new one grows in its place, doesn't it? . . . And it is the same way with the moon" (unp).

Annie, a Navajo child in Miska Miles's *Annie and the Old One*, tries to prevent a loved one's death by literally interpreting a warning. Annie, who is fond of Grandmother, watches her mother weave a rug. Grandmother tells the family she will return to Mother Earth when the rug is complete. Annie thinks she is preventing the Old One's death by unraveling the rug, but Grandmother explains the inevitable to her. Then Annie learns to accept death as part of life.

Mary Perrine's *Nannabah's Friend* tells how a lonely young

Navajo shepherdess, grazing Grandmother's sheep alone for the first time, creates clay playmates. From the red mud near a pool, she makes two dolls, "Baby Brother" and "Little Sister," and a *hogan*, or home, for them. She leaves these toys behind and returns the next day to find a girl playing with them. This is the beginning of their friendship.

For mood contrast, Thomas Rockwell offers humor in *How to Eat Fried Worms*, which shows how Alan Phelps, after betting Billy Forrester fifty dollars he cannot eat a worm daily for fifteen days, plots against him. Conniving with Joe O'Hara, Alan tries to sicken Billy by gluing two crawlers together before Billy catches them. Alan and Joe take Billy to a baseball game and stuff him so full of hot dogs, they think without an appetite, he will forget to eat a worm—but he remembers. After they lock Billy in a barn, he escapes. They even try to scare him by forging the name of Billy's doctor on a note they write warning of death from eating worms. However, Billy, who cleverly disguises the worm taste with condiments, wins the bet and declares, "I even like the *taste* now" (116).

Eight-year-old Maggie Rose Bunker is a spunky model for her lazy six siblings and parents in Ruth Sawyer's *Maggie Rose: Her Birthday Christmas*. Maggie's birthday is on December 24, but because her family is poor, she never celebrates her birthday or Christmas. All summer, Maggie picks raspberries and sells them to earn party money so that she can invite villagers who have been kind to her family. When Maggie goes to the woods to retrieve forty dollars she's saved and hidden, a tramp sees her, takes her money, and escapes. Her parents and two older brothers change enough to get jobs to replace the money. By December, they save enough money to help Maggie Rose decorate their house and invite friends to a party with delicious food.

In the black urban community is another poor girl, nine-year-old Lilly Etta Allen, who uses ingenuity to help the evicted Brown family in Sharon Bell Mathis's *Sidewalk Story*. Evicted for being three months arrears in rent are Mrs. Louise Brown and her seven children, including Tanya, Lilly Etta's best friend. Although the girls' mothers are good friends, Mrs. Allen seems scared to object when the marshal puts Mrs. Brown's furniture on the sidewalk. Lilly Etta goes with Tanya to a phone booth and makes a futile protest call to the police. Then she calls a newspaper and is lucky enough to speak to Frazier, a newsman, who says, "The only thing unusual in all this is you. How old did you say you were?" (46) It rains that night, so Lilly Etta covers the furniture at the curb and sleeps on the covers to hold them down. Frazier photo-graphs her there and prints a story which gets Mrs. Brown a job, nursery care for her young children, and a larger apartment.

In Ellen Conford's *Lenny Kandell*, nine-year-old Leonard ("Lenny") Kandell, who lives with his sister and widowed mother in Flushing, New York, repays a debt resourcefully. He needs to pay for cleaning his Aunt Harriet's furpiece that he soiled in a game, so he announces a dime charge for a Sunday afternoon show on the roof of his apartment building. He is to be the shows's comic but worries that a bully, Maurice ("Mousie") Blatner, will attend. Sure enough, Mousie comes, threatening a rooftop fight. Facing his forty-two guests, Lenny later reports, "I got up and walked on the ledge and told him to come and get me" (116). Frightened Mousie leaves and never bothers Larry again.

Corinne Gerson in *Son for a Day* tells about another New York lad, eleven-year-old Danny Turner who helps "zoodaddies" (divorced fathers who spend a custody day on the weekend with a son at the Bronx Zoo.) Danny understands their problems since his own parents are divorced. The zoodaddies appreciate the way Danny eases communica-tion with their sons, and most of them want him to join them again. He keeps a weekend appointment book for zoo visits, other sightseeing, and dining with these new friends. After he helps a "zoomommy," Gretchen Anderson, she invites him to speak on her television program where she explains to the audience, "I can only tell you that he's like another precious son to me. Son for a day" (110).

Appelsap, New York is the setting for Janet Taylor Lisle's *The Dancing Cats of Appelsap*, a humorous tale of ingenuity in keeping a store open. Shy, ten-year-old Melba Morris and old Angela Toonie, a clerk who coddles a hundred cats in Jiggs's Drug Store, lead a cats' parade through the town to prevent permanent closing of the store. When curious folks follow the cats, they see them dance to the unusual guitar music of the store's owner, old Jackson Jiggs. Taken by surprise, Mr. Jiggs sends people home, and the humane society collects the cats. The local newspaper, however, gets the cats out in time to restage their dance. Viewers become regular customers, so the store continues. Melba gets publicity in *Guinness Book of World Records* about the cats' weekly dance, and Mr. Jiggs announces plans to build a cat dormitory. He says, "We've got to smarten up if we're to be a national landmark" (163).

Athena V. Lord's *Today's Special: Z.A.P. and Zoe* presents six humorous episodes that take place in another small New York town, Cohoes, in the summer of 1939. An eleven-year-old Greek-American boy, Zachary Athanasius Poulos (Z.A.P.), has to baby-sit with his precocious four-year-old sister Zoe so that Mother can work in the family's luncheonette. One night, Zach takes Zoe to a carnival, buying two bingo cards—one for him and one for Zoe, who is a distance from him. During the game, Zoe stands on a table and shrieks in Greek, "Zaharia, *prepi na kano pee-pee!*" (86). Everyone laughs and blushing Zach takes her behind a bush. Then Zach learns most of the vendors are Greek. One gives Zoe free popcorn and tells Zach to say *parakalo* (please) at other booths. Acting as a shill, Zach gets a free ride for Zoe and himself on an elephant, and he wins a teddy bear for Zoe.

Four of Dale Fife's books about Lincoln Farnum show him to be a resourceful, black New York City lad. The first one, *Who's in Charge of Lincoln?* begins the series. This book tells how eight-year-old Lincoln solves problems on his own when his mother is in a hospital to have a baby. His baby-sitter cannot tend him and his sisters are away. While the boy is outside playing, a man tosses him a brown paper sack and gives him fifteen dollars to watch his "lunch" until he returns. Lincoln sees money in the sack, tries to deposit it in a bank, and finds the bank closed. He wants to tell Officer Roberts, but the police are too busy with a robbery to listen to a child. He uses the fifteen dollars for round-trip fare to Washington, D.C., hoping to find his oldest sister, Sara, whose class is visiting the capitol. He still has not seen her when he is at the Lincoln Memorial, so he leaves the money there where authorities find it, and he returns home.

Who'll Vote for Lincoln? by Dale Fife, shows Lincoln Farnum running for class president. When his opponent, a bully called "Mooch," distributes free peanuts, Lincoln says that he will buy everyone a chocolate shake if he wins. He solves his self-created problem by confessing his false promise to the class before they vote, and he is surprised when he is elected. Later, after he helps expose a bookie joint, he gets permission for a class garden next to school.

Fife's *What's New, Lincoln?* tells how Lincoln uses a Christmas gift, a printing set, to start a neighborhood newspaper, *The Plum Street Informer*. Cartoons in that paper lead to the identity of a phantom prowler who has been stealing drugstore items. The cartoonist, Bunky Hanson, draws a bull dog, Fats Butch, looking heavier after he leaves the store than when he arrives. Lincoln shows Officer Roberts, and they find four-year-old Willie Woods, the druggist's son, is angry that a dog is not allowed in the store. He has been hiding things under the dog's coat. The druggist rewards Lincoln, the detective, telling him, "I guess I can spare that empty space in back of my store for a meeting place for the Plum Street Boys Athletic Club" (58).

Finally, Dale Fife's *What's the Prize, Lincoln?* depicts Lincoln Farnum, about nine years old, in the neighborhood club occupying the drugstore's fenced-in backyard and unused coal bin. To get club equipment, Lincoln suggests entering contests for prizes. The best thing he wins is a camera. Lincoln and his friends have a flea market in front of the drugstore to sell prizes and raise money for the club. The boys photograph the flea market with Lincoln's new camera, and the camera store displays their snapshots, bringing honor to the druggist for sponsoring the boys. Although previously denying them use of his cellar, the druggist now has a change of heart.

Eleven-year-old Janie Golden is also enterprising in Susan Beth Pfeffer's *Kid Power.* When her father says he will pay half the cost of a new bicycle for Susan and her thirteen-year-old sister Carol if the girls earn the rest, Susan starts a money-making business, " 'Kid Power.' No job too big or small" (11). As business expands, she gives assignments to friends, like a gardening job to Lisa, and she keeps 10 percent of their wages. She thinks, "Earning money really seemed easy when you had other people doing it for you" (117).

Having acquired a ten-speed bicycle, twelve-year-old Janie Golden is saving for a home computer in Susan Beth Pfeffer's sequel, *Kid Power Strikes Back.* On winter walks Janie helps aged people, like a man she calls Mr. Rotten since he seems to hate everybody. He does help her trick Johnny Richards, who is stealing her snow-shoveling jobs by pretending to be part of Kid Power. She gets her sister Carol and her best friend Lisa to tell Johnny that Mrs. Dell pays twenty-five for shoveling her long driveway. After shoveling, Johnny tries to collect, expecting twenty-five dollars, but he only receives twenty-five cents. Johnny finally agrees, "You shovel your turf, I shovel mine" (111). Janie's agency is such a success that she inspires Mother to start "Something Extra," involving ten women who cater and organize a town carnival with the help of Mr. Rotten's daughter, Mayor Rhazhnophski.

Eleven-year-old Duffy Moon also opens a no-job-is-too-tough-for-us business in Jean Robinson's *The Strange but Wonderful Cosmic Awareness of Duffy Moon*. To combat being short in stature, Duffy buys Doctor Flamel's course on "cosmic awareness" and says that his success is due to projecting what he wants to happen. However, Duffy's partner and best friend, Peter, thinks success comes from Duffy's creativity and the fact that both boys willingly tackle every job. That is why Duffy Moon, Incorporated competes favorably with a junior high odd-job organization. Duffy finally concedes the limitations of cosmic awareness when it does not cure an injured parakeet.

Two other best friends, fourth graders Adam Tyler and Noah Carter, are resourceful in spending Saturdays together, as noted in Ann Sharpless Bond's *Saturdays in the City*. In a theater, they find a diamond ring in their popcorn. They realize a thief from a nearby robbed jewelry store gave them his popcorn by mistake, and they help catch the criminal. When they are at the airport, they find a wallet with two boarding passes and enjoy a free round-trip flight with lunch. While they visit a television studio, a commentator interviews them on the air. They promote city institutions so well that the production manager says, "I bet people will be lining up for the zoo and the Natural History Museum" (146).

Ilse Kleberger's *Grandmother Oma* features a grandmother who lives in Germany with her son and his wife, helping in a wise way with their five children: Ingeborg, Jan, Bridget, Peter, and the baby. The youngsters invite friends to watch Oma roller-skate. Grandmother helps Ingeborg become a veterinary student. When Jan wants to run away to America, he is surprised that Oma boards his same train and pretends she wants to accompany him. He confesses that he does not know English and agrees when she suggests postponing the trip. Oma even saves Jan's friend who falls through the ice while skating.

China seems to be the setting of Patricia Miles Martin's *The Pointed Brush*, a tale of a student who, with ingenuity, teaches his father the value of education. Chung Yee, Chung's sixth son, tells Elder Uncle that he is sad since he, who is least needed in the fields, is the only family member going to school. A farmer, Ling Po, gets authorities to arrest Elder Uncle for stealing his water buffalo. When his older brothers cannot free their uncle, Chung Yee uses his pointed brush to write a letter which he puts on the village wall asking the elder fathers to free his innocent uncle and find the missing animal. The boy, acting without permission, suffers when Father disciplines him. However, the elders free his uncle. Then Father says, "The man who knows the written word has strength. . . . All of our sons shall go to the teacher" (unp). In the end, the farmer's water buffalo wanders back.

Two imaginative eleven-year-old schoolmates, April Hall and Melanie Ross, originate a game about ancient Egypt in Zilpha Keatley Snyder's *The Egypt Game*. April, a new white girl, plays with her black neighbors, Melanie and a younger brother, Marshall; a Chinese child, Elizabeth Chung; Ken Kamaki; and Toby Alvillar. They amuse themselves in the abandoned storage yard behind the Curio Shop of the Professor, Dr. Huddleston, an anthropologist. The Professor develops new interests after watching them, and his vigil prevents a murder. Melanie says of their make-believe world, "Imagining games are just about all I ever play because most of the time I never have anybody to play with" (32–33). The story ends as April and Melanie plan a gypsy game.

Zilpha Keatley Snyder also has quick-witted characters in her trilogy, *The Headless Cupid*, *The Famous Stanley Kidnapping Case*, and *Blair's Nightmare*. In *The Headless Cupid*, Professor Jeff Stanley has four children: eleven-year-old David, six-year-old Janie, and four-year-old twins, Blair and Esther. When he marries a divorced artist, Molly, with an eleven-year-old daughter, Amanda, they move to a haunted country house with a headless cupid carving on the stairs. Amanda acts as if she has occult gifts, but Blair actually does since he talks to animals and to Harriette who lived in the house long ago. In a seance, Amanda initiates the children into occultism with nine ordeals, such as avoid touching anything with your hands. David cleverly suggests the use of gloves for this ordeal and helps his siblings cope with each ordeal. A poltergeist house visitor turns out to be Amanda.

In Snyder's *The Famous Stanley Kidnapping Case*, Molly's Italian uncle leaves her his Florence house and money that must be spent in Italy, so the Stanley family moves to Italy for a year. When Amanda brags that her father is rich, poor Italians kidnap her but have to take the other siblings as well. The children escape after resourcefully exploiting the kidnappers' religious superstition. The book ends with the family once more united in Italy.

Blair's Nightmare by Snyder takes place in California two years after *The Headless Cupid*. Jeff forbids the children to have a dog but at night, Blair sees a huge one he calls Nightmare. Its owner locks this Irish wolfhound in a dark shed during the day. Another dog lover, big fourteen-year-old Peter Garvey, visits Amanda, secretly giving the children kibbles dog food. They resourcefully hide Nightmare's food in pillow cases, so their parents are none the wiser. Finally, the parents welcome Nightmare into the family.

It often takes ingenuity to survive, as fantasy and realistic fiction depict. William Steig's fantasy, *Abel's Island*, which takes place in 1907, shows a personified mouse, Abel, who tries to retrieve his wife's scarf in a storm, but winds sweep him from his hometown, Mossville, to a deserted island. He tells himself, "It was his family tradition never to give up but to keep gnawing away until problems were solved" (42). Though unaccustomed to work, he manages to gather his own food and survive for a year until he can swim back to his wife, Amanda.

More serious is Uri Orlev's realistic fiction, *The Island on Bird Street*, a World War II tale set in the Warsaw ghetto. An eleven-year-old Jewish boy, Alex, suffers when his mother disappears and the German army "selects" his father for an unknown destination. Father's farewell is a whispered message to Alex to wait for him in an abandoned building at 78 Bird Street, so Alex survives the harsh winter of 1943–44 in that building with a white mouse, Snow, as his only friend. With ingenuity, he takes a homemade rope ladder to the jagged third-floor remains of an apartment hidden from the street. With further cunning, he lowers himself to forage for food and fuel in the abandoned ghetto. Alex kills a German soldier attacking Jewish partisans and helps a wounded partisan recover. Just in time, as Germans raze the ghetto wall, Alex's father returns and the boy's lonely vigil ends.

BOOKS FOR LATER YEARS

Keith Robertson's *Ice to India* is historical fiction about a sea captain, John Mason, whose crew includes Hooker Hance, a man with a hook in place of a left hand. Undecided about what cargo to carry, the owner accepts Hance's brilliant suggestion to load ice packed in sawdust from wintry New England and carry it to hot India. Although agents of Mason's enemy, Traskill, join the crew and wreak havoc on board, Hance ruins their plot and fights them with his hook. One of Traskill's henchmen kills Traskill before authorities can punish him. Mason delivers the ice for a good price and avoids bankruptcy.

In another book by Keith Robertson, *Henry Reed's Baby-sitting Service*, adolescent Henry Reed spends the summer in Grover's Corner,

New Jersey with his Uncle Al and Aunt Mable. A neighbor, Midge Glass, becomes his partner in a baby-sitting service. A lanky lad with a lively imagination, Henry suffers through a variety of clients. Bespectacled young Belinda, for example, has a passion for hiding until Midge and Henry track her with walkie-talkies and cure her wanderlust. As a tribute to their handling of emergencies, the Surburban Woman's Club names the two partners' enterprise their Business of the Month.

Arthur D. Stapp's *The Fabulous Earthworm Deal* tells how a plucky junior-high student, Marshall ("Marsh"), raises and sells earthworms, assisted by a promotional friend, J. T. At first, Marsh sells worms to fishermen who pass his home en route to the docks. When Marsh posts signs showing customers his house, fishermen arrive at 3 A.M., so Father orders the removal of all signs. Undaunted, Marsh builds a backyard pit in which he adds 4,000 breeder worms before he launches a national mail-order worm business. When a power failure blacks out lights that have been shining on the pit to keep worms within bounds, most worms escape. Marsh's four-year-old brother, Paul, runs away, feeling he is to blame, but Marsh brings him home. J. T. cleverly directs national television attention to the great worm escape.

Several books in John Fitzgerald's Great Brain series, set in a Utah village, Adenville, in 1898, stress resourceful scheming by twelve-year-old Tom Fitzgerald, known as the Great Brain. In *The Great Brain Reforms*, Tom, home for school summer vacation, becomes a genius at making money through trickery. Tom builds a wooden raft and charges peers for river rides. One rainy afternoon, Tom and two other boys on the raft almost drown. Then Tom's younger brother and frequent victim, John, joins neighborhood boys in giving Tom a mock trial, citing his avarice. "Judges" hear Tom say, "When this trial started, I thought it was a big joke and that my great brain would make you all look like fools. Instead, for the first time in my life, I see myself as others see me" (160).

John Fitzgerald's sequel, *The Great Brain Does It Again*, shows that Tom's reform is short-lived. In eight humorous episodes, Tom continues to be a clever swindler. For example, Tom wagers against village children that an old mustang, Dusty, can win a race with Parley's fast quarter horse. The quarter horse could win a quarter-mile race, but Tom makes the course one mile, and Dusty has more endurance, so Tom wins the bet. When Tom becomes thirteen, he has to work for Father, and John, his brother, complains that life is less exciting. John concludes, "Things had been so darn dull since Tom started working that if he wanted to bet I couldn't jump over our barn, I would have taken the bet" (128).

Judie Angell's *A Word from Our Sponsor or My Friend Alfred* depicts twelve-year-old Alfred Caro, Gillian Tenser, and Rudy Sugarman from Briarfield School in Manhattan ingeniously exposing consumer fraud. When Alfred's six-year-old brother, Douglas, has chicken pox, Father brings him a Sandalwood Sam drinking cup given away with Choco-Rich syrup, an account in the advertising agency that employs Mr. Caro. Alfred notices that the cup fades after one dishwasher cycle, and he conducts tests to show that the cup's lead content makes it dangerous inside and outside. Mr. Caro gives Alfred's formal report to his boss who reacts with scorn. Seeing the cup advertised on television, Alfred and his friends call the Food and Drug Administration and the one consumer group that listens to children, Help Our Children Grow. That group corroborates the cup's lead concentration, exposing facts on a television program in which the three children participate with reluctant Mr. Caro. The next day, the main boss fires Mr. Caro but rehires him and fires his immediate superior instead. The ending is positive, for "Alfred proved that kids can have clout after all" (138).

John McNamara's *Revenge of the Nerd* shows how fourteen-year-old Bertram Cummings avenges himself against a group of Master's High School students who call him "nerd." Although he is the smartest in his class, Bertram causes a small fire when simply preparing toast, and he makes a fool of himself in trying to talk to a girl he admires, beautiful Louise Baker. In a science class, when Bertram exposes Michael ("Mike") Godey, who claims to have seen a UFO, Mike retaliates with help from Charles ("Chuck") Benson and Dennis Hutchinson. They send Bertram a love note with Louise's forged signature. Bertram responds, but the three boys and Louise laugh at him. Then Bertram uses his original science class Big Project which enables him to appear on any television set within five miles of his home. Dressed in a green costume, pretending to be Non of Zenka, an alien from the Andromeda galaxy, he talks on television to each of the four who had laughed at him. He makes this request:

You must set up a receiver at the meeting of . . . student council. We plan to make contact on what you earthlings call

Tuesday. . . . Our message is of the utmost importance, and
your help will be rewarded. (78)

At the meeting, Bertram shows how gullible the four are, becomes a
school hero, and later establishes rapport with Louise.

Avi's *S.O.R. Losers* portrays the clever way in which a losing
South Orange River (S.O.R.) seventh-grade soccer team accepts the
fact that their players are good students but poor athletes. The book is a
humorous spoof on sports as the basis of school spirit. Ed Sitrow is a
substitute player whom the fledgling coach names as goaltender and
captain, only because he is tall. Ed refers to his teammates when he
says, "I mean, we are good, good at *lots* of things. . . . Doesn't bother
me to lose at sports. At least, it didn't bother me until I let other people
make me bothered" (77). Before the final game, after losing all previous
games, Ed and a teammate secretly add on their shirts below the printed
school initials, S.O.R., the word, "Losers." When the team suffers
defeat again, the captain cheers that they are "Champions of the bloody
bottom" (89). He says, "Aced it. *Our* way" (90).

In New York in 1940, seventeen-year-old Frances Green, who is
intelligent yet unhappy, looks upon her good-natured eighth-grade
brother, Marv, as a daydreamer in Marilyn Sachs's *Marv*. Marv thinks
he is a failure because Frances belittles him, and she challenges him to
finish a useful project for someone other than himself. Then Marv
creates an unusual pond, bridge, weather vane, and revolving birdbath
in his front yard. He announces, "I made it for you, Frances" (156).
Although she is dismayed, he is pleasantly surprised since his project
gives so much summer fun to neighborhood children.

A pretty, tall, sixteen-year-old farm girl, Trish Harker, is a sophomore who conducts an ingenious campaign to be Pratt High's junior
class president in Lael Littke's *Trish for President*. The reason Trish is a
candidate is to make her ambitious opponent and unrequited love,
Jordan Amery, notice her. Jordan likes strong women and his campaign
manager, unscrupulous Susu Smith, is obnoxiously strong. Trish's
manager, Roger Gregory ("R. G.") Cole, and her poster-painting best
friend, Dannalee Davis, help Trish create a campaign mystery. Trish
announces a treasure chest to be opened on election day and a slogan,
"The real treasure is in the chest" (157). The treasure consists of
enormous dollar bills with Trish's picture instead of Washington's and
the inscription, "The real treasure of Pratt High is Trish" (159). After

her opponent displays posters of Trish and her dog, Snyde, labeled "The Harker and the Barker," R. G. brings Snyde to rallies in disguise as "Aunt Beulah" with blonde wig and shawl, a mascot used successfully the previous year by Trish's brother, Marv. When opponents put ice cubes under Aunt Beulah's wig, the dog runs away with sophomores in pursuit. Ninety percent write in Aunt Beulah's name for president, "she" declines, and the class awaits a runoff.

In M. E. Kerr's *Dinky Hocker Shoots Smack*, an obese fourteen-year-old Brooklyn Heights girl, Susan ("Dinky") Hocker, tries a dramatic way of announcing her problems to her parents, especially her mother. Mrs. Hocker donates her time to rehabilitating drug addicts, failing in her own home with her niece, Natalia Line, who has been in a schizophrenic therapeutic center, and with her overweight daughter, who is not a drug addict. At a dance, Natalia dates Tucker Woolf and Dinky dates obese P. John Knight. P. John and Dinky later join Weight Watchers, and he is successful. But Mrs. Hooker sabotages Dinky's reducing efforts by ejecting P. John from her home since he is conservative politically. When Mrs. Hocker interferes between Natalia and Tucker, Natalia retreats to a schizoid's compulsive rhyming. The night the community honors Mrs. Tucker at a banquet with a Heights Samaritan Award for working with ex-addicts, fat Dinky, tired of parental indifference, uses ingenuity. In bright Day-Glo paint, she sprays a message, "Dinky Hocker Shoots Smack!" (183) on walls near the banquet hall. Tucker explains to Dinky's father that his daughter should be called Susan, adding, "People who don't shoot smack have problems, too" (194). Then the Hockers show they care about their daughter by taking her on a European trip.

Solving a mystery requires ingenuity, as Isabelle Holland indicates in *The Empty House*. Fifteen-year-old Betsy Smith and her twelve-year-old brother, Roddy, search for clues that may free their divorced father, Geoffrey Smith, now jailed for tax fraud. The Smith children are staying with wealthy maternal relatives, Uncle Paul and Aunt Marian MacTiernan, so "Aunt Mayflower" worries that snobbish friends may learn about her former brother-in-law. Friendly seventeen-year-old Ted Lockwood becomes Betsy's romantic interest. Unfortunately, his father, Max Lockwood, has written newspaper columns that helped jail Mr. Smith. In an apparently empty house, Betsy and Roddy meet two disabled recluses, seventy-eight-year-old Ellen Whitelaw and her mentally impaired fifty-year-old daughter, Miranda, friends of Ted. After the young people learn that the accountant, who unscrupulously tried to defraud the Whitelaws, also testified against Smith, they try to clear Father's name.

In Rosemary Wells's *The Man in the Woods*, Helen Curragh, a fourteen-year-old New Bedford, Massachusetts high school newspaper volunteer, solves a mystery, with the help of Pinky Levy, a colleague. They see a woman and child nearly killed as a figure throws stones and hits cars. The figure, humming "The Wanderer" melody, goes into the woods, and Helen follows him. Police arrest a delinquent, Stubby Atlas, refusing to listen to Helen and Pinky who search for the guilty figure. When Helen and Stubby get notes typed on an ancient Thurber typewriter, they go to the library and historical society, learning a Thurber typewriter may be at the Lucy Fairchild Mansion Museum. (Fairchild had been a traitor to the north, storing Confederacy supplies, including morphine, in her basement.) Helen and Pinky locate a drug-dealing punk rocker who had broken into the Fairchild mansion, and they get police to arrest him, clearing Stubby.

Charlotte MacLeod's *We Dare Not Go A-Hunting* tells about a red-headed, blue-eyed adolescent sleuth, Molly Bassett, in a New England resort, Netaquid Island, during the summer of 1932. The previous summer, wealthy six-year-old Annette Sotherby pretended to be kidnapped for a week, her father paid a ransom, and she returned. Mr. Sotherby gets wealthy friends to boycott hiring islanders, kidnapper suspects. The Truells, however, hire an islander, Molly, to baby-sit their four-year-old son, Sammy, while they are away. Mrs. Truell returns, allowing Sammy to ride in a runabout boat with Annette and her "psychiatrist," Dr. Putnam. Then kidnappers seize both children. It is Molly who solves the mystery, recovering the children and five adult plotters. Molly uses a lingering oil slick as one clue and implicates former show business people, only two of whom face arrest. Molly is such a fine example, summer residents regain their confidence in hiring islanders.

Barbara Cohen's *Lovers' Games* depicts enterprising matchmakers. After Aunt Carrie's divorce, she and her glamorous daughter, Lissa, live with sixteen-year-old Amanda ("Mandy") Jane and her parents. When Carrie marries Peter Rasmussen, he joins the household. Before the marriage, Lissa tells Mandy that she dreams of her parents being reunited. That is the first time bright Mandy, who idolizes popular Lissa, is aware that her cousin "had troubles, like anyone else" (27).

After the marriage, Mandy and Lissa visit a Yale student, Lissa's new stepbrother, Rory Rasmussen. Rory's cousin, Connor Borne, is the intermediary as Mandy and Lissa try matchmaking each other with Rory. Their clever schemes backfire since both girls find Rory boring, enjoying each other and Connor.

In New York City in 1976 (eleven years into the future at publication time), Jean Merrill shows through a fantasy, *The Pushcart War*, how 500 pushcart peddlers resourcefully win a war with 20,000 truck drivers. The struggle begins on March 15th when Mack of Mammoth Moving Company runs his truck into the pushcart of Morris the Florist. Tensions mount as truckers print viscious newspaper articles against pushcart owners. In a fight with street-monopolizing truckers, pushcart operators start an ingenious pea-pin shooting campaign, flattening trucker's tires. Finally, both sides agree that "to talk is better than to fight" (176), and they negotiate the Courtesy Act which makes it a crime for a larger vehicle to take advantage of a smaller one.

Malcolm J. Bosse's *Ganesh* depicts the wisdom of a fourteen-year-old orphan uprooted from India, Jeffrey Moore, who fights for midwestern United States justice. In India, Jeffrey is called Ganesh, the name of a Hindu god. After both parents die in India, he begins a new life in the United States with his Aunt Betty in his father's family home. Father had told him, "Try America. Then if you wish, return to India" (64). Jeffrey wants to bridge the gap between the world he has not wholly left and the one he has not wholly entered. His friendship with a top basketball star, Tom Carrington, helps. To save his aunt's home from destruction for a highway, he, his aunt, and school friends have an eleven-day hunger strike called *satyragraha*. The *satyragraha* "is a means of achieving agreement by assuming your oppressor can change to your way of thinking—learn by examining your own motives" (159). After the direct action is successful, Jeffrey elects to stay in America.

Ingenuity in surviving is a value stressed in Felice Holman's *Slake's Limbo*. A thirteen-year-old orphan, underfed Aremis Slake, sleeps on a cot in the run-down kitchen of a cruel aunt's apartment. After teachers and classmates treat him like a worthless lump, he escapes a gang by running into a New York subway tunnel. When he finds a small room in the tunnel, he hides there for four months, resourcefully selling old newspapers in the terminal and cleaning a coffee shop's floor for a daily meal. Slake is secure from those who mistreat him until the tunnel collapses. After hopelessly staying in his hideout without food or water,

Slake feverishly wanders onto the tracks where a subway motorman, Willis Joe, finds him and takes him to a hospital. Slake recovers, aided by a true friend, Willis Joe, and hoping for a better life.

Anne Holm's *North to Freedom* describes the ingenuity of twelve-year-old David during World War II in escaping from an Eastern European concentration camp and traveling north to freedom. David speaks several languages fluently, but he avoids people because he is afraid. "He was aware only of fear, of the need to be constantly on his guard" (121). David walks to Salonika, stows away on a boat to Italy, and in Lugano, Switzerland, meets a Danish painter who notices how closely he resembles a former concentration camp friend. The artist tells David his father is dead but shows him a picture of his mother and gives him her address in Denmark. He walks to Germany where a farmer holds him captive for months before he escapes, continuing his walk to Denmark. After he knocks at the right door, "The woman looked into his face and said clearly, 'My son!' " (190). Reunited with Mother in a free country, David at last learns to trust some individuals.

Scott O'Dell tells about an American girl, Karana, who survives alone on San Nicolas Island near California from 1835 until 1853 in *Island of the Blue Dolphins*. When Karana's people sail from the island, she discovers that her brother, Rama, is left behind. She swims back to him, but wild dogs soon kill him. Near a spring she builds her home, fenced with whale rib bones which she describes: "They were long and curved, and when I had scooped out holes and set them in the earth they stood taller than I did" (74). The fence keeps wild animals away, but Karana brings home a wounded dog pack leader, nurses him, and calls her new friend Rontu ("Fox Eyes"). She also tames several birds. Despite taboos against women fishing, hunting, and making weapons, Karana does these things to survive, using a dead sea elephant's teeth as spear points. She eats seeds and sea food; weaves her own baskets and nets; make clothes of yucca fiber, sealskin, or cormorant feathers; and fashions her own canoe. Karana begins to feel reverence for nature. In the end, this female Robinson Crusoe willingly ships with hunters to California.

In futuristic science fiction, *Z for Zachariah* by Robert C. O'Brien, sixteen-year-old Ann Burden uses her ingenuity to survive after a nuclear war. The title paraphrases Ann's alphabet book, "The first page said A is for Adam. The last of all was Z is for Zachariah" (75). Ann believes that she is the last person left in the world, lucky to be in a

Pennsylvania valley that escaped nuclear bombing so that she could use the water and cultivate food. She reflects, "I had all summer to understand how things were, to get over being afraid, and to think about how I was going to live through the winter" (13). She meets another survivor, John R. Loomis, a New York chemist wearing a radiation-proof safe suit. He becomes ill after swimming in a radioactive creek, but Ann nurses him back to health. After he insanely attempts to kill her, Ann steals his safe suit and leaves the valley, hoping to survive elsewhere.

Cleverness keeps ten-year-old twins, Adam and Eva, permanently out of an orphanage in Berniece Rabe's *The Orphans*, set in 1932 in the midwest. After their parents' death, the twins live with their uncles until a train accident kills the men; their aunts cannot keep the children. When the state refuses Adam's request to stay with their step-grand-mother, G-Mama, authorities send the twins to an orphanage. Adam gets Sheriff Erica Wheeler to take him and his sister to the home of G-Mama, who has broken her hip and secretly needs their help. Eventu-ally Sheriff Erica adopts them. The two take this oath: "We promise to take this woman, Erica Wheeler, as our legal mother, and G-Mama as our legal grandmother, to honor and obey, to cherish and love till death do us part" (183).

Characters are resourceful in tales of adventure, like Gloria Skur-zynski's *Trapped in the Slick-Rock Canyon: A Mountain West Adven-ture*. Twelve-year-old Gina Farrell and her cousin, Justin Farrell, climb 7,000 feet up a mountain to see an ancient American Indian petroglyph while their fathers are ascending Muleskin Cliff. The adolescents witness an archaeologist's death by gunfire while he is trying to photograph two men removing the petroglyph. The gunman also sees the cousins and chases them. As the young people quickly descend, Justin hurts his ankle, and they cleverly hide in a cave on the mesa wall. Eventually their fathers rescue them.

Charlene Joy Talbot's *The Great Rat Island Adventure* shows the growing ingenuity of fat, eleven-year-old Joel Curtis. He spends the summer with his divorced father, Marshall Curtis, an ornithologist on Great Rat Island off Long Island, New York. Uncomfortable with Father, Joel feels like a peer with Father's college student assistants—Gary, Horace, and D. J.—who band and count terns. They teach him to swim, drive a motor boat, and help him lose weight. While bird watching from a tower, Joel unexpectedly sees Vicky Owners, whose wealthy family owns Little Rat Island, hiding on the island instead of being at camp. She is the sole person on the island. Joel makes his first friend when he rescues her and her dog, Sirius, during a hurricane. Vicky has pneumonia, so he puts her in a protected building and builds a signal fire that attracts rescuers. Then Joel has a warm reunion with Father who has searched for him during the hurricane.

Twelve-year-old Jim from an Arizona Apache reservation ingeniously tracks his dog, Quick, in Patsey Gray's *Barefoot a Thousand Miles*. His school enemy, Billy, gives Jim's border collie, Quick, to the Johnsons, tourists who live in Santa Barbara, California. Jim follows them to Santa Barbara after hitchhiking, hopping a train, working for meals, and walking a thousand miles barefoot when he loses his shoes. He phones his father at intervals to tell him his location. Jim finally finds Quick, starving and injured, at the Los Angeles stockyards. Since he has never before left the reservation, he is surprised that others show no bias toward him as an Indian and help him. The tale ends as Jim hitchhikes home before Quick has puppies. He gives Father some credit for his resourcefulness, saying, "My dad doesn't believe in luck just happening. He claims we make our own" (60).

Stephanie Tolan's *The Liberation of Tansy Warner* shows the spunk of a ninth-grade student, Tansy Warner, in paying bills and managing the household when her mother leaves the family, taking with her most of their money. Tansy's father becomes an unshaven recluse, refusing to help in the house and unwilling to search for his wife. Tansy confides in two friends, Vickie and her mother, who help Tansy schedule Warner household chores, giving tasks to Tansy's older siblings, Gwen and Dennis. Tansy cleverly traces Mother through a repeated listing on a telephone bill of a Chicago phone number, then goes to Chicago and finds Mother working in a friend's craft shop. She learns Father had wanted Mother to have an abortion when she was pregnant with Tansy. Mother left her husband in order to find herself. Vickie says, "I think it's possible that your mother left *to save her life*" (93). Tansy returns home alone but wiser as she accepts the challenge of holding her family together.

In a lighter vein, Joan Carris's *Pets, Vets, and Marty Howard* describes the clever way a twelve-year-old animal lover, Marty Howard, gives away puppies and kittens. Marty, who works after school at Doc Cameron's Veterinary Hospital, likes to clean cages and help in operations but cannot bear to see unwanted animals put to sleep. Marty's brothers help him hide puppies in a home closet until he finds friends to take them. He even sells two to an orphan home director. As for extra kittens, Marty aggressively tells a department store owner, Mr. Stone, Jr., "I have a great way to bring people into the store. Who wouldn't love watching this kitten chase his tail? It'd turn your window into a real live barn. It'd be the *only* window in town" (163). He is correct when he suggests this window sign: "FREE CHRISTMAS KITTENS. Ask inside" (163).

Another animal lover, twelve-year-old Arliss Coates, has a cunning way of proving his manhood in Fred Gipson's historical Western, *Little Arliss*, a sequel to *Old Yeller* (see chapter 3, "Friendship and Love of Animals"). Arliss is tired of being told he is too little to do grown-up things, as his teacher, Hoot Owl Weatherby, and Papa discover. When men are unable to catch an outlaw stallion, Salty, Arliss listens to a pioneer girl, Judy, who accompanies him on his horse, Nellie, following new horse tracks. It is Judy's bright idea to scatter corn below Nellie and to let her nicker for a stallion while both children wait above, hidden in a treetop. When the palomino, Salty, comes below the tree to join Nellie, Arliss lassos him. Later, Arliss impresses the adults by riding Salty.

Eth Clifford's *The Rocking Chair Rebellion* shows problem-solving abilities of the elderly and their friends. After fourteen-year-old Penelope ("Opie") Cross visits Mr. Pepper at the Maple Shade Home for the Aged, she does volunteer summer work there four days a week. She finds one resident, Mrs. Sherman, raising money for her tombstone by crocheting a bedspread and raffling it to the public. Opie persuades the Maple Shade Home to change the site of its annual Family Fair to the public street, so neighbors and residents can mingle. On that street, Mr. Pepper and some of the home's active residents buy a home where they can share chores. When neighbors take Mr. Pepper to court to prevent communal living, Opie's father, a lawyer, defends him and wins the case. In time, neighbors value these self-sufficient senior citizens.

SUMMARY

Ingenuity is a stressed value in the eighty-nine books discussed in this chapter. Thirty-two of the books are geared for early years, twenty-eight for middle years, and twenty-nine for later years, so there is fairly even distribution.

References

Alexander, Martha. *Sabrina*. Illustrated. The Dial Press, 1971. Unpaged. (E)

———. *We Never Get to Do Anything*. Illustrated. The Dial Press, 1970. Unpaged. (E)

Angell, Judie. *A Word from Our Sponsor or My Friend Alfred*. Bradbury Press, 1979. 140 p. (L)

Avi. *S.O.R. Losers*. Bradbury Press, 1984. 90 p. (L) (Friendship, Self-respect)

Barry, Robert E. *Faint George*. Illustrated. Houghton Mifflin Company, 1957. 32 p. (E)

Behrens, June. *Soo Ling Finds a Way*. Illustrated by Taro Yashima. Golden Gate Junior Books, 1965. Unpaged. (E)

Bond, Ann Sharpless. *Saturdays in the City*. Illustrated by Leonard Shortall. Houghton Mifflin Company, 1979. 147 p. (M) (Friendship)

Bosse, Malcolm J. *Ganesh*. Lippincott & Crowell, Publishers, 1981. 185 p. (L) (Humaneness, Maturing)

Carris, Joan. *Pets, Vets, and Marty Howard*. Illustrated by Carol Newson. J. B. Lippincott, 1984. 186 p. (L)

———. *Witch-cat*. Illustrated by Beth Peck. J. B. Lippincott, 1984. 154 p. (M)

Clifford, Eth. *The Rocking Chair Rebellion*. Houghton Mifflin Company, 1978. 147 p. (L) (Friendship)

Coatsworth, Elizabeth. *Lonely Maria*. Illustrated by Evaline Ness. Pantheon Books, 1960. Unpaged. (E)

Cohen, Barbara. *Lovers' Games*. Atheneum, 1983. 239 p. (L)

Conford, Ellen. *Lenny Kandell, Smart Aleck*. Illustrated by Walter Gaffney-Kessell. Little, Brown & Company, 1983. 120 p. (M)

du Bois, William Pène. *Lion*. Illustrated. The Viking Press, 1956. 37 p. (E)

Elkin, Benjamin. *Gillespie and the Guards*. Illustrated by James Daugherty. The Viking Press, 1956. 62 p. (E)

Fife, Dale. *What's New, Lincoln?* Illustrated by Paul Galdone. Coward-McCann, 1970. 59 p. (M)

———. *What's the Prize, Lincoln?* Illustrated by Paul Galdone. Coward, McCann & Geoghegan, 1971. 64 p. (M)

———. *Who'll Vote for Lincoln?* Illustrated by Paul Galdone. Coward,

McCann & Geoghegan, 1977. 63 p. (M) (Maturing, Responsibility, Self-respect)

———. *Who's in Charge of Lincoln?* Illustrated by Paul Galdone. Coward-McCann, 1965. 61 p. (M)

Fitzgerald, John D. *The Great Brain Does It Again.* Illustrated by Mercer Mayer. The Dial Press, 1973. 165 p. (L) (Friendship, Humaneness)

———. *The Great Brain Reforms.* Illustrated by Mercer Mayer. The Dial Press, 1973. 165 p. (L) (Friendship, Humaneness)

Gannett, Ruth Stiles. "*My Father's Dragon.*" Illustrated by Ruth Chrisman Gannett. Random House, 1948. 86 p. (M)

Gauch, Patricia Lee. *Christina Katerina & the Box.* Illustrated by Doris Burn. Coward, McCann & Geoghegan, 1971. Unpaged. (E)

Gerson, Corinne. *Son for a Day.* Illustrated by Velma Ilsley. Atheneum, 1980. 140 p. (M)

Gipson, Fred. *Little Arliss.* Illustrated by Ronald Himmler. Harper & Row, Publishers, 1978. 83 p. (L) (Courage, Animal Friendship)

Gray, Patsey. *Barefoot a Thousand Miles.* Walker & Company, 1984. 92 p. (L)

Hoban, Lillian. *Arthur's Honey Bear.* Illustrated. Harper & Row Publishers, 1974. 62 p. (E)

Hoban, Russell. *A Bargain for Frances.* Illustrated by Lillian Hoban. Harper & Row, 1970. 62 p. (E) (Animal Friendship)

Holland, Isabelle. *The Empty House.* J. B. Lippincott, 1983. 218 p. (L) (Friendship, Responsibility)

Holm, Anne. *North to Freedom.* Translated from Danish by L. W. Kingsland. Harcourt, Brace & World, 1965. 190 p. (L)

Holman, Felice. *Slake's Limbo.* Charles Scribner's Sons, 1974. 117 p. (L) (Maturing)

Keller, Holly. *Geraldine's Blanket.* Illustrated. Greenwillow Books, 1984. Unpaged. (E)

Kerr, M. E. *Dinky Hocker Shoots Smack.* Harper & Row Publishers, 1972. 242 p. (L)

Kleberger, Ilse. *Grandmother Oma.* Illustrated by Wallace Tripp. Atheneum, 1967. 124 p. (M)

Leaf, Munro. *Wee Gillis.* Illustrated by Robert Lawson. The Viking Press, 1938. Unpaged. (E)

Lexau, Joan M. *Benjie.* Illustrated by Don Bolognese. The Dial Press, 1964. Unpaged. (E)

————. *Benjie on His Own.* Illustrated by Don Bolognese. The Dial Press, 1970. Unpaged. (E)

Lionni, Leo. *Frederick.* Illustrated. Pantheon, 1967. Unpaged. (E) (Cooperation)

————. *Inch by Inch.* Illustrated. Astor-Honor, Inc., 1960. Unpaged. (E)

Lisle, Janet Taylor. *The Dancing Cats of Applesap.* Illustrated by Joelle Shefts. Bradbury Press, 1984. 169 p. (M)

Littke, Lael. *Trish for President.* Harcourt Brace Jovanovich, 1984. 165 p. (L) (Friendship)

Lobel, Arnold. *A Holiday for Mister Muster.* Illustrated. Harper & Row, Publishers, 1963. Unpaged. (E)

Lord, Athena V. *Today's Special: Z.A.P. and Zoe.* Illustrated by Jean Jenkins. Macmillan Publishing Company, 1984. 150 p. (M) (Friendship, Responsibility)

MacLeod, Charlotte. *We Dare Not Go A-Hunting.* Atheneum, 1980. 188 p. (L) (Responsibility)

McNamara, John. *Revenge of the Nerd.* Delacorte Press, 1984. 118 p. (L) (Friendship)

Martin, Patricia Miles. *The Pointed Brush.* Illustrated by Roger Duvoisin. Lothrop, Lee & Shepard Company, 1959. Unpaged. (M) (Maturity)

Mathis, Sharon Bell. *Sidewalk Story.* Illustrated by Leo Carty. The Viking Press, 1971. 71 p. (M) (Friendship)

Merrill, Jean. *The Pushcart War.* Illustrated by Ronni Solbert. William A. Scott, 1964. 222 p. (L)

Miles, Miska. *Annie and the Old One.* Illustrated by Peter Parnell. Little, Brown & Company, 1971. 44 p. (M) (Friendship)

Molarsky, Osmond. *Right Thumb, Left Thumb.* Illustrated by John E. Johnson. Addison-Wesley Publishing Company, 1969. Unpaged. (E)

O'Brien, Robert C. *Z for Zachariah.* Atheneum, 1975. 249 p. (L) (Courage)

O'Dell, Scott. *Island of the Blue Dolphins.* Houghton Mifflin Company, 1960. 184 p. (L) (Courage, Maturing)

Orlev, Uri. *The Island on Bird Street.* Translated from Hebrew by Hillel Halkin. Houghton Mifflin Company, 1984. 162 p. (M)

Peet, Bill. *How Droofus the Dragon Lost His Head.* Illustrated. Houghton Mifflin Company, 1971. 46 p. (E)

Perrine, Mary. *Nannabah's Friend*. Illustrated by Leonard Weisgard. Houghton Mifflin, 1970. 23 p. (M) (Friendship, Responsibility)

Pfeffer, Susan Beth. *Kid Power*. Illustrated by Leigh Grant. Franklin Watts, 116 p. (M)

——. *Kid Power Strikes Back*. Franklin Watts, 116 p. (M)

Pomerantz, Charlotte. *The Half-Birthday Party*. Illustrated by DyAnne DiSalvo-Ryan. Clarion Books, 1984. Unpaged. (E)

Rabe, Berniece. *The Orphans*. E. P. Dutton, 1978. 184 p. (L)

Robertson, Keith. *Henry Reed's Baby-sitting Service*. Illustrated by Robert McCloskey. The Viking Press, 1966. 204 p. (L) (Responsibility)

——. *Ice to India*. Illustrated by Jack Weaver. The Viking Press, 1955. 224 p. (L)

Robinson, Jean. *The Strange but Wonderful Cosmic Awareness of Duffy Moon*. Illustrated by Lawrence Di Fiori. The Seabury Press, 1974. 142 p. (M)

Rockwell, Thomas. *How to Eat Fried Worms*. Illustrated by Emily McCully. Franklin Watts, 1973. 116 p. (M)

Sachs, Marilyn. *Marv*. Illustrated by Louis Glanzman. Doubleday, 1970. 160 p. (L) (Self-respect)

Sawyer, Ruth. *Maggie Rose: Her Birthday Christmas*. Illustrated by Maurice Sendak. Harper & Brothers, 1952. 151 p. (M)

Schertle, Alice. *The April Fool*. Illustrated by Emily McCully. Lothrop, Lee & Shepard, 1981. Unpaged. (E)

Skurzynski, Gloria. *Trapped in the Slick-Rock Canyon: A Mountain West Adventure*. Illustrated by Daniel San Souci. Lothrop, Lee & Shepard, 1984. 123 p. (L)

Snyder, Zilpha Keatley. *Blair's Nightmare*. Atheneum, 1984. 192 p. (M) (Friendship)

——. *The Egypt Game*. Illustrated by Alton Raible. Atheneum, 1967. 215 p. (M)

——. *The Famous Stanley Kidnapping Case*. Atheneum, 1979. 212 p. (M)

——. *The Headless Cupid*. Illustrated by Alton Raible. Atheneum, 1971. 203 p. (M) (Friendship, Responsibility)

Stanek, Muriel. *Left, Right, Left, Right*. Illustrated by Lucy Hawkinson. Albert Whitman & Company, 1969. Unpaged. (E)

Stapp, Arthur D. *The Fabulous Earthworm Deal*. Illustrated by George Porter, 1969. 160 p. (L) (Friendship, Loyalty, Responsibility)

Steig, William. *Abel's Island*. Illustrated. Farrar, Straus, Giroux, 1976. 119 p. (M) (Courage)

———. *Doctor De Soto*. Illustrated. Farrar, Straus and Giroux, 1982. 32 p. (E)

Talbot, Charlene Joy. *The Great Rat Island Adventure*. Illustrated by Ruth Sanderson. Atheneum, 1977. 164 p. (L) (Courage, Friendship)

Thurber, James. *Many Moons*. Illustrated by Louis Slobodkin. Harcourt, Brace & World, 1943. Unpaged. (M)

Titus, Eve. *Anatole*. Illustrated by Paul Galdone. McGraw-Hill Book Company, 1956. 32 p. (E)

———. *Anatole and the Cat*. Illustrated by Paul Galdone. McGraw-Hill Book Company, 1957. 32 p. (E)

Tolan, Stephanie S. *The Liberation of Tansy Warner*. Charles Scribner's Sons, 1980. 137 p. (L) (Loyalty, Maturing, Responsibility)

Udry, Janice May. *Mary Jo's Grandmother*. Illustrated by Eleanor Mill. Albert Whitman & Company, 1970. Unpaged. (E)

———. *The Sunflower Garden*. Illustrated by Beatrice Darwin. Harvey House, 1969. 37 p. (E)

Watson, Pauline. *Curley Cat Baby-sits*. Illustrated by Lorinda Bryan Cauley. Harcourt Brace Jovanovich, 1977. Unpaged. (E)

Wells, Rosemary. *The Man in the Woods*. Dial Books, 1984. 217 p. (L)

———. *Stanley & Rhoda*. Illustrated. Dial Press, 1978. 40 p. (E) (Animal Friendship, Responsibility)

Yolen, Jane. *The Seeing Stick*. Illustrated by Remy Charlip and Demetra Marsalis. Thomas Y. Crowell Company, 1977. Unpaged. (E)

Zimelman, Nathan. *Mean Murgatroyd and the Ten Cats*. Illustrated by Tony Auth. E. P. Dutton, 1984. Unpaged. (E)

Zion, Gene. *The Plant Sitter*. Illustrated by Margaret Bloy Graham. Harper & Row, Publishers, 1959. Unpaged. (E) (Responsibility)

VII

Loyalty

Loyalty refers to faithfulness to family, friends, country, customs, and ideals. It is a difficult concept for young children to understand. Most books on loyalty for the early years relate to steadfast friendship and love between animals, between children and animals, between children, and between children and adults; so this type of loyalty is incorporated in chapters on friendship and love. By the time children are nine or ten years old, their feeling of loyalty to family and friends can be extended to country, particularly to a symbol, such as the flag. It is not until children enter their teens that most feel allegiance to customs and ideals.

BOOKS FOR EARLY YEARS

Betty Horvath depicts family loyalty in *Be Nice to Josephine*, illustrated by Pat Grant Porter. Charlie Mitchell, who spends Saturdays playing baseball, is unhappy when his mother insists that he devote the day to a visiting cousin, Josephine. He decides to take her fishing and have a picnic. Using a roundabout route to the creek to avoid friends, he lets her carry the equipment and walk behind him. When he finds that Josephine digs worms, eats unusual sandwiches, and knows how to be quiet, he returns home through the schoolyard where his friends are playing ball. He answers jeers about being with a girl by saying, "I didn't have to spend the day with her. I wanted to. She's my cousin. Didn't anybody ever tell you that blood is thicker than water?" (unp).

BOOKS FOR MIDDLE YEARS

Joan M. Lexau's *Striped Ice Cream* reveals a black family's loyalty. Eight-year-old Becky, youngest of five children, resents her older brother and sisters excluding her from activities. She hopes to have striped ice cream (vanilla, chocolate, and strawberry) for her birthday but knows money is scarce. Mama, who works in a button factory, refuses welfare. Becky resents wearing hand-me-downs from her sisters and people for whom Mama does odd jobs. When opening a bag from Mrs. Robbins, Mama says, "There's charity and there's charity. The word means love you know" (26). Becky complains about her sisters to her mother, "But they act mean and nice to me at the same time. They're nice when I'm there but they don't want me around" (78). Becky understands their love for her when they give her a new birthday dress of pink, white, and brown stripes.

As children move outside the family into the community, there may be loyalty between generations, as shown in *Ellen Grae* by Vera and Bill Cleaver. Eleven-year-old Ellen Grae Derryberry is torn between loyalty to Ira, a simple-minded peanut vendor, and feeling responsibility to speak when she knows his parents did not abandon him and go to Canada. Ira claims they died from snake bite, and he shows her where he buried them in a swamp. When the problem makes Ellen Grae ill, Mrs. Magruder, with whom she lives during the school year, sends for her parents. She tells them the story which they insist she repeat to the sheriff. Her father says:

> Moral responsibility is what you feel toward Ira. You feel that
> a moral wrong has been committed and because you have a
> conscience you are troubled and concerned and distressed.
> Because you know about this wrong you feel responsible. (69)

All the townspeople, familiar with Ellen Grae's imaginative tall tales, laugh at her story. The sheriff does tell her Ira is safe from punishment even if his account were true.

Rumer Godden's *Mr. McFadden's Hallowe'en* is a sad but heartwarming story of friendship and loyalty between generations. When young Selina Russell's Great Aunt Emily dies, she wills money for the village of Menock, Scotland to create a much-needed public park. The owner of the best land is old Angus McFadden, who lives alone on a farm with a dog, Lady, and a gander, Big Wullie. His refusal to sell the land turns the town against him. Selina rescues McFadden when a boulder crushes his leg. With the help of her father and Tim, an orphan friend, Selina temporarily takes care of the old man and his farm, earning the villagers' enmity. McFadden, appreciating Selina's and Tim's loyalty, says, "They can throw stones at me, aye, and put turfs on m'chimney, but when it comes to the bairns . . . I dinnae ken what taa dae. . . . How can I sell the bluidy field without losing face?" (110). Selina suggests that he *give* the field to the village. "Then you won't have to take their auld money because you won't sell them the field, you'll give it. You won't lose your face. That will make them talk on the other side of theirs" (111) The story has a happy ending as the village gets its park and Tim, adopted by McFadden, lives with Selina's family.

It is painful for children to divide their loyalty. In *Walking Away* by Elizabeth Winthrop, thirteen-year-old Emily enjoys spending the summer on her grandfather's farm, helping him with chores, and having intimate talks. She looks forward to a visit from her best friend, Nina. However, Nina, whose viewpoint is different, sees Grandfather as a broken-down old man. Emily feels guilty because, while she helps Nina prepare for a square dance, Grandfather hurts his back fixing a dam. Emily, desolate at Grandfather's death, remembers his explanation that a relationship can be altered by outside forces. He urged her to make up her own mind when facing divided loyalties.

An aspect of loyalty is patriotism or devotion to the homeland and its ideals, symbolized by its flag. In *The Fragile Flag*, Jane Langton's characters demonstrate to the government against potential horrors of a new "peace missile." When eleven-year-old Georgie Dorian Hall of Concord, Massachusetts misses the deadline to mail her essay on "What the Flag of My Country Means to Me" to the United States president, she decides to carry an old tattered attic flag to Washington to read the president her essay. Georgie, a thin, wispy little girl with rockbound determination, carries the flag with her parents' blessing. Joining Georgie on the 450-mile walk to Washington are her cousins Eddy and Eleanor, classmate Frieda Caldwell, and the United States president's grandson, Robert Toby. The walk becomes a children's crusade as thousands join from around the country. The organizer, Frieda, who calls herself the Media Interface Person, insists that every child have a permission slip, adequate equipment, and supplies. Despite bad weather, sore feet, exhaustion, and poor treatment, the children eventually reach Washington and meet the president. Although he maintains the flag stands for strength, after meeting the marchers, he acknowledges that Georgie is right when she says, "The flag means American people being friends with other people" (1).

Leonard Todd's *The Best Kept Secret of the War* involves an unusual extension of patriotism. In Pinehill, North Carolina during World War II, ten-year-old Cam Reed wants to help the war effort. His father, fighting with American forces in Europe, takes part in the Normandy invasion, which he says "was the best kept secret of the war" (19). Cam discovers old Jeddah Whitmire hiding in the woods after escaping from depressing Cawley Home for the Aged, and the boy keeps the hiding place a secret. He declares, "I guess it'll just have to be a secret, a war secret" (31). He sees a parallel between the treatment of lonely, exhausted soldiers and Jeddah. The old man rescues the boy from attackers and stays at his home with him, his mother, and his great aunt, until the home for the aged forces him to return. When Cam visits Jeddah at the home, there is a fire and Jeddah saves the lad a second time. The home burns and residents stay at Cam's until a new place opens with improved management. Cam feels that by helping Jeddah, he has been part of a war in which there is suffering, not medals.

When eleven-year-old Kate Harris volunteers to join a project to read aloud to Concord School first graders, she does not expect unpopular Maudie Schmidt to be her partner or to involve the community in a censorship battle. In *Maudie, and Me and the Dirty Book*, Betty Miles shows how an innocent act can lead to city-wide confrontation and how loyalty to an ideal can cause heartbreak and confusion. Kate and Maudie get acquainted with some of the first graders before choosing books to read to them. Quiet Simon tells them about his new puppy, so Kate selects *The Birthday Dog*, a story about a dog having puppies. The pupils love the book and talk about reproduction as they know it. One mother, who hears words used in the discussion, demands book censorship. She writes the newspaper a letter lamenting that innocent sixth graders must hear about reproduction and "moral values are being corrupted by smut" (105). Seeing a petitioner getting signatures to censor children's books, Kate's mother says:

> I think you're prejudiced. I think it's a sad day for this community when a little group of parents take it upon themselves to stand in judgment on all the rest of us who support our teachers and our librarians. (117)

At a school board hearing, Kate bravely defends the book on reproduction and her teacher's project.

In the mid-1800s, even children witness the conflict between conscience and law as thousands of runaway slaves follow the North Star in the Big Dipper, the drinking gourd, to freedom on the Underground Railroad. In F. N. Monjo's easy "I Can Read History Book," *The Drinking Gourd*, a boy in New England, Timothy Fuller, must return home early after misbehaving in church. When he comes to his barn, he discovers Jeff, Vinnie, and their children, four black runaways, hidden in the hay loft. Father explains that he works on the Underground Railroad and gets Timothy to help take them to the next station. Father also explains the moral dilemma of obedience to law versus obedience to conscience. The next morning, Father tells Timothy, "I believe in obeying the law. But you and I broke the law last night. Someday it will all be changed" (58). Timothy says, "But Jeff and Vinnie are people" (60). Father replies, "Yes, that's why I can't obey the law. That's why I hate it. It's wrong" (61).

BOOKS FOR LATER YEARS

Marcus Miles begins to blink his eyes and stutter again, torn between loyalty to his father and loyalty to his mother in Eve Bunting's *Blackbird Singing*. His father wants to kill a horde of blackbirds that are destroying his cornfields. His mother, an artist, wants to paint the beautiful birds. Marcus loves his parents and realizes they "will never be able to change each other" (91). Only when a doctor explains that Marcus may suffer from histoplasmosis, a disorder transmitted by bird droppings, does his mother accept the spraying of fields and destruction of maple trees. Here is a poignant story of a child caught between an environmental problem and economic survival.

Loyalty to friends is a key issue in four books. In *The Flight of the Sparrow* by Julia Cunningham, fourteen-year-old Mago, a Parisian street urchin, rescues nine-year-old Cigarette from an orphanage and takes her to an abandoned shed to live with him and several other orphans, including retarded Drollant. When Drollant runs into a street and a car injures him, Cigarette feels responsible. To pay for Drollant's care in a private clinic, Cigarette agrees to steal a painting for evil Eel. Eel gets Mago to sell the painting to a gallery but keeps the money and says that Mago and Cigarette must work for him or he will go to the police. Cigarette confronts Eel, and Mago dies rushing to her defense.

Cigarette then lives with Madame Bruneau, who gives her opportunities that Mago never had. Before he died, Mago told her, "You must stay free for yourself and for me. You must be my chance, the one I never had. . . . Your chance will become mine because I am giving mine to you this moment" (178).

Another tragedy is Lynn Hall's *Uphill All the Way*. Seventeen-year-old Callie Kiffin wants to be a farrier, or blacksmith. She earns money for a truck by doing summer work for Dr. Fulcher, a veterinarian. Callie befriends the doctor's stepson, Truman Johnson, who spent his senior year at Tumbleweed Ranch for selling marijuana on school grounds. She has never had a boyfriend and is thrilled to date Truman, ignoring warning signs that he is a con man and thief. The climax occurs when Truman steals Callie's new truck to commit a robbery. After she informs police about Truman, her father says, "You did everything a friend could be expected to do and more. If you'd gone on shielding him after what he's done tonight, you'd have been committing a crime yourself" (112).

Boys as well as girls can be loyal friends, as Tom Berry shows in *Four Miles to Pinecone* by Jon Hassler. Tom works in Mr. Kerr's grocery. He is in the basement when he hears a robbery upstairs and thinks the robber's voice is that of his best friend, Mouse Brown. He does not tell a detective because he feels sorry for Mouse, who comes from a large family living below the poverty level. He does wonder where Mouse gets so much spending money but thinks, "Is a guy supposed to squeal on his best friend? . . . Wasn't it the job of the police to find the guilty?" (51) Tom decides to tell the detective about Mouse after another thief almost injures him during the Labor Day weekend while he house-sits at his uncle's camp near the Canadian border. Tom returns home, sees Mouse in jail, and feels less guilty when the detective explains:

> Sometimes doing right is harder than doing wrong—but never in the long run. If you feel wrong about reporting Mouse, think how rotten you'd feel if you didn't report him and after a year or two he was picked up for something worse, like murder. (114)

Is That You, Miss Blue? by M. E. Kerr revolves around loyalty as a central theme. When fourteen-year-old Flanders Brown comes to a private school, she cannot conform with the "in" group and is ostracized for defending her religiously fanatical science teacher, Miss Ernestine Blue. Flanders thinks, "I wasn't the only one under Miss Blue's spell in the classroom. Most of us came away with sort of a full, silent feeling that you have after you've seen a really good movie" (93). When some students succeed in getting Miss Blue dismissed, Flanders and two friends steal a painting of Mary, Queen of Scots that Miss Blue loves, and they give it to her with a forged note from the headmistress. Flanders explains, "The idea was that if we could not prevent this cruelty about to be inflicted on Miss Blue, we could at least soften it" (139).

When individuals are opposed to a war their nation is fighting, there is a conflict between loyalty to country and to personal conscience. Among the war stories that show such conflict is Lorna Beer's fiction about the Revolutionary War, *The Crystal Cornerstone*. Sixteen-year-old Thaddeus Long from Newtown, Pennsylvania "wanted to be with Washington's army and fight for Liberty, Freedom, and the Rights of Man" (I). His family wants him to go to Prince Town to become a minister, but the night before he is to leave for school, he runs away and joins Captain Hardy's company at Fort Lee. Ragged, independent volunteers cross the Delaware with Washington. Near the end of their enlistment, the men are ready to go home, but Washington urges them to stay, pleading:

> If you will stay with me one month more, for the sake of liberty and your country, you will serve your country as you will never be able to serve it again. For this is the crisis. This is the hour that will decide your destiny. (171)

Later, based on General Washington's words, Thaddeus preaches a sermon, entitled "It Is Your Right to Go, I Entreat You to Stay," in which he says:

> In imploring us, he lifted our spirits up to his high understanding of and his faith in the sacred principles of the Revolution. It was in that moment he laid the crystal cornerstone of the Republic. (216)

A story showing the futility of war and how it destroys family life is *My Brother Sam Is Dead* by James L. and Christopher Collier. Sixteen-year-old Sam supports the Americans in the Revolutionary War when he tells his father, "Sir, it's worth dying to be free" (21). His father replies, "I will not have treason in my house. We are Englishmen, we are subjects of the King, this rebellion is the talk of madmen" (21). Sam, ordered to leave home, joins the rebels. Twelve-year-old Tim is torn by arguments for and against resistance. After rebels capture his father who eventually dies, Tim says, "It seems to me that everybody was to blame and I decided that I wasn't going to be on anybody's side any more. Neither one of them was right" (167). When Sam is stationed near home, he visits his mother one night without permission. Hearing her cows bellow, he chases two soldiers who capture him, accusing him of stealing cattle. General Putnam charges Sam with leaving his post and thievery, executing him despite pleas from Tim and his mother. Fifty years later, Tim remembers his father declaring, "In war the dead pay the debts of the living" (211).

In *Rifles for Watie*, Harold Keith portrays war's horrors, shows the value of personal loyalty in love and war, and questions the wisdom of any war. During the Civil War, sixteen-year-old Jeff Bussey joins the Union Army to preserve the nation and help the new state of Kansas become pro-Union. After falling in love with a rebel girl and being captured by Watie's Cherokee rebels, Jeff changes his opinions about war and the rebels. He says, "If I wasn't fighting to hold the Union together and clean up the border trouble in Kansas, I could change sides mighty quick in this war" (280).

A story of wartime loyalty to an individual is Bette Greene's *Summer of My German Soldier*. At her father's store in Jenkinsville, Arkansas during World War II, a twelve-year-old Jewish girl, Patty Bergen, meets twenty-two-year-old Anton Reiker, a German prisoner of war from a nearby camp. When he escapes, she and the Bergen's black housekeeper, Ruth, hide him in an abandoned building and care for him. Unloved by her parents, Patty finds happiness in her friendship with Anton as he helps her develop a positive self-image. Before he leaves, he gives Patty an heirloom ring, declaring, "I want you to always remember that you are a person of value, and you have a friend who loved you enough to give you his most valued possession" (134). When Patty displays the ring, authorities arrest her for aiding an enemy soldier and send her to the reformatory. Her only visitor there is Ruth, still loyal to Patty.

M. E. Kerr deals with post-World War II problems in *Gentle-hands*. A policeman's son, adolescent Buddy Boyle, takes his friend, Skye Pennington, to visit his grandfather, Frank Trenker, a cultured, wealthy recluse. Later, at the Penningtons', Buddy meets a journalist, Nick De Lucca, who is hunting a man responsible for his cousin's death at Auschwitz. The hunted Nazi's ironic nickname is Gentlehands. Though De Lucca's clues point to him, Frank Trenker denies accusations but refuses to confront his opponent. Buddy must choose between loyalty to his grandfather and loyalty to his ideals. After Grandfather disappears, leaving Buddy a note saying he is Gentlehands, Buddy tells authorities where they might locate the elderly man. Buddy explains why he cooperates: "I could hear him telling me that once I knew something was wrong, I was responsible—whether you see it or hear about it, and most particularly when you're a part of it" (172).

Virginia Sorenson's *Lotte's Locket* shows a different type of divided loyalty. Eleven-year-old Lotte, daughter of a deceased World War II pilot, lives on a farm in Denmark with her mother, Mor, and her paternal grandmother, Farmor. Lotte, who represents the eighth generation of her family to live at Lottegaard, looks forward to confirmation day when she will receive the locket that belonged to the first Lotte. After her mother falls in love with an American who knew Lotte's father and marries him, she goes to the United States, expecting Lotte to follow after school ends. Lotte wants to stay in Denmark, though Farmor counsels her to join her mother. While Farmor tells stories about the first Lotte and Lottegaard, Farmor adds, "The world is changing, yes, and people move about. They don't stay in their old homes anymore. And yet—I think the old stories should be remembered and told to the children." (38). Only when Lotte becomes ill and her mother flies home does Lotte accept that she can be loyal to Denmark and yet live in the United States.

William Hallstead's *The Man Downstairs* is an unusual story of loyalty: idealism in politics. Twenty-year-old Don Ellison, a Millbury Streets Department draftsman, refuses to contribute voluntarily to a political party campaign. After his department head pressures him, Don is so horrified that he tells his story to a friend, a newspaper reporter. Harassed by police, ignored by co-workers, lectured by his father-in-law who helped him get his job, Don firmly maintains his principles. Munro, the "man downstairs," or the boss, says, "The world is run by practical men not idealists. That's the way things work best" (79). Pegler, who replaces Munro after the scandal, adds, "The people change but the system goes on. But the trick is to learn to live with it the best way you can" (155). Despite personnel shifts, Don realizes there is no fundamental change and leaves town. His one comfort is praise from his estranged father who tells him, "Remember I told you some sell out cheap, some sell out high. But you're one of them that don't sell out at all" (158). Though the book is not a literary masterpiece, it may help young people not to "sell out at all."

It is difficult for children to remain loyal to ideals when adults put them in a bad light. *Revolt at Ratcliffe's Rags* by Gillian Cross is an English story about three children—Abigail Proctor, Susan Grantley, and Chris Benton—who are assigned to a home town factory for a school project. They choose Ratcliffe's Rags where Chris's mother works. They discover that employees are underpaid and have miserable job conditions. Abby tells Susan and Chris, "They ought to do something. They ought to get organized. They ought . . ." (37). When employees strike, Mr. Ratcliffe closes his plant, and this turns some workers against the children. Abby gives up, but Chris and Susan continue to support the strikers. Susan says, "I don't think we should desert them all just because things have got nasty" (136). There is a hopeful ending because employees plan to use their redundances (a British term that describes money workers receive when a plant closes) to buy machines and operate the business themselves.

A story for mature readers is *Old Ramon* by Jack Schaefer. During school vacation, old Ramon, a loyal employee and friend, lets his patron's son accompany him while he pastures the sheep. The father wants his son to learn about life from experience as well as from books. Old Ramon teaches the boy how to accept responsibility for sheep, endure loneliness, and cope with sand storms, snakes, and coyotes. Old Ramon counsels, "I think that the way to learn is to do" (28). The boy notices the dogs' loyalty to their master and to the sheep, and he sees a shepherd's loyalty both to his sheep and his patron.

In Anne Mason's *The Dancing Meteorite*, sixteen-year-old Kira Walden chooses between loyalty to a friend who is wrong and loyalty to a hated supervisor who is right. Kira has replaced her mother as E-comm specialist, an expert in languages and communication with aliens from other planets. Kira had watched Captain Andlers let her parents die as they explored a strange planet, but she knows, "laws of the sector permitted Captain Andlers no other choice than to abandon her parents" (1). Kira's only friend, Arreglon, a young girl, is a captive with other Thangians at the space station. One day, Kira sees a meteorite moving in a peculiar fashion. It damages two space ships and could have damaged the space station if Kira had not pulled an emergency switch. Discovering that Thangians can "mind move" objects, Kira is sure Arreglon caused the dancing meteorite. When Captain Andlers and Captain Ertrex go on trial for not sighting the meteorite while on duty, Kira must choose between truth or loyalty to her friend, Arreglon. She realizes that the truth will free Captain Andlers, the supervisor she hates for allowing her parents to be abandoned. She questions, "Could she live with herself if she betrayed her best friend in the name of justice? Could she live with herself if she betrayed justice for her best friend?" (199) Finally, she favors justice and is self-critical for not winning Arreglon's loyalty. She explains how she feels to Sector Control commissioners:

> I don't know if any other Thangians are involved beside my friend, but I do know this. I am the E-comm on this station, and one of my duties is to promote understanding among aliens. I failed in my duty, so whatever punishment you choose to give to my friend, you must also give to me. (202)

Fortunately, colleagues appreciate Kira's honesty and do not punish her.

Another futuristic book, James D. Forman's *Doomsday Plus Twelve*, tells about a crusade led by young people with the patriotic ideal of preserving civilization in the year 2000. The unusual title refers to a 1988 nuclear holocaust, Doomsday, and an anti-militaristic protest that occurs twelve years later. After a nuclear holocaust, Fort Blanco, Oregon is among the few pockets of life left on the west coast of the United States. Japan is the only surviving industrial nation. Fort Blanco residents put radiation sickness behind them and live their lives in peace. In the year 2000, a People's Army in San Diego acquires a nuclear submarine aimed at Japan and comes north to recruit, trying to remilitarize the surviving Americans. A Fort Blanco resident, fifteen-year-old Valerie Tucker comes under the influence of a World War III veteran, Vic Ellis. She wins an essay contest with this view of patriotism: "What if I were to write about living well for one's country, instead of having but one life to give and all that dying gloriously stuff?" (76). Ellis gets her to represent youth at a Doomsday Plus Twelve rally and to lead a peace crusade to San Diego. When the enemy colonel there seizes Valerie, other crusaders march past a firing line to the People's Army stronghold. The firing line is more loyal to the crusaders than to their few hated officers. The crusaders free Valerie, assure scuttling of the nuclear submarine, and celebrate their victory as they end the People's Army.

SUMMARY

Of the twenty-five books chosen for this chapter, only one is for the early years, eight are for the middle years, and sixteen are for the older years. Every book exemplifies additional values, such as courage, friendship, responsibility, and self-respect.

References

Beers, Lorna. *The Crystal Cornerstone.* Harper & Row, Publishers, 1953. 45 p. (L) (Maturing)

Bunting, Eve. *Blackbird Singing.* Illustrated by Steven Gammell. Macmillan Publishing Company, 1980. 92 p. (L)

Cleaver, Vera, and Bill Cleaver. *Ellen Grae.* Illustrated by Ellen Raskin. J. B. Lippincott Company, 1967. 89 p. (M) (Friendship)

Collier, James L., and Christopher Collier. *My Brother Sam Is Dead.* Four Winds Press, 1974. 224 p. (L) (Courage)

Cross, Gillian. *Revolt at Ratcliffe's Rags.* Oxford University Press, 1980. 144 p. (L) (Responsibility)

Cunningham, Julia. *The Flight of the Sparrow.* Pantheon Books, 1980. 144 p. (L) (Friendship)

Forman, James D. *Doomsday Plus Twelve.* Charles Scribner's Sons, 1984. 230 p. (L) (Courage, Responsibility)

Godden, Rumer. *Mr. McFadden's Hallowe'en.* Viking Press, 1975. 127 p. (M) (Friendship)

Greene, Bette. *Summer of My German Soldier.* Dial Press, 1973. 230 p. (L) (Friendship, Humaneness, Self-respect)

Hall, Lynn. *Uphill All the Way.* Charles Scribner's Sons, 1984. 121 p. (L) (Friendship)

Hallstead, William Finn. *The Man Downstairs.* Elsvier-Nelson Books, 1979. 158 p. (L) (Courage, Responsibility)

Hassler, Jon. *Four Miles to Pinecone.* Frederick Warne, 1977. 117 p. (L) (Friendship)

Horvath, Betty F. *Be Nice to Josephine.* Illustrated by Pat Grant Porter. Franklin Watts, 1970. Unpaged. (E) (Humaneness, Maturing)

Keith, Harold. *Rifles for Watie*. Thomas Y. Crowell Company, 1957. 322 p. (L) (Humaneness, Maturing)

Kerr, M. E. *Gentlehands*. Harper & Row, Publishers, 1978. 183 p. (L) (Maturing)

————. *Is That You, Miss Blue?* Harper & Row Publishers, 1975. 170 p. (L) (Friendship)

Langton, Jane. *The Fragile Flag*. Illustrated by Erik Blegvad. Harper & Row, Publishers, 1984. 224 p. (M) (Ingenuity)

Lexau, Joan M. *Striped Ice Cream*. Illustrated by John Wilson. J. B. Lippincott Company, 1968. 95 p. (M) (Friendship, Ingenuity)

Mason, Anne. *The Dancing Meteorite*. Harper & Row, Publishers, 1984. 214 p. (L) (Friendship)

Miles, Betty. *Maudie and Me and the Dirty Book*. Alfred A. Knopf, 1980. 144 p. (M) (Friendship)

Monjo, F. N. *The Drinking Gourd*. Illustrated by Fred Brenner. Harper & Row, Publishers, 1970. 62 p. (M) (Humaneness)

Schaefer, Jack. *Old Ramon*. Illustrated by Harold West. Houghton Mifflin Company, 1960. 102 p. (L) (Responsibility)

Sorensen, Virginia. *Lotte's Locket*. Illustrated by Fermin Rocker. Harcourt, Brace & World, 1964. 253 p. (L) (Maturing)

Todd, Leonard. *The Best Kept Secret of the War*. Alfred A. Knopf, 1984. 165 p. (M) (Friendship, Responsibility)

Winthrop, Elizabeth. *Walking Away*. Illustrated by Nöelle Masseña. Harper & Row, Publishers, 1973. 219 p. (M) (Friendship)

VIII
Maturing

Probably the major challenge a boy or girl faces is growing up or maturing—going from a carefree child to a caring adult. Maturing is an ongoing process toward the goal of maturity. Through books, young people can relate to characters who share their fears and problems— physical, mental, and emotional. Realizing that others have (or have had) their same dilemmas, readers may see ways in which to mature with minimum heartbreak and maximum hope for the future. Through book characters, a child can begin to understand why parents, siblings, peers, and adults act as they do. A well-developed book character can be a reader's role model.

BOOKS FOR EARLY YEARS

A young boy or girl can relate to animals as easily as to human beings when animals cope or gain insights. In *Petunia*, written and illustrated by Roger Duvoisin, a silly goose, Petunia, carries a book, thinking it will make her wise because Mr. Pumpkin says, "He who owns books and loves them is wise" (unp). Other animals accept Petunia's "wisdom" until she tells them a box is full of candles instead of firecrackers. When animals remove the box lid, there is an explosion which opens Petunia's book. Seeing printing on its pages, she knows she cannot read. She states, "Now I understand. It was not enough to carry wisdom under my wing. I must put it in my mind and in my heart. And to do that I must learn to read" (unp).

Children and animals mature physically, mentally, and emotion-ally at different rates. A hopeful story is *Leo the Late Bloomer*, written by

Robert Kraus with Jose Aruégo's striking illustrations. Leo, a young tiger, cannot do what other tigers his age do, such as read, write, draw, or talk. His father worries but his mother says, "Patience. A watched bloomer doesn't bloom" (unp). Suddenly, Leo reads, writes, eats neatly, and speaks in complete sentences, declaring, "I made it" (unp).

Rufus is a bat who sleeps all day and hunts at night in *Rufus*, written and illustrated by Tomi Ungerer. One night, Rufus sees a drive-in color movie and becomes "dissatisfied with his own dull costume" (14). After he paints himself in bright colors and joins the day shift, frightened people try to shoot him. A rare butterfly collector, Dr. Tarturo, rescues him. "Rufus soon realized that the sun hurt his eyes and he had to wear dark glasses and swallow pills for his headache" (29). When he sees a black and white televised show, Rufus decides he is nocturnal after all.

An odd-shaped book on the importance of privacy is Beatrice Schenk De Regniers's *A Little House of Your Own*, illustrated by Irene Haas. The narrator thinks everyone needs a secret house which may be under a dining room table, in a box, or under a blanket over two chairs. It is a place for solitude or for sharing with a friend. Father may be in his own little house "when he is behind his newspaper. Mother may be in her own little house when taking a nap. . . . Everyone has to have a little house of his own" (unp).

Knowing when to let go of a loved one is the theme of Efner Tudor Holmes's *Amy's Goose*, illustrated by Tasha Tudor. Amy, who lives on a farm with her parents, feeds corn to wild geese who stop on their way south. Finding a goose injured by a fox, she and her father take it to the barn to nurse it. Since the flock stays nearby, a gander flies every day over the barn. Though the goose is well, Amy shuts her in the barn, saying, "I'm going to shut you up. You're not strong enough for flying yet. Next spring they'll be back" (unp). When only one bird of the flock remains circling, Amy rushes to the barn to free the goose.

Comparing one's own growth to that of siblings is normal for young children. In *Much Bigger than Martin*, written and illustrated by Steven Kellogg, Henry is tired of being Martin's little brother. He tries to make himself bigger by stretching, watering himself, and eating apples. After he tells his parents why he eats apples that sicken him, Father says, "When Martin was your age, he was just your size. You're wearing his old blue pajamas" (unp). Martin asks him to play ape hunt, but Henry is secure enough to refuse because he is making stilts.

Recognizing a difference between fact and fantasy can be difficult for imaginative young children. In *Sam, Bangs & Moonshine,* written and illustrated by Evaline Ness, Samantha ("Sam") lives near the ocean with her fisherman father and Bangs, her cat. Sam claims her mother is a mermaid. Her father, who warns her about lying, says, "Today, for a change, talk REAL not MOONSHINE. Moonshine spells trouble" (unp). After Sam tells her friend, Thomas, there is a baby kangaroo in a cave behind Blue Rock, Thomas goes to the cave, followed by Bangs. When they are caught in a storm, Bangs returns alone and her father rescues Thomas. Sam apologizes, "Oh, Daddy! I'll always know the difference between REAL and MOONSHINE now. Bangs and Thomas were almost lost because of MOONSHINE" (unp). Sam takes her father's gift, a gerbil, to Thomas, telling him it is a gerbil, not a baby kangaroo.

Brinton Turkle is author-illustrator of two delightful books about a little Quaker boy, Obediah Starbuck, who lives on Nantucket Island. In *Thy Friend, Obediah,* a seagull follows Obediah, even to the meeting house. When Father says, "Thee has a friend, Obediah" (unp), Obediah, upset by family teasing, shouts, "That bird is not my friend" (unp). However, when the seagull is not near his bedroom window one night, Obediah goes to the wharf and finds it with a rusty fishhook caught in its beak. Obediah lectures, "That's what happens when thee steals from a fishing line. Serves thee right" (unp). He removes the hook and the seagull follows him. Obediah tells his mother, "That seagull is my friend. . . . Since I helped him, I'm *his* friend too" (unp).

In Turkle's *The Adventures of Obediah,* Obediah tells tall tales. Even the teacher sends a note home about his lying. Mother says, "What is to be done about thy fancies, Obediah? . . . Thee must learn to tell the truth" (unp). When Obediah gets separated from his family on Sheep Shearing Day, he rides a ram, dances in a sideshow area, sees a fire eater, and gets his fortune told. After he finds his family, however, no one believes his story until a neighbor returns Obediah's hat, confirming his tale. Then Mother kisses him and laments, "It was true. Oh, Child! Was thee hurt?" (unp).

BOOKS FOR MIDDLE YEARS

A prolific writer who understands growing-up problems is Beverly Cleary. In *Henry Huggins,* she tells about an ordinary third grader with loving parents. Henry feels nothing exciting happens to him until police bring him home with Ribsy, a mongrel dog. Henry buys two guppies that multiply. Since he loses a football belonging to his friend, Scooter, he has to catch thousands of night crawlers to earn money to replace it. He avoids playing a little boy in the school's Christmas operetta after Ribsy knocks a can of green paint on him. When Ribsy's former master appears, Ribsy shows he prefers to stay with Henry.

Four of Beverly Cleary's books about Ramona Quimby deal with maturing. In *Ramona the Pest*, Ramona waits anxiously for the first day of kindergarten. "Ramona thought growing up was the slowest thing there was, slower even than waiting for Christmas to come. She had been waiting years just to get to kindergarten, and the last half hour was the slowest part of all" (14). She misunderstands her teacher who tells her to sit there for the present and refuses to move, waiting for a present. She looks forward to show-and-tell, although the class of her older sister, Beezus, no longer has it. "Ramona was not discouraged. She was used to Beezus' growing out of things as she grew into them" (43). When a classmate, Susan, tells Ramona, "You're a big pest" (162), Ramona pulls Susan's corkscrew curl as she says, "Boing." After the teacher sends Ramona home, the child does not return to school until she gets a letter from her teacher and a tooth she lost in class.

In Cleary's *Ramona the Brave*, Ramona, now in first grade, has her own bedroom. Unhappy with her strict teacher, the child cries because her report card lists two behavioral complaints. She feels everyone is against her, but Father tells her to show spunk.

Ramona enters third grade in *Ramona Quimby, Age 8*. Mother works as a dentist's receptionist while Father is in college. Things go wrong from the first day when her new sandals squeak and she cracks an egg on her head (as everyone does), but hers is not hardboiled. While sitting with wet hair near the principal's office, she listens to her teacher's complaint, "I hear my little show-off came in with egg in her hair. What a nuisance" (68). Because her teacher finds her annoying, Ramona is afraid to confide on another day when she is sick, so she throws up on the floor. After she gives a book report in the style of a television commercial, her teacher compliments her, telling her she is not a nuisance, only the egg in her hair was.

Ramona is still in third grade in *Ramona Forever*. Neither she nor Beezus want to stay with Howie Kemp's grandmother after school, preferring to be home alone. Father asks Ramona how she can improve her relationship with Mrs. Kemp, but "Ramona did not want the responsibility of thinking what she should do. She wanted help from a grown-up" (33). Mother is pregnant and after the new baby arrives, Ramona is amazed that she loves it. She says, "You know what I think? I think that it is hard to be a baby" (180). Father replies, "Growing up is hard work" (180).

Allie Pratt, whose father died in Vietnam when she was ten months old, lives with her mother in a boarding house in Crosby Bonsall's *The Goodbye Summer*. Allie's invented stories cause trouble and she resists change. After Mother makes her clean her room, she has fourteen bags of trash plus a broken bedstead. She hops on the trash truck, causing a traffic jam at the dump. When Wanda Lenya, a poor, visually impaired, former actress, rents a room for the summer, she helps Allie accept her life. As summer began, Allie remembers thinking that "all she wanted was to hang on to everything and everybody so her world wouldn't change. It was better that way. You knew where you stood. There were no surprises. There were no goodbyes" (28).

Jeannette Grisé tells about a boy who plays jokes on peers and adults in *Robert Benjamin and the Great Blue Dog Joke*. After pretending to stutter, he goes to a psychiatrist who detects his trick and explains a difference between showing off and entertaining, saying, "An entertainer diverts and amuses people. . . . A show-off tries to annoy people . . . to impress people he is smarter than they are" (57). He gets into trouble at school by painting a dog blue that a classmate makes out of leather. Benjamin finally decides that "the best kind of joke takes an audience by surprise. A really great one has to be on yourself" (117).

It is difficult for a child to mature with an overprotective mother, as LouAnn Gaeddert shows in *The Kid with the Red Suspenders*. Rob, a new pupil, gets others to help him jeer, "Ham, Ham, Mommy's little lamb" (8), because Hamilton's mother walks him to school, prepares nutritious school lunches, and makes him wear red suspenders. Hamilton retaliates by deliberately making homework mistakes, hiding the suspenders, and giving away his lunches. Rob coaxes Hamilton and his best friend, Jerry, to skip school and joins them on a trip to the Bronx Zoo. Then Rob leaves Hamilton stranded with no money. After Hamilton returns home, Father convinces Mother to buy her son a belt and let him walk to school alone. She says, "If you can get yourself home from the Bronx, you can walk to school" (71).

Overcoming a problem of a unique appearance is a challenge, as Babbis Friis shows in *Kristy's Courage*, a tale of a little girl whose face and tongue are damaged in an automobile accident. When Kristy appears with a facial scar and speaks with difficulty as she enters second grade, classmates are cruel. Big boys circle her, teasing as if she were a bull in a ring. After boys pour water on her and her newly covered books, Kristy runs to the hospital to see Inger, her former roommate. Inger understands her problem and so does the chief surgeon who finds her sleeping in the bed next to Inger. Kristy says that she wants to stay in the hospital until "I is made all right. I am ugly" (120). The chief surgeon puts a big bandage on her face, telling her father the story, and her parents talk to the school principal and teacher. When bandaged Kristy returns to school, children accept her, but she knows she is cheating with the bandage, so she removes it and peers still welcome her.

In *Dear Mr. Henshaw* by Beverly Cleary, Leigh Bolts lives with his divorced mother in California but misses his father, a cross-country trucker. When his teacher tells the class to write an author, he chooses Boyd Henshaw whose *Ways to Amuse a Dog* is his favorite book. Though Leigh annually writes Mr. Henshaw, this time he includes ten questions. The author replies with his own questions and suggests Leigh keep a correspondence journal. Regular diary entries help Leigh as a writer and as a son, clarifying his feelings about his father. He thinks, "I don't have to pretend to write to Mr. Henshaw anymore. I have learned to say what I think on a piece of paper. And I don't hate my father either. I can't hate him" (73). Leigh finds appreciation at school after he rigs an alarm system in his lunch box and has a story accepted in the *Young Writers' Yearbook*. He thinks, "Maybe I'm not so medium after all" (102).

Ten-year-old Anastasia Krupnik matures rapidly in Lois Lowry's *Anastasia Krupnik*. Anastasia likes to make lists and writes in her green notebook, *Things I Love* and *Things I Hate*. When she learns her mother is pregnant, she puts babies on the hate list and plans to leave home. Father says, "If by some chance you should decide to stick around, you may name the baby" (25). She dislikes her old, forgetful grandmother who often talks about her deceased husband, Sam. Anastasia, who enjoys poetry, asks Father about the "inward eye" in Wordsworth's poem, "I Wandered Lonely as a Cloud." He tells her, "The inward eye can mean memory. Solitude means being alone. And bliss means happiness" (72). Anastasia begins to understand, missing her grandmother when she dies. She names the baby Sam for Grandfather and retains only one word on her hate list: liver.

Ten-year-old Martha Albright is sure she is adopted because she is the only family member with green eyes in Anne Lindberg's *Nobody's Orphan*. When her family moves to Georgetown, she does not make friends as easily as her seven-year-old brother, Kermit. She does introduce herself to an older couple, the Ables, and fantasizes that she is their granddaughter. Gradually, Martha accepts that she is an Albright. Amory Able says, "She has been our sunshine. . . . Ornery little thing, though" (137).

BOOKS FOR LATER YEARS

Characters may mature in any historical period, as Marguerite deAngeli shows in *The Door in the Wall*. Ten-year-old Robin, son of a knight and a lady-in-waiting, is alone with servants in his London home, soon to begin knighthood training with Sir Peter deLindsay. Robin awakens one morning, paralyzed from the waist down, only to find the servants have fled the plague. Brother Luke comes for frightened, angry Robin, reminding him that, as with the wall around his father's estate, "Thou has only to follow the wall far enough and there will be a door in it" (16). At the monastery, Brother Luke teaches Robin to whittle, read, write, and swim, saying, "Whether thou'lt walk again soon I know not. This I know. We must teach thy hands to be skillful in many ways, and we must teach thy mind to go about whether thy legs will carry thee or no. For reading is another door in the wall" (29). After Robin makes himself a pair of crutches, Brother Luke takes the lad to Sir Peter deLindsay's castle. During a surprise Welsh attack, Robin slips out of the castle and swims across the river for help. When Robin says he will be a sorry page, Sir Peter replies, "Each of us has his place in the world. . . . If we do what we are able, a door always opens to something else" (71).

In the 1850s, seventeen-year-old Sam Chase does not own slaves although his father is a prosperous cotton broker. In *Looking for Orlando* by Frances Williams Browin, Sam visits his Quaker grandparents in Pennsylvania. Wesley Owens, a brother of Sam's classmate, comes there looking for his father's runaway slave, Orlando. Sam explains, "You can't blame Wesley's father for wanting his slave back, can you? After all the fellow's Mr. Owens' property. . . . the Underground is the sneaky gang of people who hide runaway niggers and help them get to Canada" (12). When Sam finds Orlando, he hides him and is surprised to hear his grandfather's farm is a station of the Underground Railroad. Sam remembers Orlando's words, "You think the Lord give any man the right to own another man?" (57). After Sam decides to help runaways, Grandfather says, "Thee has learned that, when the laws of man conflict with the laws of God, the laws of God are what we must obey" (59).

During the 1860s, Caddie Woodlawn is a nonconformist tomboy in Carol Ryrie Brink's *Caddie Woodlawn: A Frontier Story*. Her parents give Caddie a boy's freedom to help her recover from illness, but the circuit rider wants to know when they are going to begin making her into a young lady. Caddie asks herself, "Who wants to be a young lady? . . . But still there were times when it was uncomfortable *not* to be one even with Father's loyal support" (17). Father, who traces his beliefs about freedom and justice to his English father, a nobleman, says about his parents, "In those days the worst vice in England was pride. I guess the worst vice of all because people thought it was a virtue" (94). Caddie bravely warns some American Indians about a plot to massacre them. However, when she teases Cousin Annabelle, Father punishes her, confiding, "It's a strange thing, but somehow we expect more of girls than of boys. . . . I want you to be a woman with a wise and understanding heart, healthy in body and honest in mind" (244).

Wartime children may mature as quickly as Jethro Creighton, a southern Illinois farm boy, in Irene Hunt's *Across Five Aprils*. In 1861, Jethro thinks war means "loud brass music and shining horses ridden by men wearing uniforms finer than any suit in the stores in Newton. It meant riding like kings" (17). When Jethro asks Mother why Lincoln cannot decide on war, she says, "He's like a man standin' where two roads meet, and one road is as dark and fearsome as the other" (20). After Jethro's brother Bill becomes a rebel, Union sympathizers burn the family's barn, despite the fact that two brothers and a cousin are in the Union army. His father becomes ill, so Jethro does the farm work and becomes a man. When the cousin deserts and returns home, Jethro, knowing the punishment, must decide about hiding a deserter. He "had faced sorrow and fear . . . had felt a terrible emptiness . . . and deep anger but in his eleven years he had never been faced with the responsibility of making a fearful decision like the one confronting him" (165). Jethro, who writes to President Lincoln about his cousin, is responsible for amnesty for all deserters.

Among stories about children maturing rapidly during World War

II, none is more realistic than Els Pelgrom's *The Winter When Time Was Frozen*. Twelve-year-old Noortje Vanderhook and her father take refuge on the Everingen family farm in the last year of World War II. Noortje enjoys the new experiences of farm life and Evert Everingen's company but feels war's horror. She hides in the woods once as British planes fly overhead and hears Evert say, "That was a beautiful sight, wasn't it?" (215) "Yes," says Noortje, "It was a beautiful sight. But it was terrible too, Evert. How can it be both?" (215).

A sequel to *When Hitler Stole Pink Rabbit* (see chapter 5, "Humaneness") is Judith Kerr's *The Other Way Round*. In the second book, fifteen-year-old Anna and her family are in England after fleeing from Switzerland and France. Anna's father, a famous Jewish writer, has to leave Germany before Hitler's rise to power. Her brother, Max, has been released from internment, and is with them. Father has trouble getting work, and her parents do not adjust well to exile, but Anna feels, "Everything will be different. . . . We'll survive the war and I shall grow up" (126). After an unhappy love affair with her art school instructor, Anna interrupts her art training. While wondering how their parents will handle peace, Max says, "You remember what you used to say in Paris? That as long as you were with Mama and Papa you wouldn't feel like a refugee. . . . Now, I suppose it's the other way round" (255). Max's words are prophetic because the children do assume protective roles toward their parents.

Learning to adjust to life after a war can be difficult. In Michelle Magorian's *Back Home*, twelve-year-old Virginia Dickinson returns from America to England to her mother and four-year-old brother, Charlie. She offends her mother when she says initially, "You can call me Rusty. Everyone back home does" (16). Her American manners, accent, and clothes antagonize all except a neighbor, Beth, whom she tells, "I wish I was grown up. Then I could go wherever I wanted instead of having someone else tell me where I was going to and where I had to live" (77). Disliked by classmates, she thinks, "Sometimes she had the feeling that she was disappearing altogether. . . . Often she had to pinch herself to make sure she was still there" (178). Rusty runs away to the empty house where she first met her mother. There she reflects that though "she still didn't know an awful lot about her mother, . . . she had grown to love her and she didn't want to leave her again" (352).

Being responsible for an animal is one way of helping a child grow into adulthood. Mary O'Hara's *My Friend Flicka* is a modern classic about maturing ten-year-old Ken McLaughlin. He dreams so much in class that he may have to repeat fifth grade. He begs his father for his own colt, but his father refuses because Ken is irresponsible. His father tells him and his brother, Howard, "There's a responsibility we have towards animals. . . . We use them. . . . Shut them up. . . . Take their freedom away" (40). After Ken is upset at watching horse gelding, Mother explains about taking the good with the bad, "That's the way grown-up people do. You've just had a little bit of growing up today" (74–75). Before giving him a colt, Father says, "This giving you a colt is a kind of bargain between us. I give you the colt, you give me more obedience, more efficiency, than you ever have in your life before" (81–82). Ken trains Flicka, a filly, and when she nearly dies from injuries, he cares for her. While his family leaves for a rodeo, Ken stays behind with Flicka and Father announces, "All right, kid—leaving you in charge!—*It's all yours*" (181).

Another modern classic about maturing through devotion to an animal is Marjorie Rawling's *The Yearling*. Twelve-year-old Jody Baxter lives with his parents on a northern Florida farm. He is lonely until he finds Flag, a fawn whose mother is dead. When his parents let Flag be his pet, "It did not seem to him that he could ever be lonely again" (164). As Flag grows, he "was in increasing disgrace. . . . When he was free, he raised havoc. . . . He was wild and impudent" (357). Mother helps Jody replant crops and build a fence around them, but Flag destroys the plants. Finally, Father orders Jody, "Take the yearling out in the woods and tie him and shoot him" (376). After Flag dies, Jody runs away, gets lost, and nearly starves. He thinks, "This then was hunger. . . . the thing was terrifying. It had a great maw to envelope him and claws that raked across his vitals" (390). Then Jody realizes his family's survival is more important than his love of the fawn.

A unique pet is in Robert Newton Peck's *The Day No Pigs Would Die*. Thirteen-year-old Robert Peck lives on a Vermont farm with his father, Haven Peck, the local hog butcher. Running away from school one day, Robert finds a neighbor's cow having trouble giving birth. After getting mauled helping her, Robert explains, "I'd just wound up running away . . . from the schoolhouse. I was feathered if I was going to run away from one darn more thing" (5). After his neighbor gives him a piglet, Pinky, Robert dreams of large litters. Learning Pinky is barren, Rob has to help Papa butcher her "because he had to. Hated to and had to" (139). His dying Papa insists Rob finish school and learn about farming. Papa says, "Come spring, you aren't the boy of the place. You're the man" (122). On Papa's funeral day, his boss and co-workers attend services, so Rob reasons, "There would be no work on this day. The day no pigs would die" (146).

Stepparents have special parental problems, as William Corbin shows in *Smoke*. Fourteen-year-old Chris Long, who adored his father, lives on a ranch with his mother and stepfather of three months, Calvin Fitch, a man he resents. Chris finds a stray German shepherd, Smoke, and with the help of his eleven-year-old sister, Susie, feeds and hides the dog. Cal surprises Chris by defending his right to privacy with the dog, saying, "I happen to believe in personal privacy, and that every-body's entitled to [it] unless he's doing something criminal, in which case it's police business" (62). A local veterinarian, Cal, and a hired hand named Leeroy, help Chris cure Smoke, who is ill. Cal advertises the dog, and when the real owner comes for him, Chris runs to the mountains with Smoke. In the mountains, he recalls Leeroy's words, "It's easy to run away—easiest thing in the world—but it's hard—cruel hard to go back" (203). Chris finally realizes he must. When he calls home, he learns that Cal has bought Smoke for him.

There may be a child-parent communication gap in a broken home, as twelve-year-old Nina Beckwith experiences in Stella Pevsner's *A Smart Kid Like You*. On her first day in junior high, Nina is horrified to find her father's new wife is her mathematics teacher. After trying to get the teacher to quit by having peers harass her, Nina talks with her teacher and they agree to work together. At home, Nina is unable to accept Phil, whom Mother dates, and she complains that Mother "never talks about *feelings*. Just about things" (64). Nina confides in an older friend, Merlaine, who encourages change, stating, "A smart kid like you should be able to figure that out. . . . Just start talking!" (64). And Nina does.

In 1949 in Nebraska, thirteen-year-old Addie Mills falls in love with her teacher, handsome, young Douglas Davenport in *Addie and the King of Hearts* by Gail Rock. Since Addie snubs a potential date, Billy Wild, she has to go to the school Valentine dance with her father and his girlfriend, Irene Davis, whom she resents. Upset at meeting Mr. Davenport's fianceé, Addie removes her shoes and plays basketball with the boys on the dance floor. When others choose Billy to be King of Hearts and the teacher disbands the basketball group, Addie, ashamed, goes home with her father. Dad tells Addie, "Love isn't something you get. It's not like winning a game or something. It doesn't happen at first sight. You have to know somebody a long time and work at it" (75). After Billy delivers Valentine candy following the dance, Dad says, "The right person might be there all along and you wouldn't see him— somebody like Billy" (77).

A poignant family story is *Far from Home* by Ouida Sebestyen. Before mute Dovie Yeager dies, she leaves a note for her thirteen-year-old son, Salty, to take his eighty-four-year-old great-grandmother to Buckley Arms boarding house where Dovie worked for many years. When Salty questions the great-grandmother why the landlord, Tom Buckley, accommodates the two of them, the old woman asks, "Who do you think let us live here rent-free all these years? Whose money do you think paid for your Momma's doctor's bills and funeral?" (25). Salty suspects Tom is his father. After Salty complains that Tom will not recognize him, Hardy, a boarder, tells him, "Salty, the only thing wrong with you is that you're Dovie's boy, and not Babe's" (104). Salty likes Babe, Tom's wife, and finally accepts that Tom will not recognize him as a son because, as Tom says about Babe, "I loved her first. I've shared my life with her. I owe her more. I promised to honor her. . . . So I make it up to her now" (187).

Twelve-year-old Carrie learns to communicate sensitively with her eighteen-year-old half-brother, Ben Felix, in Paula Fox's *Blowfish Live in the Sea*. Carrie loves Ben, although he is a school dropout, refuses to get a job, speaks to no one, and writes, "Blowfish live in the sea," (1) on everything. Ben's father sent him a ceramic blowfish when Carrie was born. After Ben's father invites him to Boston for a visit, Ben asks Carrie to join him. They find the alcoholic father is a defeated man. Ben plans to stay with him to help him, suggesting it will be better this way, "and Carrie knows that people always say it'll be better when they do what they want" (105). Ben comes home for clothes. After he leaves, Carrie finds the blowfish under her bed because Ben does not need it anymore.

In Virginia Hamilton's *M. C. Higgins, the Great*, thirteen-year-old Mayo Cornelius Higgins, known as M. C., lives with his family on a side of Sarah's Mountain. The mountain's name honors Great-grandmother Sarah who sought refuge there from a slave master. Strip mining causes a spoil heap that can ooze down the mountain and cover the Higgins's home. A talent scout tells M. C. that the heap is slipping. "Waves of fear swept over M. C. as if they had been holding back, waiting for the time they could let loose at once. It was his nightmare come to life" (41). M. C. tries unsuccessfully to get his parents to leave before he starts building a wall to control the danger.

In *Sycamore Year*, Mildred Lee depicts how important it is for an adolescent to submit some sensitive problems to an adult. Fourteen-year-old Wren Fairchild and her family move to a small town, Syca-more, where her father is the school principal. Wren becomes friends with fifteen-year-old Anna Lewis who loses her head over a seventeen-year-old boy and becomes pregnant. The girl's secret becomes known when Wren writes Grandma, requesting asylum for Anna. After Mother suggests adults talk to Anna, Wren thinks, "She only wanted to spare me but that too angered me. Why should I be spared? In trying to ease Anna's distress I had only added to it. The least I could do was to tell her myself" (168). Her older sister, Chess, suggests to Wren, "I've been thinking. I suppose anything you learn—especially the hard way—is bound to be of some value" (189).

A boy can be aware of a parent's needs, as fourteen-year-old Billy Catlett shows in *Pistol* by Adrienne Richard. In Montana during the depression, Billy, employed on a small ranch, waits for a ranch hand, Tom, to break in the boy's promised horse, Sundance. Tom says, "A whole lot of living is like horse breakin! You get corralled and then you learn what you got to know and it's better to learn it gentle than to learn it mean" (50). After his meat-packing business fails, Billy's father, Mr. Catlett, prospers by moving his family from Great Plain to a shanty town in a wild, open area where Billy realizes his mother is unhappy. A friend there, a teacher, tells Billy, "You know about illusions. . . . Wordsworth thought they were very important to youth, that they even aided in the process of development" (196). Billy gets his father to agree to return to Great Plain as soon as they have enough money. Billy, who likes to travel, declares, "I want to be able to say I took a look at the world and made my choice. Chicago's only my first stop" (235).

A socio-economic environment can influence values. In *Connie* by Anne Alexander, Connie Colburn, an eighth-grade student, is ashamed when her father loses his job and Great-aunt Berta comes to stay. Connie feels there are "not many people you dared be honest with. She was always covering up, hiding stuff. It was as if there were a real Connie and a pretend one. But she wasn't always sure which was which" (43). Connie learns every family has problems and ceases to be embarrassed over Aunt Berta or ashamed of her father.

In Frieda Friedman's *Carol from the Country*, eleven-year-old

Carol hates it when her family moves from a lovely rural home to a tiny city apartment. Feeling superior to classmates, she tries to prove it by entering a library art contest. She is devastated when a girl in her building, Christine, wins first prize and she, second prize. While caring for her younger siblings, Jinny and Johnny, Carol is surprised that a neighbor, Miss Tyler, does not bang for quiet. Using the dumb-waiter, Carol gets Johnny into Miss Tyler's apartment where he finds the woman on the floor with a broken leg. Carol calls police and neighbors cheer as hospital attendants come for Miss Tyler. Then Carol realizes that "helping a person was more important than winning a prize" (183).

In *By the Highway Home* by Mary Stolz, thirteen-year-old Cathy Reed experiences the death of her brother, Beau, in Vietnam and Father's unemployment. When Father announces they are moving to Vermont to help Uncle Henry run a small inn, Cathy is confused. She thinks, "She'd told them [her family] that thirteen was old enough to share. Sorry that she'd asked, wishing she'd stayed in the ignorance of grown-up problems that being thirteen should entitle her to" (28). At Beau's funeral she learns that "when you are in pain, when you know that what you are feeling now is sorrow, grief, those words in a book, you are quite alone even if people you love are all around you" (47). The elderly Vermont inn residents help Cathy and her family relate to each other.

In *Basketball Girl of the Year* by Amelia Walden, Pat Palmer, a high school senior, wants to win the Basketball Girl of the Year award. Living with her grandparents in a low-income, multi-ethnic area, she tells Chris Landry, a photographer, "Life is a jungle where there is a certain law you may not have heard about. It's called survival of the fittest" (144). Pat plays basketball with her black friends at the Mansion recreation center where she feels "most comfortable, most *right*, in all the world" (9). The photographer and a new coach, Madge Dickson, help Pat begin to relate to her father and recognize that being a woman does not mean being rejected.

Both girls and boys get help from older persons as they mature. In *The Lilith Summer* by Hadley Irwin, twelve-year-old Ellen, who wants a ten-speed bicycle, earns money by sitting with seventy-seven-year-old Lilith Adams. The girl is horrified to learn Mother is paying sitter's fees to Lilith, who plans to buy aluminum screens. On the first day with Lilith, Ellen discovers both are being paid to take care of the other. Ellen is dismayed, questioning, "Why did Lilith's daughter offer money? Why did my mother offer *me*? . . . Why did Lilith have to be so old?" (5). After talking together, Ellen and Lilith decide to take the money and say nothing. Toward summer's end, they have a week's vacation from each other, and Ellen discovers she thinks of Lilith constantly. On the last day, Ellen tells Lilith, "I think, I think when I grow old . . . mean grow up . . . I want to be just like you, Lilith. I think you're very brave and I don't think you're so old . . . or useless . . . or junky" (80).

Thirteen-year-old Emma Williams learns she is not as mature as she thinks in Gen LeRoy's *Emma's Dilemma*. Emma, who baby-sits for six-year-old Herbie Johnson, considers Pearl, her sheepdog, to be her only true friend. Emma's grandmother moves in with the family but she is allergic to Pearl. Herbie's mother refuses Pearl, saying, "Sometimes we all have to give up something or someone we love but life goes on" (71). The upset grandmother tells Emma, "It's just that I've always been so careful about the people I love. And I've always been able to take *care* of them. This is the first time I've felt so . . . absolutely useless" (85). All ends well when a New Jersey aunt accepts Pearl and Emma realizes age does not detract from friendship.

Callie Burke tells about her ties to a bedridden, mute, elderly woman at the Crane Home in Ruth Wallace-Brodeur's *Callie's Way*. Callie feels she is a family misfit since her father is a minister and her mother and sister are fine musicians. Seeing the word, "Help," spelled on a frosted window pane, Callie secretly visits Margaret Megal Reid. Callie thinks, "The more I talked to Megal, the more I had to say. I even talked to her in my head when I wasn't with her" (56). Callie describes crying with Megal for no particular reason: "I sat down on her bed, put my head in her lap, and bawled. Megal's hand was heavy on my head, a great comfort that let me cry until I was ready to stop" (66). After Megal dies, Callie realizes, "I'd been thinking about the people around me more since Megal died. Even if I didn't like some of them very much, they kept me from being alone, like Megal had been before I answered her Hello" (116).

An aged person can help a boy mature through friendship, as W. E. Butterworth shows in *LeRoy and the Old Man*. Eighteen-year-old LeRoy Chambers leaves Chicago to stay with his Mississippi grandfather to avoid testifying at a trial of thugs he saw beat an old woman in his housing project. His welcoming grandfather, a shrimp fisherman with strict moral values, offers LeRoy these supportive words, "I could go back up there with you, when you testify against those bums" (25). After Chicago police come for him, LeRoy reluctantly decides to return, saying, "I'm not brave. . . . It's just that I'm more afraid of the old man cutting me off, shutting me out of his life" (152).

Another story of friendship between a boy and an aged man is Gary Paulsen's *The Foxman*. After his drunken mother abuses him, a fifteen-year-old boy goes to be with relatives in the Minnesota north woods, enjoying hard farm work and trapping. During a storm, he and his cousin take refuge in a cabin with a man who has lived there alone for thirty years. The man's face is disfigured from World War II, but the boy calls him the Foxman, visiting him often. When the boy cannot reconcile his uncle's war stories with the Foxman's experience, the old man says, "The men telling those stories are only trying to remember some of the parts of the war that might be worth remembering—trying to find some use in all that waste" (95). The Foxman rescues the boy in a storm and instructs him, upon his death, to burn the cabin and its contents except for books and valuable hides. When the man dies, the boy burns all except one fox pelt and acknowledges, "Actually, he [Foxman] taught me new ways to look at the same old things, taught me always to question things and make sure they are right before accepting them" (100).

Fourteen-year-old Dave Mitchell's story is about father-son antagonism in Emily Neville's *It's Like This, Cat*. Dave lives in New York City near his best friend, eccentric, elderly Kate, who owns many cats. Feeling his father does not understand him, Dave lavishes affection on a cat. Through his pet he meets a college student, Tom, who is at odds with his own father. Tom says, "*You* talk like *your* Dad is a real pain, and that's the way *I* always have felt about *mine*. But your Dad looks like a great guy to me, so well, maybe mine could be too, if I gave him a chance" (84). Dave's father, a lawyer, helps Tom get a job. When Kate inherits her brother's fortune, Dave's father handles her affairs. Kate leaves money for Children's Aid as well as for stray cats "because there are a lot of stray children in New York City that need looking after as well as cats" (161). Tom tells Dave that he and his father are alike: "You're both impatient and curious, got to poke into everything. As long as there's a bone on the floor, the two of you worry it" (173).

In Stella Pevsner's *Cute Is a Four-Letter Word*, Clara Conrad enters eighth grade determined to be popular, calling it the Year of the Clara. Her best friend, Angel, quits the Pom Pon Cheerleading Squad and helps Clara take her place. After the squad elects Clara captain, she knows she is secure because Skip Svoboda, star athlete, always dates the Pom Pon captain. Clara feels, "As if by magic, I had suddenly become somebody at Harrison Junior High" (74). Angel and Fergy McNutt begin a rat experiment in the Conrad basement, helped by Jay Frank Fogarty, the next-door neighbor for whom Clara baby-sits. During a crucial game, Jay Frank calls Clara to come home. Knowing she will lose the captaincy, Clara questions, "What could I do? Jay Frank needed me. I'm his first, best friend" (180).

Another girl who learns the difference between outer appearance and inner feelings is fifteen-year-old Billie Quinn in June Foley's *Love by Any Other Name*. Billie enjoys dating Bubba Umlauf, school sports star, but wishes he could converse beyond sports and do something besides making out. When she meets Alex Cameron in her drama class, she finds the two have much in common. On prom night, she leaves Bubba and awakens Alex to talk to him. When her younger sister, Jennifer, asks her to explain sex she says:

> Sex doesn't have to do with private parts of your body. It has to do with . . . secret parts of your heart. It has to do with caring about a person so much, wanting to share with that person so much, trusting that person so much. . . . It's real special. (198)

Outward appearance can deceive boys, as fifteen-year-old Jørn Endresen learns in Finn Havrevold's *Undertow*. Though Jørn's parents object to his friendship with seventeen-year-old Ulf, Jørn says about Ulf, "He was really a friend worth having, one who gave me a feeling of growing up just by being with him" (24). Jørn insists on vacationing with Ulf and Ulf's folks in a cabin in Notterö. Jørn learns Ulf, a cruel liar, is alone and plans to sail a stolen boat. Jørn stays because he feels he can save Ulf, who has no moral code, from a life of crime. Ulf wrecks the boat in a storm and drowns. After being rescued, Jørn realizes his parents' wisdom, declaring, "I think that for the first time I had seen the good and the bad in people and I'd found the good and bad in myself" (183).

Guilt is a strong emotion and accepting that fact is important in the process of maturing. In *The Big Hang-up* by William E. Huntsberry, Corey Chance feels responsible for an automobile accident in which one girl dies; the community ostracizes the driver, Rick; and

Corey himself is seriously injured. Rick is driving his mother's new car after a school prom when Corey urges him to race it. After Corey makes known that the accident is his fault, the doctor replies, "I agree that you are partly responsible. No man is an island. . . . No matter what you suggested or did, Rick was the one who was driving the car. . . . What's past is past" (45). Rick leaves school to work for his father, who is ruined by the accident, and Rick asks Corey not to make him feel more guilt. Discussing "Hamlet" in class, the teacher quotes Hamlet, "Give me that man that is not 'passion's slave'—who is not wiped out every time he faces some emotional crisis" (124). A supportive student says in agreement, "A strong man looks ahead, not backward. . . . What's done is done. He's going to keep moving" (124).

All-American by John R. Tunis explores the subjects of guilt and racial bias in the development of a high school athlete, Ronald ("Ron") Perry. In a football game between his private Academy and Abraham Lincoln High School, Ron and a teammate tackle Myer Goldman from Lincoln High and break his neck. Ron visits Myer in the hospital and tells classmates of his guilt feelings, but they argue, "When you had the responsibility of hitting a man high enough or hard enough to break his neck, or worse, you didn't care much about victory. You were in a different world. You suddenly became a man" (29). Ron transfers to Lincoln High where students do not accept him, and Myer cautions him to learn to take it. Ron thinks, "At the Academy he hadn't taken it. . . . He'd gotten up and walked out. Now he had to learn to take it" (77). The team is to play in Miami without Ned LeRoy, a top black player, so Ron and Jim Stacy lead a team rebellion. The coach says, "This is just one of those things. . . . We have to accept the situation. That's life. . . . You can't change human nature" (209). Withstanding civic pressure, the team refuses to go to Miami and gets an invitation instead to the Chicago Intersectional.

Carolyn Meyer's *The Summer I Learned About Life* is a story about fifteen-year-old Eleanor ("Teddie") Schneider who wants to be an aviatrix in 1928 when girls are supposed to act like her sister, Hannah. Teddie thinks about Hannah, "She was a Perfect Girl who wanted to be a Perfect Woman, get married, and become a mother and have Perfect Children" (13). Teddie secretly reads the diary of her older brother, Rob, to learn about problems with his girl. She reflects, "But now I knew things I didn't want to know. And once you've got someone's private thoughts, there's no way you can give them back or get rid of them" (29). Teddie feels sorry for her friend, Julia, who has an unlucky love affair. She looks favorably at Warren, a potential boyfriend, who compliments her after she rides in a small plane. He says, "Teddie's the heroine around here. . . . She's got brains and nerve. And common sense too" (198).

Stella Pevsner understands the emotions of girls trying to mature in *And You Give Me a Pain, Elaine.* Thirteen-year-old Andrea Marshall tells her mother's friend, Rosemary, "I don't know what I'm really like. And I don't know where I'm going, or what I can do" (53). She has difficulty understanding her sixteen-year-old sister, Elaine, who is contentious, sarcastic, and selfish. Andrea feels responsible for the motorcycle death of her adored brother, Joe, as he is en route home from college to see her in a play. Joe's girlfriend, Cassie, tells her to stop feeling guilty about Joe's death. Joe considered Andrea, "someone strong. Someone special. Steady. A girl who knows what is worthwhile and how to keep her balance. No matter what" (174).

Ann Rinaldi's *Term Paper* shows a way of removing guilt. A ninth grader, Nicki DeBonis, lives with her older married brother, Tony, who is a school football and basketball coach *and* her English teacher. Tony assigns her a term paper on death in their family, hoping she will release long-suppressed emotions. After her mother's death, Nicki shows she hates her father for being unfaithful to her mother, for interfering in the love life of her brother Larry, and for forcing her Aunt Rosemary to return to Paris. Tony, her surrogate father, tells Nicki, "You know how far you can go with him, and if you go any further, you're an idiot. Besides, then you violate something, a trust he has in you. And you come off feeling rotten" (6). When she complains she is not at fault, Tony replies, "Don't tell me it wasn't your fault. We all have to assume responsibility for our own actions in this world" (9). Though she knows her father has had a heart attack, Nicki accuses him, "We got all screwed up. Maybe you loved Mom. I'm not saying you didn't. But the rest of us, Daddy, you hurt us all. All the time" (142). Her father has another heart attack and dies. Only after Tony reads her term paper can he explain to her she was not responsible for her father's death, helping end her guilt.

Two selections that portray a main character maturing in relation to the death of a loved one are Lois Lowry's *A Summer to Die* and Peggy Woodford's *Please Don't Go.* Lowry's *A Summer to Die* shows birth, death, and maturing. The Chalmers family moves to the country so that Mr. Chalmers can finish writing a book. Fifteen-year-old Molly easily makes friends. Thirteen-year-old Meg says of herself, "Being both determined and unsure at the same time is what makes me the way I am, I think: hasty, impetuous, sometimes angry over nothing, often miserable about everything" (3). Meg shares a love of photography with a young college couple living nearby, Ben Brady and Maria Abbott. When Molly goes to the hospital with leukemia and dies, devastated Meg says, "It isn't fair" (121). Dad replies, "Of course it isn't fair. But it happens and we have to accept that" (121). What helps Meg is watching and photographing the birth of the son of Ben and Maria. Afterwards, Meg comments, "I had been afraid to see Molly, and now I wasn't. There isn't anyway to explain that" (134).

In Woodford's *Please Don't Go*, fifteen-year-old Mary Meredith spends a month in France with the Menards after fifteen-year-old temperamental, egotistical Marie Claire ("Mío") Menard had spent a month with Mary's family in England. Mary makes friends with sixteen-year-old Joël Joubert and becomes infatuated with an older man, Antoine Malmaison. When she goes back home, she realizes, "My month in France had given me confidence, and things like a snub or a spot on my face did not bother me as they used to. . . . I had a secret past now to my life, and secrets give you power" (105). Joël visits Mary during Easter and tells her, "Mary, don't you find, when you think of last summer, that we were still children then, and we aren't anymore" (121–122). When Mary returns to the Menards in the summer, she realizes she loves Joël, not Antoine. After Joël dies suddenly of meningitis, Mary goes to the funeral. She thinks, "Though I did not weep at this public ceremony, I found my grief had acquired two levels, for the tragic waste of his death, and for my own personal loss" (181). Monsieur Menard insightfully suggests that Mary might study archaeology, knowing Joël's and her interests. Mary reflects, "It was not a new possibility. Deep inside me I felt a stirring of hope for the future, of life holding promise again" (184).

Growing up Jewish is not easy whether in Russia in 1905 or today in the United States. In Chaya M. Burstein's *Rifka Grows Up*, twelve-year-old Rifka lives in a small Russian village where she dreams of furthering her education. Russia in transition is harsh to Jews generally, particularly to young Jewish revolutionaries fighting for improvements. Rifka's father quotes Rabbi Hillel, "If I am not for myself who will be for me—but if I am for myself alone, what good am I?" (6). When Rifka's revolutionary teacher is in jail, Rifka studies alone. Rifka fails the examination because there is a Jewish quota. Although the czar gives the people a constitution, fearful peasants in Rifka's village attack the Jews. Rifka and a friend stop the fighting by setting peasant homes on fire. The ending is hopeful because Rifka plans to join her brother in America.

In *Other Sandals*, a sequel of *To Build a Land* (see chapter 5, "Humaneness"), Sally Watson relates a second-generation story of life in a kibbutz and in Haifa. On a kibbutz, twelve-year-old Devra Meyer hates Arabs who injured her parents in the Israeli War of Liberation. She is a bouncy stutterer, never thinking before she speaks or leaps into a situation. Her cousin, Eytan, crippled in an accident, lives with his parents in Haifa and refuses to make friends. The parents exchange children for the summer. Devra tells her uncle about Arabs, "You *know* they're the most wicked, c-cruel, t-treacherous . . ." (72). After she becomes a friend of Serita, an Arab girl, she admits, "Well, of course there's b-bound to b-be a few exceptions like the K-Khateehs" (98). Max, an African kibbutz student, teaches Eytan judo and tells him, "There are two things you can always be sure of, when you see someone with a nasty disposition. One is that he believes it's the rest of the world who's nasty, and the other is that this person isn't on good terms with himself" (156) Eytan changes, becoming a group member. Devra decides, "You could hate unknown people, but you couldn't very often go on hating ones you know" (195).

A Canadian, Kate Bloomfield, has a different problem in *Kate* by Jean Little. Her father, a nonpracticing Jew, has been alienated from his family since he married her Anglican mother. Dr. Rosenthal, who had once been her father's friend, tells Kate, "You're just like him—thinking yourself a cut above the rest of the world and not caring who knows it" (72). After his daughter, Sheila Rosenthal, is unkind, Kate's friend, Emily, says, "There are prejudiced people. . . . Maybe Sheila's prejudiced too—against people like you" (52). Kate thinks, "Maybe that's partly what prejudice is—feeling without thinking" (130).

In Molly Cone's *A Promise Is a Promise*, eleven-year-old Ruthy Morgan sometimes wishes she were not Jewish. After a Sunday School party with Sandra, her friend, Ruth considers joining Sandra's church. At her brother's bar mitzvah, she decides she wants a bas mitzvah. The rabbi tells Ruthy, "It's what you do that counts. A person sometimes cannot control his thoughts but he can and should control his actions"

(98). When Ruthy questions lighting Friday night candles, Grandmother says, "A promise is a promise" (94). Ruthy promises to care for the cats of a neighbor, Mr. Harvey, while he is in the hospital. She is surprised at an offer from another neighbor, Mrs. Byrd, whom she dislikes, to keep the cats during the girl's bas mitzvah ceremony. Now Ruthy understands the rabbi's words, "To a Jew there are no endings. There are only beginnings" (141).

Charlotte Herman's *The Difference of Ari Stein* is a story of a boy trying to retain his culture. When the Steins move to Brooklyn's Nass Street, Ari wears his yarmulke, or skull cap, to public school. He befriends Max Friedman, a nonpracticing Jew and hustler. Max gets Ari into trouble, encouraging the boy to steal money from his mother for a shoeshine business. Ari plans to fast on Yom Kippur to atone for stealing Mother's money, but he finally confesses to her. Ari's Aunt Marilyn wants the family to drop Jewish ways for "melting pot" blending, so Ari says:

> But Aunt Marilyn, I am old enough to know what the melting pot means. . . . It doesn't mean that everyone should become like everyone else. It means that all kinds of people from all kinds of backgrounds can come and live together and contribute something of themselves.

In E. L. Konigsburg's *About the B'nai Bagels*, twelve-year-old Mark Seltzer has problems when his mother becomes manager of his B'nai B'rith baseball team and his twenty-one-year-old brother, Spencer, becomes coach. Spencer advises Mark, "[Become] more sure of yourself" (59). The team wins its last game after twins trick Mrs. Seltzer and exchange positions. When Mark finally tells his mother, she forfeits the game.

Among girls' most popular books is Judy Blume's *Are You There, God? It's Me, Margaret.* Twelve-year-old Margaret Simons, whose parents have different religious backgrounds, tries to decide between being Jewish or Christian and talks to God about her problems. She thinks she is a failure when she submits a school report on religions, adding, "If I ever have children I will tell them what religion they are so they can start learning about it at an early age. Twelve is very late to learn" (143). Margaret also worries about being underdeveloped until she gets her period. Then she thanks God, announcing, "Now I am almost a woman" (148).

Blume's tale of growing up in a New Jersey suburb in the 1960s differs from growing up in rural Arkansas in the 1940s, as Robbie Branscum depicts in *Johnny May*. But girls' curiosity about their physical development remains constant. Ten-year-old Johnny May lives on a farm with her grandparents and two aunts. She suspects Aunt Irene's suitor of murdering his four dead wives until he saves Johnny May from drowning in flooded Big Creek. When eleven-year-old Aron McCoy moves to the next farm, Johnny May has a friend and begins to have physical and emotional feelings toward the other sex. While they swim naked in the creek, she sees physical differences between males and females for the first time. After school starts, Johnny May consents when Aron asks, "Johnny May, will you walk to school with me and be my girl?" (134).

Natalie Savage Carlson has written two tales of the Savage girls growing up in 1915 in Maryland. In *The Half Sisters*, eleven-year-old Luvvy wants to be one of the girls, like her half-sisters in a residential convent school. Only seven-year-old Maudie and three-year-old Mary-lou are children, not she. Luvvy is smart, quick, and always in trouble. When a rescued baby dove dies and the other escapes, Sam, the hired man, advises, "You've got to learn to give them up when they go, Luvvy. You wouldn't want to be penned up in a cage all your life, and he doesn't neither" (47). After Maudie dies from being kicked by a horse, Sam says, "Just think of the good things. It's no use to think about the bad—only hurts you inside" (137). Luvvy shows she is maturing when she lays out dry clothes for her sisters after they are caught in a storm.

In *Luvvy and the Girls*, Luvvy goes to boarding school with Hetty and Betsy but is upset when grouped with "little girls." It is hard for her to adjust until she befriends Agatha Mulcahy, a school nun's orphaned niece. When Agatha spends Easter vacation on Luvvy's farm, they meet two neighboring girls and Luvvy notes, "Agatha made getting acquainted with them an adventure" (117). Back at school, Luvvy has other chums, deciding, "All girls were different and you had to accept them as they were if you wanted friends" (158).

Harriet the Spy by Louise Fitzhugh is popular because eleven-year-old Harriet M. Welsch is a nonconformist. Harriet, who lives in Manhattan, wants to be a writer, like her friend's father. She spends her spare time spying on neighbors and classmates to gather data. Classmates find her notebook, isolating her after they read it. Harriet's mother writes for advice to Ole Golly, a favorite nursemaid, now in Canada. Ole Golly responds to Harriet:

> Remember that writing is to put love in the world, not to use against your friends. But to yourself you must always tell the truth. . . . You don't need me now. You're eleven years old which is old enough to get busy at growing up to be the person you want to be. (276)

In *Five Summers*, Jo Ann Bren Guernsey tells a tale of Mandy who develops from an impatient twelve-year-old farm girl into a young woman able to cope with illness, death, and first love. Mandy complains about her old, disagreeable grandmother coming to live with them. Mother replies, "Old age is a gift but not without its drawbacks" (14). The next summer, her five-year-old cousin, Charles, Jr. ("Chicky"), moves in with them after his parents die in an automobile accident, and Grandma goes to a retirement home. During the third summer, Mother has a cancer operation, so Grandma comes back to help. When Grandma praises Mandy for her "good instincts for cooking" (90), Mandy says, "I was beginning to agree with Grandma on some things" (90). During the fourth summer, Mandy imitates Mother's unique way of helping Chicky mature. Mandy notes, "She would give Chicky credit for things he had never thought of doing, and then he would go do them" (106). The overwhelming affection of eighteen-year-old Peter, a new farm worker, makes Mandy cry. She reports, "There were more picnics and more concerts and more kisses with Peter after that. . . . He did understand that I was not quite ready for him" (141). Mother dies after another cancer operation the next summer. Although Mandy runs from the hospital, she realizes her responsibility and calls home, only to find Grandma is also dead.

Irene Hunt portrays the confusion and dilemmas of maturing in *Up a Road Slowly*. Julia Trelling is seven years old when her mother dies and she and her nine-year-old brother, Chris, move into the home of unmarried Aunt Cordelia and her alcoholic brother, Haskell. Julie resents Aunt Cordelia's affection for Chris and for Danny, a pupil in the one-room school where the aunt is the teacher. Julie also resents the friendship between Chris and Danny. Uncle Haskell gives her some hard-to-take advice, "Accept the fact that this is a man's world and learn how to play the game gracefully" (31). After visiting Laura, her married sister, Julie feels even more alone. In high school, Julie likes a self-centered, handsome, popular boy who eventually tires of her. When Danny tells her he loves her, she admits, "That was the moment of my greatest security and confidence; it was the time when I realized that love makes one a better person, a kinder and a gentler one" (161). After graduation, Julie thinks, "Let people who have forgotten their childhood say that the early years are the happiest. . . . For me, it was good to be over that stretch of the road which was beset by half-formed anxieties and resentments" (185).

Mollie Hunter's *A Sound of Chariots*, set in Scotland, tells about a girl's ties to her father and her eventual acceptance of his death. Bridie McShane's first memory is of hearing her father say, "You can have the other bairns, Agnes. *This one is* mine" (14). Her revolutionary father tells her, "The world is no better now than it was in Christ's time, and it won't change till everyone is prepared to fight for truth and justice" (34). When she is nine years old, Bridie is devastated by her father's death and for years afterwards, has nightmares about it. At age seventeen, she hears a teacher advise that she can overcome her father's death by living her own life to the fullest. Bridie plans to do so, remembering a line from Andrew Marvell's poem, "To His Coy Mistress": "Time's winged Chariot hurrying near" (194).

Eleven-year-old Claudia Kincaid, bored with life, decides to run away for adventure in *From the Mixed-up Files of Mrs. Basil E. Frankweiler* by E. L. Konigsburg. Since her nine-year-old brother, Jamie, has money, Claudia takes him with her. For a week, she and Jamie live at New York City's Metropolitan Museum of Art, eluding guards and becoming fascinated with an unknown sculptor's angel. Claudia thinks, "She would solve its mystery; and it, in turn, would do something important to her, though what this was, she didn't quite know" (65). She says, "I, Claudia Kincaid, want to be different when I go back. Like being a heroine is being different" (119). She and Jamie discover where the statue's donor, Mrs. Frankweiler, lives and visit her to learn the sculptor's name. Mrs. Frankweiler agrees to show them proof that Michaelangelo is the sculptor if they keep her secret and return home. To her lawyer, Saxonberg, who happens to be the children's grandfather, Mrs. Frankweiler writes, "She [Claudia] could carry the secret of Angel inside her. . . . Now she wouldn't have to be a heroine when she returned home . . . except to herself" (151).

Mother embarrasses thirteen-year-old Anastasia Krupnik in Lois Lowrey's *Anastasia, Ask Your Analyst*. The girl feels she herself may be disturbed and needs a psychiatrist, but her family refuses, so she talks to a Sigmund Freud bust which she buys at a garage sale. When she tells Mother her friends think their mothers are weird, Mrs. Krupnik says:

It's something that happens around the time you become thirteen. . . . The mothers stay the same but the thirteen-year-olds change, and the mothers seem disgusting. . . . I bet it's hormones. When people begin to mature, all those hormones start rushing around or something. (22–23)

In spite of Mother's rodent phobia, Anastasia mates gerbils as a science project. After giving the baby gerbils to a little girl, Anastasia explains to Freud, "First, the gerbils disappeared, and then the hormones did. Life is just one weird surprise after another" (112).

Eleven-year-old Galadriel ("Gilly") Hopkins moves to her third foster home in three years in *The Great Gilly Hopkins* by Katherine Paterson. Gilly, who wants a home with her real mother, takes out her unhappiness on others. At Maime Trotter's foster home, Gilly frightens seven-year-old William Ernest ("W. E."), a slow-thinking foster child, and steals money from a blind black neighbor, Mr. Randolph. Since Trotter, W. E., and Mr. Randolph win her affection, "Gilly knew in the marrow of her bones that if she stayed much longer this place would mess her up" (60). She thinks, "I can't go soft—not so long as I'm nobody's real kid" (71). After she writes her mother, her grandmother, Nonnie, takes her home. When her mother visits, Gilly realizes her mother will never want her. Though she starts another school and likes her grandmother, she wants to return to Trotter, W. E., and Mr. Randolph. She understands that "she loved those stupid people" (131). Responding to her phone call, Trotter tells Gilly to stay with her grandmother who needs her. Gilly goes back to Nonnie, saying, " 'Sorry to make you wait. I'm ready to go home now.' No clouds of glory perhaps, but *Trotter would be proud*" (148).

Anorexia nervosa is the subject of several books about maturing girls. In *The Hunger Scream* by Ivy Ruckman, a high school senior, Lily Jamison, diets because she feels too fat. Her mother, a high fashion illustrator with a model's figure, is a poor example. Lily envies Mother and the attention her five-year-old sister, June, gets. She also admires a neighboring college sophomore, Daniel Perry. Lily enjoys being thin, thinking, "Her senses were so acute since she'd lost weight. Sounds were sharper, smells were keener and penetrating colors were somehow more intense" (99). Dr. Coburn, who hospitalizes the girl when conferences fail, works with the family and helps Lily understand "that her anorexia was a plea for independence, but *knowing* and *doing* were still two different things" (177).

Author-illustrator Kate Seredy shows how two cousins mature in Hungary in *The Good Master*, whose sequel is *The Singing Tree* (see chapter 5, "Humaneness"). Ten-year-old Jancsi Nagy, a farm boy, has never attended school. Before a visit by his city cousin, Kate Nagy, her widowed father warns her uncle, Marton Nagy, about his disobedient daughter, stating, "When she looks like an angel she's contemplating something disastrous" (32). Kate, who teaches Jancsi to read and write, learns to love people and country life. She is comfortable with Uncle Marton Nagy, called "the good master" by his farm workers. Kate describes preparing for winter, "Now she saw that every bite of bread meant hard work—months of planning, worry, anxiety. Having had a small share in all of this, every bite of bread was all the sweeter to her" (141). During his Christmas visit, Father is pleased to see how healthy and busy Kate has become.

Jean Ure's *See You Thursday* portrays sixteen-year-old Marianne Fenton as a reserved, lonely girl who goes to private girls' school even though she would rather attend public school. Her mother rents a room to twenty-six-year-old Abe Shonfeld, a blind music teacher at a private school. Marianne takes Abe to socials and joins his choral group. After Mother asks Abe to leave because Marianne spends too much time with him, Marianne lies to Mother and continues visiting Abe. When she fights with Mother, she runs to the woods to hide. Abe, knowing her hideout, follows her, falling into a quarry. Marianne thinks, "It wasn't fair, running out on someone who couldn't run after you. . . . And she had done that, hadn't she? She had taken the meanest advantage of him that anyone could" (191). Finally, Marianne recognizes that Mother is not mean but caring since she plans to move Abe into his own apartment.

Mildred Pitts Walter's *Because We Are* shows problems of a mixed marriage in a middle-class black community. Seventeen-year-old Emma Walsh has a black professional father and a white mother. After insulting a teacher in an integrated high school, Emma gets a transfer to Manning High, an all-black school. Her upset mother says, "They told me how, here lately, you have been isolating yourself with the black kids. And how you don't participate in school activities the way you did"

(19). Emma's only friend at the new school is a loner, Allan Davis. When attendance at Manning High prevents her debut into society, Emma is brokenhearted. Gradually, her friendship with Allan helps her achieve her father's image of her. She remembers a statement from a former Howard University dean: "It is not the treatment of a people that degrades them, but their acceptance of it" (179).

Growing up is as difficult for boys as for girls. Joseph Krumgold discusses three different life styles in his trilogy about maturing boys: . . . *And Now Miguel, Onion John,* and *Henry 3.* In . . . *And Now Miguel,* twelve-year-old Miguel Chavez lives near Taos, New Mexico where his family herds sheep. Miguel wants to accompany men and sheep to the summer pasture in Sangre de Cristo Mountains, but Father will not let him travel. On San Ysidro Day, Miguel prays to the saint:

> Dear Sir. If you think it is a good idea, please arrange it I should go up into the mountains, the Sangre de Cristo. I know it's a hard thing to do but whichever way you do it, no matter how, is all right with me, Miguel, thanks. (116)

Miguel realizes his wish when his brother Gabriel gets drafted. Then he prays to San Ysidro to withdraw his wish and apologizes to Gabriel who says, "Wishing is risky. Unless you don't care what happens" (198). Gabriel realizes he himself had made a wish to see the world.

Onion John shows a father-son conflict. Twelve-year-old Andy Rausch is a loner, and his father, a dynamic business man, wants Andy to be a scientist with a more exciting life than his father's. While playing outfield at a ballgame, Andy makes friends with Onion John, who lives in a shack on Hessian Hill and speaks a foreign language. Andy decodes his speech, spending a lot of time with him. Mr. Rausch heads the Rotary Club committee which builds a new house for Onion John. Andy asks Father, "Wouldn't it be just as good, as far as Onion John goes, to leave him alone?" (175). Once Onion John occupies the newly furnished house, he lights a fire, accidently burns the place down, and leaves town. After the fiasco, Father is more cautious as he advises Andy occupationally, "All I'm saying is, when the time comes you make up your own mind" (244).

In *Henry 3,* the main character, Henry, lives with his family in a wealthy suburb, Crestview, so his father, a corporation vice-president, can commute to New York City. Henry befriends Fletcher Larkin whose family once farmed potatoes where Crestview now is. There is community dissension when Henry's father builds a backyard bomb shelter to test if his company should sell shelters. Henry says bomb shelters are unnecessary if people end wars his way: "Just suppose that every last insurance policy in the United States was sold here by Russia. And just suppose every last life insurance policy in the U.S.S.R. was sold over there by the U.S." (143). During a hurricane, Henry's father shows his organizing ability, and Fletcher Larkin's guardian grandfather dies. Henry, who wants Fletcher to live with his family, tells his mother about the Larkin lad's consistency in trying to do his best daily, not just in an emergency. Henry praises Fletcher, "It's just as honest with him one day as it is the next. The thing is, with Larkin, you don't have to wait until it's dangerous to do your best. You're always trying" (244).

There are a lot of basketball games in Walter Dean Myers's *Hoops.* Seventeen-year-old Lonnie Jackson, who lives in Harlem, is a top athlete befriended by a former professional player, Cal Jones. Cal, forced to quit after a point-shaving scandal, is an alcoholic, determined to prevent Lonnie from repeating his mistake. Regarding the scandal in which another player, Davy Blue, was proved innocent, Cal says, "Davy Blue was used and I was used. The only difference was that he didn't know he was being used because he didn't see it. I didn't know I was being used because I didn't want to see it" (59). After gamblers kill Cal, Lonnie concludes:

> I figure that there are going to be a lot of Tyrones and O'Donnels, you know, good guys and bad guys, that I'm going to have to learn to deal with. I know I can't win all the time, but I got to keep myself in the game, got to keep my game together, so at least I have a chance. (183)

Two strong black men guide sixteen-year-old John Brown, a summer visitor in Harlem with his aunt and uncle, in Mary Elizabeth Vroman's *Harlem Summer.* His father in Alabama is in a wheel chair since a policeman shot him for not moving to the back of a bus. When John leaves Alabama, Father says, "Son, I want one thing out of you. I just want you to be a man. . . . A man tries to do what he knows is right no matter what" (73). John gets a Harlem grocery job, becoming a friend to another employee, Marcus Garvey, who lives with Old Paul, his grandfather. Old Paul tells John, "Our people need lots of help. . . . I think what we need most is men" (50). John, who sees the good and bad, explains to Marcus, "The way I see it, most people want to be the best they can. They're trying to respect themselves. And nobody has the right to tear them down for trying" (96).

Australia is the setting for Joan Phipson's *Peter and Butch*. Fourteen-year-old Peter Watson, who resents smothering attention from his widowed mother and older sister, takes the nickname Butch. When he helps thwart a robbery by his gang, he knows he is on the wrong path. Joining the police boy's club, he makes friends with David Miller, a counselor. Peter has curly hair, the features of a cherub, and an uncontrollable temper. When Peter attacks a boy who calls him Curly, David warns, "Fightin's all right. Savagery isn't. And hurting someone just because you feel like it is the stone end" (132). After spending a weekend at David's, seeing how a strong man, David, enjoys cultural activities, Peter realizes he can have ideals and still be masculine. When two boys try to jump Peter, he does not run. He thinks, "This time he knew he was right. He would be fighting in self-defense under complete control. David would approve. It was wonderful—intoxicating—not to feel frightened any more" (221).

Another boy, who is overprotected by his mother, is twelve-year-old Lloyd Albert in *Last Was Lloyd* by Doris Buchanan Smith. Fat, clumsy, slow Lloyd, who has no friends, is always chosen last to play ball until a new girl, Ancil, appears. After three husbands, Lloyd's mother, who was only fourteen when he was born, is afraid authorities may take him from her and she keeps him near all the time. Lloyd plays hookey, so the truant officer, Mr. Duggan, advises, "I think you are old enough to start being responsible for yourself" (41). When Lloyd tells Mr. Duggan he likes to make classmates angry, Mr. Duggan replies, "I think we all feel that way sometimes. When someone hurts our feelings, we want to do something to get back at them" (55). Lloyd relates to Ancil that he does not care whether anyone likes him, but she says, "Anyone who doesn't care if anyone likes them or not is either stupid or crazy. I do care if someone likes me or not, and I wish I didn't because no one does, anyway" (92). Then Lloyd and Ancil become friends.

Pete by Alison Morgan begins in Wales. Thirteen-year-old Pete Jenkins loses his place on a class trip to Germany because he is accidently involved in a robbery.

Pete found himself quite alone, between two groups. To the rebels, he was the turncoat and possibly the traitor who had

given the show away. To the righteous, he was the one who
had shared in the spoils while pretending to be the thief-
catcher. (77)

Afraid to tell his mother and principal the truth, he runs away to see his
father, a construction worker on the island of Kell, Scotland. In Cardiff,
someone beats him up. After rescuing him, Alan, a classmate's cousin,
follows him to the island. Pete learns his father is a loner, a slow
thinker, and a person who places dynamite blasts. Near the dynamite
blasting site, Father jeopardizes his own life to save Alan. Pete thinks,
"He had come all this way to discover a father he had never learned to
know and he had discovered him, but not as the mysterious romantic
figure he had imagined, and yet . . . and yet . . ." (210).

In *Enoch's Place* by Joyce Rockwood, fifteen-year-old Enoch
Callahan plans to live with Uncle Ned in the city. Enoch's parents,
hippies in the sixties, came to the North Carolina mountains for a
simple life. He explains to his younger sister, Mercy, why he wants to
leave: "Have you ever been in town watching television, watching some
documentary about something current and modern, and got the feeling
you were watching a show from a country that wasn't yours?" (14).
Once in the city, Enoch cannot accept the lazy, dishonest life with
alcohol and drugs of his cousin and friends. When his mountain home
burns, he wants to return to his family, telling his uncle, "I think I have
more advantages at home. I've had more advantages all along than most
of the kids around here" (188).

An unusual story of a maturing boy is *The Hard Way Home* by
Richard Shaw. Various people tell a story of sixteen-year-old Gary Hutt
who, despite his charm, is irresponsible, lazy, and feels hassled. His
parents send him to survival camp, but he sells the equipment and runs
to a nearby town. When his parents do not come after him, Gary gets a
job as a bus boy in a cafeteria. Father, who hires an off-duty policeman
to watch over the boy, cautions Mother, "If we give in, Laura, he'll
have us under his thumb. This is a little bit of blackmail, and I'm not
buying" (46). Gary joins a commune where he does not do his share of
the work and breaks rules. He gets fired from his job for being late and
lazy. His boss says, "Growing up means a lot more than getting bigger.
It means being able to handle yourself right, not dumping on other
people" (96). Gary decides to return home and accept responsibilities.

Jean Craighead George has written two excellent books on maturing boys. In *Gull Number 737*, sixteen-year-old Luke Rivers is frustrated and resentful of Father's dedication to pure science as they spend a fifth summer on Block Island studying seagulls. Luke helps Father band birds. Holding a baby gull as a jet flies overhead, Luke drops it and afterwards, Gull Number 737, or Spacecraft, as Luke calls it, hides from jets. Luke complains about the gull project until Father tells him:

> A man can only do what he must, even if it seems to hurt those he loves. If I'm honest with myself, you'll learn to be honest with yourself. As far as I'm concerned there's nothing more to living than knowing what you are. (63)

After seagulls cause a plane disaster and Dr. Rivers gets a call to help, Luke goes with him. Seeing a female gull hiding as jets depart, Luke wants to mate it with Spacecraft to produce a breed frightened of jet sounds. Though Dr. Rivers does not agree with Luke's proposal, he recognizes the boy's newfound maturity.

In *My Side of the Mountain* by Jean George, thirteen-year-old Sam Gribley leaves home in May to see if he can survive independently on Great-grandfather Gribley's Catskill Mountains land. Sam does research at a library about animals and natural foods to help him survive. He captures a baby falcon, Frightful, and befriends a weasel, the Baron, as well as a raccoon, Jesse Coon James. Sam learns how to cook and preserve foods, to fish, and to use deer killed by hunters. A college professor, Brando, visits him with a newspaper clipping headlined, "Wild boy suspected of living off deer and nuts in the wilderness of Catskills" (125). His father visits on Christmas Day. In the summer, reporters and photographers appear, followed by Sam's family members who plan to build a house so that he can stay on the land.

Audree Distad's *The Dream Runner* focuses on twelve-year-old Sam McKee who enjoys running. He thinks, "The little heaviness that followed him into vacation was left behind when he ran" (4). An old man, Clete, whose grandfather was an American Indian, tells Sam about a vision quest boys took in their passage to manhood. Clete says, "To give them power, sort of helps them over rough spots . . . kind of magic. Not muscle power, exactly, but inside power" (9). When Clete dies, Sam plans to see a mountain vision site. He meets a retired teacher, Mrs. Em, who gives him directions. On his way up the mountain, he injures his ankle. As he starts down, he loses his way and has no food. Ms. Em finds him and takes him to a hospital. He tells

her, "There was a runner, right up there in the hills with me. A boy.
. . . He just called up strength from the bottom of the barrel . . . the way
a runner does" (149).

   Cynthia Voigt tells a powerful story of a boy maturing in *A Solitary
Blue*, which also has some characters that are in *Homecoming* and
Dicey's Song (see chapter 9, "Responsibility"). When Jeff Greene is
seven years old, his mother, Melody, leaves home to help starving
children and endangered ecology. Feeling rejected by his father, the
Professor, a history instructor, Jeff takes care of the house, respecting the
Professor's wish for peace and order. The summer he is twelve, Jeff visits
his mother and grandmother, Gambo, in South Carolina. He has such
a wonderful time that, on the return bus ride, he thinks, "Maybe
someday he would have to choose between his parents. . . . He knew
who he would choose, he knew why, and he said her name" (45). The
next summer, he visits his mother again, but this time, after learning
that she lies to him and Gambo, Jeff says to his mother, "What you do
to people. Lying to them so you'll get what you want" (87). Jeff is so
disturbed on his return, he fails the next grade in school. He moves
with his father to a cabin in the marshes, where he goes to school and
makes friends. Following Gambo's death, Melody tries to lure him with
his inherited estate, but Jeff tells her he does not love her. A school
friend, Dicey Tillerman, compares him to the loner among birds, the
blue heron. She adds that Gram likes him and reports, "[Gram] . . .
says you've got staying power and a gentle spirit. She says you're a rare
bird" (184).

   Both fantasy and science fiction can portray characters who mature
in the course of the story. A good example is Carol Kendall's *The
Gammage Cup* which tells about Minnipins living in Slipper-on-the-
Water, a village ruled by the Periods. They traditionally wear the same
clothes, paint house doors the same color, and never question authority. Five defiant people who get banished are a poet, Gummy; a
historian, Walter the Earl; a museum supervisor, Muggles; a painter,
Curley Green; and the town treasurer, Mingy. While surviving in the
woods, the five learn that Hairless Ones plan to attack through a
mountain passage, so they warn villagers who band together and force
the enemy to retreat. Villagers welcome the five back while the mayor
says, "We have had differences in the past, but when danger threatened,
we found there were no differences in our hearts" (217). After discredit-
ing Fooley, originator of the Period dynasty, Muggles tells the people,

"About Fooley . . . it makes no difference what we thought of him yesterday or what we think of him today. . . . Our village is what it is" (218–219). Judges who evaluate villages give the reformed Minnipins the Gammage Cup.

A frightening story about what could happen in the future is John Rowe Townsend's *Noah's Castle*. Sixteen-year-old Barry Mortimer and his sister, Nessie, are upset when the family moves to an isolated house where their father fills a basement with food and other survival items. The country faces economic disaster and a short food supply. Mr. Mortimer tells his family why he is hoarding: "It's all very well helping others, but nobody's going to help you" (54). When Barry sees acquaintances starving, he is torn between reporting his father for hoarding and keeping quiet. The boy reflects, "In a way I felt more loyal to Father than I had done a few weeks ago. There was something heroic about his stand, however wrong he might be. But did loyalty mean I had to support him in whatever he saw fit to do?" (191) Barry decides to betray his father and give basement items to SHARE ALIKE, a group helping the elderly, poor, and sick. Before he does, raiders steal nearly everything.

The five books in the Prydain series by Lloyd Alexander are adventurous tales of the battle between good and evil and the maturing of Assistant Pigkeeper Taran. The characters in the imaginary land of Prydain are from Welsh myths except for Taran and Princess Eilonwy. In the first volume, *The Book of Three*, Taran lives with an old enchanter, Dallben; a blacksmith, Coll; and an oracular pig, Hen-Wen. Taran joins Prince Gwydion and an unusual animal, Gurgi, in opposing the Horned-King who wants to conquer Prydain. An enchantress, Achren, locks them in a dungeon, but Princess Eilonwy, with her ball that glows when needed, leads Taran and a bard, Fflewddur Flam, safely out of the castle while the others escape. Prince Gwydion kills the Horned-King, having learned his secret name from Hen-Wen. Gwydion says, "Once you have courage to look upon evil, seeing it for what it is and naming it by its true name, it is powerless against you and you can destroy it" (209). Before returning, Gwydion offers gifts. He gives Fflewddur Flam a harp string that does not break when he bends truth. He gives invisibility to Dwarf Doli and to Princess Eilonwy, a ring of gold. Taran refuses a gift, saying, "I ask no reward. I want no friend to repay me for what I did willingly, out of friendship and for my own honor" (211).

In the second Prydain book, *The Black Cauldron*, despite the Horned-King's death, evil Arawn wants Prydain. He puts live and dead bodies in a black cauldron to make them invincible. Gwydion tries to destroy the cauldron, enlisting help from Taran and Prince Ellidyr who joins only to make a name for himself. When Taran tells Princess Eilonwy that jealousy is a black beast on Ellidyr's shoulder, she agrees, commenting, "It does makes a person think there is some hope for you after all" (109). After the companions find the cauldron, Prince Ellidyr knows the only way for it to be destroyed is for a living person to jump willingly into it. Taran offers himself but Ellidyr jumps in first and the cauldron explodes. Later, Gwydion says, "It is easy to judge evil unmixed. But, alas, in most of us good and bad are closely woven as the threads on a loom" (217).

Alexander's third book in his series, *The Castle of Llyr*, finds Taran and Gurgi taking Princess Eilonwy to the castle of her betrothed, clumsy Prince Rhun, on the Isle of Mona where she is to learn royal behavior. The bard, Fflewddur Flam, and Gwydion, disguised as a shoemaker, are already at the castle. Prince Ruhn tells Taran that, although he is not clever, he wants to be a worthy member of royalty, and Taran replies, "For a man to be worthy of any rank, he must strive first to be a man" (90). The evil enchantress, Achren, steals Eilonwy, taking her to the empty Castle of Llyr. Taran, Gwydion, and their friends rescue her, later witnessing the castle's destruction. Eilonwy gives Taran an ancient battle horn before he goes home and she and Prince Ruhn return to the Isle of Mona.

In *Taran Wanderer*, Taran is in love with Eilonwy but feels he must know who he is before he can declare his love. Dallben suggests a search for Taran's parents throughout Prydain, believing, "Though you may not find what you seek, you will surely return a little wiser—and perhaps even grown to manhood in your own right" (20). In the villages, Taran learns to be a blacksmith, a weaver, and a potter. After defeating bandits led by Dorath, Taran and Gurgi go to the Mirror of Llunet, a pool of water in a cave. In the water, Taran sees Dorath who followed him, hoping for treasure. Dorath escapes and Taran returns to Annlaw, the potter, telling him:

> I saw myself. In the time I watched, I saw strength—and
> frailty. Pride and vanity, courage and fear. Of wisdom a little.
> Of folly, much. . . . I saw alike as men may seem, each is

different as flakes of snow, no two the same. . . . As for my parentage, it makes little difference. . . . True kinship has naught to do with blood ties. . . . manhood is not given but earned. (252–253)

In the Prydain finale, *The High King*, Taran, back at Caer Dallben, joins the good Sons of Don who attack the stronghold of evil Arawn. Prince Rhun, now king of Mona, and Coll, a blacksmith, die in battle, but Arawn loses his power after Taran takes his sword, Drnwyn, and restores Prydain's peace. Gwydion tells the Sons of Don to leave Prydain and go to Summer Country, the land from which they came, "a land of no strife or suffering, where even death itself is unknown" (264). Gurgi and Hen-Wen may go. Taran becomes High King when he decides to help rebuild Prydain. Eilonwy relinquishes powers of enchantment to stay with him. The book ends, "And so they lived many happy years, and the promised tasks were accomplished" (285).

SUMMARY

This chapter deals with 100 realistic and fanciful books. Nine are for early years, twelve are for middle years, and seventy-nine are for later years. Obviously, there are more books for older children who are struggling to achieve their own maturity and choose to read about this value.

References

Alexander, Anne. *Connie*. Illustrated by Gail Owens. Atheneum, 1976. 179 p. (L)

Alexander, Lloyd. *The Black Cauldron*. Holt, Rinehart & Winston, 1965. 224 p. (L) (Courage)

———. *The Book of Three*. Holt, Rinehart & Winston, 1964. 217 p. (L) (Courage)

———. *The Castle of Llyr*. Holt, Rinehart & Winston, 1966. 201 p. (L) (Courage)

———. *The High King*. Holt, Rinehart & Winston, 1968. 285 p. (L) (Courage, Responsibility)

———. *Taran Wanderer*. Holt, Rinehart & Winston, 1967. 256 p. (L) (Courage)

Blume, Judy. *Are You There, God? It's Me, Margaret*. Bradbury Press, 1970. 149 p. (M)

Bonsall, Crosby. *The Goodbye Summer.* Greenwillow Books, 1979. 148 p. (M) (Friendship)

Branscum, Robbie. *Johnny May.* Illustrated by Charles Robinson. Doubleday & Company, 1975. 135 p. (L)

Brink, Carol Ryrie. *Caddie Woodlawn: A Frontier Story*, rev. ed. Illustrated by Trina Schart Hyman. Macmillan Company, 1973. 275 p. (L)

Browin, Frances Williams. *Looking for Orlando.* Criterion Books, 1961. 159 p. (L) (Loyalty)

Burstein, Chaya M. *Rifka Grows Up.* Illustrated. Bonim Books, 1976. 184 p. (L)

Butterworth, W. E. *LeRoy and the Old Man.* Four Winds Press, 1980. 154 p. (L)

Carlson, Natalie Savage. *The Half Sisters.* Illustrated by Thomas Di Grazia. Harper & Row, Publishers, 1970. 163 p. (L)

———. *Luvvy and the Girls.* Illustrated by Thomas Di Grazia. Harper & Row, Publishers, 1971. 159 p. (L) (Friendship)

Cleary, Beverly. *Dear Mr. Henshaw.* Illustrated by Paul O. Zelinsky. William Morrow & Company, 1983. 135 p. (M)

———. *Henry Huggins.* Illustrated by Louis Darling. William Morrow & Company, 1950. 155 p. (M)

———. *Ramona Forever.* Illustrated by Alan Tiegreen. William Morrow & Company, 1984. 182 p. (M)

———. *Ramona Quimby, Age 8.* Illustrated by Alan Tiegreen. William Morrow & Company, 1981. 180 p. (M)

———. *Ramona the Pest.* Illustrated by Louis Darling. William Morrow & Company, 1968. 192 p. (M)

Cone, Molly. *A Promise Is a Promise.* Illustrated by John Gretzer. Houghton Mifflin Company, 1964. 153 p. (L) (Self-respect)

Corbin, William. *Smoke.* Coward-McCann, 1967. 253 p. (L) (Courage, Responsibility)

deAngeli, Marguerite. *The Door in the Wall.* Illustrated. Doubleday & Company, 1949. 121 p. (L) (Courage)

DeRegniers, Beatrice Schenk. *A Little House of Your Own.* Illustrated by Irene Haas. Harcourt, Brace & Company, 1954. Unpaged. (E)

Distad, Audree. *The Dream Runner.* Harper & Row, 1977. 151 p. (L)

Duvoisin, Roger. *Petunia.* Illustrated. Alfred A. Knopf, 1950. Unpaged. (E)

Fitzhugh, Louise. *Harriet the Spy.* Illustrated. Harper & Row, Publishers, 1964. 298 p. (L) (Friendship, Responsibility)

Foley, June. *Love by Any Other Name*. Delacorte Press, 1983. 216 p. (L) (Friendship)

Fox, Paula. *Blowfish Live in the Sea*. Bradbury Press, 1970. 116 p. (L)

Friedman, Frieda. *Carol from the Country*. Illustrated by Mary Barton. William Morrow & Company, 1950. 191 p. (L)

Friis, Babbis. *Kristy's Courage*. Illustrated by Charles Geer. Translated from Norwegian by Lise Sømme McKinnon. Harcourt, Brace & World, 1965. 159 p. (M) (Courage, Humaneness, Self-respect)

Gaeddert, LouAnn. *The Kid with the Red Suspenders*. Illustrated by Mary Beth Schwark. E. P. Dutton, 1983. 71 p. (M) (Friendship)

George, Jean Craighead. *Gull Number 737*. Thomas Y. Crowell Company, 1964. 198 p. (L) (Ingenuity)

—————. *My Side of the Mountain*. Illustrated. E. P. Dutton & Company, 1959. 166 p. (L) (Courage, Ingenuity)

Grisé, Jeannette. *Robert Benjamin and the Great Blue Dog Joke*. Illustrated by Alex Stein. Westminster Press, 1978. 121 p. (M)

Guernsey, JoAnn Bren. *Five Summers*. Clarion Books, 1983. 180 p. (L)

Hamilton, Virginia. *M. C. Higgins, the Great*. Macmillan Company, 1974. 278 p. (L) (Responsibility)

Havrevold, Finn. *Undertow*. Translated from Norwegian. Illustrated by Cathy Babcock Curry. Atheneum, 1968. 186 p. (L) (Friendship, Self-respect)

Herman, Charlotte. *The Difference of Ari Stein*. Illustrated by Ben Shecter. Harper & Row, Publishers, 1976. 150 p. (L) (Cooperation, Friendship, Loyalty, Self-respect)

Holmes, Efner Tudor. *Amy's Goose*. Illustrated by Tasha Tudor. Thomas Y. Crowell, 1977. Unpaged. (E)

Hunt, Irene. *Across Five Aprils*. Illustrated by Albert John Pucci. Follett Publishing Company, 1964. 223 p. (L) (Responsibility)

—————. *Up a Road Slowly*. Illustrated by Don Bolognese. Follett Publishing Company, 1966. 192 p. (L)

Hunter, Mollie. *A Sound of Chariots*. Harper & Row, Publishers, 1972. 242 p. (L)

Huntsberry, William E. *The Big Hang-up*. Lothrop, Lee & Shepard Company, 1970. 127 p. (L)

Irwin, Hadley. *The Lilith Summer*. The Feminist Press, 1979. 109 p. (L)

Kellogg, Steven. *Much Bigger Than Martin*. Illustrated. Dial Press, 1976. Unpaged. (E)

Kendall, Carol. *The Gammage Cup*. Illustrated by Erik Blegvad.

Harcourt, Brace & World, 1959. 221 p. (L) (Humaneness, Self-respect)

Kerr, Judith. *The Other Way Round*. Coward, McCann & Geoghegan, 1975. 256 p. (L) (Humaneness, Responsibility)

Konigsburg, E. L. *About the B'Nai Bagels.* Illustrated. Atheneum, 1969. 172 p. (L) (Friendship, Responsibility)

———. *From the Mixed-up Files of Mrs. Basil E. Frankweiler.* Illustrated. Atheneum, 1967. 162 p. (L) (Self-respect)

Kraus, Robert. *Leo the Late Bloomer*. Illustrated by Jose Aruégo. Windmill Books, 1971. Unpaged. (E)

Krumgold, Joseph . . . *And Now Miguel.* Illustrated by Jean Charlot. Thomas Y. Crowell Company, 1953. 245 p. (L)

———. *Henry 3.* Illustrated by Alvin Smith. Atheneum, 1967. 268 p. (L) (Friendship)

———. *Onion John.* Illustrated by Symeon Shimin. Thomas Y. Crowell Company, 1959. 248 p. (L) (Friendship)

Lee, Mildred. *Sycamore Year.* Lothrop, Lee & Shepard Company, 1974. 190 p. (L) (Friendship)

LeRoy, Gen. *Emma's Dilemma.* Harper & Row, Publishers, 1975. 123 p. (L) (Friendship)

Lindberg, Anne. *Nobody's Orphan.* Harcourt Brace Jovanovich, 1983. 160 p. (M) (Friendship)

Little, Jean. *Kate.* Harper & Row, Publishers, 1971. 162 p. (L) (Humaneness)

Lowry, Lois. *Anastasia, Ask Your Analyst.* Houghton Mifflin Company, 1984. 119 p. (M)

———. *Anastasia Krupnik.* Houghton Mifflin Company, 1979. 114 p. (M)

———. *A Summer to Die.* Illustrated by Jenni Oliver. Houghton Mifflin Company, 1977. 154 p. (L)

Magorian, Michelle. *Back Home.* Harper & Row, Publishers, 1984. 375 p. (L) (Humaneness)

Meyer, Carolyn. *The Summer I Learned About Life.* Atheneum, 1983. 198 p. (L)

Morgan, Alison. *Pete.* Harper & Row, Publishers, 1972. 241 p. (L)

Myers, Walter Dean. *Hoops.* Delacorte Press, 1981. 183 p. (L)

Ness, Evaline. *Sam, Bangs & Moonshine.* Illustrated. Holt, Rinehart & Winston, 1966. Unpaged. (E)

Neville, Emily. *It's Like This, Cat.* Illustrated by Emil Weiss. Harper & Row, Publishers, 1963. 180 p. (L) (Friendship)

O'Hara, Mary. *My Friend Flicka*. Illustrated by Dave Blossom. J. B. Lippincott Company, 1941. 253 p. (L) (Friendship, Responsibility)

Paterson, Katherine. *The Great Gilly Hopkins*. Thomas Y. Crowell Company, 1978. 148 p. (L)

Paulsen, Gary. *The Foxman*. Thomas Nelson, 1977. 125 p. (L) (Friendship)

Peck, Robert Newton. *A Day No Pigs Would Die*. Alfred A. Knopf, 1972. 150 p. (L)

Pelgrom, Els. *The Winter When Time Was Frozen*. Translated from Dutch by Maryka and Raphael Rudnik. William Morrow & Company, 1980. 253 p. (L)

Pevsner, Stella. *And You Give Me a Pain, Elaine*. The Seabury Press, 1978. 182 p. (L)

———. *Cute Is a Four-Letter Word*. Clarion Books, 1980. 190 p. (L)

———. *A Smart Kid Like You*. The Seabury Press, 1975. 216 p. (L)

Phipson, Joan. *Peter and Butch*. Harcourt, Brace & World, 1969. 222 p. (L)

Rawlings, Marjorie Kinnan. *The Yearling*. Illustrated by Edward Shenton. Charles Scribner's Sons, 1938. 400 p. (L) (Friendship)

Richard, Adrienne. *Pistol*. Little, Brown & Company, 1969. 245 p. (L) (Responsibility)

Rinaldi, Ann. *Term Paper*. Walker & Company, 1980. 202 p. (L)

Rock, Gail. *Addie and the King of Hearts*. Illustrated by Mike Ludlow. Alfred A. Knopf, 1976. 85 p. (L)

Rockwood, Joyce. *Enoch's Place*. Holt, Rinehart & Winston, 1980. 205 p. (L)

Ruckman, Ivy. *The Hunger Scream*. Walker & Company, 1983. 188 p. (L)

Sebestyen, Ouida. *Far from Home*. Little, Brown & Company, 1980. 191 p. (L)

Seredy, Kate. *The Good Master*. Illustrated. The Viking Press, 1935. 196 p. (L)

Shaw, Richard. *The Hard Way Home*. Thomas Nelson, 1977. 127 p. (L)

Smith, Doris Buchanan. *Last Was Lloyd*. The Viking Press, 1981. 124 p. (L) (Friendship)

Stolz, Mary. *By the Highway Home*. Harper & Row, Publishers, 1971. 194 p. (L)

Townsend, John Rowe. *Noah's Castle.* J. B. Lippincott Company, 1975. 255 p. (L) (Loyalty)

Tunis, John R. *All-American.* Illustrated by Hans Walleen. Harcourt, Brace & Company, 1942. 245 p. (L) (Humaneness)

Turkle, Brinton. *The Adventures of Obediah.* Illustrated. The Viking Press, 1972. Unpaged. (E)

———. *Thy Friend, Obediah.* Illustrated. The Viking Press, 1969. Unpaged. (E) (Friendship)

Ungerer, Tomi. *Rufus.* Illustrated. Harper & Row, Publishers, 1961. 32 p. (E)

Ure, Jean. *See You Thursday.* Delacorte Press, 1981. 211 p. (L)

Voigt, Cynthia. *A Solitary Blue.* Atheneum, 1983. 189 p. (L)

Vroman, Mary Elizabeth. *Harlem Summer.* Illustrated by John Martinez. G. P. Putnam's Sons, 1967. 190 p. (L) (Friendship, Humaneness)

Walden, Amelia. *Basketball Girl of the Year.* McGraw-Hill Book Company, 1970. 224 p. (L) (Self-respect)

Wallace-Brodeur, Ruth. *Callie's Way.* Atheneum, 1984. 119 p. (L) (Friendship, Self-respect)

Walter, Mildred Pitts. *Because We Are.* Lothrop, Lee & Shepard, 1983. 192 p. (L) (Friendship, Humaneness)

Watson, Sally. *Other Sandals.* Holt, Rinehart & Winston, 1966. 223 p. (L) (Humaneness, Self-respect)

Woodford, Peggy. *Please Don't Go.* E. P. Dutton & Company, 1972. 187 p. (L)

IX

Responsibility

When parents or parent substitutes are dead, absent, or unreliable, child characters in juvenile books often assume adult responsibilities. Many tales depict children caring for each other and failing to report to authorities when parents or guardians neglect them for fear of being separated in foster homes or institutions. Stories show dependability, in terms not only of family members, but also of friends; students; the helpless or needy, such as elderly persons; animals; a career or business; a dwelling place; or the community at large. The latter includes everything from emergency action by lighthouse keepers to the action of guilty persons who turn themselves in to police. In a variety of books, characters are responsible for their own survival or that of a group of people.

BOOKS FOR EARLY YEARS

Some picture storybooks show personified vehicles that render an important service. For example, *Little Toot* by author-illustrator Hardie Gramatky depicts a small tugboat, Little Toot, often ignored by other tugs for his frivolity, who shows he can be serious when he guides an ocean liner through a storm into a harbor. Before Little Toot acts, he blows an S.O.S. signal from his smokestack to alert other tugs, but they cannot reach the liner in the rough sea. They treat Little Toot like a hero when he is successful.

Similarly, *Katy and the Big Snow* by author-illustrator Virginia Burton portrays a personified red crawler-tractor that plows streets after a ten-inch snowfall. When truck-type snowplows are stuck, Katy clears the most difficult roads for the police, firemen, and employees of the post office and utilities. She plows a road to the hospital for the doctor and clears airport runways. Exhausted, she plows side streets for traffic to move freely. "Then . . . and only then did Katy stop" (unp).

Some books show responsible characters who are honest though they may suffer as a result. Joan Lexau's *I'll Tell on You*, illustrated by Gail Owens, presents a young black boy, Mark, with his dog, Spud. Mark is walking his dog when they stop in front of the baseball coach's house and see his daughter, Mary Wells. The dog wants Mary to pet him, but the scared girl hits and kicks him, so he bites her. Mark hides Spud's involvement until he realizes Mary must get rabies shots. Urged by his friend, Rose, whom he is training to be a baseball catcher, Mark admits his dog is guilty. Taking a chance that the coach won't use him on the team, Mark tells him, "It was my dog [that] bit Mary. She hit him and he got scared" (16). Since the dog does not have rabies, Mary is safe. Coach Wells puts both Mark and Rose, the first female, on the team.

BOOKS FOR MIDDLE YEARS

Frank Asch sets his animal fantasy, *Pearl's Promise*, in Mr. Adams's Pet Store. A caged white mouse, Pearl, sees both her parents sold and obeys her mother's last request, "Take good care of little Tony" (1). Pearl does her best to protect her young brother, Tony. Mr. Adams puts Tony into the cage of an evil snake, Prang, as future food, and a boy named Jay buys Pearl. Although she likes her owner, Pearl feels she must rescue Tony, so she escapes and returns to the pet store. When she frees Tony, he says, "If it weren't for you, I wouldn't be alive today" (151). She places Tony with a pair of kind field mice, Oliver and Josephine. Then she returns to Jay to share her cage with Wilbur, a mouse friend Jay bought in her absence.

John Reynolds Gardiner's *Stone Fox*, which takes place in Wyoming's horse-and-buggy days, focuses on reliable ten-year-old Willy. Facing his bedridden guardian grandfather, the boy declares, "I'll make Grandfather want to live again" (11). Willy hitches his dog, Searchlight, to the plow and harvests the potato crop alone; then he discovers Grandfather's demoralization is not due to crop problems but to taxes. If the old man does not pay $500 in overdue taxes, he will lose his farm. Willy uses his fifty-dollar college savings as an entrance fee to compete in the National Dogsled Races for a $500 purse, despite the fact that a tall American Indian, Stone Fox, is sure to win. Willy tells Stone Fox why he is racing and, although Searchlight dies a hundred feet from his goal, Stone Fox guarantees that Willy, holding his dog, walks across the finish line first. Willy draws comfort from Grandfather's words, "There are some things in this world worth dying for" (63).

Also about ten years old is Caroline ("Angel") O'Leary who feels responsible for her four-year-old brother, Theodore ("Rags") O'Leary, in Judy Delton's *Back Yard Angel*. (Rags earned his nickname from carrying an old blanket.) Since Mr. O'Leary has left the family, Mrs. O'Leary works part-time and shares baby-sitting with Angel, warning her, "Baby-sitting is not just a job, Angel. It means being responsible for someone's very life" (3). After trying to rescue her brother who climbed on a television antenna, Angel hopes that "she could keep Rags healthy, or at least alive, until he started kindergarten in the fall" (64). Finally, Mother gives Angel time off to visit a school chum.

Eleanor Clymer tells about another older sister who cares for her younger brother in *My Brother Stevie*. After Father's death, Mother deserts them, and twelve-year-old Annie Jenner with her eight-year-old brother, Stevie, go to their paternal grandmother's urban project apartment. As Mother leaves, she tells Annie, "Take care of your brother" (7). It is not easy because Stevie plays hookey or breaks into candy machines and Grandma is ineffective. Annie gets help from Stevie's new teacher, Miss Stover, who teaches a social studies unit on trains after Annie privately tells her Stevie throws rocks at trains. After school, Miss Stover lets Stevie walk her dog. When the teacher leaves town, Stevie reverts to attention-seeking behavior. Annie sacrifices to buy train tickets to Hacketsville, New York, so she and Stevie can visit Miss Stover. Following that visit, Stevie changes, Grandma stops hitting him, and Annie's burden lightens.

In Nutbrush, Mississippi, a black couple, Matt and Luvenia Carson, assume responsibility for their interracial niece, four-year-old Ethel Hardisen, in Eleanora E. Tate's *Just an Overnight Guest*. Matt's brother in St. Louis, Jake Carson, is Ethel's father. Her white mother, Mary Hardisen, an alcoholic prostitute, abuses her daughter, keeping her filthy and locked in their trailer without regular meals. Mrs. Carson, a high school English teacher, brings Ethel home. Her husband, a long-distance trucker, and her daughters, thirteen-year-old Alberta and nine-year-old Margie, are not enthusiastic since Ethel is noisy, undisciplined, and destructive. When Ethel wears Margie's old dress to church, Margie is jealous. Mrs. Carson explains, "If we hadn't taken her in, no one else would have because everybody says she's bad" (76). Margie begins to understand when she questions, "Was Ethel bad only because she'd never had anyone to show her how to be good?" (105).

Eve Bunting's *The Skateboard Four* portrays Morgan, a leader of three other skateboard enthusiasts, who turns down a dare dangerous for his group. Albert, a new boy with a shark-shaped skateboard, defies Morgan and his group to skate around the rim of an empty, dilapidated swimming pool. Morgan agrees to do it himself until he hears about the accident of Corky Annon, a motorcycle club leader who always accepted a bet. Morgan, feeling leadership responsibility, rejects the challenge, explaining, "There's a lot to being a leader. He felt a new confidence, a new certainty. A leader had to be wise. A leader had responsibilities. Not everybody understood that" (63).

Beverly Cleary's *Henry and the Paper Route* shows Henry Huggins being a responsible boy, once he gets the job. The district manager, Mr. Capper, rejects Henry when he first applies because, with four kittens inside his jacket, he seems immature. Henry tries to impress Mr. Capper by substituting on the route of his friend, Scooter. As his eleventh birthday nears, Henry is successful when he applies again since an older boy, Murph, resigns. Murph objected to four-year-old Ramona Quimby following him and collecting his papers. Henry finally gets "*his route* . . . doing what he wanted to do—something important" (191). He keeps Ramona from interfering by getting her to imitate a mechanical man who "can't move very fast" (189).

Another book in Beverly Cleary's Henry Huggins series is *Henry and the Clubhouse*, which depicts Henry carrying his papers past mean dogs and in uncomfortable weather, despite pesky Ramona. Henry builds a clubhouse with neighborhood boys, but Ramona locks him inside. He has to be free by six o'clock to deliver papers, so he sends Ramona to get her sister, Beezus. He tells Beezus the key's location and she releases him after he teaches her the club's secret entry words. Another day when it snows, Henry lets Ramona ride on his sled and a "Dear Editor" letter appears in his newspaper, commending him on "his work" and kindness to a "little girl" (184).

Clyde Robert Bulla's *Shoeshine Girl* focuses on spirited ten-year-old Sarah Ida Becker who is so irresponsible that her parents send her to Palmville to spend the summer with Aunt Claudia. When her aunt denies her spending money, Sarah becomes a shoeshine girl at Al Winkler's Grand Avenue stand. She and Al become friends. After a car hits Al and he goes to the hospital, Sarah handles the business independently, giving Al all profits. He tells her, "Everybody thinks it's wonderful the way you're running the stand all by yourself" (70). Al recuperates, but Sarah's mother becomes ill, so the girl returns home.

After his father's death, sixteen-year-old John Haskell, a fur trapper, becomes "the man of the family" in Walter D. Edmonds's *Two Logs Crossing: John Haskell's Story*. When John tries to collect a one-dollar debt from wealthy Judge Doane, he learns Father owed the judge forty dollars. By summer's end, John has grown winter food for his family, but he has not made enough money from part-time work to pay Judge Doane. The lad borrows seventy-five dollars from the judge for equipment so that he can trap in the winter with Seth, an American Indian. John starts for home in the spring with enough skins to pay both debts to the judge but does not listen to Seth's warning to cut two logs to lay across the creek before crossing it. Hurriedly John cuts one log, tries to cross, falls into the creek, and loses everything. He sadly confesses to the judge. However, John's eventual success justifies the judge's continued faith in him.

M. S. Stolz's *A Dog on Barkham Street* centers on a fifth-grader, Edward Frost, whose parents deny him a dog because he is not dependable. Edward admires carefree, wandering Uncle Josh who arrives with a collie, Argess. The boy changes enough to take care of Argess. While Edward fights a next-door neighbor, Martin, "Barkham Street's Bully," Argess defends Edward. The boy is so shocked when his uncle leaves with Argess that he skips school and jumps on a freight train with a friend. Awaiting him on his return is Uncle Josh who gives him Argess. "Edward . . . couldn't help realizing that he no longer wanted to grow up to be like Uncle Josh, that no one could ever depend on, and who didn't really care about anybody. Not even Argess" (183).

An eleven-year-old black boy, Dolph Burch, befriends a dog, Tory, and helps other animals in Charlotte Baker's *Cockleburr Quarters*, named for a section of town where Burch lives. Under a church, the boy finds Tory and her eight puppies, feeds her, and moves the "family" to a shack where he discovers a black drifter, Jake, who also cares for Tory. When a fire destroys the shack and dependent puppies, Jake and Tory escape, moving into a vacant house. There Jake advises neighborhood children to remove garbage, so animals will not get worms from spoiled food. When the children need medicine for Tory and their pets, they earn money by collecting returnable bottles. After the sale of Cockleburr Quarters, Dolph's family moves nearby, keeping spayed Tory.

In Mary Perrine's *Salt Boy*, a ten-year-old Navajo shepherd, Salt Boy, lassos an animal in an emergency. He practices lassoing rocks or sheep while tending his flock and wants to use his roping skill to train horses. Father, who thinks he is too young, makes him promise to stop roping sheep. When a flash flood in a cave endangers a lamb, Salt Boy breaks his solemn promise by lassoing and rescuing the lamb. Father arrives in time to appreciate his skill and to forgive him.

Paula Fox's *One-eyed Cat* tells about eleven-year-old Ned Wallis, a boy who helps an old neighbor after school. Ned worries about blinding an eye of a wild cat one night when he secretly fires a birthday gun his folks forbade him to use. The person who sees him is not his father, Reverend Wallis, nor their snort-and-bellow housekeeper, Mrs. Scallop, but his rhumatoid mother. The boy communicates superficially with his mother after the shooting since he is afraid of her insight. When chrysotherapy gold injections put Mrs. Wallis in remission, he confesses to her his feeling of responsibility for the cat and eases his conscience.

In *The Light at Tern Rock*, Julia L. Sauer shows that working at a lighthouse involves year-round and around-the-clock responsibility. Tern Rock's regular lighthouse keeper, Byron Flagg, tricks Martha Morse into being his substitute before and during Christmas. Since Martha has lived at Tern Rock during the fourteen years her now-deceased husband was its keeper, she knows how to manage the place. She brings her nephew Ronnie with her. Flagg assures them he will return from shore leave on December 15, but by December 23 he still has not come, so Aunt Martha cooks, bakes, and cleans for the holiday. After Christmas dinner, Martha and Ronnie find gifts from Flagg and a letter from him that says:

> I have played you a mean trick. . . . But let me tell you the reason. I am more than sixty years old and I have never yet spent a Christmas with a parcel of young ones. . . . Last Christmas I promised myself I would spend this one with my niece's family. . . . And when I couldn't get relieved, I took this way. (60)

Mrs. Morse admits she has enjoyed being of holiday service.

Around the world, young and old alike learn to be of service, especially to their families. Meindert DeJong's *Journey from Peppermint Street*, set in Weiram, Netherlands in the early twentieth century, tells how ten-year-old Siebren must baby-sit with his brother, Knillis, who says only one word, "Da." Relief comes when Grandpa takes Siebren on a journey from his Peppermint Street home. On the walking trip, the boy befriends a dog, Wayfarer, leaving the dog where Father will see a note to bring it home. At night, they come to a marsh where Grandpa would have drowned had Siebren not thrown a ball to keep him afloat. They call for help and tiny Great-aunt Hinka, who lives in a former monastery with her huge deaf-mute husband, retrieves them in her boat. Hinka identifies with Siebren, explaining, "I live in a marsh with a deaf-and-dumb husband, you sit endless hours with a baby brother who can't talk, so both of us have to make up things within ourselves—for ourselves" (198). Armed with this advice, Siebren returns home to his dog and a brother who now says, "Sieb."

Dorothy Rhoad's modern Maya story in the Yucatan, *The Corn Grows Ripe*, traces how carefree twelve-year-old Dionisio (nicknamed "Tigre") assumes a man's responsibilities after Father breaks his leg. Tigre walks alone through the forest to fetch a distant bonesetter, and while Father recuperates, fulfills Great-grandmother's edict, "Tigre will make our *milpa* [cornfield]. We can always depend on our men in *this* family" (37). When Mother has a new baby, Tigre plants extra corn and vegetables for the growing family. He even continues his studies at night. A drought ends in time for Tigre's crops to be a success, and Father is well enough to join him in harvesting them.

In a tale about Japan, Masako Matsuno's *Taro and the Tōfu*, honest Taro goes to the house of the old *tōfu* [bean curd] seller to buy two tōfu cakes for supper. The seller says his grandson is ill. With his change, Taro buys two chocolates at another store. Then he finds that the tōfu seller has given him too much change and, though it is late, Taro returns the extra money to him, leaving his grandson a chocolate. Taro is responsible enough to tell the shopkeeper, "You gave me the wrong change. Forty extra yen. For your grandson, *ojiisan* [old man]" (unp). Returning home, Taro is happy.

Shirley L. Arora's "*What Then, Raman?*" revolves around Raman, a shy boy in India who is the first in his village to learn how to read. He reluctantly leaves school to help support his family by gathering hill plants for an American teacher. She prods Raman until he realizes that with learning comes a responsibility to teach others in his village. He fulfills that obligation well.

Korea is the setting for Pearl Buck's *Matthew, Mark, Luke and John*, a tale about four half-Korean, half-American outcasts. Eleven-year-old Matthew, who has never known his American father, makes a home in a cave under a bridge when his Korean mother deserts him. He goes to an American army camp to beg and meets an abandoned six-year-old boy whom a soldier names Mark. The soldier tells them they are brothers and mutters a prayer about Matthew, Mark, Luke, and John. A policeman brings them an eight-year-old he caught stealing. The children name him Luke and when they find a four-year-old rummaging for food, they call him John. The burden of providing food and shelter for them falls on Matthew. On Christmas, he takes them to the American camp. When Luke tries to steal food, Matthew cries, telling his troubles to Sam, a friendly American soldier, and Sam arranges for the four to be at the children's center. Later, Sam adopts Matthew, taking him to America where the boy tries to get others to adopt Mark, Luke, and John.

Natalie Savage Carlson's *A Brother for the Orphelines*, which takes place in a village near Paris, focuses on Josine, the smallest of twenty girl orphans (*orphelines* in French). When an Arab worker, temporarily at the orphanage, asks Josine if she gets enough to eat, she replies positively, and she questions if he has children. He says, "Too many" (13). Soon Josine finds an Arab baby boy, a fondling left in the orphanage bread basket. Calling him Coucky, Josine wheels him in a padded shopping cart, or *pousette*, with a lampshade sunshield. The teething baby cries before the girls go on a trip, so Josine responsibly stays with him. She declares, "Oh, I can't leave him. All the time I would wonder if he was still crying" (36). The day before authorities are to send the baby to an orphanage for boys, Josine secretly takes him, searching for a possible foster father. She gets caught in the midst of a bicycle marathon, and a newspaper reporter writes about her. As a result, executives combine male and female orphanages, so Josine and Coucky can remain together.

A Parisian tale by Natalie Savage Carlson, *The Family Under the Bridge*, tells how old Armand Pouly changes from a carefree hobo to a workingman who supports three "grandchildren" and their mother. Armand looks upon youngsters as being like pesky starlings until he finds the poor Calcets—Suzy, Paul, Evelyne, and their mother—unable to pay rent and staying under the very bridge he always occupies in winter. Now that he feels needed, Armand becomes an apartment caretaker. Part of his pay is a three-room dwelling for his "family."

BOOKS FOR LATER YEARS

In some high-adventure books, characters feel responsible for each other. This is apparent in Joan Aiken's *Bridle the Wind*, historical fantasy about a trip from England to Spain of orphaned thirteen-year-old Felix Brooke. Felix is shipwrecked trying to return to his mother's folks in Spain after visiting his father's unhappy English family. Insane, supernatural Father Vespasian imprisons him in a French monastery. Nearby, Felix finds the small hanging figure of thirteen-year-old Juan Esparza, supposedly dead, left by evil Mala Gente bandits. Felix leads Juan to the monastery, they escape, and Felix feels he must guide mysterious Juan to safety. Felix thinks, "With what relief I would deliver Juan to his uncle, and rid myself of this perplexing responsibility" (123). Using money brought from England, Felix buys ponies, and they ride into Spain. Juan's Uncle León is not home but is hiding for political reasons. Juan leaves a grateful farewell note to Felix, asking him not to follow because Juan knows where his uncle is. After Felix joins his maternal grandfather, the lad receives Uncle León's letter of thanks for helping his *niece*, Juana. No longer is Felix's traveling companion mysterious.

Elizabeth George Speare's *The Sign of the Beaver*, which takes place in 1760, tells about thirteen-year-old Matt Hallowell who reliably guards Father's newly built Maine cabin as he waits for Father to return from Quincy, Massachusetts with Mother and his siblings. Matt survives in the forest with the help of Attean, a lad in the nearby Beaver clan, and Attean's grandfather, Saknis. The sign of the beaver guides the boys to the American Indian community where visiting Matt gradually finds acceptance. When Attean's people move in winter to better hunting grounds, they invite Matt to join them, but he says, "Thank you, I'd like to go on the hunt. But I can't do that. If—when my father comes, he wouldn't know where I had gone. . . . Something might happen to the cabin. He's trusting me to take care of it" (112). Attean leaves Matt his dog as the two friends part.

Fourteen-year-old Gerry, who is in a new school, proves more

responsible than the self-appointed class leader, Bert, in Roderic Jeffries's *Trapped*. After Father's death, Gerry and Mother move to a small
town on the English coast where Bert provokes Gerry. One cold
afternoon, Bert "borrows" a boat and entices Gerry to go downstream to
a mud flat to hunt ducks. When snow falls and they cannot find their
beached boat, it is Gerry who copes. In the darkness, Gerry forces Bert
to keep moving until help finally arrives.

In Peter Zachary Cohen's *Bee*, fourteen-year-old Herb Dexel
learns to fulfill responsibilities as apprentice to an experienced herder,
Rudy Kemp, on his small Wyoming ranch near Cheyenne. Rudy
teaches Herb to ride nervous Bee and tells him, when searching for stray
cows, to stay on the ridge. After Herb disregards Rudy's instructions,
Rudy breaks his ribs saving the boy from being carried on Bee into
timber. Herb is reliable in getting an ambulance for Rudy and in
thwarting three cattle rustlers. Later, he helps bring Rudy home from
the hospital and takes care of Rudy's livestock.

Fifteen-year-old Jonas, after a lonely year at a boarding high
school in southern Alaska, returns to his Eskimo village, resuming a
hunter's life to feed his family in Ann Turner's *A Hunter Comes Home*.
Eight years before, his father and twelve-year-old brother Samik froze to
death while hunting seals. Grandfather, Owl-man, supports his mother
and younger sister, Oolah, but Jonas thinks:

> Sons are meant to care for their mothers, and I had not done
> that. I must find some way to help, to take away the thinness
> in her face, to make Oolah grow taller. I had to find some way
> that did not mean giving in to Owl-man [sic] and doing things
> his way (49).

Jonas and Grandfather go on a fishing trip and dry many fish for winter
before Grandfather loses his footing in the river and drowns, dying "a
hunter's death" (116). When Jonas returns with Grandfather's body and
the fish, Mother says, "A hunter comes home" (118).

Hunting as a way of providing for a family is also central in Jane
and Paul Annixter's *Horns of Plenty*. Gary Luckett, about seventeen,
lives with his folks in a log cabin in the Montana Rockies where Mr.
Luckett makes a haphazard living shooting game and guiding trophy
hunters. When the best-paying client, Mr. Fraser, finds Mr. Luckett ill,
he gets Gary to guide him. Fraser fails to shoot a bighorn sheep, Big
Eye, and offers $1,000 for its horns. After a cougar injures Gary, Mr.

Luckett becomes a more responsible provider. It is Gary, however, who finds Big Eye dead after a storm and happily claims his reward without shooting the animal.

In *Pickpocket Run*, Annabel and Edgar Johnson portray a high-school graduate, Dix, who is more trustworthy than his father, owner of an automobile repair shop. The father creates business by surreptitiously damaging cars brought to him for repair. His mother is apathetic about her dishonest husband, and Dix's older sister has her own problems, but Dix refuses to help his father cut good wires on cars. Another lad, Keno, beats up Dix because he will not help rob a motel. The police chief is uncooperative and Father refuses to help stop the robbery, so the youth confides in a newcomer, Matt Burnham, who turns out to be a famous racket-busting district attorney. After Keno threatens Dix's sister, Matt counsels the boy to leave on a bus and return secretly. Dix arranges for the police to catch Keno committing the crime, but authorities come late, and Dix must face armed Keno and another thug alone until police arrive.

Louise Moeri's *Downwind* focuses on twelve-year-old Ephraim Dearborn who often cares for his nine-year-old brother, Bones; his younger sister, Jocelyn; and the baby, Caleb. There are televised warnings to flee following an Isla Conejo nuclear power plant accident, so the boy tries calming Mother and does the packing. After Father returns from work, the family uses a truck and trailer to escape with Ephraim in charge of his siblings in the trailer. When Jocelyn gets a concussion from a severe jolt, a nurse, Murdock, arranges for a helicopter to take the girl with her mother to a Reno hospital. (The strength of Nurse Murdock balances a poor female image cast by the neurotic mother.) Ephraim helps Father overpower several ruthless refugees, and once it is safe to return, the boy reflects about the future:

> The little ones would be there inside the comfortable old yard
> for some time yet, and he would be there to help take care of
> them part of the time, but . . . more and more, as time
> passed, he would be outside the fence, out here with Dad and
> people like the Murdocks. (121)

Responsibility to others extends beyond the family. In Jerome Brooks's *Make Me a Hero*, twelve-year-old Jake Ackerman is conscientious when, one spring day during World War II, he gets a job learning to emboss desk pads. Old Izzie Gold tells the boy, "Take your time and do it right, Ackerman. . . . That's all that counts: making everything into something" (37). Jake decides to prepare for his bar mitzvah in imitation of Harry Katz, a fellow employee his same age. Jake is so conscientious about helping Harry study Hebrew that he goes to Harry's house at 5:30 A.M. in a snowstorm and gets pneumonia as a result. There is no reciprocation since Harry forgets Jake's bar mitzvah and Jake is disillusioned with his former friend.

The Mock Revolt by Vera and Bill Cleaver tells about thirteen-year-old Ussy Mock who lives with his family in a small Florida town in 1939. Wanting to be independent, Ussy finds a summer truck farm job and plans to save his money so he can run away from "deadlies," or dull people. On the farm, he meets thirteen-year-old Luke Wilder and his destitute migrant family. Wanting to help Luke, Ussy gives him money and brings fruit and soap from home for him. After Luke steals his money, Ussy avoids contact until authorities arrest Mr. Wilder for attacking a truck farm supervisor. Ussy finds Luke a job, assists the boy and his mother to move, and gives them rent money. When Luke loses his job, Ussy is disgusted with his shiftlessness but feels responsible for helping Luke to improve. Then Ussy abandons his own departure plans.

In Louise Lawrence's *The Dram Road*, poor sixteen-year-old Stuart Roper, sick with pneumonia, is a bum in Birmingham, England when he commits a crime. Accompanied by two thugs, Stuart hits a jeweler with a pipe and tries to rob him before running away. In this fantasy, Stuart takes several buses to a village, Green Edge, where two ghosts lead him on Dram Road to old Ted Nelmes's home. Ted's neighbor—April Jarrett, a doctor's wife—calls on Ted and nurses Stuart. When Stuart recovers, he fixes the cottage and cares for his host until the man dies. Believing himself to be a murderer, Stuart wants to pay for his crime and returns to Birmingham with Dr. Jarrett as his character witness. At first, Stuart thinks he will spend the next fifteen years in jail, but he learns the jeweler is not dead, so he hopes for probation.

Walter Dean Myers's *The Young Landlords* describes a cluster of organized Harlem teenagers who talk to the landlord about improving their apartment building. The landlord, in turn, sells them the place for a dollar. When tenants complain about not having the money to pay their rent, the young landlords try to avoid evictions by suggesting a street fair and rent party to raise funds. In the end, one young landlord, Paul, admits:

I had wanted the fun of owning a place, but I hadn't wanted
the responsibility. . . . I learned to accept the idea that
answers were a lot easier to come by when you stood across
the street from the problem. What was a lot harder to accept
was that there weren't good answers to every problem, and
when there weren't good answers you had to make do the best
you could. (195)

Corinne Gerson features a daughter who is more responsible than
her mother in *How I Put My Mother Through College.* Jessica ("Jess")
Cromwell lives on Long Island with her nine-year-old brother, Ben,
and her recently divorced mother, Ann, a thirty-two-year-old college
enrollee. In a role reversal, Mom now expects Jess to cook, clean, do
the laundry, and solve problems. Mom asks her daughter for advice
about college courses, dating, and how late she should stay out with
men. Nightly, Mom comes into Jess's room for a "little talk," reporting
on college experiences and questioning which groups to join. Ben asks,
"Hey, Jess, did you ever get the feeling that Mom was just another kid in
the family?" (58). After Mom injures herself cheerleading, she tells Jess,
"You'll even have to help me dress and undress. Ha! Now you'll be *my*
mother!" (70). Life becomes more complex when Daddy remarries and
Mom brings home boyfriends, like slovenly Randy, whom Ben detests.
Ben's maneuver ends Mom's ties to Randy. When Mom dates Professor
Dante Reynolds, she assumes more domestic responsibility.

Elisabet McHugh's *Raising a Mother Isn't Easy, Karen's Sister,*
and *Karen and Vicki* reflect the views of capable pre-adolescent Karen
Bergman that she is the central household manager. The trilogy begins
when Karen is eleven years old and ends eighteen months later. In the
first book, adopted Karen describes life with her mother, a pretty,
blonde, blue-eyed, twenty-nine-year-old veterinarian, Barbara
Bergman, who even tunes up her own car: "I don't know how my
mother managed before she had me. . . . I was four and a half when I
came from Korea to be adopted, and I have taken care of Mom
practically ever since" (3). Karen adds:

Every day after school I have chores to do. This time of year I
have to carry firewood in first of all. That's for our stove in the
kitchen. Then I feed the animals [seven cats, two dogs, one
pig, six rabbits, eleven ducks, fourteen geese, two guinea pigs,
and lots of chickens] and start dinner. I fix most of the meals
in this house. (7)

The first book ends as the veterinarian announces that she is adopting a five-year-old Korean girl, and Karen comments, "I'm glad I finally gave up trying to find a husband for my mother. Getting a new sister is more fun" (156).

Grandmother Eulalia Bergman visits to welcome her second granddaughter in McHugh's sequel, *Karen's Sister*. Mom, Karen, and her new sister are returning from the airport after midnight when their car gets a flat tire. Karen insists on waiting with Mom on the roadside although it is cold. Karen says, "I felt sorry for Mom. After all, it wasn't her fault that we had a flat tire, and I knew she must be just as tired as I was" (28). The mother names her second daughter Meghan. When Grandmother leaves, Mom tells Karen she is going to marry John Carlson, a university researcher and widower with three children, whom she met when he changed her flat tire.

In McHugh's third book, *Karen and Vicki*, Karen, aged twelve and a half, and her sister, Meghan, are living in the home of their stepfather, John Carlson, with his three children: Vicki, aged sixteen; Marcus, aged fourteen; and Ryan, aged six; and Grandma Carlson, the main housekeeper. Karen's project in a class for gifted children is a time efficiency study (TES). She announces, "I'd like to work on getting my family more organized" (2). After Karen's pregnant mother gives birth to a son, Jonathan, household chores multiply. Irresponsible Vicki, who monopolizes the bathroom, is lax with both home and school tasks. When Karen tries to change Vicki, the older girl replies, "Tell Miss Goody-Goody to get off my back and mind her own business instead" (99). Only when Grandma Carlson has a heart attack does Vicki change. Karen plans to enter her TES project in the school science fair, but her stepfather comments that the report will hurt Vicki's feelings, so Karen thinks about a new project.

Bruce Clements's *Anywhere Else but Here* portrays Mollie Smelter, a mature thirteen-year-old girl who helps her widower father when his Schenectady, New York printing business goes bankrupt. While Father auctions personal effects to pay debts, Mollie meets Mr. Potrezeski, who was saved in Poland during World War II by Mollie's maternal grandfather. Feeling obligated to this fine family, he offers to finance Mollie's eventual college education and pays $500 for a dollhouse she is selling. She uses the money as a deposit on a printing shop for Father in Willimantic, Connecticut. Mollie and Father move, bringing an abandoned eight-year-old boy, Claude, for whom, "We'll be taking responsibility . . . like parents" (147).

In Julia First's *Move over, Beethoven,* a talented junior high student, Gina Barlow, tries to follow her piano teacher's instructions to practice four hours daily. She says:

> I was about to become the only twelve-year-old girl in the second half of the twentieth century in the United States of America with such restrictions imposed on her that the word *freedom* would be an unknown quantity. (11–12)

It is no wonder Gina feels guilty when she secretly joins an after-school orchestra, partly to be with a clarinetist, Joshua Jackson. Joshua also sings in the Metropolitan Opera chorus. When Gina's widowed mother wants to buy her daughter an expensive baby grand piano, Gina gets Mother's approval for extracurricular activities. Joshua makes a date with Gina, admiring the "cool" way she handles responsibilities.

Living with a retarded sibling involves special obligations. Twelve-year-old Neil Oxley has a retarded thirteen-year-old sister in Marlene Fanta Shyer's *Welcome Home, Jellybean.* The presence of Geraldine (whose pronunciation of her name sounds like "Jellybean") is traumatic for her family and other apartment house tenants. She pushes an emergency button as she enters an elevator and a siren wails. In anger she pulls down drapes and throws a bag of groceries down a garbage chute. After Gerri puts applesauce on the keys of Father's prized piano, he moves into his own apartment. Seeing her brother paste photographs in an album, she removes food can labels and glues labels on two school reports her brother must submit. Father invites Neil to live with him, but Neil says, "I wouldn't really want to leave Mom and Gerri" (130). When tenants petition for the family to move, the building superintendent, noting Gerri's progress, destroys the petition. At Neil's piano performance in school, Gerri rushes onstage during his piece. Neil tries to move in with Father, but the boy's conscience pricks him, so he stays with Mom, learning to be proud of Gerri's slightest gains.

In Norway, thirteen-year-old Mikkel Grabseth copes with a similar problem in *Don't Take Teddy* by Babbis Friis-Baastad. Teddy is Mikkel's fifteen-year-old brother who has the mind of a two-year-old. While playing baseball, Mikkel tries to baby-sit Teddy, who knocks out an opponent's teeth. Afraid of Teddy's possible arrest, Mikkel runs away with his brother to Uncle Bjarne's summer cottage. Both boys develop pneumonia from the ordeal and are delighted when Father and Uncle Bjarne rescue them. After they recuperate, Teddy attends Lillebo, a special school. Seeing Teddy's contentment as a day pupil, Mikkel begins to shed his burden.

Fifteen-year-old Sara Godfrey accepts responsibility for her ten-year-old retarded brother, Charlie, in Betsy Byars's *Summer of the Swans*. Sara, Charlie, and their nineteen-year-old attractive sister, Wanda, live with Aunt Willie. Father deserted the family after Charlie's birth, and Mother died. Sara envies her sister's beauty but is bitter about her estranged father's neglect, mainly of Charlie. She complains about her brother, "I never get to do anything by myself. I have to take him everywhere" (30). However, when Charlie gets lost trying to see swans, Sara frantically searches for him, finds him in a ravine, and brings him home.

Caring for the aged is a task only sensitive friends and relatives do well. Lillian Eige's *The Kidnapping of Mister Huey* tells about fourteen-year-old Willy Goodwin. On his paper route, Willy meets Mister Huey who wants to return to his home town in Wisconsin though his grandson prefers placing him in Happy House Boarding Home. Willy's parents leave for California after arranging for their son to attend Falcon Survival Camp in northern Wisconsin. Instead of going to camp, Willy takes Mister Huey to Wisconsin by bus, unaware of the worry their disappearance causes. When they return, the grandson agrees to Mister Huey's staying in his own home while Willy looks after him.

Vera and Bill Cleaver have written about responsible granddaughters in several books, such as *Queen of Hearts*, featuring twelve-year-old Wilma Omalie Lincoln. She becomes housekeeper and companion for difficult Granny Lincoln who has had a stroke. Granny accuses Wilma and her six-year-old brother, Claybrook, of stealing a goldpiece Father finds in Granny's hiding place. Claybrook refuses to return, so Wilma copes alone. During the summer, Granny learns to accept help and appreciate Wilma. It is a maturing experience for the girl who worries when she studies Granny, "Every line of her sagged. Here was decay, ruthless, forsaken, and terrible, without consolation" (29).

In *The Whys and Wherefores of Littabelle Lee*, Vera and Bill Cleaver show another dutiful granddaughter, orphaned sixteen-year-old Littabelle Lee, who lives in the Ozark Mountains with her grandparents, Paw Paw and Maw Maw, and Aunt Sorrow, an herb doctor. When lightning destroys their house and winter food supply, the family moves into the barn loft while Paw Paw builds a log house. After she falls off a horse, Sorrow suffers mentally, discontinues her practice, and joins a hermit she loves. To support the family, Littabelle becomes a substitute teacher, though pay is meager. When Littabelle notices Paw Paw is sick, she begins to do his chores and fights her own illness with these words, "I am sick but I cannot be sick. I have got two old, helpless people depending on me" (113). Finally, Littabelle gets a judge to force her city-dwelling uncle and two aunts to help their parents while she tries to become a teacher.

When a family caregiver dies, a loving person often tries to substitute. Isabelle Holland's *Alan and the Animal Kingdom* details the problems of Alan MacGowan, orphaned since he was three and shunted from one relative to another. After Uncle Ian dies and Alan has to move, authorities kill three of his pets. At the age of nine, Alan, who stutters when nervous, prefers animals to human beings. He moves in with Great-aunt Jessie. Before she dies from a heart attack, Alan visits her in the hospital and destroys her identifying documents so that he can return to their home and live alone with his pets. When Alan takes his sick kitten to a veterinarian, Dr. Harris, the boy confesses the lie he is living, and the doctor similarly confesses he is an alcoholic. After a car strikes his dog, Alan, unable to reach Harris, goes to another veterinarian. He tries to get money from Harris for the bill but finds him drunk, so he steals from school. When he learns the boy's story, the school headmaster takes Alan home with him. Then the lad learns that Dr. Harris is trying to rehabilitate himself to become a responsible foster parent for Alan.

In Betsy Byars's *The Night Swimmers*, young Loretta ("Retta") Lynn has to assume a mother's role since her own mother is dead. Retta cares for her two younger brothers, Johnny and Roy, and her father, Shorty, a Country Western singer. Since Father is away at night, busy during the day, and inattentive to his children, Retta must meet all family needs. "Retta has always been his [Roy's] daytime mother. Even when her real mother was alive, it had been Retta who looked after him" (21). In a neighbor's private pool, without permission, Retta gives her brothers the pleasure of night swimming, but she feels guilty when Roy almost drowns. The ending holds out hope that Retta may have less responsibility if Father remarries.

Ruth Whitehead depicts another motherless home in *The Mother Tree*, set in western Texas in the early 1900s. After Mother's unexpected death, ten-year-old Tempe Foster becomes responsible for the household and her four-year-old sister, Laurie, who still cannot understand

Mother's absence. When Father works for six weeks in Oklahoma, taking his teasing fourteen-year-old son, Philip, grandparents let Tempe and Laurie stay with them. Tempe feels lighthearted while Granny is in charge. With Granny's help, Tempe comes to recognize little Laurie's reliance on her and her own special role as elder daughter in a home without a mother.

Mildred Lee's *The Rock and the Willow* focuses on thirteen-year-old Enie Singleton who helps care for her brothers and sisters. She loves school and, with her English teacher's encouragement, wants to become a writer. She describes her special place for thinking: "Her secret place was down beyond the curve of the branch, a little nook under a clump of willows whose drooping boughs screened her into rare and delicious privacy" (17). When her little sister, Sue Ann, dies, Enie "tremble[s] in the face of adult sorrow, knowing no way to touch it with her own" (94). Mother becomes so ill that she cannot attend Enie's graduation as valedictorian. After Mother's death, Enie resents Father's courting the choir mistress until she realizes that Miss Elsie Mae cares about Father and his children and will help Enie go to college.

Jean Slaughter Doty's *If Wishes Were Horses* tells about orphaned thirteen-year-old Stephany and her older sister, Camilla ("Cam") Reed, who manage their Virginia family horse farm, Thunder Rock, after their father's death. (Dad had never recovered from Mother's death.) Cam cancels nursing studies and "gently [takes] over the running of the farm" (29). She oversees the stables until Stephany replaces her after school and Cam leaves for an office job. Stephany says, "Cam and I had helped Dad with the new foals for years. It was always a terrific responsibility—newborn foals are so terribly fragile—but we enjoyed working with them, and we were good at it" (11). They even deliver twin foals. After the farm burns, the bank forecloses on its mortgage, claiming all animals except a mare, Rosie, the girls' personal property. A young rancher who dates Cam, Jimmy Conner, secretly mates Rosie to a famous racing colt, Northern Dancer, before the colt's death, so an expected foal gives the sisters new hope.

Mary Stolz's *The Edge of Next Year* shows the disintegration of a happy, prosperous farm family when the mother dies in an automobile accident. Ten-year-old Victor withdraws, creating an attic vivarium for his "crawlies." Mr. Woodward seeks solace in alcohol. Thirteen-year-old Orin assumes the responsibilities of cook, housekeeper, and caretaker, refusing involvement with peers, including an interested young girl. With the approach of spring, the edge of next year, Orin puts behind his several months of grieving and focuses on living. Father, realizing Orin's concern about his drinking, enlists in Alcoholics Anonymous and announces to his sons, "Then we can make it" (193).

In *Trouble in the Jungle*, John Rowe Townsend's economically deprived characters live in a northern English slum, or "jungle." The characters include orphaned thirteen-year-old Kevin and his twelve-year-old sister, Sandra. Since their parents' death, Kevin and Sandra have lived with their irresponsible Uncle Walter; his friend, Doris; and his children, Harold and Jean. When Walter and Doris desert them, Kevin moves the children into an attic of an empty warehouse, earning food money by delivering newspapers. Kevin finds that smugglers, aided by Uncle Walter, are storing goods in the warehouse. Walter, who soon turns against the smugglers, assures police that the children will now have a stable home with him.

Townsend's sequel, *Good-bye to the Jungle*, begins two years later. An urban renewal program demolishes Walter's run-down slum house, so he and his friend, Doris, take the four children to a new suburban house where they feel out of place among middle-class neighbors. Complaining about the rent, Walter drinks and gambles away his paycheck. Realizing Doris is trying to be neater, Kevin and Sandra borrow money to buy second-hand furniture, but they find that Doris has used credit to buy new furniture, which Walter sells for gambling money. Walter gets a job at a furniture warehouse. Kevin, suspicious of his uncle, trails him, and sees him set fire to the building. After Walter goes to jail, Doris, who really cares about the children, becomes more responsible. She stays with the family while Kevin rejects a scholarship to take a job.

Fourteen-year-old Mary Call Luther lives in the North Carolina mountains with her siblings and sharecropper father, Roy Luther, in Vera and Bill Cleaver's *Where the Lilies Bloom*. The siblings include a "cloudy-headed" older sister, Devola; a ten-year-old brother, Romey; and a five-year-old sister, Ima Dean. Since Roy Luther knows he is dying, he pleads with Mary Call to bury him secretly, keep the family together, never accept charity, and never let their landlord, Kiser Pease, marry Devola. Mary Call worries about the "responsibilities he has charged me with" (14), but tells Kiser, "I aim for me and my family to stay on here in this house you gave us and come spring we'll work the land you gave us and we'll be our own people" (42). When Roy Luther dies, Mary Call and Romey bury him, concealing his death to prevent the welfare department from sending them to the county home. They support themselves by "wildcrafting," or picking medicinal plants for a drug company. Mary Call keeps all promises except one: She lets Devola, no longer "cloudy headed," marry Kiser. He, in turn, helps the family.

Vera and Bill Cleaver's sequel, *Trial Valley*, takes place two years later. Mary Call Luther insists on raising her younger brother and sister in a small Blue Ridge house while the Kiser Peases, their legal guardians, live nearby. The youngsters complain that Mary Call is a hard taskmaster, but they love her. One day, they find five-year-old Jack Parsons in a cage nailed to a tree. He knows nothing about his parents, only that the "Widder Man" left him. Jack wants to stay with Mary Call, but authorities place him with the Peases as a ward. When he runs away, Mary Call leads searchers to his cage. Among the searchers are Mary Call's suitors—an honest, hard-working neighbor and a well-to-do social worker from Virginia. When Jack rushes from the cage, he falls into a rain-swollen creek, and Mary Call dives in to save him. The neighbor suitor rescues the boy and the social worker saves Mary Call. She decides to assume responsibility for Jack and marry the boy's rescuer.

A white sixteen-year-old neighbor, Sarah West, becomes a substitute parent for three black children of the Saunders family in Irene Hunt's *William: A Novel*. As the story unfolds, Elizabeth Saunders, a widow with cancer, befriends Sarah, an unmarried, pregnant artist who moves next door. Sarah, in turn, names her newly born daughter Elizabeth. Her neighbor dies, and with the help of eighteen-year-old Robert Norris, Sarah assumes responsibility for the Saunders children: thirteen-year-old Amy, eight-year-old William, and their four-year-old blind sister, Carla. Sarah assures William, "There'll be no 'orphan places,' William. Amy and I promised Mama that. We'll be the two big sisters, you'll be the man of the family, and the three of us will look after the little sprouts" (71). In the course of four years, Sarah takes Carla to Boston for surgery that removes cataracts and gives the child clear vision. As the story ends, Amy and Robert marry and live in the Saunders's home. The enlarged family will tend young Elizabeth while Sarah goes to a Chicago art school on a scholarship. Robert tells Sarah, "As for the children, you've had the responsibility of them for a long time, and you've worked yourself to the bone for them. Surely Amy and I can take over now . . ." (177).

Richard Peck's *Father Figure: A Novel* portrays seventeen-year-old Jim, a New Yorker, whose terminally ill mother commits suicide by carbon monoxide poisoning. Jim still has not recovered from his father's unexplained departure eight years earlier. While living with his grandmother, Jim assumes the role of a father figure to his eight-year-old brother, Byron. At the funeral, Jim notices a tanned stranger whom Grandmother acknowledges as their father, a man who soon leaves. When a street gang hurts Byron, Jim explodes in front of Byron's principal. The principal complains to Grandmother who calls upon the boys' father in Florida to take them for the summer. In Florida, Jim gets Father's answer about why he left home eight years ago, and Byron decides to stay with Father. Jim returns alone to New York, to Grandmother, and to school.

Another protective big brother is orphaned twenty-two-year-old Keith Rennie in Thomas Baird's *Walk Out a Brother*. In a summer cabin near Wyoming's Yellowstone Park, sixteen-year-old Don Rennie is with his older brother until their father's funeral. Don envied the closeness between Dad and Keith and resents the fact that Keith is his guardian. Keith invites Don to live in an Oregon apartment he shares with a fellow law student, Shirley. Wanting space and guided by Dad's maps, Don runs away into the wild Absaroka Mountains where he meets secretive Lester Pratt, a murderer. Lester steals Don's maps and follows them to Keith. Don, fearing what Lester might do to Keith, overcomes his desire for freedom and returns home, capturing Lester. Don minimizes his courageous return, confessing, "You're not much of a hero if all you do is try to fix something up when you've been the cause of its going wrong in the first place" (267). Significantly, he tells Keith, "I walked into the mountains a stranger to you, I walked out a brother" (276). This book is unusual because the protagonist is less admirable than the brother he dislikes.

When one or both parents or guardians prove irresponsible, it may be children who keep the family together. In *Celebrate the Morning* by Ella Thorp Ellis, fourteen-year-old April stays in a ramshackle house with her mother, Mary, who lives in another world most of the time. April's best friends, Allan and Dolly, live on farms outside town. When Mary, suffering from pneumonia, goes to a hospital and then a mental institution, April's next-door neighbor, Fermine, arranges with a social worker to become April's guardian. Mary runs away from the hospital, and Dolly and Allan help April search for her. Dolly tells April, "Your mother's a grown woman. She can take care of herself. Who made you her watchdog? Now, April, don't get your dander up. I only mean that you can go find her now, but you can't run her life for her" (99). After locating Mother, April looks forward to the future, assisted by Fermine and the social worker.

In Marilyn Sachs's poignant *The Bears' House*, nine-year-old Fran Ellen Smith, ridiculed by fourth graders since she sucks her thumb and smells bad, skips school to look after her baby sister, Flora. After Father left them, Mother has been so depressed, the children must fend for themselves. Fletcher, her twelve-year-old brother, tells the others to keep their troubles a secret to avoid separate foster home placements. He tries to shop and pay bills. When he delegates jobs, he refers first to Florence, his eleven-year-old sister, saying, "Florence will take care of the baby and do the cooking. You, Fran Ellen, will do the cleaning" (20). Fran Ellen does lazy Florence's tasks and her own. She sneaks home during recess to give the baby a bottle of Kool-Aid and helps her five-year-old sister, Felice. Fran Ellen's main joy is fantasizing she is Goldilocks in a classroom dollhouse fixed for the three bears. Her teacher, Miss Thompson, visits the Smith apartment to complain about Fran Ellen's truancy, not knowing the girl is taking care of the baby. The teacher also delivers the dollhouse gift and promises help, a rather positive ending to this story of despair.

Mavis Thorpe Clark's *The Min-Min* shows a capable Australian teenager, Sylvie. She copes with life in a railroad shanty; an eleven-year-old brother, Reg, who is in trouble with the police; four young children who need her now that Mother, expecting another child, is ill most of the time; and a drunken father who was once convicted of theft. After police warn Reg he will be sent to a correctional institution if he gets into further trouble, he destroys a teacher's phonograph. Fearful, Sylvie walks with Reg for two days under the outback's scorching sun to see wise, trustworthy Mrs. Tucker. Since floods delay the children's return, the kind woman helps Sylvie relax and forces Reg to face his undisciplined behavior. When they return home, Reg enters reform school. Sylvie draws inspiration from a teacher who encourages her to go to high school. Father asks her to care for her siblings because Mother must go to Sydney for a rest, but they will move from the railway camp. Because of Reg's good conduct in reform school, authorities give him another chance and let him work for Mr. Tucker.

In Patricia A. Engelbrecht's *Under the Haystack*, thirteen-year-old Sandy faces the fact that her mother and stepfather have abandoned her and her sisters, eight-year-old Marie and six-year-old June. To keep the welfare department away, Sandy says her parents are vacationing. The girls run the farm and care for their three-room shack while Sandy has the added responsibility of curing Marie's leg wound caused by a rusty pitchfork. After the onset of puberty, Sandy discusses her fears with a neighbor, Mrs. Baxter, who says that the girls' mother will return. Realizing townspeople know of Mother's disappearance, Sandy prepares her sisters for a welfare worker's visit. One afternoon, the girls hide under a haystack when they see what they believe is a sheriff's car at their door. The next evening, the girls bathe and dress neatly while they await the dreaded car which proves to be a taxi returning their mother.

Cynthia Voigt's *Homecoming* and *Dicey's Song* focus on a sister caring for children of absentee parents. In *Homecoming*, a single mother cannot cope after she loses her job, and she abandons her beloved children: Dicey, aged thirteen; James, aged ten; Maybeth, aged nine; and Sammy, aged six. Mother's last words are, "You little ones, mind what Dicey tells you. You hear? . . . That's all right then" (5). Dicey, afraid authorities will separate them, seeks a home. They walk down Route 1, a long trip, to Bridgeport, Connecticut, where they stay briefly with a cousin who wants them to show constant gratitude. When they learn their maternal grandmother, Abigail Tillerman, lives in Crisfield, Maryland, they push on to her run-down coastal farm. Gram, who cherishes her freedom, tells the weary travelers they cannot stay permanently. Dicey gets the children to do productive work and James has income-generating ideas, so Gram changes her mind. When Gram and Dicey disagree about how to discipline Sammy, Dicey removes a privilege, not a meal, from the boy who has been hungry enough. Feeling responsible, she reflects that she "had learned that she had to do what she thought was right for her family, not what someone else thought" (284).

In Voigt's sequel, *Dicey's Song*, Dicey gradually relinquishes some responsibility for her siblings to feisty, eccentric Gram with whom she feels a growing bond. Dicey, earning seven dollars weekly in an after-school grocery job, gives a dollar allowance to each child with the balance to Gram. The boys also work. Quick-witted James tutors slow-learning Maybeth, letting Sammy continue his former paper route. After Gram adopts the children, she announces, "You are now, legally and officially and permanently—and any other lee they could think of—my responsibility" (150). Gram knits the girls sweaters and bakes cookies for visitors. Isaac Lingerle gives free piano lessons to musically talented Maybeth. Lingerle also baby-sits and pays for Gram and Dicey to go to Boston, where Momma is dying. As Dicey carries her mother's ashes home in a box, Gram teaches her to let go of ties to her parent. When Dicey questions, "How long was she going to have to spend worrying about her brothers and sister?" (67), Gram replies, "For as long as you live, the attachments hold" (67).

In Bianca Bradbury's *Those Traver Kids*, sixteen-year-old Terry feels responsible for her ten-year-old sister, Pat, and her three-year-old brother, Hugo ("Hugger") Traver, although her seventeen-year-old brother, Dan, helps her. Their father deserted them three years before, so Dan gives his family earnings from his work at a gas station. Evelyn, their mother, who seems unaware of them, has brought lazy, brutal Ben Green into the home as a stepfather. Ben almost kills their German shepherd, Colonel. Terry, an "A" student, works part-time as a super-market checker and library assistant to buy food and pay for a psychiatrist for Pat, who appears on the verge of a mental breakdown. Terry and Dan are desperate to get rid of their stepfather. They tell police the truth—that he steals their Aid to Dependent Children money—and police confirm that Ben has a criminal record. The officers learn that Terry barely escaped Ben's pass at her and she is worried about Pat, but they cannot arrest the man until he commits a serious crime. When drunken Ben cruelly beats Hugger for wetting his bed, Dan and Terry take the boy to the hospital and call the police. At Ben's trial for child beating, the young people learn he and Evelyn are not legally married. Authorities sentence Ben and forbid him to see the children again. With Ben gone, they now have to focus on living just with their mother, "a third child who had to be looked after" (196).

SUMMARY

As expected, there are more books for older children than for younger ones stressing the value of young persons' assuming responsibility. This chapter cites only three books for the early years, twenty-two for the middle years, and forty-four for the later years—a total of sixty-nine books. One-fourth of the selected books for the later years emphasize a similar idea: If parents are deceased or irresponsible, children may try to fend for themselves without informing authorities so that the siblings can stay together.

References

Aiken, Joan. *Bridle the Wind.* Delacorte Press, 1983. 242 p. (L) (Courage)

Annixter, Jane and Paul. *Horns of Plenty.* Holiday House, 1960. 203 p. (L)

Arora, Shirley L. *"What Then, Raman?"* Illustrated by Hans Guggenheim. Follett Publishing Company, 1960. 176 p. (M)

Asch, Frank. *Pearl's Promise.* Illustrated. Delacorte Press, 1984. 152 p. (M) (Friendship, Ingenuity)

Baird, Thomas. *Walk Out a Brother.* Harper & Row, Publishers, 1983. 278 p. (L) (Courage)

Baker, Charlotte. *Cockleburr Quarters.* Illustrated by Robert Owens. Prentice-Hall, 1972. 175 p. (M) (Ingenuity)

Bradbury, Bianca. *Those Traver Kids.* Illustrated by Marvin Friedman. Houghton Mifflin Company, 1972. 204 p. (L) (Courage)

Brooks, Jerome. *Make Me a Hero.* E. P. Dutton, 1980. 152 p. (L) (Humaneness, Self-respect)

Buck, Pearl. *Matthew, Mark, Luke and John.* Illustrated by Mamoru Funai. The John Day Company, 1967. 80 p. (M)

Bulla, Clyde Robert. *Shoeshine Girl.* Illustrated by Leigh Grant. Thomas Y. Crowell, 1975. 84 p. (M) (Friendship, Ingenuity, Maturing)

Bunting, Eve. *The Skateboard Four.* Illustrated by Phil Kantz. Albert Whitman & Company, 1976. 63 p. (M) (Maturing)

Burton, Virginia. *Katy and the Big Snow.* Illustrated. Houghton Mifflin Company, 1943. 36 p. (E) (Cooperation)

Byars, Betsy. *The Night Swimmers.* Illustrated by Troy Howell. Delacorte Press, 1980. 131 p. (L) (Ingenuity)

———. *Summer of the Swans.* Illustrated by Ted Coconis. The Viking Press, 1970. 142 p. (L) (Maturing)

Carlson, Natalie Savage. *A Brother for the Orphelines.* Illustrated by Garth Williams. Harper & Brothers, 1959. 100 p. (M)

—— *The Family Under the Bridge.* Illustrated by Garth Williams. Harper & Brothers, 1958. 99 p. (M)

Clark, Mavis Thorpe. *The Min-Min.* The Macmillan Company, 1969. 216 p. (L)

Cleary, Beverly. *Henry and the Clubhouse.* Illustrated by Louis Darling. William Morrow & Company, 1962. 192 p. (M)

——. *Henry and the Paper Route.* Illustrated by Louis Darling. William Morrow & Company, 1957. 192 p. (M) (Friendship, Ingenuity)

Cleaver, Vera and Bill. *The Mock Revolt.* J. B. Lippincott Company, 1971. 159 p. (L)

——. *Queen of Hearts.* J. B. Lippincott Company, 1978. 158 p. (L)

——. *Trial Valley.* J. B. Lippincott Company, 1977. 158 p. (L) (Loyalty)

——. *Where the Lilies Bloom.* Illustrated by Jim Spanfeller. J. B. Lippincott, 1969. 174 p. (L) (Ingenuity)

——. *The Whys and Wherefores of Littabelle Lee.* Atheneum, 1973. 156 p. (L) (Ingenuity)

Clements, Bruce. *Anywhere Else but Here.* Farrar, Straus & Giroux, 1980. 151 p. (L) (Maturing)

Clymer, Eleanor. *My Brother Stevie.* Illustrated by Estal Nesbitt. Holt, Rinehart & Winston, 1967. 76 p. (M) (Friendship)

Cohen, Peter Zachary. *Bee.* Illustrated by Richard Cuffari. Atheneum, 1975. 187 p. (L) (Courage)

DeJong, Meindert. *Journey from Peppermint Street.* Illustrated by Emily Arnold McCully. Harper & Row, Publishers, 1968. 242 p. (M)

Delton, Judy. *Back Yard Angel.* Illustrated by Leslie Morrill. Houghton Mifflin Company, 1983. 107 p. (M)

Doty, Jean Slaughter. *If Wishes Were Horses.* Macmillan, 1984. 125 p. (L)

Edmonds, Walter D. *Two Logs Crossing: John Haskell's Story.* Illustrated by Tibor Gergely. Dodd, Mead & Company, 1943. 82 p. (M) (Maturing)

Eige, Lillian. *The Kidnapping of Mister Huey.* Harper & Row, 1983. 153 p. (L) (Humaneness)

Ellis, Ella Thorp. *Celebrate the Morning.* Atheneum, 1972. 177 p. (L) (Friendship)

Engelbrecht, Patricia A. *Under the Haystack.* Thomas Nelson, 1973. 124 p. (L) (Maturing)

First, Julia. *Move over, Beethoven.* Franklin Watts, 1978. 121 p. (L) (Friendship)

Fox, Paula. *One-eyed Cat.* Bradbury Press, 1984. 216 p. (M) (Courage, Friendship)

Friis-Baastad, Babbis. *Don't Take Teddy.* Translated from Norwegian by Lise Sømme McKinnon. Charles Scribner's Sons, 1967. 218 p. (L)

Gardiner, John Reynolds. *Stone Fox.* Illustrated by Marcia Sewall. Thomas Y. Crowell, 1980. 85 p. (M) (Courage)

Gerson, Corinne. *How I Put My Mother Through College.* Atheneum, 1981. 136 p. (L) (Maturing)

Gramatky, Hardie. *Little Toot.* Illustrated. G. P. Putnam's Sons, 1939. Unpaged. (E)

Holland, Isabelle. *Alan and the Animal Kingdom.* J. B. Lippincott Company, 1977. 190 p. (L) (Animal Friendship)

Hunt, Irene. *William: A Novel.* Charles Scribner's Sons, 1977. 188 p. (L) (Cooperation)

Jeffries, Roderic. *Trapped.* Harper & Row, Publishers, 1972. 150 p. (L)

Johnson, Annabel & Edgar. *Pickpocket Run.* Harper & Row, Publishers, 1961. 185 p. (L) (Courage)

Lawrence, Louise. *The Dram Road.* Harper & Row, Publishers, 1983. 218 p. (L) (Maturing)

Lee, Mildred. *The Rock and the Willow.* Lothrop, Lee & Shepard, 1963. 223 p. (L)

Lexau, Joan. *I'll Tell on You.* Illustrated by Gail Owens. E. P. Dutton, 1976. 25 p. (E) (Friendship)

McHugh, Elisabet. *Karen and Vicki.* Greenwillow Books, 1984. 150 p. (L) (Friendship, Ingenuity)

———. *Karen's Sister.* Greenwillow Books, 1983. 149 p. (L) (Friendship)

———. *Raising a Mother Isn't Easy.* Greenwillow Books, 1983. 156 p. (L) (Friendship)

Matsuno, Masako. *Taro and the Tōfu.* Illustrated by Kazue Mizumura. World Book Company, 1962. Unpaged. (M)

Moeri, Louise. *Downwind*. E. P. Dutton, 1984. 121 p. (L) (Courage)

Myers, Walter Dean. *The Young Landlords*. The Viking Press, 1979. 197 p. (L)

Peck, Richard. *Father Figure: A Novel*. Viking Press, 1978. 192 p. (L) (Maturing, Self-respect)

Perrine, Mary. *Salt Boy*. Illustrated by Leonard Weisgard. Houghton Mifflin Company, 1968. 31 p. (M)

Rhoads, Dorothy. *The Corn Grows Ripe*. Illustrated by Jean Charlot. The Viking Press, 1956. 88 p. (M) (Maturing)

Sachs, Marilyn. *The Bears' House*. Illustrated by Louis Glanzman. Doubleday & Company, 1971. 81 p. (L)

Sauer, Julia L. *The Light at Tern Rock*. Illustrated by Georges Schreiber. The Viking Press, 1951. 62 p. (M)

Shyer, Marlene Fanta. *Welcome Home, Jellybean*. Charles Scribner's Sons, 1978. 153 p. (L) (Courage, Maturing)

Speare, Elizabeth George. *The Sign of the Beaver*. Houghton Mifflin Company, 1983. 135 p. (L) (Courage, Friendship)

Stolz, M. S. *A Dog on Barkham Street*. Illustrated by Leonard Shortall. Harper & Row, Publishers, 1960. 184 p. (M)

Stolz, Mary. *The Edge of Next Year*. Harper & Row, Publishers, 1974. 195 p. (L)

Tate, Eleanora E. *Just an Overnight Guest*. The Dial Press, 1980. 182 p. (M) (Maturing)

Townsend, John Rowe. *Good-bye to the Jungle*. J. B. Lippincott Company, 1967. 184 p. (L) (Courage, Loyalty)

———. *Trouble in the Jungle*. Illustrated by W. T. Mars. J. B. Lippincott Company, 1969. 158 p. (L)

Turner, Ann. *A Hunter Comes Home*. Crown, 1980. 118 p. (L) (Courage, Ingenuity)

Voigt, Cynthia. *Dicey's Song*. Atheneum, 1982. 196 p. (L) (Friendship)

———. *Homecoming*. Atheneum, 1981. 312 p. (L) (Courage, Friendship, Ingenuity)

Whitehead, Ruth. *The Mother Tree*. Illustrated by Charles Robinson. The Seabury Press, 1971. 149 p. (L)

X

Self-respect

The value that may contribute most to a human being's mental health is self-respect: a positive self-image and regard for personal dignity. Individuals must feel comfortable with themselves in order to relate to others. Books in this chapter recognize the importance in the formative years of finding identity and contentment with one's own character and appearance.

BOOKS FOR EARLY YEARS

Animals appear often in picture storybooks because young children may relate to them better than to people. In *Arthur's Nose*, written and illustrated by Marc Brown, an anteater, Arthur, unhappy with his own nose, wants another from Dr. Louise, the rhinologist (a nose doctor). After trying on pictures of different animals' noses, he decides, "I'm just not me without my nose" (unp).

Once a Mouse: A Fable Cut in Wood, written and illustrated by Marcia Brown, introduces a mouse whose character changes. A hermit sees a mouse about to be caught by a crow. He protects him from larger animals by changing him into a cat, a dog, and finally a tiger. When the tiger begins acting superior, the hermit turns him back into a mouse, saying, "You are ungrateful! Go back to the forest and be a mouse again" (unp).

Ellen Conford's *Just the Thing for Geraldine*, illustrated by John Larrecq, is about a young opossum who likes to juggle. Her mother sends her to ballet school, a weaving class, and finally to Schuyler's School of Sculpture. Her performance is so poor that her mother lets her study juggling because it is what she enjoys and does well.

Roger Duvoisin is the author-illustrator of *Veronica* which features an inconspicuous hippopotamus, Veronica, who wants to be famous. When Veronica goes to a city, her size is a problem, so a policeman lets her sleep in a parking lot. After the hungry animal steals vegetables, she finds herself in jail. An old lady pays her fine, sending her home in a moving van when Veronica says, "I only want to go home to my mud bank, to my river, to all my hippopotamuses" (unp).

Another author-illustrator, Don Freeman, is creator of *Dandelion*, a story of a lion who beautifies himself after Jennifer Giraffe invites him to a party. Dandelion gets his mane shampooed and curled, wears a fancy new jacket and cap, and carries a walking stick. Jennifer does not recognize him, so she slams the door in his face. When a storm messes his hair and jacket, blowing away his cap, he returns to her party where she welcomes him, telling him about the previous silly-looking lion. Dandelion explains that he arrived earlier, adding, "I promise I will never try to turn myself into a stylish dandy. From now on I'll always be just plain me" (48).

Kay Chorao's soft illustrations complement Marjorie Weinman Sharmat's text in *I'm Terrific*. His friends do not like it when Jason Everett Bear gives himself stars for superior deeds. He tries doing the opposite—mean acts—like tying knots in the fur of a raccoon, Marvin, and kicking the nuts of a squirrel, Raymond, but his friends still do not like him. He apologizes to them, eliminates the gold stars, and says, "Mother, I am what I am. I am Jason Everett Bear, and I am glad of it" (unp).

Phyllis Krasilovsky's *The Shy Little Girl*, illustrated by Trina Schart Hyman, portrays shy Anne who does not like her looks, is afraid to raise her hand in class, and is always too slow to join recess games. Claudia, a new pupil, admires Anne's clothes and her freckles. After the two pick dandelions during recess, Anne, gaining confidence, begins to participate in class and on the playground. "Anne discovered she liked to talk and that it was fun to make someone laugh" (30).

Illustrations tell a story in *Andy (That's My Name)* by author-illustrator Tomie dePaola. Andy's cart holds huge block letters of his name, but when other children use his letters to make words, they do not let him play. Finally, he puts his letters in his cart and says as he leaves, "I may be little. . . . But I'm very important" (unp).

Nils loves the wool stockings with black and white roses and stars from his grandmother in Norway. In *Nils*, written and illustrated by Ingri and Edgar Parin D'Aulaire, the boy wears the stockings to school, but after peers call him a sissy, he hides them. One bitter winter day, he gets the stockings, wears them under his jeans, and feels toasty warm at school while others freeze. He shows his stockings, thinking, "I don't have to freeze to show I am not a sissy. Who cares if I am different!" (unp).

A sad story with a happy ending is *How I Faded Away* by Janice Udry, with illustrations by Monica DeBrwyn. Robbie feels visible only in summer at his grandmother's. Thinking he made mistakes in first grade, he does nothing to be noticed in second grade. In third grade, his teacher says, "Robbie, I can hardly see you or hear you. Speak up! Sit up! You don't want to be counted absent, do you?" (unp). When his teacher has insufficient recorders to give him one, he buys one with his Christmas money, learns to play it, and becomes visible when he plays it at school. He reflects, "Sometimes I wonder if my recorder is a magic one. I guess I'll never know, but whether it is magic or not, I love to play. I'm hardly invisible anymore. And when I am, I don't care now" (unp).

Feminists enjoy *Everybody Knows That!* by Susan Pearson with illustrations by Diane Paterson. Although they were best friends, when they are in kindergarten, Herbie does not let Patty play with trucks or be an airplane pilot. Another boy, Jason, says, "Boys aren't stewardesses and girls aren't pilots" (unp). After Patty questions why not, Jason replies, "Everybody knows why not" (unp). When Herbie spends Saturday with Patty, she does not let him bake cookies and he wants to know why not. Patty states, "Everybody knows why not. Only girls can bake cookies" (unp). Mother intervenes to let them both lick the bowl.

Beverly Keller's *The Beetle Bush*, illustrated by Marc Simont, is easy to read. It tells about young Arabelle Mott who feels she is a failure because nobody interprets her pictures correctly or knows she is doing cartwheels. She puts outside her bedroom door a sign, "Arabelle Mott Failure." Adopting her father's idea of trying gardening, she works hard, but snails eat her tomatoes, moles gnaw her carrots, and beetles consume her bush beans. After the landlord enjoys her beetle bush, Arabella Mott, ex-failure, writes a poem excerpted below:

> . . . Bugs and weeds
> Have simple needs.
>
> . . . So now that I am a success
> I do not love them any less. (64)

BOOKS FOR MIDDLE YEARS

A picture storybook that young children enjoy hearing and that middle-grade pupils read for themselves is Margery Williams's *The Velveteen Rabbit: Or How Toys Become Real*, illustrated by Michael Hague. A little boy loves Velveteen Rabbit until it becomes shabby and other toys replace it. The Skin Horse tells Rabbit what it means to be real, "When a child loves you for a long, long time, not just to play with, but *really* loves you, then you become real. . . . Once you become real you can't be ugly, except to people who don't understand" (16–17). In this poignant story, Velveteen Rabbit does become real.

Children may find it difficult to choose between traditional and modern customs, as Jane Flory shows in *One Hundred and Eight Bells*. Although twelve-year-old Setsuko Sagawa goes to a modern school and her brother, Jo, is in college, her family follows traditional Japanese customs, like attending a temple on New Year's Eve to hear 108 bells that cleanse worshippers of sins. Her father is an artist, and she would like to be one. After her father receives a commission to paint scenes in Kyoto, he takes Setsuko with him for a week, and both enjoy sightseeing or sketching. When the man who commissions her father praises Setsuko's art, her mother says, "But Setsuko is only a girl. She should learn her place and learn how to fill it well" (91). Aunt Toshiko replies, "The old world in which we were raised is changing and Setsuko will be a modern woman whether we approve or not" (91). Her encouraging brother Jo tells her, "You can do anything if you do it one step at a time" (219).

In *The Gift-giver* by Joyce Hansen, a fifth-grade black girl, Doris, resents her overprotective family's restrictions. She befriends a new neighbor, Amir, a loner who gets along with all. Amir stands up to teasing boys, telling Doris, "They would bother me more if I ran home scared. It's better to face it and get it over with" (24). Helping Doris gain self-confidence, Amir says, "If you can't do what other people do, so what? Do something else" (55).

Twelve-year-old Anna Glory is the unmusical member of the Glory Gospel Singers in *The Glory Girl* by Betsy Byars. Anna sits at the back of a hall to sell albums while her family performs. She feels closer to Uncle Newt than to her family after his release from jail for an inept attempt at bank robbery. When the Glorys' old bus is in an accident, Uncle Newt appears and helps Anna save her family. Before leaving he tells Anna, "You're the best of the bunch—you know that? You've got a generous kind way about you, and don't you ever lose it" (119).

A story with a touch of fantasy is Elizabeth Coatsworth's *Marra's World*. Marra lives on an island with her grandmother who hates her and her father who ignores her. Her mute mother, Nerea, has disappeared. She communicates only with a storekeeper, Mr. Pratt, until Alison Dunbar, a doctor's daughter, arrives and becomes her friend. Mrs. Dunbar teaches Marra manners and makes her clothes. When the two girls are out in a boat and a fog envelopes them, a seal guides them home. Marra feels that seal is her mother, Nerea. Gradually, her grandmother and other islanders accept Marra and she changes. Marra thinks, "Something of the assurance of being loved by Nerea had entered into her even if Nerea was forgotten" (64).

Tink in a Tangle by Dorothy Haas features eight-year-old, red-haired Tink, whose mother works at the Fountain of Beauty. Tink says, "Red hair's terrible. It always gets me into trouble" (6). For example, she starts a home beauty salon which ends in disaster. She has friendship problems because Jane Ellen wants to be her best friend and she prefers Poppy. Tink's mother suggests, "You don't have to like everyone, but you've got to be nice to everyone. . . . Include her in. One of these days when she's nice to everyone all the time, she'll find a best friend" (118–119).

In *The Unmaking of Rabbit* by Constance C. Greene, Paul's classmates call him Rabbit. A timid loner, he lives with his grandmother because his mother is irresponsible. He thinks, "He never told his mother that he didn't have any friends to speak of and that on the block where his grandmother lived there weren't any flowers and trees" (19). On the night of a robbery, a bully, Freddy, tries to make Paul steal, but he follows an older boy's advice and pretends to "puke," so he gets out of it. A grocer, Mr. Barker, says, "You should tell people how you feel about them" (92). In a school composition on Freddy, Paul states, "The moral to this is: A clear conscience is worth more than friends" (121). When Freddy calls him Rabbit, he replies, "My name is Paul. It's not Rabbit . . . and don't you forget it" (123). No matter what happens, he has taken one positive stand.

Paula Fox exposes secret feelings of ten-year-old Gus, who has two older and two younger siblings, in *The Stone-faced Boy*. To show he does not care when others tease him, Gus wears a blank facial expression. He reflects, "When he first noticed how stony his face was getting, he hadn't minded. . . . But now Gus ha[s] a new kind of trouble. The stone face seemed to have stuck" (12–13). While Great-aunt Hattie visits, she shows Gus a geode, explaining, "The stone must have a crack. It must be in a special place where minerals seep into it, certain kinds of minerals" (42). After Gus braves a snowstorm to search for an old dog his sister Serena loves, he discovers his face, like the geode, has a crack.

John D. Fitzgerald's *Me and My Little Brain* tells about the time Tom, the Great Brain, is in boarding school and nine-year-old J. D. tries to be a substitute Great Brain, but everything goes wrong. When he gets two poor boys to do his chores for half his weekly allowance, his parents give him miserable tasks, such as spreading manure and helping clean house. After he tries to trade things, he confesses, "I'm just a born loser" (86). Papa replies: "There is no such thing as a born loser. But there are people who continually overreach themselves. . . . Find your own identity and say to yourself, 'This is me, and I can't be anybody but me' " (36–37). In the end, J. D. captures a murderer and saves a boy, concluding, "I know I haven't got a great brain like Tom. But I'm satisfied with my own little brain" (135)

Janet Schulman presents a problem and solution in *Jenny and the Tennis Nut*. Jenny's father, an enthusiastic tennis player, wants her to follow his example, but she is an able gymnast. When Father sees her expertise on a swing, he promotes her interest by buying proper gymnastic equipment and letting her take lessons. He says, "You have found your game all by yourself. You do it well and you really enjoy it. Gymnastics is right for you" (49).

Children empathize with Ramona Quimby, a first-grade pupil, in Beverly Cleary's *Ramona the Brave*. After her unsympathetic teacher, Mrs. Griggs, praises an owl Susan copied from Ramona, the Quimby girl crushes Susan's owl. The teacher then complains to Mrs. Quimby about Ramona's lack of self-control. On the way to school one day, Ramona defends herself by throwing her shoe at a dog. In class, Mrs. Griggs compliments her because she wears a slipper she makes from paper towels. After police return her shoe to school, the secretary tells Ramona that she is brave. The girl reflects, "Brave Ramona, that's what they would think, just about the bravest girl in the first grade. And they would be right. This time Ramona was sure" (190).

Eight-year-old best friends, Gabrielle and Selena, tire of being themselves and decide to change identities in *Gabrielle and Selena* by

Peter Desbarats. Their families insist they role play accurately, so Selena has to eat omelets and Gabrielle, turnips. Deciding they prefer to be themselves, they laugh at the joke their parents play on them. Only the illustrations tell the reader that Selena is black and Gabrielle, white.

Apologizing is always difficult, as Amy Hadley discovers in Julia First's *Amy*. The daughter of a lawyer who favors integration, Amy considers Donald Randall a bigot. He insults a black classmate and starts a fight at Amy's Hallowe'en party. Amy competes with him to be class president, wins, and has to disqualify herself for failing mathematics. She admits she destroyed her teacher's warning note to her parents. After she leaves during the first class meeting Donald conducts, he goes to her house and says, "I'm sorry you walked out. I guess I have to remember not to-uh-talk so much. . . . I'm sorry you flunked math" (82–83). Ashamed, Amy asks Mother, "Mums, . . . do you think it is possible for people to change?" (84). Then she calls Donald and apologizes.

Five-year-old Teddy and his seven-year-old sister, Nora, live with their mother, who is allergic to cats, in a New York City apartment where they cannot have a dog. In *Superduper Teddy* by Johanna Hurwitz, Teddy takes the job of feeding his neighbor's cat and finds a perfect family pet, a giant turtle. He decides he no longer needs his Superman cape to feel secure after his neighbor tells him, "You are a super cat-sitter!" (48). When Nora adds, "Teddy you were smart to find him (the turtle)" (69), Teddy donates his cape to the kindergarten costume box, saying, "I'm getting too big for it" (79).

Two poignant stories help readers identify with girls who have learning disabilities. In *Sue Ellen* by Edith Fisher Hunter, eight-year-old Sue Ellen hates school. She has five siblings, an invalid mother, and an industrious, illiterate father. She has a loving, understanding teacher, Miss Kelly, in a special school with only eleven classmates. Polly Smith, an older girl who often assists Miss Kelly, rides a bus with Sue Ellen. As Sue Ellen begins to learn to read, her attitude changes. She thinks on the weekend, "This was a no-school day. Sue Ellen lay in bed wishing it was a school day" (39). When the child helps Polly make a crazy cake, Polly explains the terms, "crazy, dummies or retards," saying, "Lots of people use the word 'crazy' when they just mean 'different.' Some of my friends think I'm crazy because my ideas are different from theirs" (128). Sue Ellen's teacher helps the family get on its feet. During a class visit to a pet farm, Sue Ellen sees a sign over a barn, "The Pet Farm," and she knows she can read.

In *Will the Real Gertrude Hollings Please Stand Up?* by Sheila Greenwald, Gertrude feels she is two different people, stupid at school and, with toy owls, imaginative at home. Teachers say she "needs more confidence in her ability to master skills. She is afraid of being hurt, afraid to get involved and afraid to fail" (15). While her parents are in Greece on business, Gertrude unhappily stays with relatives. She discovers that her cousin, Albert, a genius and super-achiever, lives a miserable, regimented life. Gertrude assumes the job of helping Albert to accept his mother's pregnancy. When Gertrude returns home, Albert runs away to find her "because he missed me. I showed him the benefits of being part of a multiple family, of sharing and . . . companionship and flexibility" (161). In a surprise ending, Gertrude learns that her own mother is pregnant.

Bette Greene shows problems of very intelligent children in stories set in rural Arkansas, *Philip Hall Likes Me, I Reckon Maybe* and *Get on Out of Here, Philip Hall*. Eleven-year-old Beth Lambert, who helps her classmate, Philip Hall, with his farm chores, is second to him in arithmetic, spelling, and reading. Her mother questions if she is letting him star so he will like her. After Beth questions herself, her grades improve. She opens a vegetable stand and helps catch turkey thieves. Her entry does better than Philip's at a country fair where she wins a blue ribbon. He sulks until they compete as a couple in a square dance contest. She says, "This contest is for partners. Win together or lose together" (135).

In the sequel, *Get on Out of Here, Philip Hall*, Beth, a top student, is president of the all-female Pretty Pennies Club. When she loses a church award to Philip Hall, causes the Pretty Pennies' defeat in a relay race, and discovers her club's secret vote to replace her as president, Beth feels so ashamed that she moves to her grandmother's Walnut Ridge home. She asks, "Haven't I already spent too much of my life being bossy? Trying to use my ideas to become the number-one best leader?" (115). However, she shows genuine leadership as she guides the town's Happy New Year's Day party. With her self-confidence rebuilt, Beth returns home.

The poor self-image of a bully may be due to physical appearance or home environment. Gene Kemp's *Gowie Corby Plays Chicken* is set in England, but the catalyst for change is an American black girl, Rosie

Angela Lee. Gowie Corby tells his wife and four children how a Nobel
Peace Prize nominee, Dr. Rosie Angela Lee, changed his life. The
flashback focuses on twelve-year-old Gowie Corby, a smart, imaginative class terror whose father is in jail and whose mother works in a bar.
Gowie's pranks plague his teacher and a classmate, fat, clumsy Heather.
After causing a star football player, Stewart, to break his arm, Gowie
refuses to join the team. Stewart declares, "You are the rottenest,
meanest, horriblest kid who ever came here. You've never done nuthin'
for nobody in the whole of your mean, miserable life" (42). In a gang
beating, Rosie saves Gowie. When the gang dares Gowie to stay in the
school's haunted cellar, Rosie hides with him. He lets the gang call him
chicken, but he becomes a successful adult who marries Heather.

Tall, fat Martin Hastings reacts to teasing by bullying smaller
children in *The Bully of Barkham Street* by Mary Stolz. When his
parents give away Rufus, the dog he loves, Martin feels, "Everywhere
he looked, everything he thought about, just was more trouble. Borrow-
ing, lying, getting into fights" (41). After his teacher, Mr. Foran,
compliments him, Martin reflects, "Hearing himself praised, during
recess or any time, was highly agreeable to him" (74). Martin is
surprised to learn that his older sister feels he is the favored child. His
mother tells him, "Remember it's one of the surest signs of maturity the
day you find yourself accepting people for what they are, with their good
points and their bad" (142). Martin tries to quit lying and ignore teasers.
He discovers that admitting a mistake makes it easier to bear.

Learning to swim is a problem for some children. In *The Hatching
of Joshua Cobb* by Margaret Hodges, ten-year-old Josh hates camp
because he can swim only with one foot on the lake's bottom. His father
is dead, his mother is overprotective, and his camp counselor is a bully.
When his team loses a relay race because he cannot find a sneaker, he
thinks, "What was the use? He was a loser, no matter what he tried to
do" (46). In a treasure hunt, he helps his partner find the way back to
camp. His new counselor tells him, "Sometimes your first summer at
camp can be the start of feeling right about yourself" (113). At the
camp's awards night, Josh wins a silver star for highest score at a track
meet, consistently winning second place four times. Then Josh decides
to stay two more weeks at camp.

In Delores Beckman's *My Own Private Sky*, eleven-year-old
Arthur Livingston Elliott has allergies, buckteeth, and is afraid to swim.
His sitter, Mrs. Jennifer Kearns, tells him a person can do anything he

feels like doing, so he throws away his allergy pills but is still afraid of swimming. When Mrs. Kearns loses a leg in an accident, she refuses to use her prothesis. After she asks him to practice diving, Arthur says: "You think it's all right for me to jump on a board into the water when I'm scared, but you're afraid to get up on your leg and walk. . . . You know what I think? I think you're a great big fakeroo!" (148). Arthur goes to the pool and when he sees Mrs. Kearns on two legs, he dives off the board.

Catherine Woolley's *Ginnie Joins In* can help any fifth grader who has a poor self-image. Feeling she is homely and without talent, Ginnie Fellows is afraid to make swimming mistakes. On a lakeside vacation with her family, Cousin Anna, and best friend, Geneva, Ginnie begins to gain self-confidence. Mother cautions, "Don't copy other people, Ginnie. It never works out. Just be yourself—only try and remember to be happy. Everybody loves a happy little girl" (40). With effort Ginnie learns to swim and dive. "I dived, I dived, she kept thinking, hardly able to believe it. And I stayed in the woods all night, even if I was scared" (104). The illustrations may be dated but not the story.

In *Arthur for the Very First Time* by Patricia MacLachlan, ten-year-old Arthur Rasby finds it easier to write journal entries than to have enriching experiences. In summer he is with his great-aunt Edda and great-uncle Wrisby because his mother has a difficult pregnancy about which Arthur knows nothing. The veterinarian's niece, Moira, befriends him, calling him Mouse because he is fearful. Moira tells him, "You spend so much time writing in that journal of yours, that you don't really see what is going on around you" (53). While his aunt and uncle are shopping, Arthur and Moira help the pregnant sow, Bernadette, deliver. Since Arthur keeps the runt of the litter alive, Moira says, "Arthur did it. Arthur really did it all" (117). He grins at Moira who calls him Arthur for the very first time.

Doug Meets the Nutcracker by William H. Hooks appeals to boys who like to dance but are ashamed of taunts. After ten-year-old Douglas Simpson sees his sister, Julie, dance in "The Nutcracker," he wants to be a dancer. When other children discover his secret lessons and tease him, he gets hurt in a fight with them and has to go to the hospital. One boy, Matt Egan, says apologetically, "You're no sissy. You put up a good fight. That don't mean I go for that ballet stuff. But I won't bug you no more about it. And I guess I speak for the whole gang. See you around" (72).

BOOKS FOR LATER YEARS

Regardless of their backgrounds, most young people in foster homes find it difficult to have a positive self-image. In *The Pinballs* by Betsy Byars, successful foster parents, the Masons, accommodate three children with sad histories. Eight-year-old Thomas J., abandoned when he was two, lived with elderly twin sisters until both were hospitalized. The intoxicated father of thirteen-year-old Harvey ran over him in a car, leaving him with two broken legs. Teen-aged Carlie, beaten by her second stepfather, tells Mrs. Mason:

> Harvey and me and Thomas J. are just like pinballs. Some-
> body put in a dime and punched a button and out we came,
> ready or not, and settled in the same groove. That's all. . . .
> Now, you don't see pinballs helping each other, do you?"
> (29).

When Harvey is depressed because his mother never answers his letters, his two friends help. Carlie says, "Harvey, you *have* to make it. Because you're one of us—you and me and Thomas J. are a set. And I've got used to you, Harvey. When I get used to somebody, I don't want anything to happen to them" (85). Carlie and Thomas J. secretly bring him a puppy as a birthday gift, and Harvey cries for the first time. Thomas J. hears Carlie confide,"Pinballs can't help what heppens to them and you and me can" (136).

Fifteen-year-old Kep Lanning, featured in Zachary Ball's *Kep*, accidently kills his father while duck hunting. He goes to live with Oda and Chester Maskew, whose son was born the same year as Kep and died from polio. However, Oda is still grief-stricken and Chester does not know how to be Kep's pal. Link Wybel, an antiques restorer and "town bum," becomes Kep's friend. When Ken rescues a baby fox from hunters, he tells Link, "I wish I could like Chester the way I like you" (99). Link replies that humans and animals are the same in not liking everyone. After an otter kills a puppy Link has given him, Kep vows to kill the otter. He finds two bobcats attacking the otter, so he scares them away. Link says he has learned that hatred is not the answer to everything.

In *Queenie Peavy*, Robert Burch describes life in a small Georgia town during the depression. Queenie's father is in prison for stealing and her mother works in a cannery. Thirteen-year-old Queenie throws rocks and talks back to teachers to hide feelings of shame when others tease her about her father. She thinks, "Besides hating them for what they said, she hated them for what they made her say and do" (50). Her understanding principal tells her, "It *is* their own sadness if they are crude enough to tease you. . . . I'm firmly convinced that people who are inconsiderate hurt themselves in the long run more than they hurt anyone else" (67). The judge admires Queenie's loyalty but says that "each of us is responsible for what we do" (104). When Queenie's father comes home, he pays no attention to her and returns to prison for violating parole by carrying a gun. Queenie, realizing he causes his own troubles, determines to "make something of myself! There's no telling what I can do if I try" (151).

Children from wealthy families may also have self-image problems. In *Boy on the Run* by Bianca Bradbury, twelve-year-old Nick Fournier tests his self-sufficiency by running away from his mother's luxurious New York City apartment. He pawns personal items to buy camping equipment and instead of going to Grandmother's home, gets off the ferry on a nearby island. After being alone for several days, he befriends a puppy and another loner, Fred. He mails postcards to his family so they know he is alright. Nick stops taking pills from a psychiatrist and discovers that he can "get along with people" (91). Before visiting Grandmother, he calls her housekeeper, Angie, who says, "I hope that headshrinker can see you're not a disturbed boy. You're just an average, normal, rotten brat" (105). After being with Grandmother, he plans to try communicating with Mother.

The main character in M. E. Kerr's *The Son of Someone Famous* is sixteen-year-old Adam, who has been expelled from several schools. He moves to a small Vermont town to be with his dead mother's father. At a drugstore, he meets Brenda Belle Blossom, another misfit. In alternate chapters, she and Adam tell about the year when they help each other develop positive self-images. Adam says, "My father was the last man you could imagine having an inferiority complex. . . . I *did* have an inferiority complex. . . . I was plain inferior" (57). Brenda Belle's aunt suggests, "The right way is what you grow to learn is right for you. . . . From time to time you'll change your own way of seeing things, too" (141). Adam's grandfather and stepmother help him to appreciate his father.

Life in the entertainment world seems glamorous to outsiders, but not to thirteen-year-old Sunday Donaldson in *Adorable Sunday* by

Marlene Fanta Shyer. Her mother, a former professional skater, pushes Sunday into television commercials. Sunday says, "In my dream I was famous and rich and people asked me to sign their menus in restaurants. How could anything that exciting ever stop being fun?" (10). But her grades suffer and she attracts so much attention that her younger brother gets solace only from his fish tank. Sunday buys him a lion fish with her first check, thinking, "I knew Edward felt out of things. Maybe even a little bit lonely" (111). On a trip for a commercial in Florida, Sunday prevents suicide by an older girl who has disappointed her family because no employer wants her to perform now. The experience changes Sunday who cuts her braid, a trademark, to avoid jobs.

In *A Special Gift* by Marcia L. Simon, Peter Harris must choose between his love for ballet and his love for basketball. "It scared Peter to have to admit now that ballet really was a secret he kept on purpose. It must mean something pretty terrible would happen if the secret got out" (18). After Peter gets a role in "The Nutcracker," all goes well until a basketball game occurs on rehearsal day. Sneaking from the rehearsal early, he hurts himself during basketball. Dancing damages his ankle, so the doctor puts him on crutches. As Peter watches the conductor at a performance, he understands:

> It was wonderful, that it was a rare and precious gift for a person to get such pleasure from just making music. And for the first time in his life, Peter accepted his own love of dancing as that same kind of special gift. (112)

Twelve-year-old Jay Sharp and his family spend the summer on an island, but Jay resents the confidence and popularity of his brother, Mal, in Bianca Bradbury's *The Loner*. Jay works at a marina and befriends another loner, Eddie Prince. Starting a dog-walking service, they save enough money to buy a boat. Eddie teaches Jay to swim, but neither boy knows how to handle the boat when they first use it. After Mal and some friends rescue them, the boys let Mal claim a third of the boat. Jay remembers his father saying, "Jay, you think Mal ought to be perfect. Are you sure you're perfect, son? You have to take Mal the way he is. You have to take the world the way it is, with all its faults" (118).

In *Save the Loonies* by Joyce Milton, a twelve-year-old girl, Jenny Schulman, begins to accept herself and helps seventeen-year-old David Bidwell accept himself. Jenny is spending a week with Nicole Bidwell and her parents in a New Hampshire cabin. Jenny, taller and physically more mature than classmates, is often humiliated, "like the time in gym class when no one could find the soccer balls and one of the boys had joked that Jenny must be hiding them under her tee shirt" (42). Nicole's brother, David, secretly leaves camp and hides near his parents' cabin. He and Jenny become friends by saving a baby loon. David, Nicole, and their father agree to try communicating better.

Maria Gripe's *The Green Coat* depicts thirteen-year-old Fredrika who wants to be strong, like her dentist mother. She buys a green coat similar to one worn by an alderman's daughter. Britt, an insecure, wealthy classmate and Fredrika's admirer, purchases a duplicate green coat. When Fredrika becomes a class leader, she still feels lonely, so she helps Britt excel in sports. "Fredrika encouraged Britt, went with her everywhere, urged her on, applauded her" (143). After Britt gains self-confidence, Fredrika, realizing she has inner talents and resources, discards her green coat.

Sara Louise and Caroline Bradshaw are fraternal twins living on a Chesapeake Bay island in *Jacob Have I Loved* by Katherine Paterson. Pretty, sickly Caroline is a talented musician whom her family pampers. By contrast, Sara Louise toils on boats to help her father and a male buddy, Call. Aware of her poor self-image, Sara Louise questions, "Didn't they know that worry proves you care? Didn't they realize that I needed their worry to assure myself that I was worth something?" (33). Sara Louise hates her sister at times, reflecting, "She would not fight with me. Perhaps that was the thing that made me hate her most" (64). Grandmother aptly quotes the Bible, "Romans nine thirteen. Jacob have I loved, but Esau have I hated" (156). When Caroline receives money to study music in Baltimore and Sara Louise's only friend, Call, admits he loves Caroline, Sara Louise is devastated. Though she wants to be a doctor, Sara Louise goes to the University of Kentucky School of Midwifery on a scholarship. Afterwards, she works in an Appalachian village where she marries a widower with children and begins to feel important.

Mary Stolz writes about a loner in *Wait for Me, Michael*. Fifteen-year-old Amy lives with her widowed mother and three boarders. Amy knows friendship and love vicariously through books. When Michael Vye comes to board, she begins to live without books. A popular classmate, who is interested in Michael, becomes Amy's friend. After Michael leaves, Amy still receives party invitations but discovers she neither enjoys nor needs crowds and social drinking.

In *Portrait of Ivan* by Paula Fox, when Ivan's wealthy father orders his son's portrait painted, Ivan discovers a new world. Matt Mustazza, the artist, gets old Miss Manderly to read while Ivan poses, so the three become friends. Ivan tells Matt his wish to know more about his mother. The boy, who has never seen Mother's picture, knows only that she, Grandmother, and Uncle escaped from Russia in a sledge, or sleigh. Father never mentions her. When Matt gets a commission to sketch a Florida plantation, he takes Ivan and Miss Manderly with him. On their return, Matt gives Ivan his sketch of a sledge with three people escaping. Previously feeling tied to an adult by a rope, Ivan thinks, "But since he had met Matt, space has been growing all around him. It was frightening to let go of that rope, but it made him feel light and quick instead of heavy and slow" (105).

Children raised in two worlds may have difficulty knowing where they belong. Laurence Yep, who writes about Chinese-Americans in the San Francisco area, portrays twelve-year-old Casey Young in *Child of the Owl*. After robbers beat her gambling father who becomes a hospital patient, Casey stays with her maternal grandmother, Paw Paw, in Chinatown. Casey begins to love her grandmother and appreciate her culture, though she does not think of herself as Chinese until girls in school tease her. She reflects, "My skin color and different-shaped eyes were like theirs. Only I didn't want to be like them because they made me feel rotten and fat and ugly" (39–40). Showing Casey a lovely jade owl pendant, Paw Paw confides, "Did you feel that you were all alone inside? All of our family go through that. I did. Your mother did too. We're all children of the Owl Spirit, you see?" (57). The jade owl is stolen, then retrieved, and Paw Paw sells it to a museum to pay the gambling debts of Casey's father. Casey tells herself: "Some Chinese still know how to look deep inside themselves and I'm gonna be one of them. I'm a child of the owl" (203).

Another book by Laurence Yep, *Sea Glass*, shows a Chinese-American boy, Craig Chin, whose father, a former all-American, wants his son to excel in sports. The Chins move to a small town near San Francisco where fat, clumsy, unathletic Craig is unhappy. He makes friends with a seaside-dwelling, old Chinese man, Uncle Quail, who explains the sea's beauty, teaches him to swim, and says, "You have to learn how to pay attention to things. But first you have to like yourself. People who don't like themselves, they spend all their time looking at their faults. They don't have time to look at the world" (77–78). Craig befriends another misfit, Kenyon. He makes Father, Uncle Quail, and Kenyon angry with him until he follows Mother's advice, "Don't try to force things. Just leave them alone for a while and wait until you have something to agree on. . . ." (181)

Pulga, the Spanish word for flea, is the nickname of a fourteen-year-old Bogotá, Colombia slum boy, the subject and the title of S. R. Van Iterson's powerful book. Apparently orphaned, Pulga tries to provide for his crippled brother Pedro, his sisters, and grandmother. Pulga is resting under a truck when the driver, Gilimon Naranjo, hires him as a helper on a haul to the Caribbean. Gilimon stops en route to visit his godmother, Mamá Maruja, who says she needs a boy like Pulga to assist her. When Gilimon compliments Pulga for keeping him awake on the long ride, "Pulga blushed to his ears. Never before had anyone praised him" (111). Gilimon buys Pulga tennis shoes that someone steals at a rest stop. Pulga is heartbroken because "they were the symbol of all his awakening feelings" (137). With many adventures behind him, they return to Bogotá to find Grandmother dead, the sisters in a home, and Pedro hiding. After taking Pedro to Mamá Maruja as her helper, Pulga returns to work with Gilimon.

Seventeen-year-old Alfred Brooks, a high school dropout, lives in Harlem with his aunt and cousins. In *The Contender* by Robert Lipsyte, Alfred works at a grocery. One night, his best friend, James, a drug-using gang member, gets caught trying to rob the grocery store. After the gang beats Alfred for not revealing the store's alarm, Alfred goes to Donatelli's gymnasium to become a champion boxer. Donatelli says everyone wants to be a champion, but "That's not enough, you have to start by wanting to be a contender, the man coming up" (27). When Alfred wins three fights, Donatelli makes him quit because he lacks a killer instinct. Alfred decides to finish school and help addicted James, declaring, "Gonna get you clean, [M]an, and gonna keep you clean" (182).

Anna Marie Reichert's family from Alsace continues old-world traditions in *Spring Comes First to the Willows* by Helen Marie Pundt. Fifteen-year-old Anna Marie still wears a long braid. She is attracted to a rich, selfish classmate, Alan Newbury. After Alan tries to make love to her in his car, she realizes, "She had thought she had known what love was, and she hadn't known anything, not anything at all" (181). When friends visit, she reflects:

She thought of the countless times she had imagined herself different or out of place or not belonging. Yet wasn't everyone there on the lawn "different"? Of the girls that she knew even moderately well, each one of them could have set up some barrier in her mind and said, "I don't belong because!!!" (214).

Evelyn Sibley Lampman's *The Potlatch Family* is exemplary in showing American Indian pride. Thirteen-year-old Plum Langor, a Chinook, lives with her grandmother, half-brothers and half-sisters, and alcoholic father. Plum's returned brother, Simon, an injured veteran, involves his community in a potlatch, or feast for tourists, to develop cultural pride and make money. Plum's white classmate and only true friend, Mildred Schwartz, helps in the potlatch. Simon announces:

I'm not a revolutionary and I'm not an advocate of Red Power. I just want my people, my tribe, to hold up their heads and take pride in being what they are. The potlatch can show people, our people, as well as the whites, that the Indian had a culture of his own. (105)

In the successful project, Plum becomes a celebrity. When Simon dies, family members honor him by continuing the potlatch.

In *Jemmy* by Jon Hassler, seventeen-year-old Jemmy Stott tries to struggle out of poverty while discovering her identity as a woman and an artist. Her mother, a Chippewa, was married to a weak, alcoholic white man. In school Jemmy attends the white assembly and the Indian one, commenting, "Being half Indian and half white didn't seem to add up to one total person. You remained two persons" (15). Her father orders her to quit school to care for her younger siblings. When she is caught in a blizzard after resigning from school, an artist and his wife, Otis and Ann Chapman, rescue her. Otis, the painter of a Minneapolis mall mural on the American Indian heritage, gets Jemmy to pose for his main character, the Maiden of Eagle Rock. "For the first time in years Jemmy was glad to be an Indian" (65). The Chapmans befriend the Stotts, and Otis, a reformed alcoholic, shames Mr. Stott into going to work while reducing his drinking. Noting Jemmy's artistic talent, Otis gives her lessons. After Jemmy sees the finished Minneapolis mural, she realizes that "there was nothing so difficult about being two people if you didn't fight it. Weren't most people really two people after all?" (171).

Beverly Butler's A *Girl Named Wendy* shows both militant and conservative attitudes among American Indians. Fifteen-year-old Wendy Gerard and her seven-year-old sister, Jill, who are part Menominee, attend a mission school. After their father deserts them, their mother moves around seeking work. Wendy tries living with her Indian aunt and white uncle who have taken in Russell, a militant Indian college student. Russell wants Wendy to renounce everything that is white, and her aunt wants her to shed everything that is American Indian. She thinks, "Their ideas were at opposite poles, but they were agreed that Wendy should be someone else, someone who was not Wendy Gerard" (101). Wendy finally comprehends:

> It was a person's whole self that counted, the knowledge of what was right for her by nature and what was wrong. To be true to that knowledge, though, to act on it—she was beginning to understand how that would not always be easy. (209)

In the 1900s in a small Swiss village, Nicola, who lives with her grandmother, wants to make her father, a widower, proud of her. Ruth M. Arthur's *Nicola, My Daughter* describes the central character as a small scrapper who complains, "There lay my early troubles. I did not grow, not noticeably anyhow. I was always taken for much younger than my age, and how I hated it! . . . My temper was easily aroused" (5). She plans to explore a nonworking mine to show she is as good as a boy. When a companion cancels their date, she goes alone, accidently drops her father's watch down the shaft, tries to find it, and cannot get out until a friend rescues her. Father says:

> Nicola, Nicola, my dear. You did not have to show me anything. I *know* your worth. I know you have [the] courage of a boy and the gentleness of a girl. . . . You could offer me any boy in our valley, and I would still choose my daughter, Nicola. (120)

Paula Danziger is the author of two books on girls with poor self-images. In *The Cat Ate My Gymsuit*, thirteen-year-old Marcy Lewis, fat and mousy, uses "The cat ate my gymsuit" (11) as her excuse for skipping gym. Her new English teacher, Ms. Finney, tells her class, "I decided to become an English teacher because I care about people" (8).

After making students excited about English, Ms. Finney starts an after-school group dynamics club. The principal suspends Ms. Finney because he does not like her dress, teaching methods, or refusal to recite the "Pledge of Allegiance." Both Marcy and her mother, the P.T.A. president, defend Ms. Finney. The board of education finally reinstates Ms. Finney, but she resigns, declaring, "This community has been split on this issue so badly that I doubt I can ever walk back into my classes and teach effectively" (42). Through their joint endeavor, however, Marcy and her mother communicate. Marcy feels good enough about herself to begin losing weight.

In *The Pistachio Prescription* by Paula Danziger, another thirteen-year-old, Cassie Stephen, has asthma and eats red pistachio nuts when upset. She thinks she has been adopted because she does not look like others in her family. With her friend, Vicki, she plans "Operation Overthrow" to upset a clique running the school. When Cassie plucks her eyebrows to impress a neighbor, Bernie Howard, her face is such a mess that her mother gives her dark glasses to wear to school. Defying her teacher's order to remove the glasses, Cassie becomes a heroine. At home, the children try unsuccessfully to reunite their parents. Cassie realizes that even the fall of her young brother, Andrew, from a tree house has not brought the parents together. She thinks, "I want to tell him the truth that it'll never work out, that it'll never be the way it was or the way we want it to be. That we're going to have to accept things the way they are now. That we'll survive" (153).

A fat, tall, homely, and gawky thirteen-year-old, Tibb, reads the newspaper horoscope religiously in *Leo the Lioness* by Constance C. Greene. Tibb, upset because her best friend, Jen, and her older sister, Nina, giggle about boys, evaluates her mean nature: "I can be very nasty at times. I have a cutting tongue. But not without provocation" (15). She confides in Carla, her former baby-sitter, who says, "It's your age. It's a tough one. I remember feeling the same way when I was your age" (41). When Carla has to marry, Tibb refuses to go to the wedding and then changes her mind, realizing:

> I hope I have learned not to sit in judgment on people. I hope I've learned not to think I am always right and the other guy is always wrong. . . . [A]s long as my standards remain mine, and I stick to them, then it shouldn't matter what other people's standards are. (118)

With mainstreaming of the disabled important in current education, *Belonging: A Novel* by Deborah Kent is excellent for teenagers. Fifteen-year-old Meg Hollis decides she wants to go to a public school rather than the Institute for the Blind. She wants to know what girls her age do. Finding acceptance difficult, she joins two other nonconformists, Lindy Blake and Keith Leonard, in publishing the magazine, *Messenger*. Lindy Blake has a paper route and likes bicycling. Keith Leonard, who loves opera, often sings Wagnerian operatic excerpts. Meg cancels going to the opera with Keith, Lindy, and their emotionally unstable English teacher, Miss Kellogg, so that she can go to a party of popular students. Miserable with party kissing and pot smoking, Meg apologizes to Lindy and Keith. When Miss Kellogg loses her job, the three write an editorial in her defense. Meg, who decides to continue at high school, tells her parents, "I guess nobody's happy all the time anywhere. I've made friends here, I'm learning a lot—I really do want to stay. I can't go through life without being hurt once in a while" (196).

In Robert Lipsyte's *One Fat Summer*, fourteen-year-old Bobby Marks decides to get a summer job caring for Dr. Kahn's property. Fat Bobby is unpopular with everyone except his neighbor, Joanie, who considers her big nose a problem. After people tease Bobby, calling him the Crisco Kid, he thinks, "Rule number one: Never let people know they can get to you or they'll never stop trying" (2). Willie Rumson, an ex-marine, resents summer people, especially Bobby, for getting a job. When Bobby refuses to relinquish his job, Willie and his friends strip him naked and dump him on an island. Bobby tells himself, "On your feet. You're not gonna let those bastards kill you. You beat the lawn, you can beat them. You're tough. You ran, you fought, you'll do it again. You'll do it till you win" (84). He does. He loses weight and defies the bullies. Dr. Kahn says Bobby should pay him for making "a miserable fat boy into a fairly presentable young man" (150). Bobby replies, "You didn't do it, Dr. Kahn, I did" (150).

Thinking he is a born loser, Gary Getz refuses to participate in organized sports in Mike Neigoff's *Runner-up*. Since Gary enjoys running, his friend, Tubby, who tries out for every sport, gets him to join the track team. His coach says, "Most coaches look for kids who will win and help the team make points. I look for kids like you and Tubby who need the team" (30). Tubby calls Mike a quitter because he gives up when he is losing a race. Dad says, "It's not foolish to try, even if you fail. Almost everything in life is competitive. You don't expect to win all the time, but if you keep trying, you'll win more times than you fail" (41). Realizing his weakness, Gary thinks, "It didn't make him feel good at all" (62). After he really runs, he does win a race.

In another book about a runner, Kin Platt's *Brogg's Brain*, fifteen-year-old Monty Davis likes running but refuses to be on a team for fear of losing. His father had been a fast miler and so had his English teacher who tells him, "Enduring is only instinct. Courage is something else. Not as exciting. Sometimes it has its own rewards. I'm talking about the courage to dare to be unpopular, to please yourself. To do only what you want to do" (21). Monty lacks the competitive spirit of his father, who was not Mr. Nice Guy in races. Father says, "I let those guys know from the start, this was competition. . . . Anybody who could stop me winning was my enemy. And that made them a little uptight" (94). Monty draws inspiration from a movie, "Brogg's Brain," about a 200-year-old scientist who posthumously has his brain saved, and it guides people. In an important race, Monty lets his brain spur him to victory.

In *The Telltale Summer of Tina C.* by Lila Perl, a twelve-year-old girl, who is 5' 9" tall, has personal and family problems. Tina Carstairs's nickname is "Tina C.,—the teen age twitch," because she twitches her nose when nervous. She lives on Long Island with her father, grandmother, and younger brother, Arthur. Tina and several troubled friends form the Saturday Sad Souls Club. Visiting her mother in New York City, she meets a Dutch boy at the Museum of Natural History. He shows that he likes her and helps her find her missing brother. Feeling more secure and accepting her mother's marriage to a younger man, Tina returns home to cancel her club membership. She tells the girls:

> I don't feel like a sad soul anymore. Oh, I'm not going to try being one of those teen-age model types, either. I'm just going to try to be me, not so critical of myself anymore or of anybody else either. It makes life too hard. . . . We've got to start living our lives instead of sitting around and talking about them. (143)

Eighth-grader Paul Griffin likes noncompetitive fishing, though friends encourage him to join a team sport in *The Summer I Was Lost* by Paul Viereck. Paul thinks, "It seemed as if nothing turned out right, and I began to wonder if anything would. I didn't have much faith in myself, needless to say. The way I look back at it, I was really lost before the summer began" (47). Paul enjoys his sixth-grade teacher, Mr.

Perker, who says, "You will have to *think* to survive in this world" (9).
Mr. Perker is a counselor at a camp that Paul enjoys attending, even
with brief survival sessions. While the boy is hiking in the White
Mountains, a storm occurs. In panic, Paul goes down the wrong side of
the mountain. For days, he stays alive by catching fish, and he stays
calm as he tries to find his way to camp. Once he returns, there is a
special campfire in his honor. The Colonel declares:

> Most important item you take into the woods to help you
> survive is yourself. Your determination will usually see you
> through. As long as you are not ready to admit defeat and are
> convinced that you can save yourself. (153)

Being overweight can devastate a girl, as fat, clumsy Ellen DeLuca
knows in *The Fat Girl* by Marilyn Sachs. Jeff, a senior, unhappy with
his home life, tries to help Ellen. Driving to her house before the senior
prom, he thinks, "When I met her she was ready to kill herself. Tonight
she'll be going to the prom in a magnificent golden gown [he chose for
her], and her joy will be written all over her face. Because of me" (152).
Earlier she thanked him for his support by saying, "I think you must
have understood that I really wanted to change" (141). But Ellen has
begun to respect herself and selected her own prom dress. After the
prom, she tells him, "You think you own me. You think I can't do
anything by myself. . . . You locked me up again. It was the power—
that's all you wanted" (163–164). When Ellen rejects Jeff, she begins to
manage her own life.

A girl can also suffer from being too thin, as thirteen-year-old
Kathy McGruder finds in Jan Van Leeuwen's *I Was a 98-Pound
Duckling*. She and her best friend, Beth, take a suitcase of ointments,
creams, and magazines to a summer cottage. The girls try to remodel
themselves and meet two dates. Kathy learns the advice in the magazines is absurd. She can talk about sports, be herself, and have fun. Her
date, Keith, invites her to football week at his private school. When she
weighs in the fall, she is up to 102 pounds and says, "I figure this may be
significant" (102).

In Ester Wier's *The Rumptydoolers*, fifteen-year-old Whit Stewart
develops a positive self-image. After his parents' death, Whit leaves an
expensive school and goes to Uncle Mike's Arizona sheep ranch. His
uncle, who feels the boy is a spoiled snob, tells him: "Out here you take
a person at his worth. . . . Every once in a while I find a real champion.

. . . He's learned courage, loyalty, a sense of honor, and it doesn't matter how he looks or what color skin he has" (25). Digger, an Australian, teaches Whit that Rumptydoolers is an Aussie slang term for champions. Whit and Chihu, an Apache lad, accompany Uncle's men on a 200-mile trek to pasture sheep in the mountains for the summer. Whit "couldn't decide what hurt most, his uncle's failure to make friends with him or his lack of confidence in him. I'll show him, he repeated to himself" (59). In the long, difficult, and miserable trip, he finds himself caring well for the sheep. "He wondered why he worked so hard. . . . He found himself wanting to take care of them. . . . Because they needed him" (116–117). After he becomes Chihu's blood brother, Whit understands what his uncle means about giving people a chance to prove themselves.

SUMMARY

Of the seventy-one books discussed in this chapter, twelve are for the early years, twenty-five are for the middle years, and thirty-four are for the later years.

References

Arthur, Ruth M. *My Daughter, Nicola.* Illustrated by Fermin Rocker. Atheneum Publishers, 1965. 122 p. (L) (Courage)

Ball, Zachary. *Kep.* Illustrated by E. Harper Johnson. Holiday House, 1961. 207 p. (L) (Friendship, Maturing)

Beckman, Dolores. *My Own Private Sky.* E. P. Dutton, 1980. 154 p. (L) (Friendship, Maturing)

Bradbury, Bianca. *Boy on the Run.* The Seabury Press, 1975. 126 p. (L) (Friendship, Maturing)

———. *The Loner.* Illustrated by John Gretzer. Houghton Mifflin Company, 1970. 140 p. (L) (Friendship, Maturing)

Brown, Marc. *Arthur's Nose.* Illustrated. Little, Brown & Company, 1976. Unpaged. (E)

Brown, Marcia. *Once a Mouse: A Fable Cut in Wood.* Illustrated. Charles Scribner's Sons, 1961. Unpaged. (E)

Burch, Robert. *Queenie Peavy.* Illustrated by Jerry Lazare. The Viking Press, 1966. 159 p. (L) (Maturing)

Butler, Beverly. *A Girl Called Wendy.* Dodd, Mead & Company, 1976. 211 p. (L) (Maturing)

Byars, Betsy. *The Glory Girl*. The Viking Press, 1983. 121 p. (M)

————. *The Pinballs*. Harper & Row, Publishers, 1977. 136 p. (L)
(Friendship, Maturing)

Cleary, Beverly. *Ramona the Brave*. Illustrated by Alan Tiegreen.
William Morrow & Company, 1975. 190 p. (M) (Courage)

Coatsworth, Elizabeth. *Marra's World*. Illustrated by Krystyna Turska.
Greenwillow Books, 1975. 83 p. (M) (Friendship)

Conford, Ellen. *Just the Thing for Geraldine*. Illustrated by John
Larrecq. Little, Brown & Company, 1974. 32 p. (E)

Danziger, Paula. *The Cat Ate My Gymsuit*. Delacorte Press, 1974. 147
p. (L)

————. *The Pistachio Prescription: A Novel*. Delacorte Press, 1978.
154 p. (L)

D'Aulaire, Ingri, and Edgar Parin. *Nils*. Illustrated. Doubleday &
Company, 1948. Unpaged. (E)

dePaola, Tomie. *Andy (That's My Name)*. Illustrated. Prentice-Hall,
1973. Unpaged. (E)

Desbarats, Peter. *Gabrielle and Selena*. Illustrated by Nancy Grossman.
Harcourt, Brace & World, 1968. Unpaged. (M)

Duvoisin, Roger. *Veronica*. Illustrated. Alfred A. Knopf, 1961. Unpaged. (E)

First, Julia. *Amy*. Prentice-Hall, 1975. 84 p. (M)

Fitzgerald, John D. *Me and My Little Brain*. Illustrated by Mercer
Mayer. The Dial Press, 1971. 137 p. (M) (Ingenuity)

Flory, Jane. *One Hundred and Eight Bells*. Illustrated. Houghton
Mifflin Company, 1963. 219 p. (M) (Maturing)

Fox, Paula. *Portrait of Ivan*. Illustrated by Saul Lambert. Bradbury
Press, 1969. 131 p. (L)

————. *The Stone-faced Boy*. Illustrated by Donald A. Mackay. Bradbury Press, 1968. 106 p. (M)

Freeman, Don. *Dandelion*. Illustrated. The Viking Press, 1964. 48 p.
(E)

Greene, Bette. *Get on Out of Here, Philip Hall*. The Dial Press, 1981.
150 p. (M) (Maturing)

————. *Philip Hall Likes Me, I Reckon Maybe*. Illustrated by Charles
Lilly. The Dial Press, 1974. 135 p. (M) (Cooperation, Friendship)

Greene, Constance C. *Leo the Lioness*. The Viking Press, 1970. 118 p.
(L) (Maturing)

————. *The Unmaking of Rabbit*. The Viking Press, 1972. 125 p. (M)

Greenwald, Sheila. *Will the Real Gertrude Hollings Please Stand Up?* Little, Brown & Company, 1983. 162 p. (M) (Ingenuity)

Gripe, Maria. *The Green Coat*. Translated from Swedish by Sheila La Farge. Delacorte Press, 1977. 170 p. (L)

Haas, Dorothy. *Tink in a Tangle*. Illustrated by Margot Apple. Albert Whitman & Company, 1984. 136 p. (M) (Friendship)

Hansen, Joyce. *The Gift-giver*. Houghton Mifflin/Clarion Books, 1980. 118 p. (M) (Friendship)

Hassler, Jon. *Jemmy*. Atheneum, 1980. 175 p. (L) (Humaneness, Responsibility)

Hodges, Margaret. *The Hatching of Joshua Cobb*. Illustrated by W. T. Mars. Farrar, Straus & Giroux, 1967. 135 p. (M) (Friendship)

Hooks, William H. *Doug Meets the Nutcracker*. Illustrated by Jim Spanfeller. Frederick Warne & Company, 1977. 79 p. (M)

Hunter, Edith Fisher. *Sue Ellen*. Illustrated by Bea Holmes. Houghton Mifflin Company, 1969. 170 p. (M) (Friendship)

Hurwitz, Johanna. *Superduper Teddy*. Illustrated by Susan Jeschke. William Morrow & Company, 1980. 80 p. (M)

Keller, Beverly. *The Beetle Bush*. Illustrated by Marc Simont. Coward, McCann & Geoghegan, 1976. 64 p. (E) (Ingenuity)

Kemp, Gene. *Gowie Corby Plays Chicken*. Faber & Faber, 1979. 136 p. (M) (Friendship)

Kent, Deborah. *Belonging: A Novel*. Dial Press, 1978. 200 p. (L) (Friendship, Maturing)

Kerr, M. E. *The Son of Someone Famous*. Harper & Row, Publishers, 1974. 226 p. (L) (Friendship)

Krasilovsky, Phyllis. *The Shy Little Girl*. Illustrated by Trina Schart Hyman. Houghton Mifflin Company, 1970. 32 p. (E)

Lampman, Evelyn Sibley. *The Potlatch Family*. Atheneum, 1976. 135 p. (L) (Humaneness)

Lipsyte, Robert. *The Contender*. Harper & Row, Publishers, 1967. 182 p. (L)

————. *One Fat Summer*. Harper & Row, Publishers, 1977. 151 p. (L)

MacLachlan, Patricia. *Arthur for the Very First Time*. Illustrated by Lloyd Bloom. Harper & Row, Publishers, 1980. 117 p. (M) (Friendship)

Milton, Joyce. *Save the Loonies*. Four Winds Press, 1983. 151 p. (L)

Neigoff, Mike. *Runner-up*. Illustrated by Fred Irvin. Albert Whitman
    & Company, 1975. 128 p. (L)

Paterson, Katherine. *Jacob Have I Loved*. Thomas Y. Crowell, 1980.
    215 p. (L) (Maturing)

Pearson, Susan. *Everybody Knows That!* Illustrated by Diane Paterson.
    Dial Press, 1978. Unpaged. (E)

Perl, Lila. *The Telltale Summer of Tina C.* The Seabury Press, 1975.
    160 p. (L) (Maturing, Responsibility)

Platt, Kin. *Brogg's Brain*. Lippincott & Crowell, Publishers, 1981. 123
    p. (L) (Courage)

Pundt, Helen Marie. *Spring Comes First to the Willows*. Thomas Y.
    Crowell, 1963. 231 p. (L) (Maturing)

Sachs, Marilyn. *The Fat Girl*. E. P. Dutton, 1983. 176 p. (L)

Schulman, Janet. *Jenny and the Tennis Nut*. Illustrated by Marylin
    Hafner. Greenwillow Books, 1978. 56 p. (M)

Sharmat, Marjorie Weinman. *I'm Terrific*. Illustrated by Kay Chorao.
    Holiday House, 1977. Unpaged. (E)

Shyer, Marlene Fanta. *Adorable Sunday*. Charles Scribner's Sons,
    1983. 182 p. (L) (Maturing)

Simon, Marcia L. *A Special Gift*. Harcourt Brace Jovanovich, 1978.
    132 p. (L) (Courage, Humaneness, Maturing)

Stolz, Mary. *The Bully of Barkham Street*. Illustrated by Leonard
    Shortall. Harper & Row, Publishers, 1963. 194 p. (M) (Maturing)
    ———. *Wait for Me, Michael*. Harper & Row, Publishers, 1961. 148
    p. (L) (Friendship, Maturing)

Udry, Janice May. *How I Faded Away*. Illustrated by Monica De-
    Brwyn. Albert Whitman & Company, 1976. Unpaged. (E)

Van Iterson, S. R. *Pulga*. Translated from Dutch by Alexander and
    Alison Gode. William Morrow & Company, 1971. 240 p. (L)

Van Leeuwen, Jean. *I Was a 98-pound Duckling*. Dial Press, 1972. 105
    p. (L)

Viereck, Phillip. *The Summer I Was Lost*. Illustrated by Ellen Viereck.
    The John Day Company, 1965. 158 p. (L) (Courage, Ingenuity)

Wier, Ester. *The Rumptydoolers*. Illustrated by W. T. Mars. The
    Vanguard Press, 1964. 159 p. (L) (Maturing)

Williams, Margery. *The Velveteen Rabbit: Or How Toys Become Real*.
    Illustrated by Michael Hague. Holt, Rinehart & Winston, 1983.
    33 p. (M)

Woolley, Catherine. *Ginnie Joins In.* Illustrated by Iris Beatty Johnson. William Morrow & Company, 1951. 192 p. (M) (Maturing)

Yep, Laurence. *Child of the Owl.* Harper & Row, Publishers, 1977. 217 p. (L) (Humaneness, Maturing)

———. *Sea Glass.* Harper & Row, Publishers, 1979. 213 p. (L) (Friendship, Humaneness)

Title Index

Author Index